THE UNITY OF I

Sir Rabinder Singh has been one of the leading lights in the recent development of the common law, most notably in the field of human rights and the law of privacy. Here, for the first time, he reflects on the defining themes of his career as advocate and judge.

Combining his trademark originality of thought and impeccable scholarship, he selects previously published and unpublished writings to track the evolution of his approach to the common law. A substantial introduction gives context to the book, while opening introductions to each piece reflect on their relevance to contemporary legal thought.

The essays explore themes as diverse as judicial review, equality, and privacy and personal autonomy. Insightful, erudite and thought-provoking, this collection is a must-read for all those interested in the law and its role in society.

The Unity of Law

Rabinder Singh

·HART·

OXFORD · LONDON · NEW YORK · NEW DELHI · SYDNEY

HART PUBLISHING

Bloomsbury Publishing Plc

Kemp House, Chawley Park, Cumnor Hill, Oxford, OX2 9PH, UK

1385 Broadway, New York, NY 10018, USA

29 Earlsfort Terrace, Dublin 2, Ireland

HART PUBLISHING, the Hart/Stag logo, BLOOMSBURY and the Diana logo are
trademarks of Bloomsbury Publishing Plc

First published in Great Britain 2021

Copyright © Rabinder Singh, 2021

A catalogue record for this book is available from the British Library.

Library of Congress Cataloging-in-Publication data

Names: Singh, Rabinder, author.

Title: The unity of law / Rabinder Singh.

Description: Oxford, UK ; New York, NY : Hart Publishing, an imprint of Bloomsbury Publishing,
2021. | Includes bibliographical references and index.

Identifiers: LCCN 2021041868 (print) | LCCN 2021041869 (ebook) | ISBN 9781509949427
(hardback) | ISBN 9781509949472 (paperback) | ISBN 9781509949441 (pdf)

Subjects: LCSH: Legal polycentricity. | Law—Philosophy. | Jurisprudence. | Judicial review. |
Equality before the law. | Privacy, Right of.

Classification: LCC K236 .S575 2021 (print) | LCC K236 (ebook) | DDC 340.9—dc23

LC record available at https://lccn.loc.gov/2021041868

LC ebook record available at https://lccn.loc.gov/2021041869

ISBN: PB: 978-1-50994-947-2
        HB: 978-1-50994-942-7
        ePDF: 978-1-50994-944-1
        ePub: 978-1-50994-943-4

Typeset by Compuscript Ltd, Shannon
Printed and bound in Great Britain by CPI Group (UK) Ltd, Croydon CR0 4YY

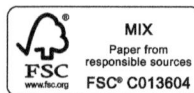

MIX
Paper from
responsible sources
FSC® C013604

To find out more about our authors and books visit www.hartpublishing.co.uk.
Here you will find extracts, author information, details of forthcoming events
and the option to sign up for our newsletters.

Permissions Note

The author and publisher gratefully acknowledge all of the publishers of previously printed material which appears in this book. In particular:

1. Taylor & Francis Group

The Honourable Mr Justice Singh, 'Divided by a Common Language: American and British Perspectives on Constitutional Law' (2017) 22(2) *Judicial Review* 165–81, DOI: 10.1080/10854681.2017.1315899

The Right Honourable Lord Justice Singh, 'Tribute for Lord Steyn' (2018) 23(2) *Judicial Review* 102–05, DOI: 10.1080/10854681.2018.1485359

www.tandfonline.com/

2. Oxford University Press

Rabinder Singh QC, 'Interpreting Bills of Rights' (2008) 29(2) *Statute Law Review*. By permission of Oxford University Press

https://global.oup.com/

3. Cambridge University Press

Rabinder Singh, 'The Development of Human Rights Thought from Magna Carta to the Universal Declaration of Human Rights' in *Magna Carta, Religion and the Rule of Law* (Cambridge, Cambridge University Press, 2015)
Reproduced with permission of the Licensor through PLSclear

www.cambridge.org/

4. Thomson Reuters (Professional) UK Limited

Rabinder Singh, 'Equality: The Neglected Virtue' in *European Human Rights Law Review: 2003* (London, Sweet & Maxwell Ltd, 2004)
Reproduced with permission of The Licensor through PLSclear

Rabinder Singh, 'Racial Equality and the Law' in *European Human Rights Law Review*. ISBN: 9780414073685
Reproduced with permission of The Licensor through PLSclear

Rabinder Singh, 'Privacy and the Media after the Human Rights Act' in *European Human Rights Law Review*. ISBN: 9780414073685
Reproduced with permission of The Licensor through PLSclear

*This book is dedicated to my wife and our two sons,
without whom none of this would have been possible.*

Contents

EQUALITY

PRIVACY AND NATIONAL SECURITY

INTERNATIONAL LAW

The Author

Rabinder Singh is a Lord Justice of Appeal (a judge of the Court of Appeal of England and Wales) and President of the Investigatory Powers Tribunal.

Introduction

I HAVE HAD a fortunate career in the law. At various times I have been an academic, a practising barrister and, for the last 10 years, a judge. This has given me a variety of perspectives on the law, which together have convinced me more and more of the need to bear in mind that the legal system is one coherent whole. As I say in the first chapter of this book, although specialisation has brought many benefits, it also creates risks. One of those risks is that the law may develop in different ways in different areas of doctrine because, in an increasingly busy world, no one person has the time or perhaps the ability to keep an eye on the whole of the law. This is one of the reasons why appellate courts are important and why it is important that, in each appeal heard by them, there should be a mixture of judges who are specialists in the subject-matter of the appeal and those who are not.

In this book I have put together various essays and lectures which I have written over the last 23 years, from 1998 to 2021. I chose that start date because, in 1997, I wrote a book of essays and lectures called *The Future of Human Rights in the UK* (Hart Publishing). In some ways this book complements that earlier one but the scope of this book is much wider. Although the subject of human rights continues to interest me, there are other areas of the law which are also of interest and I touch on some of them in this book.

Some of the chapters in this book have been published previously but many have not been. Perhaps more importantly, I felt that it was time to put the various pieces together in one place, not only because I hope that will be more convenient than trying to find them on the internet, but because I believe that, taken as a whole, they reflect my thinking about the law. Each chapter was intended to be heard or read on its own, so readers who wish to do that can dip into this book as much or as little as they like but I hope that they will find reading the whole to be of interest. The chapters have been ordered thematically rather than chronologically.

I have decided not to update the text of the chapters because I hope readers will find interesting how my thinking about the law has developed over the years. Each chapter is to an extent of its own time but I hope still retains relevance today. I have included a brief paragraph at the start of each chapter, which introduces it, and in that introduction have tried to indicate if there have been any major developments in the law since the time when the chapter was originally written.

One theme that will, I think, emerge in this book is the influence which my time in the USA has had on my thinking about the law. In 1985, when I was coming to the end of my first law degree at Cambridge, I was fortunate to be awarded a Harkness Fellowship to study and travel in the USA. I chose to do my Masters at the University of California at Berkeley, a beautiful campus on the eastern side of San Francisco Bay. The new state of California was admitted to the union in 1850 and its proud citizens were keen to have their own university, which was founded in 1868. For its location (which turned out to be the first of many campuses around the state) they chose a site which reminded them of arcadia and named it after the Irish philosopher, Bishop Berkeley. I am grateful to have had two kinds of legal education. At Cambridge I received a very good education in the doctrinal aspects of law. I was also introduced to jurisprudence (legal philosophy) and legal history. In many ways, the way I think about law even now was shaped in the rooms above Great Gate at Trinity College, Cambridge, where I was taught constitutional law and jurisprudence by Philip Allott (now retired as a professor). At Berkeley I was introduced to a different but complementary way of thinking about law, which places it in its social, political and historical setting. Among the subjects which I studied were constitutional law, labour law and international human rights law. I also did a seminar course on modern social theories of law. I think that background comes across in some of the chapters in this book.

Another theme which will be apparent in this book is that I think that law reflects the values of the society which produces it. Inevitably it changes over time as society's values change. Law is not a value-free zone. The relationship between law and values is a complicated one, as I seek to explore in chapter two of this book, but, when one looks at what our forebears used to regard as obvious, perhaps even part of the natural order of the world, for example in relation to people's sexuality or issues of racial and gender equality, it becomes apparent that the values of a society are capable of changing very rapidly. The law (usually) keeps up although it may sometimes be slow to do so. Sometimes it may even lead the way.

This leads me to another theme which is reflected in this book. Law is a practical enterprise. Although it is of intellectual interest, it is intended to and does have a practical impact on the real world. Law is unlike the natural world, which is studied by physicists and other scientists. It does not exist in the same way as the material world. In the end it exists through words. This is why words are so important to lawyers. The law consists of abstract concepts (a person, ownership, a trust and so on) but we can only express those concepts in words. This then leads to the inevitable difficulty that words are imperfect instruments to convey meaning. This is what keeps lawyers busy for much of their time, as they argue about the true meaning of a statute or what legal principle a decision of an appellate court stands for (its *ratio decidendi*). It is also one of the main functions of a judge, particularly an appellate judge.

Since words are the tools of a lawyer's trade it is important to use them carefully. This is particularly true of judges, since, as I have said, our words have an impact on the real world in a way that few other words do. For example, when a judge pronounces the sentence of a criminal court, a real person may be taken to prison for a very long time. More generally, when a judge writes a judgment, they should bear in mind the different audiences which may read their words. First, of course, there will be the parties to the case in which the judgment is given. Most importantly, the losing party must know why they have lost and feel that they have received a fair hearing even if they do not like the outcome. Another audience is other lawyers, not only practitioners but academics and also students. The judgment may also have to be used by other judges, in lower courts and tribunals, and also by others who must implement the law such as police officers, civil servants and ministers. In some cases, the audience may even include other members of the public. I think it is important to write a judgment which can be understood by a reasonably educated member of the public who is not a lawyer. They may not always agree with the decision of the court but they should at least be able to say to themselves: 'I see why the court got to that result'.

This brings me to the next theme I want to mention in this introduction: the transition from my being a practitioner to being a judge. The reader will probably detect that transition in the course of this book: I was appointed to the High Court in 2011, so roughly half way through the period when these essays and lectures were first written. I was then appointed to the Court of Appeal in 2017. I feel honoured to be a judge and have enjoyed both my time as a first instance judge and as an appellate judge. Each brings different challenges and rewards. As a Recorder and High Court judge, I did a lot of criminal trials, although criminal law had not been my field as a barrister. I think that many members of the public would agree that one of the most important functions of a High Court judge is to try a murder case with a jury. Being an appellate judge brings cases of great intellectual interest but I do miss sitting with a jury.

The final theme I want to mention in this introduction is that the law can be divided into what might be called 'vertical' and 'horizontal' areas. Vertical areas are defined by substantive doctrine (contract, tort, equity etc); or are sometimes just areas of practice that have grown up over time (criminal law, commercial law, family law etc). But there are also horizontal principles of law, which cut across all areas of substantive law and practice. These include international law and human rights law, which permeate all areas of law. It is very important that what I have called 'vertical' areas of law should not become silos.

One of the dangers I have detected is that someone can be a very experienced lawyer in a field like criminal law or family law but assert that they know nothing of human rights law, as that is someone else's specialist area. It is a great shame that, 21 years after the Human Rights Act 1998 came into full force on 2 October 2000, there are still some practitioners who claim that it is not 'their area'. This brings me back to the fundamental theme of this book, which gives it its title: the unity of law.

There are many people who have helped me over the years to produce what is now contained in the chapters of this book. Some of them are acknowledged in the footnotes of the individual chapters. Others I am sure have been inadvertently omitted but will, I hope, forgive me. I must thank in particular my clerks, who have done so much of the typing of lectures and essays since I became a judge in 2011: Steve Searle, Sarah Moore and Gareth Williams. I would also like to thank Sinead Moloney, at the publishers Hart, for her kind support in putting this book together.

The Common Law

The Unity of Law – Or the Dangers of Over-Specialisation

This lecture was given under the auspices of the Society of Legal Scholars, the main association of legal academics in the United Kingdom and Ireland, in 2013 in the beautiful Barber Institute on the campus of the University of Birmingham. The theme of the lecture, which gives its title to this book, is that, while specialisation in a particular branch of the law brings benefits, it carries risks too. I looked at this issue from the various perspectives of an academic, a practitioner and a judge. At the time I was a High Court judge, often going 'on circuit' to hear cases in places such as Birmingham.

I AM HONOURED to be invited to deliver this year's Centenary lecture. At the start of my career I was briefly an academic lawyer and was a member of the Society of Public Teachers of Law, as this society was then known. So it is a particular pleasure to be here this evening.

Many of you will know the story, said to originate in India, about the three blind men who were asked to describe an elephant. The first man was able to touch only the side of the elephant and said that an elephant is shaped like a wall. The second man could only touch a leg and said that an elephant was like a pillar. The third man could only handle the tail and said that an elephant was like a rope. Each was doing his best and none was inaccurate about what he could describe.

This brings me to the theme of my lecture, which is to suggest that we need as lawyers to be able to see the bigger picture, to keep an eye on the overall unity of law, a bird's eye view as it were. One of the ways in which we can do that is to integrate so far as possible the academic discipline of law and legal practice.

Let me make clear at the outset what I am not saying. I am not calling for an end to specialisation in the law. There is obvious value in specialisation both in academia and in practice. One of the notable trends in legal teaching, it seems to me, compared to when I was briefly an academic in the 1980s, is that there are many more courses for students to take, sometimes in very specialised areas of law. This is even truer at the postgraduate stage than at the undergraduate stage. I regard these as healthy developments: they enrich the experience of students and their teachers and play an important part in improving the quality of lawyers later in practice too.

However, I also think that there are dangers in over-specialisation and that it remains important to keep an eye on the bigger picture. I will try to illustrate this by reference to the different stages of my own experience in the law, at university, in practice at the Bar and now on the bench.

I want to start with the present day and outline the different kinds of work that I have to do as a judge of the Queen's Bench Division. One of the attractions of applying to become a judge (at least for me) was the variety of the work that is done. A brief look at my diary for the last year shows that I have done several criminal trials, including murder cases. I have sat in the Court of Appeal (Criminal Division), when one is usually a member of a three-judge panel, hearing appeals against conviction and appeals against sentence. I have sat in the Queen's Bench Division itself, hearing common law claims. One particular aspect of that duty is to sit in what is now called Court 37, where a judge hears interim applications, often urgent applications for injunctions which may well be heard without notice.

A week spent in Court 37 itself can cover a wide range of subjects, from commercial arbitration to a dispute about the ownership of a dog (I recall his name was Billy) and typically includes applications for freezing orders and search orders and for injunctions restraining a former employee from breaching restrictive covenants in a contract of employment.

I have also sat in the Divisional Court, where you sit with one or two other judges, usually with a Lord or Lady Justice of Appeal. Again there can be a wide variety of cases that can come before the Divisional Court: some of the most important public law cases will be heard there but there will often be appeals from the magistrates' court and appeals in regulatory contexts, such as the discipline of solicitors.

That is the sort of work that all judges of the Queen's Bench Division have to do. In addition some judges sit in one or more specialist jurisdictions. I sit in the Administrative Court and the Employment Appeal Tribunal. Some of my colleagues sit in the Commercial and Admiralty Courts or in the Technology and Construction Court. Other colleagues sit in one or more of the chambers of the Upper Tribunal. I do not think it would be right to describe a judge of the Queen's Bench Division as a 'generalist'. However, I do think that one needs to be a versatile specialist.

You may think that what I have described is a daunting array of different areas of legal work, some of it highly specialised. And you may wonder how one person is supposed to be able to do that range of work. The answer, as often, may simply lie in the fact that that is the system we have inherited and it seems to work in practice, tried and tested as it has been over a long time. But it seems to me that two things can help.

The first is legal education and training. What is not always appreciated in this country is that judges, both full-time and part-time, receive regular training, now given by the Judicial College, which succeeded the Judicial Studies Board. They usually start as Recorders or Deputy District Judges and in practice will be expected to have sat for a number of years before they are appointed full-time, as District Judges, Circuit Judges or High Court judges. When they are first appointed, judges have to go on an intensive induction course: for example, a new Recorder of the Crown Court will not be permitted to hear their first case by themselves until they have gone through a training programme comprising a four-day residential course, which includes a mock trial, sitting in court with experienced judges and going on prison visits. No judge, even a High Court judge, is permitted to try cases involving serious sex offences without going on a specialist residential course. The same is true of homicide cases. Most judges are required to refresh their training by attending continuing education courses every year. The more senior judges from the High Court upwards are not required to do so but in practice do; and there is a regular series of shorter seminars run for them at the Royal Courts of Justice on topics of practical importance.

The other part of the answer is that judges quickly learn that the skills and experience which are needed to be a judge are often transferable. It is well recognised that they are different from those needed to be a successful practitioner. In particular the most successful advocate may not necessarily be suited to becoming a good judge. There may be a temptation to enter the arena and try to argue the case, no doubt better than the advocates appearing in it. That is a temptation which judges should resist. It is salutary to remind oneself of the notice which Lord Ackner is said to have kept on the bench in front of him at all times: 'remember, you are paid to listen'. As I have said, judges tend to learn from experience that there are certain skills which are transferable between the jurisdictions in which they sit. Those skills include the finding of facts after hearing evidence; the giving of extemporaneous judgments or rulings, often without notes and certainly without a full script; and the interpretation of legislation and understanding of case law. These are not skills which are confined to any one area of law. It should be possible to develop them by experience and, I would suggest, they can often be improved by sitting in different jurisdictions and seeing how things are done away from what may be one's comfort zone.

Nevertheless there is no doubt that the changing character of the legal profession means that there are challenges for the recruitment and training of judges. This is because of the increasing specialisation of those who practise as solicitors and barristers. As I have already said, that trend towards specialisation has brought many benefits, not least to clients. But it has a potential impact on the ability of new judges in particular to do the work required of them. For example, most judges who are appointed as District Judges or Circuit Judges find that in practice it is very unlikely that all they will do is sit in civil cases. It is most likely that they will do some family law and/or criminal law. Those are the areas where there is the greatest demand for judicial resources.

Gone are the days when legal practitioners did a bit of everything. At the Bar, the trend towards specialisation was already well-established by the time that I was called in 1989. I specialised in public law although I had a more varied practice than many of my contemporaries, including some employment law and other civil work. But even someone of my generation did not specialise immediately. When I first started I was in a magistrates' court every day of the week. I then started doing some small cases in the County Court, the Crown Court and what was then called the industrial tribunal. I also did some planning and other inquiry work. I only started doing public law after several years in practice and, in particular, after I had been appointed to one of the Attorney General's panels of counsel (sometimes called Treasury Counsel but officially Junior Counsel to the Crown).

That brings me to an interesting aspect of legal practice: government work. When I started doing government work in 1992, there were relatively few counsel who were on the Attorney General's panels. Since that time, in particular since 1998, the numbers have increased considerably and my understanding is that counsel are expected to be specialists in particular areas of law. When I was one of the Junior Counsel to the Crown I was instructed in a wide range of cases, including contractual disputes, employment law and every type of public law, ranging from immigration to planning law. In a sense it could have been said that, if I was a specialist in anything, it was in doing Government work, rather than any particular area of law.

I was also for five years the additional Junior Counsel to the Inland Revenue and did all sorts of cases for the Revenue. This included public law and human rights work. It also included very interesting work in the Court of Justice in Luxembourg involving the impact of European Union law on direct taxation. While indirect taxation in the form of VAT is the subject of direct regulation by EU legislation, direct taxation, such as income tax and corporation tax, is in principle within the exclusive competence of Member States. Nevertheless, the fundamental freedoms in the Treaty, such as free movement of workers and free movement of capital, cannot be infringed even by rules of direct taxation, in particular if there is discrimination as between the nationals of different Member States. It was fascinating for me to appear as an advocate on behalf of the Government of the United Kingdom in such cases in Luxembourg, not only where the UK was directly a party but also in cases arising from another Member State in which the UK Government had chosen to appear as an intervener. On a lighter note it was also fascinating to observe the different robes that advocates from different Member States wore in the Court of Justice: my Italian colleagues seemed to have the most glamorous robes.

In my work for the Revenue I also appeared in straight tax appeals, at every level from the Special Commissioners to the House of Lords. This was not unusual. My understanding was that it had long been the custom of the Revenue to use as standing counsel members of the Bar who had no specialist background in tax law. Although this might seem strange at first sight, I was told that the underlying rationale was that what the Revenue was looking for was not substantive knowledge of a particular area of law but what might be called the transferable skills of an advocate, both in relation to the making of legal arguments and in the context of factual disputes. It was also the case that the Revenue had some of the best instructing solicitors that one could have hoped to work with: they usually gave counsel at least an introduction to the substantive law that was needed. From my point of view, I comforted myself that the court I would be appearing in would often include non-specialist judges. If I, with no previous expertise in tax law, could be made to understand what the case was about, there was at least a chance that I would then be able to convey that understanding to the court. That at least was the theory – I will leave it to others to say whether I ever succeeded.

The point I have already mentioned about the transferable skills of an advocate deserves emphasis. Even in the time that I was at the Bar my perception was that the profession became more specialised, to the point of perhaps becoming too narrow in some cases. One stark example of this is that it is conceivable that a barrister may be very good, and may attain silk (ie become Queen's Counsel) and yet never have cross-examined a witness. This could happen in particular if a barrister specialises only in judicial review proceedings, where it is rare for evidence to be taken from live witnesses and for there to be cross-examination. Yet those rare cases do arise when cross-examination is necessary. The way in which many chambers try to address this kind of problem is to ensure that their junior members have access to more general work, so they can gain experience of all relevant skills that an advocate needs, not just being a brilliant lawyer. Some commercial chambers have formal arrangements with criminal sets so that their pupils or junior members can obtain some advocacy experience in the criminal courts.

Speaking for myself, I can see advantages if similar arrangements could be in place throughout a barrister's career, although I accept that this becomes more difficult the more senior and specialist an advocate becomes. What I advise advocates to do if they can spare the time is to go and sit at the back of a court where they do not normally practise, so they can learn how things are done by their counterparts in another jurisdiction. For example, every day in the Royal Courts of Justice in the same corridor there will be courts which are hearing Administrative Court cases and other courts which are hearing cases in the Court of Appeal (Criminal Division). I think it would be beneficial to advocates in both courts if occasionally they could go and sit in one of the other courts and see how legal arguments are presented there. I think that the civil practitioners might appreciate the importance of getting your points across succinctly, in a very limited amount of time. And criminal practitioners might see that points of law can arise in the criminal field on which light may be shed by civil law. Points of law are points of law and their resolution depends on the conventional skills of legal reasoning, like the interpretation of statutes and the analysis of precedents. Unusual points of law can pop up in any jurisdiction. One example which I recall from the Court of Appeal (Criminal Division) earlier this year was when we had to consider an appeal against sentence in a case of burglary. The issue of construction which arose in the case was whether a houseboat could constitute a 'building'. We decided that it could. The interpretation of a word like 'building' can often arise in the context of civil law, for example in planning law, although the answer may not be the same, as it always depends on the context.

I want to turn to an important development in our law which has taken place in recent times, particularly noticeably in the last decade. This is the increasing relevance of public international law in domestic public law cases. Many examples could be given. I hope that two will suffice for now.

The first example is the well-known case of *A v Secretary of State for the Home Department* (often referred to as the 'Belmarsh' case),[1] which was decided by the House of Lords in 2004. That case concerned the compatibility of Part 4 of the Anti-terrorism, Crime and Security Act 2001 (which had been enacted shortly after 9/11) with the Convention rights, as set out in Schedule 1 to the Human Rights Act 1998. In order to enact that legislation the United Kingdom had lodged a derogation with the Council of Europe from Article 5 of the European Convention on Human Rights. The House of Lords issued a declaration of incompatibility under section 4 of the Human Rights Act. One of the interesting features of the case was that the domestic courts had to consider the application of the derogation provision in Article 15 of the European Convention. That provision is not itself incorporated into domestic law; it is not set out in Schedule 1 to the Human Rights Act. However, it was conceded by the Attorney General on behalf of the Secretary of State that, if the United Kingdom's derogation from Article 5 did not comply with the requirements

---

[1] [2005] 2 AC 68.

of Article 15, then not only would that derogation be ineffective in international law, it would render the domestic legislation incompatible with the Convention rights too. The House of Lords held that the derogation did not comply with the rigorous requirements of Article 15 and, accordingly, the domestic legislation was incompatible.

My other example is the case of *Al-Skeini*, decided by the House of Lords in 2007[2] and the Grand Chamber of the European Court of Human Rights in 2011.[3] That case, which concerned the actions of British forces in Iraq, arose in the domestic courts under the Human Rights Act. In turn it required the courts to interpret and apply the provisions of Article 1 of the European Convention, in particular the concept of 'jurisdiction'. That in turn required the courts of this country to engage in extensive and difficult analysis of the meaning of 'jurisdiction' in international law, in particular the extent to which a state can be said to exercise jurisdiction when acting outside its own territory.

I want to turn to a more general point about the relevance of international law in domestic law. It has long been established that customary international law is a source of the common law. This has been recognised since 1737 in *Barbuit*'s case.[4] It used to be said that customary international law is a part of the common law. In a more recent case *R v Jones (Margaret)* in 2006,[5] Lord Bingham preferred to say that it is a source of the common law. In any event, the important point for present purposes is that customary international law, unlike treaty law, does not require any Act of Parliament to incorporate it into domestic law. Although this has been a principle of English law for centuries, I doubt if this is widely known. This is perhaps unsurprising. International law is not a compulsory subject even for those who take a law degree. It is certainly not one of the core subjects, as EU law now is but was not when I was a student. I suspect that many practitioners are quite simply unaware of this doctrine. Yet it can play an important part throughout the entire range of domestic law, both criminal and civil, as cases such as *Jones* and *A v Secretary of State for the Home Department (No. 2)*[6] (which concerned the admissibility of evidence obtained by torture) have shown.

So far I have talked about 'public law' as if it were a single area of law. It is undoubtedly an area of law that has grown in importance in practice over the course of the last generation. In 1980, when the Crown Office List was set up, there were four nominated judges who sat in that specialist jurisdiction. Today the majority of the judges of the Queen's Bench Division (and several of the judges of the Family and Chancery Divisions) sit in the Administrative Court, as the Crown Office List became known in 2000. The number of cases which were started in the Administrative Court has increased nearly threefold since the beginning of this century. However, what has perhaps been less noticed is that even public law has increasingly become divided into distinct specialisms, so that practitioners may spend little, if any, time outside their

---

[2] *R (Al-Skeini & others) v Secretary of State for Defence* [2008] AC 153.
[3] *Al-Skeini & others v United Kingdom* (2011) 53 EHRR 18.
[4] (1737) Cas *temp*. Talbot 281.
[5] [2007] 1 AC 136.
[6] [2006] 2 AC 221.

own area of law. Immigration law and planning law are two such distinct special-isms which are large and important areas of work, each of which can easily require a practitioner to do nothing else.

Other areas would include education law, housing law, social services and community care law, tax law and the law relating to prisoners. The list could go on. Many of these areas of law have their own set of dedicated law reports. No doubt there are real advantages to the profession and to the public from this increasing specialisation. But, as I have tried to suggest in this lecture, there are dangers in over-specialisation too. In particular, there is a risk that conceptual differences may arise which turn out to be unsound in law.

One illustration of this can be found in the development of the law of legitimate expectation in public law. The term 'legitimate expectation' was first used in English law by Lord Denning MR in *Schmidt* in 1969.[7] It was used in the context of the possibility that a duty to act fairly (what used to be called the rules of natural justice) might arise even where there was no legal right being taken away but only a legitimate expectation. From that time on the law developed in such a way as to recognise that the duty to act fairly could arise in such circumstances. However, 'fairness' was being used in a procedural sense, in other words a duty to afford a hearing (although not necessarily an oral hearing), rather than a substantive sense. For a long time it was thought that the concept of legitimate expectation could not give rise to any substantive right. In other words it could not be used to prevent a public authority from doing something at all, although it might be used to require the authority to go through a fair procedure before doing it and, of course, a public authority must always act in a way which is rational.

In fact the contrary suggestion, that the concept of a substantive legitimate expectation could give rise to a duty to do more than act rationally, was described as a 'heresy' by the Court of Appeal in *Hargreaves*,[8] in which Hirst LJ disapproved of what had been said by Sedley J in the first instance case of *Hamble Fisheries*.[9]

What had apparently gone unnoticed was that in the meantime, since 1985, there had emerged a line of authority in the context of tax cases, in which it was indeed recognised that fairness could have a substantive content and that the concept of legitimate expectation could give rise to substantive obligations, and not only procedural ones. This line of authority started with the decision of the House of Lords in *Preston*[10] in 1985 and included the decision of the Divisional Court in *MFK Underwriting Agents*[11] in 1990. I will return to that decision later for another reason.

A particularly important decision in this line of authority was the decision of the Court of Appeal in *Unilever*[12] in 1996. However, the importance of that decision in public law generally was not fully appreciated. This may have been because it

---

[7] *Schmidt v Secretary of State for Home Affairs* [1969] 2 Ch 149.

[8] *R v Secretary of State for the Home Department, ex p. Hargreaves* [1997] 1 WLR 906.

[9] *R v Ministry of Agriculture, Fisheries and Food, ex p. Hamble Fisheries (Offshore) Ltd* [1995] 2 All ER 714.

[10] *R v Inland Revenue Commissioners, ex p. Preston* [1985] AC 835.

[11] *R v Inland Revenue Commissioners, ex p. MFK Underwriting Agents Ltd* [1990] 1 WLR 1545.

[12] *R v Inland Revenue Commissioners, ex p. Unilever plc* [1996] STC 681.

was only reported in a specialist set of law reports, *Simon's Tax Cases*. It is easy to forget today, when almost any decision is available online, whether or not it stands for any principle of law, that less than 20 years ago it could matter where a case was reported. In any event, the general importance of the line of authority in the tax context was not noticed until the decision of the Court of Appeal in *Coughlan*[13] in 1999. Perhaps unsurprisingly, it was picked up by a court which now included Sedley LJ, as he had become. Since *Coughlan* it is now recognised in public law generally that the concept of legitimate expectation can indeed give rise to substantive duties, and not only procedural ones; and the standard of review by the court is not confined to that of rationality.

I said that I would return to the case of *MFK Underwriting Agents*. The main judgment in that case was given by Bingham LJ. In what has become a classic passage he said that what was required for a legitimate expectation to be created was a representation which was clear, unambiguous and devoid of relevant qualification. In what was a novel and developing area of law he would appear to have drawn on his experience of commercial law when setting out those criteria. They clearly have echoes of the doctrine of promissory estoppel in private law. This seems to me to illustrate the need to avoid regarding conceptual distinctions such as that between private law and public law too rigidly. However, it is also important to bear in mind the cautionary words of Lord Hoffmann in *Reprotech* that 'it is unhelpful to introduce private law concepts of estoppel into planning law' and that 'public law has already absorbed whatever is useful from the moral values which underlie the private law concept of estoppel and the time has come for it to stand on its own two feet'.[14]

Another related context in which, in my view, it would be helpful to bear in mind fundamental concepts of private law concerns the circumstances in which an officer of a public authority can bind that authority. It seems to me that care needs to be taken to distinguish between two questions which may become confused. The first question is whether a local authority (for example) has the power in law to bind itself as to its future conduct. It may or may not have that power: it is well established that a public authority cannot by its representations extend its own powers, so that it cannot bind itself to act in a way which would be ultra vires.[15] The second question is whether, even if the authority does have the power to bind itself, the particular officer who made the representation had the power to make it on behalf of the authority. Whether they did or did not have that power will depend on the principles of agency, which are familiar to private lawyers, and in particular on the concepts of actual or ostensible authority. Many of the examples to be found in the case law on agency arise from business transactions. Similar issues can arise in the field of company law, another field in which a distinction needs to be kept in mind between the powers of a company (to which the doctrine of ultra vires applies) and the powers of an officer or employee of the company (to which the principles of agency apply).

---

[13] *R v North and East Devon Health Authority, ex p. Coughlan* [2001] QB 213.

[14] *R (Reprotech (Pebsham) Ltd) v East Sussex County Council* [2003] 1 WLR 348.

[15] *Maritime Electric Co v General Dairies Ltd* [1937] AC 610.

The final topic on which I want to touch in this lecture is the academic study of law and I hope it is not thought impertinent to do so in this setting. An academic friend of mine once asked me which subjects I had studied at university which had been most useful to me for my practice at the Bar. I replied jurisprudence and legal history – this was only partly tongue in cheek. It does seem to me that the most important thing I learnt at university with the benefit of hindsight was an appreciation of the general principles of law. What is of lasting value is the ability to engage in basic legal reasoning, in particular how to interpret a statute and how to analyse a case. What is also helpful is an understanding of the overall structure of the law. Everything else is detail and may turn out to be ephemeral. The specific case law I learnt about has long since become out of date but the structure and principles of law remain of lasting value.

I would tentatively suggest that the academic study of law could concentrate on the following skills.

First, knowing that there is a problem and being able to identify the right questions to ask. In real life clients do not bring problems to their legal advisers which are already labelled, for example 'contract' or 'tort'. While it is readily understandable why legal education must divide subjects up in that way, it is helpful if a student at the end of their course appreciates that problems in practice will not come packaged in that way.

Secondly, knowing how to go about finding the answer to the question which has been identified. No lawyer can know all of the law but one of the most important transferable skills they can acquire in their legal studies is the ability to conduct legal research well.

Thirdly, a good grounding in the methods of legal reasoning, in particular the interpretation of legislation and the analysis of case law. Again this should be a transferable skill and should not depend on what particular subjects a student has chosen to study.

Fourthly, an understanding of the place of law in its historical and social setting, so that a student can appreciate how we got where we are and the way in which the law responds to social problems (whether adequately or not).

As I said at the outset of this lecture I have been fortunate to have been at different times of my life a student, an academic, a practitioner and now a judge. Each of those perspectives has led me to come to the view that, while specialisation in the law is valuable, it is also important to appreciate that we operate within one legal system, in other words the unity of law.

Law as a System of Values

Jan Grodecki was an academic at the University of Leicester. In 2013 I had the honour of giving this lecture in his memory at the university's campus. In it I explored the complicated relationship between the values of a society and its laws. I suggested that law is ultimately an expression of a society's values. It changes from time to time and varies in different societies. I also traced the history of the famous 'Hart-Devlin' debates of the early 1960s, which concerned the issue of whether the law should enforce morals, in particular in the realm of private sexual relations, and tried to bring that debate up to date by looking at what had happened in the subsequent half century. At the time of this lecture I was a High Court judge.

I T IS AN honour to give this year's Jan Grodecki lecture. I did not have the pleasure of meeting Professor Grodecki but I know that he was a courageous man, a highly respected scholar and a much loved teacher. I am also pleased to see that he was an Honorary Bencher of Lincoln's Inn, which is also my Inn. Professor Grodecki was a firm believer in the view that the academic study of law should be rooted in other disciplines such as the social sciences.

In 1981 Kevin Gray and Pamela Symes published a book called *Real Property and Real People*, which brought a refreshing new approach to the study of land law. In the preface to that book they said that the ultimate purpose of a university education in law is not the learning of rules but 'the critical perception of value'. Of course, the study of law can involve both. There is no inherent contradiction between the learning of rules, in other words a doctrinal or technical approach, and a broader study, which places law in its social context. The first approach might be compared to what Professor Hart called the 'internal point of view' and the second corresponds to the 'external point of view'.[1] Many would suggest that both are important for a full and rounded legal education.

The theme of my lecture will be the relationship between law and values, a relationship which is not a straightforward one. I will use the term 'values' broadly, to include what a society regards as most worthwhile. Often values are moral values but they need not be; and moral values certainly need not be founded on the doctrines of religion in general or any religion in particular.

To the scholar who approaches law from an external point of view, it is perhaps easier to see the relationship between law and values. The law of a given society at a certain point in time will be of interest to a sociologist, a social anthropologist or an historian because it may tell that scholar something of interest about the values of

---

[1] HLA Hart, *The Concept of Law* (2nd ed., Oxford, Clarendon Press, 1994) 89–91.

that society. It was for this reason that law was of interest to the pioneers of sociology in the nineteenth century, such as Durkheim and Weber.

To take one obvious example, if a society is described as being 'polygamous' or 'monogamous' one is referring not only to its culture or a social institution; one is also making a statement about the law of that society, because the institution of marriage, although it often has its origins in social custom, and in particular the norms of a religion, is also usually governed by legal rules.

To take another, perhaps less obvious, example, a society which has abolished the death penalty can be contrasted with one that retains it. This can be seen as not just a difference between two legal systems; it tells the observer something important about the character of each society, about its basic values.

As I have said, the relationship between law and values is not a straightforward one. On the one hand, it is clear that many legal rules are intended to, and do, give effect to certain basic values of a society. Indeed this could be said to provide much of the moral force which is needed to support positive rules of law, in particular the rules of criminal law. Everyone understands, for example, that a society could not function without rules prohibiting murder or theft. One thinks immediately of the Ten Commandments. Such rules reflect fundamental values which themselves may derive from religious traditions, not only the Judeo-Christian tradition, but would be needed in a wholly secular society as well.

Secondly, it is clear that rules of civil law, and not only the criminal law, will often reflect more basic values which are not themselves derived from the law. For example, the principle that promises should be kept lies beneath the law of contract; and much of the law of equity was historically founded upon principles of conscience. Indeed, the concept of 'equity' was, and sometimes still is, used by way of contrast to the 'law' in the sense of the common law.

As every law student knows, the foundations of the law of negligence were described in explicitly Biblical terms by Lord Atkin in *Donoghue v Stevenson*.[2] Six months before the decision in that seminal case, Lord Atkin had given a lecture in which he referred to the moral basis of civil law as follows:

> The idea of law is that the obligations of a man are to keep his word. If he swears to his neighbour, he is not to disappoint them. In other words, he is to keep his contracts. ... He is not to injure his neighbour by acts of negligence; and that certainly covers a very large field of law. I doubt whether the whole of the law of tort could not be comprised in the golden maxim to do unto your neighbour as you would that he should do unto you.[3]

It is clear, thirdly, that legislation sometimes also seeks to reflect and promote certain values. A good example of this can be found in discrimination law, which, ever since the first Race Relations Act was passed in 1965, was intended not merely to make certain activities unlawful but, perhaps even more importantly, to promote the value of equality between human beings irrespective of colour, ethnic origins and so on. Indeed, it may be said that the symbolic or moral force of the discrimination

---

[2] [1932] AC 562, at 580.
[3] Quoted by Lord Morris of Aberavon in 'The Contribution of Welsh Lawyers' (the Lloyd George Memorial Lecture 2006), p 11.

legislation is even greater than its legal effect. Even if the law is not always complied with and it is often difficult to enforce in practice, that legislation still sends out a powerful signal of the kind of society we are – or at least the kind of society we think that we should be.

However, fourthly, it cannot be said that the law as it happens to be at any moment in a society's history necessarily and completely reflects the values of that society. Just because something is considered by many people to be morally wrong does not necessarily mean that it will be, or should be, prohibited by the law. The classic example is adultery, which many people regard as morally wrong, but which the law does not criminalise in this country and has not done since the time of Cromwell: at the time of the Commonwealth the criminal law did prohibit adultery as the ecclesiastical courts had previously done. However, since that time the ordinary criminal law of the land has not sought to prohibit such conduct.

History suggests, indeed, that, if the law attempts to prohibit an activity thought to be morally objectionable but which many people nevertheless wish to engage in, the law may suffer and be exposed to ridicule. The best example perhaps of such a futile attempt was the constitutional amendment introducing prohibition in the United States in the 1920s.[4] Not only was prohibition ineffective to achieve its aim, it spawned further problems for society and the legal system and led to widespread criminal and gangster behaviour.

At a more general level caution is needed in case too much significance is attached to what knowing about the law of a given society tells one about its basic values. Take the relationship between religion and the state. The fact that Israel is defined by its Basic Law as being a Jewish state tells one something important about the character of that country.[5]

But the relationship is not always so straightforward. England has an established Church, which retains a legal status not afforded to other denominations of Christianity or to other faith groups, for example its bishops may sit in the House of Lords and the monarch is the head of the Church of England. However, the role that the established Church, indeed any religion, plays in the life of this country has diminished considerably over the last century.

Contrast that with a society like the USA or India. Both have legal systems which aim to create a secular state, with a clear wall of separation between church and state. Each, however, would generally be regarded as a society in which religion plays a more significant part in people's daily lives than it does in this country. As I will suggest later in this lecture, that does not mean that such a legal system is not based on fundamental values, rather its values are different from those of a society whose law gives a special status to a particular religion or denomination.

Nevertheless, the law is undoubtedly one of the most important features of any society. Indeed, it is in a fundamental sense constitutive of it. This is why it tends to be studied by sociologists and social anthropologists in order to understand what the values of a society are or may have been at a certain point in history. Although

---

[4] 18th Amendment to the US Constitution, passed in 1919 and repealed in 1933 by the 21st Amendment.
[5] Art 2 of the Basic Law.

it is recognised that this will not give the full story, it is nevertheless an important indicator of what kind of society one lives in. After all, law is the means by which a community seeks to organise itself and give effect to the basic norms which it regards as most important.

Take, for example, two of the most controversial issues facing many societies, in particular the United States, in recent times. Whether a society permits abortion to take place or prohibits it tells one something about the nature of the values of that society. A current controversy on which there are widely differing views is the question whether gay people should be permitted to enter into marriage. In this country Parliament has recently enacted legislation to this end. The fact that opinion is so divided on that issue is an indicator that the values of a society are in the process of transition.

Although we may now like to think that the law is value-neutral, and certainly neutral as between different religious views, it is worth recalling that it was not all that long ago that the English common law was said to rest on the values of Christianity. This was said to lie beneath the definition in English law of marriage as 'the voluntary union for life of one man and one woman, to the exclusion of all others'.[6] However, more recently it was said by the Divisional Court in *R (Johns) v Derby City Council* that:

> The laws and usages of the realm do not include Christianity, in whatever form. The aphorism that 'Christianity is part of the common law of England' is mere rhetoric; at least since the decision of the House of Lords in *Bowman v Secular Society Limited* [1917] AC 406 it has been impossible to contend that it is law.[7]

In that case the Court also affirmed that judges 'sit as secular judges serving a multi-cultural community of many faiths'. At paragraph 38, the Court observed that:

> Although historically this country is part of the Christian West, and although it has an established church which is Christian, there have been enormous changes in the social and religious life of our country over the last century. Our society is now pluralistic and largely secular. But one aspect of its pluralism is that we also now live in a multi-cultural community of many faiths. One of the paradoxes of our lives is that we live in a society which has at one and at the same time become both increasingly secular but also increasingly diverse in religious affiliation.

At paragraph 55, the Court endorsed what had earlier been said by Laws LJ in *McFarlane v Relate Avon Limited*:

> The general law may of course protect a particular social or moral position which is espoused by Christianity, not because of its religious imprimatur, but on the footing that in reason its merits commend themselves. So it is with core provisions of the criminal law, the prohibition of violence and dishonesty.[8]

However, I would suggest that Laws LJ is far from saying that the law does not protect certain values. It is ascertaining what those values are which is the question, a

---

[6] *Hyde v Hyde and Woodmansee* (1866) LR 1 P and D 130, at 133 (Lord Penzance).
[7] [2011] EWHC 375 (Admin), at para 39.
[8] [2010] IRLR 872, at paras 21–23.

question to which I will return later. Earlier in the passage to which I have referred, he said:

> The common law and ECHR [European Convention on Human Rights] Article 9 offer vigorous protection of the Christian's right and every other person's right to hold and express his or her beliefs, and so they should. By contrast, they do not, and should not, offer any protection whatever of the substance or content of those beliefs on the ground only that they are based on religious precepts. These are twin conditions of a free society.

That last sentence, it seems to me, although correct, is itself based upon a statement of value. It reflects the fundamental values of what in the twenty-first century English law believes should be the foundation of the law in a society such as ours.

It was not always thus. An interesting and provocative account can be found by Eve Darian-Smith in her book *Religion, Race, Rights: Landmarks in the History of Modern Anglo-American Law*.[9] In that book she argues that, as a matter of historical development: 'At times when new regimes of Western law were constructed, law makers typically invoked some concept of the sacred as a source of legitimacy for their actions'.[10] As she says later:

> Often glossed over in explorations of the development of Anglo-American Law are its histories of conflict and legal discrimination between Christians and non-Christians (i.e. colonists against native peoples), as well as between members of different Christian faiths (i.e. Protestants against Catholics). These conflicts determined a person's standing and status before the law. Just as the colour of a person's skin was and is used as a way of demarcating 'us' and 'them', a person's spiritual affiliation also historically functioned and continues to function as a marker of cultural identity and differentiation that can justify both explicit and implicit legalised intolerance.[11]

It is instructive to remind ourselves how far the law has travelled in the last half century. Just over 50 years ago the House of Lords had to consider the case of *Shaw v Director of Public Prosecutions*.[12] The question of law to be determined was whether there existed at common law a criminal offence of conspiracy to corrupt public morals. The House of Lords held by a majority, with Lord Reid dissenting, that there was such an offence at common law. What is of interest for present purposes is what the speech of Viscount Simonds (a former Lord Chancellor) reveals about what some of our most senior judges considered to be the function of the courts of this country.

Viscount Simonds said:

> In the sphere of criminal law I entertain no doubt that there remains in the courts of law a residual power to enforce the supreme and fundamental purpose of the law, to conserve not only the safety and order but also the moral welfare of the state, and that it is their duty to guard it against attacks which may be the more insidious because they are novel and unprepared for.[13]

[9] (Oxford, Hart Publishing, 2010).
[10] Page 13.
[11] Page 15.
[12] [1962] AC 220.
[13] Page 267.

Viscount Simonds conceded that the law must be related to the changing standards of life, not yielding to every shifting impulse of the popular will but having regard to fundamental assessments of human values and the purposes of society. He acknowledged that:

> Today a denial of the fundamental Christian doctrine, which in past centuries would have been regarded by the ecclesiastical courts as heresy and by the common law as blasphemy, will no longer be an offence if the decencies of controversy are observed.[14]

However he continued:

> When Lord Mansfield, speaking long after the Star Chamber had been abolished, said that the Court of King's Bench was the *custos morum* of the people and had the superintendency of offences *contra bonos mores*, he was asserting, as I now assert, that there is in that court a residual power, where no statute has yet intervened to supersede the common law, to superintend those offences which are prejudicial to the public welfare.

Although Viscount Simonds acknowledged that such occasions would be rare, the example he specifically gave of when it might be appropriate at some point in the future is still of interest:

> Let it be supposed that at some future, perhaps early, date homosexual practices between adult consenting males are no longer a crime. Would it not be an offence if even without obscenity, such practices were publicly advocated and encouraged by pamphlet and advertisement? Or must we wait until Parliament finds time to deal with such conduct? I say, my Lords, that if the common law is powerless in such an event, then we should no longer do her reverence. But I say that her hand is still powerful and that it is for her Majesty's judges to play the part which Lord Mansfield pointed out to them.

It should be recalled that Lord Reid, one of the greatest judges of the twentieth century, took a very different view about the appropriate role of the criminal law. He said:

> Notoriously, there are wide differences of opinion today as to how far the law ought to punish immoral acts which are not done in the face of the public. Some think that the law already goes too far, some that it does not go far enough. Parliament is the proper place, and I am firmly of opinion the only proper place, to settle that. When there is sufficient support from public opinion, Parliament does not hesitate to intervene. Where Parliament fears to tread it is not for the courts to rush in.[15]

Subsequently, in *Knuller Ltd. v Director of Public Prosecutions*[16] the House of Lords held that, even if *Shaw* was wrongly decided, it must stand until it was altered by Parliament. However, more importantly, it also decided that *Shaw* was in no way to be taken as lending any support to the doctrine that the courts have some general or residual power to create new criminal offences. This was more recently reaffirmed by the House of Lords in *R v Jones (Margaret)*.[17] As Lord Bingham of Cornhill said:

> There now exists no power in the courts to create new criminal offences, as decided by a unanimous House of Lords in *[Knuller]* ... while old common law offences survive until

---

[14] Page 268.
[15] Page 275.
[16] [1973] AC 435.
[17] [2007] 1 AC 136.

abolished or superseded by statute, new ones are not created. Statute is now the sole source of new criminal offences.[18]

Lord Bingham explained the underlying democratic principle which lies behind this:

> It is for those representing the people of the country in Parliament, not the executive and not the judges, to decide what conduct should be treated as lying so far outside the bounds of what is acceptable in our society as to attract criminal penalties. One would need very compelling reasons for departing from that principle.[19]

In an earlier generation a judge like Lord Devlin might have regretted the path that the law has taken, since he believed that a fundamental function of the law is the enforcement of morals. However, the modern view itself reflects a basic value of our society – the value of democracy. I shall have more to say about Lord Devlin's views about the enforcement of morals later.

Although the outside observer of a legal system may be able to see (from the 'external point of view') that a legal norm reflects a moral or other fundamental value in a society, this does not offer much assistance to the participant within the legal system, who has to adopt the 'internal point of view'. In particular a judge has to decide a case in accordance with the law and nothing else. Certainly a judge is not entitled to impose his or her own subjective views of what is morally right or wrong on society.

In this context I think it instructive to keep in mind the wisdom imparted by Benjamin Cardozo in *The Nature of the Judicial Process*.[20] Cardozo, who was later to become a Justice of the US Supreme Court, said:

> A judge, I think, would err if he were to impose upon the community as a rule of life his own idiosyncrasies of conduct or belief. Let us suppose, for illustration, a judge looked upon theatre-going as a sin. Would he be doing right if, in a field where the rule of law were still unsettled, he permitted this conviction, though known to be in conflict with a dominant standard of right conduct, to govern his decision? My own notion is that he would be under a duty to conform to the accepted standards of the community, the *mores* of the times.[21]

However, it is not always easy to detect where a person's values come from even to that person. As Cardozo put it:

> The spirit of the age, as it is revealed to each of us, is too often only the spirit of the group in which the accidents of birth or education or occupation or fellowship have given us a place. No effort or revolution of the mind will overthrow utterly and at all times the empire of these subconscious loyalties.[22]

Traditional legal education tends to take (implicitly if not always explicitly) a positivist view of law: it regards law as a system of rules. However, experience suggests that in many fields across the legal spectrum the rules are not clear-cut and perhaps even run out.

---

[18] At para 28.
[19] At para 29.
[20] (Princeton, Yale University Press, 1921).
[21] At page 108.
[22] At pages 174–75.

This can happen not just at the appellate level, where a court may have a choice as to the development of the law. It can occur every day at the level of a first instance court. Take one of the most important decisions that such a court has to make, the sentencing decision in a criminal case. Section 125 of the Coroners and Justice Act 2009 provides that the court should follow any relevant guideline issued by the Sentencing Council or its predecessor, unless it would be contrary to the 'interests of justice' to do so. A black letter lawyer would search in vain for a definition of the interests of justice; it is not to be found in an interpretation section.

Other examples could be given from the field of civil law. For example a contract may not be enforceable if it would be contrary to public policy. A covenant may be in unreasonable restraint of trade. A duty of confidentiality may be overridden where it is in the public interest to do so. How then is a judge to say when something is contrary to the interests of justice? Or contrary to public policy? Or whether a publication is in the public interest?

More generally the question may be asked: where are values to be found if not in the subjective views of the individual judge? It seems to me that the answer is to be found in using the conventional techniques of legal reasoning which are available to a judge in adjudication. The judge must strive to reach the correct answer by reference to relevant legal materials.

First, the judge will check any relevant authorities, in particular binding precedents or guidance from appellate courts.

Secondly, the judge can look to the structure and interstices of the common law itself, to detect that there are certain fundamental values which are well-established in our system of justice. To take the sentencing example I mentioned earlier, the principle of proportionality, that a sentence should be proportionate in all the circumstances of a particular offence and having regard to any personal mitigation, will provide guidance. However desirable it is to have consistency of treatment, at the end of the day the sentencing exercise is not a mechanistic one, and justice needs to be done on the facts of a particular case.

Thirdly, guidance as to the fundamental values of our legal system may be found in legislation, in particular statutes which have a constitutional character such as the Human Rights Act 1998. It is now acknowledged that the HRA, although not an entrenched bill of rights, is no ordinary statute, but a constitutional one. The rights set out in Sch. 1 to the HRA are not rights as traditionally understood in the common law but reflect basic values of a free and democratic society. They are rarely absolute: often they have to be balanced against other rights and with the general interest of the community. This calls for the exercise of judgement, especially when a judge is called upon to decide whether an interference with a right meets the test of proportionality.

However, the point I wish to emphasise in this lecture is that the rights set out in the HRA are a good guide, if not an exhaustive one, to what our society regards as fundamental values: after all the HRA was passed by Parliament. Other statutes which similarly proclaim fundamental values would include the Equality Act 2010, which has replaced earlier anti-discrimination legislation, such as the Race Relations Act 1976 and the Sex Discrimination Act 1975.

If legal positivism taught us that law can be regarded as a system of rules, the great contribution which the late Professor Ronald Dworkin made was to give us the insight that a legal system also includes principles, which are not as rigid as rules but have gravitational force.[23] They draw us in the right direction when trying to answer a legal problem: they do not necessarily dictate the result but they do suggest one that fits better with everything else we know about our legal system than the alternative answer would.

Without wishing in any way to expound a general theory of law (something which I would not in any event be qualified to do), I would suggest that such principles themselves can be regarded as being rooted in the values of that legal system.

I would not suggest that these values are necessarily inherent in any system of law in order for it to constitute law, since clearly they can change or develop over time and vary between societies, as the sociological study of law indicates. However, what can reasonably be suggested is that our legal system is based on certain values, which are well-established in its bedrock. Without attempting an exhaustive list I think that most observers of our legal system would acknowledge that its values include the concepts of fairness, equality, democracy and the rule of law.

Although the law does not any longer attempt (or even think that it should attempt) to enforce morals in the sense that Lord Devlin thought it should 50 years ago, that is not to say that the law is immoral or even amoral. It is based on values, which lie at its foundations, but one of those values is that we do not necessarily think it right to impose a subjective code of private or sexual morality on an individual. Our legal system now recognises, as the Wolfenden Report suggested in 1957, and as Professor Hart advocated in the early 1960s, that there are some things which are none of the state's business, such as homosexual acts between consenting adults in private. As the Wolfenden Report famously put it:

> Unless a deliberate attempt is to be made by society, acting through the agency of the law, to equate the sphere of crime with that of sin, there must remain a realm of private morality and immorality which is, in brief and crude terms, not the law's business.[24]

But it is interesting with the perspective of time to look back on what the dominant view was until the 1960s. It was perhaps most eloquently expressed by Lord Devlin, one of the most respected judges that this country has produced, in *The Enforcement of Morals*. He said that:

> an established morality is as necessary as good government to the welfare of society. Societies disintegrate from within more often than they are broken up by external pressures. There is disintegration when no common morality is observed and history shows that the loosening of moral bonds is often the first stage of disintegration, so that society is justified in taking the same steps to preserve its moral code as it does to preserve its government and other essential institutions. The suppression of vice is as much the law's business as the suppression of subversive activities; it is no more possible to define a sphere of private morality than it is to define one of private subversive activity.[25]

---

[23] R Dworkin, *Taking Rights Seriously* (London, Duckworth Press, 1977), esp Ch 4 on 'Hard Cases'.
[24] Report of the Committee on Homosexual Offences and Prostitution (1957) Cmd 247, para 62.
[25] P Devlin, *The Enforcement of Morals* (Oxford, OUP, 1965) 13–14.

Professor Hart's response was equally eloquent. He said, in *Law, Liberty and Morality*, that:

> The unimpeded exercise by individuals of free choice may be held to be a value in itself with which it is *prima facie* wrong to interfere; or it may be thought valuable because it enables individuals to experiment – even with living – and to discover things valuable both to themselves and others.[26]

Note Professor Hart's repeated references in that passage to 'values'. As we now know the tide of history was on the side of Professor Hart. The law has turned 180 degrees. What was criminalised until 1967 has become the subject of a fundamental human right, in particular as a result of the Human Rights Act. The right to respect for private life in Article 8 includes a power of autonomy over many decisions which are intrinsic to a human being's personality, for example consensual sexual relationships.[27]

This does not mean that the law has become a value-free zone. Far from it. It means that the values of the law are now different from what they were 50 years ago. As Professor Hart anticipated it simply means that our society has changed; not that it has been subverted. It can still be said that law is a system of values.

---

[26] HLA Hart, *Law, Liberty and Morality* (Stanford, Stanford University Press, 1963), 21–22.
[27] Eg *Dudgeon v United Kingdom* (1982) 4 EHRR 149.

First Impressions of a New Court of Appeal Judge

I gave this after-dinner talk in 2018, about six months after my appointment to the Court of Appeal, to the student law society at Trinity College, Oxford. The student law society there is named after Michael Beloff QC, who had been President of the college for about 10 years from 1996. Michael was immensely kind and supportive of me, from the moment I first met him in 1984, when I was an undergraduate. We were later members of the same chambers, at 4–5 Gray's Inn Square, where I did my pupillage and practised for 10 years between 1990 and 2000, when I became one of the founding members of Matrix Chambers.

I WOULD LIKE to thank you for your kind invitation to speak at this year's dinner. It is a particular pleasure to be here because your law society is named after Michael Beloff QC. I first met Michael Beloff when I was an undergraduate at another Trinity College (I'm afraid not at this university but somewhere in East Anglia) when I did what today would be called a 'mini pupillage'. I spent one day accompanying Michael in the Court of Appeal. If my recollection is correct he was a relatively new silk at that time acting on behalf of an immigrant before the Master of the Rolls, Lord Donaldson. I remember being struck then that there was something wonderful about this country, in which one of the greatest advocates at the Bar can just as easily act on behalf of the poorest person in the land as on behalf of the richest.

Michael has been kind enough to remark upon my own career at the Bar. I think I was very fortunate in the work that I had the opportunity to do and the clients for whom I acted. I remember one case in which I was instructed on behalf of the Inland Revenue in the House of Lords. I was still only a junior barrister at the time. I was faced on the other side of the courtroom by two silks for the taxpayer, one of whom was a specialist in tax law and the other a specialist in EU law. When they had finished their submissions Lord Nicholls, who was in the chair, announced after a brief and private deliberation with his colleagues that the House of Lords did not need to call on me. As many of you will appreciate, that is an indication by a court that you have won your case. It confirms my view that the best kind of advocacy is often to keep quiet – or (and some of you will recognise the lyrics): 'You say it best when you say nothing at all'.

As has been mentioned, I was appointed to the Court of Appeal in October last year. I have therefore only been sitting there for about five months. I thought that this evening I would share with you some of my first impressions as a new Judge of the Court of Appeal.

One of my predecessors, Lord Justice Asquith (who later became a Law Lord), had much to say on the topic of my talk this evening. He said in 1950 that:

> The neophyte in the Court of Appeal is compelled, at an age when his intellectual arteries are beginning to harden, to go back to school: to get up new branches of the law: [and] to brush up many which he has forgotten: ...

He also observed that the Court of Appeal is a friendly place:

> One's colleagues are such nice and accomplished men, [and in those days they were all men] that it is almost a pleasure to be dissented from by them. But the intellectual climate is severe. More particularly to one accustomed to browse in the lowlands of the King's Bench Division and to inhale its crass air, is the intellectual atmosphere of the Court of Appeal one of extreme, of almost Himalayan, rarefaction.

Lord Justice Asquith reminded us of the summary given by the late Mr Theobald Mathew of the functions of a Judge of First Instance. He said that:

> He should be 'quick, courteous and wrong'. 'Wrong', because otherwise there would be nothing left for the Court of Appeal to do.

But as Lord Justice Asquith observed, we should not jump to the conclusion that a Lord Justice should be 'quick, courteous and right'. After all this would run counter to the principle that there should be some work left for the House of Lords to do. He said:

> The Lords of Appeal in Ordinary must not lightly be defrauded of their statutory prey.

Lord Justice Asquith also noted the change from being a High Court Judge to going to the Court of Appeal. He said that:

> The general setting of the Court is sober, drained of colour, and devoid of excitement, contrasting in this regard with the high pomp of circuit. ... No red robes, no javelin men or trumpeters, no cathedral services, no Rolls Royce provided by a thoughtful and lavish High Sheriff, no fuss or drama ...

That reminds me of the occasion in 1983 when the 'Red Judge' (Mr Justice Woolf, who was then a Presiding Judge of the South Eastern Circuit) arrived in Cambridge. There was plenty of pomp as his entourage arrived in Great Court at Trinity College, when we undergraduates all lined up to welcome the Red Judge. Little did I suspect then that 30 years later, in 2013, I myself would be a Presider of the South Eastern Circuit and would arrive in Cambridge to try a murder case at the Crown Court. No Rolls Royce on this occasion or trumpeters. Only a standard class ticket and carrying my own bags.

Since 1966, there has been a single Court of Appeal, which includes a Criminal Division as well as a Civil Division. This replaced the old Court of Criminal Appeal, which had been created in 1907. About half the Judges of the Court of Appeal sit in the Criminal Division as well as the Civil Division, although there are some (for example those with a Chancery background) who sit only in civil cases.

The Criminal Division is in practice the final court of appeal for most criminal cases in England and Wales. Appeals can go to the Supreme Court on a point of law of general public importance but this is rare, particularly if the appeal is against sentence. When it comes to appeals against conviction, again in practice only a few appeals go there. A famous recent example was the case of *Jogee*, which concerned the doctrine of joint enterprise, in particular in the law of homicide. More common is that there will be convened a five-judge Court of Appeal, with the Lord Chief Justice presiding, to deal with the most important criminal cases, for example if an earlier decision of the Court of Appeal is to be reconsidered.

One thing that people don't always appreciate is that in the Criminal Division there will usually be sitting not only a Court of Appeal Judge but two High Court Judges or, frequently, a High Court Judge and a Circuit Judge. Those Circuit Judges are usually very senior criminal Judges from the Crown Court around the country and bring a very important criminal experience from the coalface into the Court of Appeal.

Something else that strikes some people as a little curious is that Court of Appeal Judges sit in the High Court. This is particularly true of the Divisional Court, in which there will usually be a Court of Appeal Judge sitting with a High Court Judge and sometimes with two High Court Judges. This often occurs in criminal cases, in particular appeals by way of case stated from the Magistrates' Court, which can involve interesting points of law. For example, I recently dealt with an appeal by way of case stated in the Divisional Court, in which we had to consider whether the defence of self-defence is available as a matter of law when a person is charged with obstruction of a police officer in the execution of their duty. We held that such a defence is available as a matter of law. The Divisional Court sometimes also hears the most important civil cases by way of judicial review: for example, last week we heard an application for judicial review brought by Liberty challenging the compatibility of Part 4 of the Investigatory Powers Act 2016 with fundamental rights in EU law.

In the last few years there has been a shift in the kind of work which comes to the Civil Division of the Court of Appeal. In particular most appeals from the County Court now go to the High Court and no longer to the Court of Appeal. Our own case load in the Civil Division usually consists of appeals from one of the Divisions of the High Court; from the Upper Tribunal (in particular the Immigration and Asylum Chamber); and from other Tribunals such as the Employment Appeal Tribunal.

One of the things that I am often asked about is whether we sit only in the sorts of cases in which we are specialist. The answer is that we sit in all sorts of cases. For example, I have sat in the last few months in cases arising from the Family Court as well as the Commercial Court. When the constitution of the Court is fixed there will usually be at least one, and sometimes two, Judges who are specialists in the area of law concerned. However, it is generally thought to be important that the panel should include one member who is as it were an 'outsider'. In my view the result is that the whole is greater than the sum of the parts.

By way of example I would mention the case of *Re M*, in which we gave judgment just before Christmas. That was a family law case concerning the rights of a transgender person to have contact with her children in an ultra-orthodox Jewish community. I sat in that case with the President of the Family Division, Sir James Munby, and Lady Justice Arden. Those sorts of cases can raise acutely sensitive questions about the potential conflict between different rights such as the right to freedom of religion and the right to respect for family life.

One thing that I have noticed in my first few months in the Court of Appeal is that there are very few dissenting judgments. I myself have not found myself in a Court so far where there has been a dissenting judgment at all. There are quite often concurring judgments and I myself have occasionally given a short concurring judgment. Sometime there is a single judgment of the Court in civil cases: for example the judgment in *Re M* was a judgment of the Court. In the Criminal Division there is invariably a single judgment given, although there is provision in statute which permits the Presiding Judge to allow a separate judgment to be given.[1] In my experience of sitting in the Criminal Division in the last six and a half years that has never happened. Although it is rare, occasionally the decision is in fact reached by a majority of two to one although a single judgment of the Court will still be given.

On the subject of dissenting judgments I am reminded of my favourite story about Lord Denning when he was Master of the Rolls. A new Judge had recently arrived at the Court of Appeal and was due to sit with him. When the three Judges met outside Court to have a brief discussion about the case they were about to hear the most junior Judge tentatively said that he was minded to dismiss the appeal. Lord Denning said to him:

Don't worry, you can dissent.

At this point the second Judge in the Court piped up and said that, in fact, he too was thinking of dismissing the appeal. Lord Denning said to him:

Don't worry, you can dissent as well.

One thing that may surprise you is how often we have to consider the question of precedent and whether we are bound by an earlier decision of the Court of Appeal. Many issues have come before us, not all of which have required us to reach a final view on them. For example, when is the Civil Division of the Court of Appeal bound by a decision of the Criminal Division? In what circumstances is the Criminal Division free to depart from one of its own earlier decisions? Does it have a greater freedom of manoeuvre when a change in the law would be favourable to a defendant rather than to the prosecution? What should the Court of Appeal do when faced with an apparent conflict between a decision of its own and a decision of the European Court of Human Rights?

---

[1] Section 59 of the Senior Courts Act 1981.

This brings me back to what Lord Justice Asquith said all those years ago in 1950. He asked one of his distinguished colleagues what the difference is between the *ratio* of a case and *obiter dicta*. The answer was:

> The rule is quite simple: if you agree with the other bloke you say it's part of the *ratio*; if you don't, you say it's '*obiter* ...', with the implication that he is a congenital idiot.

One issue that sometimes arises is what we should do when an earlier case gave two reasons for reaching a decision. If either alone would suffice to explain the decision, can it be said that neither is the *ratio*? Lord Justice Asquith pointed out that:

> Absurd consequences ... follow if it can validly be argued that where there are two independent reasons either of which justifies a decision, both are *obiter* because neither is 'necessary' having regard to the existence of the other. If 'having an umbrella' means 'having a necessary umbrella' then a man who has two umbrellas has no umbrella at all.

I was reminded of all of this recently when we gave judgment in a case called *Gilham v Ministry of Justice*,[2] in which we decided that a Judge does not have a contract whereby he or she undertakes to do or perform personally any work or services for another party to the contract. There was an earlier decision of the Court of Appeal, called *O'Brien*, which had decided that there is no such contract. However, *O'Brien* went to the Supreme Court, which (after a reference to the Court of Justice of the European Union) decided the case on another point. This led in our case to the interesting question of whether we were bound by the earlier decision of the Court of Appeal in *O'Brien*. This issue had itself been the subject of decision by the Court of Appeal on an earlier occasion, in *Al-Mehdawi v Secretary of State for the Home Department*.[3] In that case Taylor LJ (as he then was) had said that a previous decision of the Court of Appeal is not binding on that Court where there has been an appeal to the House of Lords albeit that the point in issue had not there fallen for decision. As Lord Justice Underhill observed in our case, Lord Justice Taylor's conclusion is indeed *prima facie* binding on the Court of Appeal. The problem, however, is that the decision itself was the subject of an appeal to the House of Lords, which declined to consider the question and decided the case on another point. As Lord Justice Underhill observed in *Gilham* (at paragraph 62):

> We are thus in the Gilbertian situation that the application of Taylor LJ's reasoning means that it is itself not authoritative.

In the end we decided to proceed on the basis that, even if we were not bound by the earlier decision in *O'Brien*, we should follow it because (in any event) we agreed with it.

Judges vary enormously when it comes to how much they should intervene in hearings in court. I am reminded of what Lord Ackner apparently had in front of him on the bench. It was a sign which read: 'Remember – you are paid to listen'.

Unfortunately not all Judges heed that advice. There is a story told about Viscount Haldane, who later became Lord Chancellor, when he was arguing a case at the Bar.

---

[2] [2017] EWCA Civ 2220.
[3] [1990] 1 AC 876.

A colleague's daughter had been taken to visit the Court to watch the great advocate in action. Afterwards, when she was asked what she had made of it all, she replied: "Who was the man who kept interrupting the Judges?"

In conclusion: The Court of Appeal is the main law-making court in England and Wales. Of course the most important cases go to the Supreme Court but, in terms of numbers, the vast majority go no higher than the Court of Appeal. Typically the Supreme Court hears about 80 appeals a year. By way of contrast, last year the Court of Appeal in its Civil Division gave judgment in more than 2, 000 cases.

I would say that our task is to develop the common law in an incremental way so as to ensure stability in society, while keeping the law in tune with the needs of a changing world. We need to apply a steady hand on the tiller, with the occasional gentle nudge, to make sure that the law is proceeding smoothly and not getting too close either to the bank or stuck in turbulent waters.

Keynote Speech to the Criminal Bar Association Conference

I gave this speech shortly after I was appointed to the Court of Appeal. I have long had an interest in criminal law, ever since I was a student. I taught criminal law for a year, when I was doing my pupillage (1989–90) and would travel up to Cambridge, to give supervisions at my old college, Trinity, at the weekend. Although I specialised in civil work when I practised at the Bar, I enjoyed sitting as a criminal trial judge, both as a Recorder from 2004, and as a High Court judge from 2011. Criminal trials were a particularly important part of my work during the four years when I was a Presiding judge of the South Eastern Circuit from 2013 to 2016. As a Lord Justice of Appeal, I no longer do criminal trials but I do sit in the Court of Appeal (Criminal Division), which hears appeals from the Crown Court, and in the Divisional Court, which hears criminal appeals from the Magistrates' Court. Since this speech was given the issue about the test for dishonesty in criminal cases has been authoritatively decided by the Court of Appeal (Criminal Division) in R v Barton [2020] 2 Cr App R 7, *in which* Ivey v Genting Casinos (UK) Ltd [2018] AC 391 *was followed.*

INTRODUCTION

I T IS A great pleasure to be invited to speak to the Criminal Bar Association Conference this year. I am looking forward to hearing other speakers and talking to as many of you as possible during the course of the morning.

Like many people in this room I was saddened last week to read the news of the passing of Jeremy Hutchinson at the age of 102. He was one of the greatest advocates at the criminal bar in the twentieth century. He was, of course, a founding member of the CBA. To mention just one of his many famous cases, he was junior counsel – led by Gerald Gardiner QC – in the *Penguin Books* case, which in many ways ushered in a new era: metaphorically as well as literally it marked the start of the 1960s. I never had the opportunity to see him in action myself but thankfully it is still possible to hear his beautiful voice. You can go to BBC i-Player and find his interview with Helena Kennedy three years ago in 2014, when he was only 99, in a series called 'A Law Unto Themselves'. Lord Hutchinson of Lullington QC, to give him his formal title, was, in the best traditions of the criminal bar, a fearless advocate. He was prepared to stand up not only to the state in the form of the prosecution but also to stand up to judges when that was necessary.

We are fortunate in this country to have an incorruptible judiciary. We are fortunate to have a fearless and independent criminal bar. We know that, even if we ourselves are never directly involved in the criminal justice system, if one of our fellow citizens is accused of a serious crime, they will have access to the best that the bar has to offer to defend them. We are also fortunate to have prosecutions conducted by advocates who must regard themselves as 'ministers of justice'. We need you at the criminal bar to make our system of criminal justice work and to work fairly and efficiently in the interests of all concerned, including the public interest.

SUBSTANTIVE CRIMINAL LAW

I intend to say very little about recent developments in substantive criminal law. We are going to hear later this morning from Dr Findlay Stark about that topic. I would briefly mention just two cases from this year which have struck me as being of particular interest.

The first is the judgment of the Supreme Court in *Ivey v Genting Casinos Ltd*,[1] in which it was said that the second limb of the *Ghosh* direction on dishonesty was wrong. Of course that case was a civil case, not a criminal case; the relevant passage was *obiter*; and so the issue awaits authoritative resolution in the criminal context by the Court of Appeal. However, the Divisional Court has very recently observed that, given the terms of the unanimous views of the Supreme Court, 'it is difficult to imagine the Court of Appeal preferring *Ghosh* to *Ivey* in the future'. See *DPP v Patterson*[2] (Sir Brian Leveson PQBD), at paragraph 16.

Ghosh[3] was decided by the Court of Appeal when I was studying criminal law at university. In practice I don't think there were many cases in which the second limb of the direction in fact had to be given, because it usually sufficed to direct the jury that dishonesty is an ordinary word of the English language, whose meaning would be well known to them. I do remember one case I tried as a Recorder in which I did have to give the second limb of the direction.

The other case I would mention is the decision of the Court of Appeal in *Rose*,[4] which concerned gross negligence manslaughter. I remember the case because at one time I was going to be the trial judge and I had to case manage it in its preliminary stages. The defendant was an optometrist. She was convicted of the manslaughter of a boy whom she had seen for an eye examination and who later died. The Court of Appeal quashed the conviction on the ground that a submission of no case to answer should have been accepted by the trial judge. The Court clarified the basis for criminal liability in such cases. In particular the Court emphasised that the risk of death must be both serious and obvious; and that, in assessing the reasonable foreseeability of serious and obvious risk of death, it is not appropriate to take into account what the defendant would have known but for his or her breach of duty.

---

[1] [2018] AC 391.
[2] [2017] EWHC 2820 (Admin).
[3] [1982] QB 1053.
[4] [2017] EWCA Crim 1168.

THE JURY

As we all know juries are a fundamental feature of our system for trying serious criminal cases. In my experience juries take their task very seriously and value the responsibility and trust which are vested in them. I want to touch on three points in the jury system when just occasionally something can go wrong.

The first is that it is important that the panel of jurors in waiting should properly understand the significance of what is being said to them when they are asked, for example, to mention immediately if they know the name of a person connected to the case. I remember a murder case I tried at Luton in 2014 in which a juror did recognise the name of a witness but said nothing at the time because he really wanted to serve on the jury in what he thought would be a very interesting case. Later he mentioned this to other jurors. Although fortunately this was before the case had got very far, and in particular witnesses did not have to be recalled to give evidence, he was arrested by the police and his case referred to the Attorney General.

The second point is this. The introductory remarks by the trial judge to the jury should mention right from the start of the trial that they should not talk about the case even to other members of the jury except when they are all together. This does not always happen and, if it does not, counsel for the parties should remind the judge of the need for this. Earlier this year I was a member of the Court of Appeal which considered a case where, unfortunately, the trial judge had not done this, although it was her usual practice to do so; and counsel did not notice the omission: see *Agera and Lansana*,[5] paragraph 16. In the end this did not affect the outcome of the appeal although some members of the jury had spoken about the case when they went out for a drink, but it is worth remembering that counsel have a responsibility in this regard as does the judge.

The third point relates to the use of IT by members of the public in a jury trial. These days a smartphone can do so many things that were undreamt of even a few years ago; and can do so almost instantaneously. When I tried a murder case at Lewes in 2013, there was a submission of no case to answer on behalf of one of the two defendants at half time. I rejected that submission. Of course all of that happened, as it must, in the absence of the jury. Very shortly afterwards my ruling was circulated on social media by someone who had been in the public gallery. Thankfully it was possible to have this material removed quite quickly and no one suggested that any member of the jury had seen it. One cannot emphasise enough the warning that the judge now gives to jurors at the start of a trial not to research the case on the internet, including the possibility of a contempt of court and penal sanctions being imposed. But one cannot guarantee that there will never be problems when the use of smartphones is so quick and easy.

DIRECTIONS TO THE JURY

I want to turn to a different topic: directions given by the trial judge to a jury. The fundamental purpose of a summing up is to help the jury in its task. Everything that

---

[5] [2017] EWCA Crim 740.

we do as judges should be directed to achieving that purpose. In recent years it has become common practice to provide directions of law to the jury in writing, after discussion with counsel. Often those directions will be accompanied by a route to verdict, certainly in the more complicated cases.

Since the new Criminal Procedure Rules and Practice Direction came into effect in April of last year, trial judges have been encouraged to consider giving a 'split summing up'. This seems to me to be something which can have great value depending on the nature of the case being tried. Often it will be helpful to have the basic directions of law given by the judge to the jury before closing speeches by the advocates. I would suggest that the route to verdict, if there is one, should also be given to the jury before closing speeches. All of this is helpful not least because it enables the advocates to tailor their closing speeches to what the real issues in the trial are and they can assist the jury by going through the issues which the jury will have in a document and which they can readily follow.

In an appropriate case it can also be helpful for the defence to make a short speech after the prosecution have opened the case, so that the jury can understand what the issues at the trial are going to be before they start hearing the evidence.

I would even urge, in the appropriate case, the giving of written directions on the law, including the burden and standard of proof, at the outset of the trial, before the evidence is heard by the jury. This is what happened in a murder trial which I tried at Lewes in the spring of last year. The reason why that was particularly helpful to the jury in that case was that it was possible to identify right at the start of the trial what the main issue in the case was going to be. That issue was diminished responsibility, as counsel for the defence explained in a short speech. Furthermore, it was possible to explain to the jury before they heard the evidence how they should approach that evidence. Of course the burden of proof shifts to the defendant in a case where he or she relies on diminished responsibility. And the standard of proof is different for a defendant compared to the normal criminal standard of proof which lies on the prosecution.

And there will be cases which fall somewhere in the middle of the spectrum. For example, before identification evidence is going to be heard by the jury, it will often now be appropriate for the judge to give the standard direction on identification evidence just before that stage is reached. Similarly, the standard direction on expert evidence should be given just before the jury are about to hear from the first expert witness in the trial.

THE EVIDENCE OF CHILDREN

In recent years we have all become more attuned to the needs of children in our criminal courts. I myself have conducted trials where the principal witnesses of fact were very young children, at least one I remember as young as five. This will often be true in sex offence cases but it can be true in other cases too, such as homicide.

I remember one such case, which I tried at the Central Criminal Court last year, in which the main witnesses for the prosecution in a manslaughter case were the brother and sister of the young child who had been killed by their father. They clearly found it very difficult to give evidence in the normal way, even from a video suite, and so it was decided that leading counsel for both sides should go the video suite and ask their questions from there, with the intermediary also present, while the jury and others could watch the evidence being given from the courtroom.

More generally the advocates' tool kit has been of enormous help in this context. In my experience, advocates have become much better at understanding the different way in which cross-examination should be conducted of young children.

ABE (Achieving Best Evidence) interviews are something we are now well used to dealing with in a criminal trial. I think it fair to say that the quality of those interviews can still be variable. Many people feel that the early parts of the interviews could perhaps be more closely edited to focus on what is really going to be required in a Crown Court trial.

One interesting development, which has been piloted as you know in a number of courts around the country, including Kingston, is the use of section 28 to record the cross-examination of a child witness. While this is still work in progress, it seems to me that one of its beneficial consequences can be that if, for some reason, a trial becomes ineffective, at least the evidence of the child witness will already be in existence in recorded form and, even if there has to be a second trial, that child will not have to come back to court to go through the process of cross-examination for a second time.

EQUALITY AND DIVERSITY

The Chair of the CBA, Angela Rafferty QC, has made it clear that one of her priorities this year is equality and diversity, including social mobility. This is a subject in which I have long taken an interest. At one time I was Chair of the Bar Council's Race Relations Committee, which later became one of its Equality and Diversity Committees. Like Angela, I think this topic has as much to with the need for greater social mobility at the Bar as with other strands of diversity, such as gender and race. This is an important issue for the judiciary too. It is a great honour to serve the public as a judge and the country deserves the best judges, from all backgrounds.

Although there is no room for complacency I have always been a 'glass half full' person. For example, in the last year there have been four women appointed as Resident Judges at Crown Courts in London, including one person of Asian origin.[6] Another woman of Asian origin has been appointed a senior circuit judge to sit at the Old Bailey.[7] These are all steps in the right direction and I hope help to provide inspiration to others, some of whom will be in this room today. If you are not a Recorder already, I would encourage you all to think about applying to become one as perhaps the first rung on the judicial ladder.

---

[6] HHJ Deborah Taylor (Southwark); HHJ Usha Karu (Inner London); HHJ Rosa Dean (Harrow); and HHJ Alice Robinson (Croydon).

[7] HHJ Anuja Dhir QC.

CONCLUDING REMARKS

All that remains for me to say is to thank you again for the work that you do in our criminal courts. I wish you well and hope that you enjoy the rest of this Conference.

Let me end as I began with the late great Jeremy Hutchinson. In the book *Jeremy Hutchinson's Case Histories* by Thomas Grant,[8] in the post-script written by Jeremy Hutchinson himself, he said:

> No one becomes a criminal barrister to make large sums of money. A criminal practice has always been the least well paid and of the lowest status at the Bar. Yet in my opinion the rewards are of the greatest. You practise in circumstances that seriously affect your fellow human beings in their personal and everyday lives. Your clients are of every kind, privileged or deprived, bewildered and weak, or street-wise and strong. ... You are privileged in your work; privileged because, first, it falls to you to uphold at all times the principles of justice and the rule of law, and, second, unreservedly to uphold the interests of your client whose case becomes yours. You share for a short time the intimate life of a person *in extremis* and stripped bare whose reputation, livelihood or liberty have been placed in your hands.

[8] London, John Murray, 2015.

Common Law, Common Heritage?
Some Reflections on
Anglo-American Law

I gave this talk in 2018 to visiting American lawyers and judges, gathered for a conference at Jesus College, Cambridge, organised by Waynesburg University in Pennsylvania. American law has inherited the common law from its colonial past but, while there are similarities, the common law has diverged in different jurisdictions. This talk enabled me to draw on my experience as a student in the USA and as a common law judge in this country, dealing with both civil and criminal cases.

INTRODUCTION

THANK YOU FOR your kind invitation to talk to you this evening. As you have heard, I had the pleasure of spending a year as a student in the United States more than 30 years ago. After I had done my Master's Degree in California I travelled with a friend all over the United States, including visiting the states of Pennsylvania and Virginia, from which many of you come. I particularly enjoyed visiting Independence Hall in Philadelphia and Monticello near Charlottesville. Much more recently, in 2016, I had the pleasure of being back in Philadelphia and visited the Constitution Center. It was an honour to see some of the original drafts of the Declaration of Independence in Jefferson's own hand.

The theme of my talk this evening is the common law, which forms part of the common heritage of our two countries. Most of the American states have continued to use that heritage in their legal systems right up to the present time, with the exception of Louisiana, which has a system of civil law based on French and Spanish law. Many of the words and procedures that we use are still the same and have a history going back many centuries in English law.

I was interested to note from your programme for this week that one of the other speakers is Judge Gary Glazer who sits in the Pennsylvania Court of Common Pleas. The Court of Common Pleas was one of the three common law Courts which originated in England in the second half of the twelfth century, the others being the Court of King's Bench and the Court of Exchequer. Those Courts no longer exist in England, having been abolished in 1873.

The common law is often regarded as having originated during the reign of King Henry II. You may think of Harry Potter as 'the boy wizard'. But in fact in this country there is a barrister and former academic lawyer also called Harry Potter. He has written a history of the common law. He describes the beginnings of the common law in the following way:

> Henry II, cosmopolitan as he was, had not turned primarily to principles of Roman law and distorted English traditions by grafting on alien institutions. The King chose to take English customary law, fragmented and localised, no longer adequate to the needs of a changing society ... The best of local laws could be applied throughout the lands. The result was a basic system of law that drew on tradition but – unlike customary law – was also capable of being built upon, and expanded or adapted in the future. Now England did not just have regional laws; it had a legal system common to the whole kingdom. A King born in France had laid the foundations upon which the immense structure of English law could be built.[1]

It was Henry II who first despatched his judges around the country on 'circuits' to dispense royal justice, which would be common to the whole of England and would not depend on local custom and the law as administered for example by the Lord of the Manor. That system of the King's or Queen's Justices going around England and Wales on circuit is something that we still have in this country. When I was a Justice of the High Court, I was a Presiding Judge on the South Eastern Circuit, which includes London. So that tradition which goes back more than 800 years is still alive and well in this country. And, of course, the United States is also divided into Circuits. It is a pleasure to see that, Brooks Smith, the Chief Judge of the Court of Appeals for the Third Circuit, is also speaking at this conference.

It might be thought therefore that the common law has never changed and remains as it was in the twelfth century. That, of course, would be absurd. The great genius of the common law is its ability to adapt and develop to meet the needs of a changing society. One of our greatest judges in the twentieth century was Lord Denning. When he was Denning LJ he said in *Packer v Packer*:[2]

> If we never do anything which has not been done before, we shall never get anywhere. The law will stand still whilst the rest of the world goes on; and that will be bad for both.

Lord Denning was one of the most distinguished judges in this country in the twentieth century. Another was Lord Reid, who gave a famous lecture in 1972 in which he dispelled the 'declaratory theory' of the common law. He said:

> There was a time when it was thought almost indecent to suggest that judges make law – they only declare it. Those with a taste for fairy tales seem to have thought that in some Aladdin's cave there is hidden the Common Law in all its splendour and that on a judge's appointment there descends on him knowledge of the magic words Open Sesame. ... But we do not believe in fairy tales any more.

[1] *Law, Liberty and the Constitution* (Woodbridge, Boydell & Brewer, 2015) 65.
[2] [1954] P 15, at 22.

It is also important always to bear in mind that the common law is a practical system of law. In *Read v J. Lyons and Co Ltd*,[3] Lord Macmillan said:

> Arguments based on legal consistency are apt to mislead for the common law is a practical code adapted to deal with the manifold diversities of human life and as a great American judge has reminded us 'the life of the law has not been logic; it has been experience'.

That of course was a reference to Oliver Wendell Holmes in his magisterial book on the common law.

As I have mentioned, one of the other Courts which originated in the twelfth century became known as the Court of King's Bench. Although the common law courts no longer exist in that form, and were abolished on the creation of the High Court and the Court of Appeal in 1873, there is still a Division of the High Court which is called the Queen's Bench Division. That is in a sense the successor to the historic Court of King's Bench. As I will mention later, it retains the important jurisdiction of judicial review over the acts of Ministers of the Crown, and all lower tribunals and public authorities.

TRIAL BY JURY

One of the distinctive features of the common law is its reliance upon the jury. The origins of the jury lie in the early thirteenth century in England but trial by jury has remained a cherished part of our traditions. It is guaranteed by the constitution of the United States. In the US you have retained types of the jury which we no longer have in this country. In particular the Grand Jury was abolished here in 1933. Also in 1933 we stopped using juries in most civil trials. They are still used in some defamation cases and also in civil actions for example brought against the police for assault or some other wrong which the police are alleged to have committed. One can readily understand why in that kind of litigation it is regarded as still being desirable that the rights of the ordinary citizen should be determined by a randomly selected jury of their peers and not by a permanent professional judge.

In the criminal field we very much still retain the jury. It is used in the Crown Court, which tries the most serious offences although numerically they represent only three or four per cent of all criminal cases in this country. In the criminal field trial by jury is still regarded, as Lord Devlin put it in 1956 the lamp that shows that freedom still lives in this country. More recently in 2005, Lord Bingham said that a trial judge can direct a jury to acquit a defendant if that is the only verdict reasonably open to a jury, the judge can never direct the jury to convict a defendant even if that judge thinks that is the only verdict available as a matter of law: *R v Wang* [2005].[4]

As a trial judge when I was sitting in the Crown Court in many parts of this country, including the Central Criminal Court at the Old Bailey, I was struck by how important the jury remains in our system of criminal justice. I also think that the jury is the most democratic and egalitarian institution which we have today in this country. Even when

[3] [1947] AC 156, at p. 175.
[4] [2005] 1 WLR 661.

people go to vote in a general election, they do so in the privacy of the ballot booth and so they don't have to talk to each other. In contrast, when 12 randomly selected members of the public go into the privacy of the jury room to deliberate on their verdict, this will probably be the only time in their lives when people of all different social backgrounds come together and have to speak to each other. Every member of the jury has an equal voice. In my experience, juries take their task very seriously and conscientiously. The decision they take, for example in a murder trial, is probably the most important decision that most people will ever take in their lives.

There are two differences between the procedure used in this country and in the United States in relation to the role of the jury. The first is that, in this country – or at least in England and Wales, for the position is different in Scotland, which has a very different legal system – when the trial judge sums up the case before the jury retire to consider their verdict, he or she not only gives directions of law but also sums up the evidence for the jury. As I understand it an American judge would not do that. We take the view that this is helpful to the jury even though we entirely accept that it is not the function of the Judge and only the function of the jury to decide questions of fact. In fact, if a trial Judge goes too far and intrudes on the proper function of the jury to decide the facts, that may well lead to an unfair trial resulting in the conviction being quashed on appeal.

The second fundamental difference is that, in our system, the jury has no part to play in the sentencing process. That is exclusively a matter for the judge if there has been a conviction. This may be in part because we abolished the death penalty more than 50 years ago, whereas some of the states in the US have retained the death penalty. As I understand it, in death penalty cases, the jury in America does have a part to play in the sentencing process.

CRIMINAL LAW

In this country the rules of criminal law are still on the whole to be found in the common law. Although there are important statutes on offences such as theft and non-fatal offences against the person, some of the most basic offences are still governed by the common law, in particular the offences of murder and manslaughter. Although many people, especially the Law Commission, have suggested that there should be a criminal code, setting out the definitions of all offences in one statute, this has never been implemented by Parliament.

Occasionally there have been statutory incursions into the law of homicide, for example in 1957 and 2009. In the latter statute Parliament abolished the old law of provocation and replaced it with a new defence of loss of control, which will reduce an offence of murder to manslaughter. The Homicide Act 1957 abolished the old felony murder rule, which I think still exists in American law.

Something that was not the felony murder rule but many people felt was unjust did continue in the common law here until 2016, when it was abolished by the Supreme Court in *R v Jogee*,[5] which overruled earlier precedents: *Chan Wing-Siu v The Queen*.[6]

[5] [2017] AC 387.
[6] [1985] AC 168.

This concerned the doctrine of joint enterprise. If two or more people agree to commit a crime, such as burglary, and one of them kills a person during the course of that crime, both may be guilty of murder, not only the principal who killed the victim. Until recently the law was that the accomplice would also be guilty of murder if he foresaw the risk that the other person might commit the offence of murder. The law has now changed as a result of the decision in *Jogee*: the accomplice will only be guilty of murder if he intended that the other person should commit the offence of murder.

The Supreme Court considered whether it was appropriate to make this change in the criminal law by development of the common law or whether it should be left to Parliament. It took the view that the injustice of the previous law had to be remedied and this could not be left to Parliament to change the law by legislation. In other common law jurisdictions, the courts have not taken the same view: for example, in Australia, the High Court, which is their supreme court, has declined to follow the decision in *Jogee* and felt that such a radical change to the criminal law was best left to Parliament: *Miller v R; Smith v R; Presley v DPP*.[7] In Hong Kong too the Court of Final Appeal has declined to follow the decision of our Supreme Court in *Jogee*: *HKSAR v Chan Kam Shing*.[8] These are good examples of how the common law can diverge around the world even though it has a common origin in England in the twelfth century.

THE RIGHT TO PRIVACY

The next topic that I want to mention is the development of a right to privacy in English law.

We did not have a tort of invasion of privacy like the one that has been developed in American law ever since the seminal article by Warren and Brandeis on the right to privacy in 1890 in the Harvard Law Review. As recently as 1991 the Court of Appeal held that there is no such right and the House of Lords subsequently said the same.

However, in the last 15 years or so there is something very similar to the tort of invasion of privacy which has developed in this country. This has come about by a very interesting combination of common law (or, strictly speaking, equitable) principles and the introduction of the Human Rights Act in 2000. This is in one sense curious because the Human Rights Act does not apply to private individuals or corporations such as newspaper companies. It only binds public authorities. In that sense it is similar to the constitutional guarantees in the US which apply only to 'state action'.

Despite that apparent limitation, it is important to bear in mind that courts are themselves public authorities and therefore are bound by the Human Rights Act. This, taken together with the doctrine of 'positive obligations' in the law of human rights, has led to the position that the courts have a positive duty to protect the

[7] [2016] HCA 30.
[8] [2016] HKCFA 87.

privacy of a person even as against invasion by media organisations like newspapers. This was established in particular in an action brought by Naomi Campbell against Mirror Group Newspapers, which led to a decision of the House of Lords: *Campbell v Mirror Group Newspapers Ltd*.[9]

A good example of a case in which the right to privacy was recognised in this way is the decision of the High Court just last Wednesday (18 July 2018) in an action brought by the famous singer, Sir Cliff Richard, against the BBC for reporting a police investigation into allegations against him. He was never arrested or charged with any criminal offence. The court held that this was an unlawful invasion of privacy and awarded damages of £210,000. I will say no more about the case since it may be the subject of an appeal to the Court of Appeal.

This does not mean that the right to privacy will prevail in all circumstances. A balancing exercise often has to be performed, not least because of the importance in a democratic society of the right to freedom of expression. That right too is protected by the Human Rights Act. Nevertheless, it is fair to observe that in this country it is possible to obtain an injunction restraining publication of speech which will unjustifiably breach someone's right to privacy. I suspect that it would be very difficult if not impossible to obtain such a 'prior restraint' in the US. This is because of the exceptionally powerful status of the right to free speech in your First Amendment and in particular the distaste for prior restraints in America.

JUDICIAL REVIEW

I said earlier that I would say a word about judicial review. In this country we tend to use the phrase 'judicial review' in a different sense from the one used in the US. You use that term to refer to the review by the courts of legislation, including Acts of Congress, a power that the courts have had ever since *Marbury v Madison* in 1803. We use the term to mean the review by the courts of administrative action. Sometimes this branch of law is called administrative law or nowadays public law because it concerns the lawfulness of the decisions and actions of public authorities. The point I want to make now is that judicial review in this sense is probably the most important development in the English common law of the last half century.

The origins of judicial review go back many centuries. As I have mentioned, the Court of King's Bench historically had the power to issue various writs to control the actions of inferior bodies, including the King's Ministers. One of those prerogative writs was called *certiorari*, a word still used in American procedure but used in a different sense, by the US Supreme Court. We have now replaced that order with what is called a 'quashing order'. Less romantic I know but we are no longer supposed to use Latin in our courts.

Judicial review is the practical manifestation on a day to day basis of this country's respect for the rule of law. This is closely linked to the right of access to the courts, which has often been described by the courts in this country as a 'constitutional right', something which may surprise you coming from America, as you may

---

[9] [2004] 2 AC 457.

have been told that, unlike the United States, the UK does not have a constitution. Of course we do not have a written constitution in the sense of a single document, as you do, but we do recognise that certain rules are fundamental to our system of government and so are constitutional in character. Those rules are often to be found in the common law.

I cannot express the importance of access to justice more eloquently than the way it was put in the Supreme Court in *R (on the application of UNISON) v Lord Chancellor*.[10] At paragraph 66, Lord Reed JSC said:

> The constitutional right of access to the courts is inherent in the rule of law. …

At paragraph 68, he continued:

> At the heart of the concept of the rule of law is the idea that society is governed by law. Parliament exists primarily in order to make laws for society in this country. … Courts exist in order to ensure that the laws made by Parliament, and the common law created by the courts themselves, are applied and enforced. That role includes ensuring that the executive branch of government carries out its functions in accordance with the law. In order for the courts to perform that role, people must in principle have unimpeded access to them. Without such access, laws are liable to become a dead letter …

CONCLUSION

I want to end in this way. You will be hearing quite a lot at this conference about Brexit. As a serving judge I cannot comment on the political rights or wrongs of Brexit. That is the decision which the people of the United Kingdom have taken by their vote in a referendum two years ago. What I think judges can say is this. Leaving the European Union will not change the nature of the English common law. The common law has remained and continued to thrive in the four decades of our membership of the European Union. Many businesses around the world choose to regulate their affairs according to the English common law. This is why English law is often made the law of the contract even if otherwise the subject has no particular connection to this country. This is also why many potential litigants choose England as a forum for resolution of their disputes.

This will continue after Brexit. The common law will continue to provide both stability and flexibility while it develops incrementally. It seems to me that our task as judges is to be guardians of the common law and its rich heritage. It is not to cause any fundamental disruption while occasionally putting a light touch on the tiller to make sure that the law continues to develop in order to meet the needs of a changing society.

---

[10] [2017] 3 WLR 409.

Antigone's Law

In 2019 I gave this talk to Lawyers for Classics, which is part of a larger charity, Classics for All, which strives to bring classics to those who have not traditionally had access to the subject, in particular in state schools. In this talk I traced the development of thinking about 'higher law' back to the defiance of Antigone in Sophocles' play, who is willing, for reasons of conscience, to violate the decree of her uncle Creon in the state where she lives, and to accept the punishment which follows. One of the constant themes of law is the conflict between the one and the many; and another perennial theme is the conflict between the positive law laid down by the state and higher law notions of morality and justice.

INTRODUCTION

IN THE YEAR 2015 it was possible in London to go to at least four major theatres and watch new productions of Greek tragedies which had been written and first performed two and a half thousand years ago in ancient Athens. At the Old Vic I saw Kristin Scott Thomas in Sophocles' *Electra*. At the National Theatre I saw Helen McCrory in Euripides' *Medea*. And at the Barbican I saw Juliette Binoche in Sophocles' *Antigone*. I am sorry that I missed Aeschylus' *Oresteia* at the Almeida that year.

That these plays continue to attract audiences in the twenty-first century in a language which is very different from their original one speaks – I think – to their timeless quality.

I had the great privilege (in the best sense of that word) of learning classical Greek when I was at school from the age of 12. This evening I want to focus on the *Antigone* and the particular role it has played in my life since I first read it at the age of 17. The *Antigone* was written by Sophocles and first performed at the Festival of Dionysus at the theatre which lies just below the Acropolis in around the year 442 BCE.

Most of you will be familiar with the basic plot of the *Antigone* even if you have not read or seen it yourselves. Antigone was the daughter of Oedipus and Jocasta in the House of Thebes. Jocasta had a brother Creon, who became King of Thebes. After the death of Oedipus there had been a civil war in which the two sons of Oedipus, Polyneices and Eteocles, fought against each other. Both brothers were killed in that war, although the rebels were defeated. As a consequence, Creon issued a decree that the rebels were not to be buried, so that the body of Polyneices would be left to be carrion outside the city walls. Antigone was not prepared to obey that decree. She gave her brother the burial which she believed was the right thing to do according to her religion and custom. In this she was opposed by her sister Ismene.

For defying the decree of Creon Antigone is brought before the king and eventually sentenced to be buried alive in a tomb. Antigone's fiancé is the son of Creon, Haemon. Ultimately (and I apologise for the spoiler) not only Antigone but Haemon and Creon's wife, Euridice, take their own lives. It is only towards the very end of the play that Creon realises that what he has done is wrong and tries (too late) to change things. It is for this reason that some commentators have suggested that the play should perhaps be called *Creon* because it is he who is the true tragic figure in the story, who brings misery upon his family as the result of his actions.

There are three passages in particular which I would like to share with you this evening.

WONDERS ARE MANY

The first passage I want to talk about is one of the most famous lines in classical literature, at line 332 of *Antigone*, where the chorus say:

Wonders are many and none more wonderful than man.

But the original Greek is as follows: 'polla ta deina; k'ouden anthropou deinoteron pelei'. The key word there is 'deina' – the nominative, neuter plural of the adjective 'deinos'.

This famous passage perhaps illustrates the difficulty of translation. Words often have ambiguity and nuance in one language which cannot be translated into another. The Everyman edition (in English verse by Sir George Young), first published in 1906, translates that line as follows:

Much is there passing strange;

Nothing surpassing mankind;

The Loeb translation of 1994 (by Hugh Lloyd-Jones) gives the following translation:

Many things are formidable, and none more formidable than man!

However, none of them perhaps conveys the true breadth of the meaning of the word 'deinos', which lies at the heart of this passage. It has the same root as the word 'dinosaur'. Dinosaur is usually translated as meaning 'terrible lizard'. So, the famous passage could be translated as:

There are many terrible things in the world and none more terrible than man.

That would give a very different sense to the famous passage; and it would be wrong in the context of what follows, as the passage does praise the achievements of mankind.

Perhaps the most accurate way of translating it might be to say:

> There are many awesome things in the world and none more awesome than man.

The word 'awesome' can have the ambiguity that the Greek word 'deinos' also has, at least when used in its American sense.

That is how Edith Hall translates the line in her book on *Greek Tragedy*, published in 2010:

> Many things arouse awe, but none is more awesome than man.

What I hope this one example illustrates is the desirability in principle of teaching the classics in their original languages. Although it is laudable that as many children as possible should have access to our classical heritage, for example by studying Classical Civilisation, you can miss the subtleties and the nuances if you cannot read the original Latin or Greek. To which I would add that Greek is even more fun because you have to learn a different script and alphabet.

To this day I think the most difficult thing I have ever had to do was an optional paper at A Level, which required us to translate an unseen piece of English verse into Greek verse. We not only had to get the vocabulary right; we had to make the lines fit into iambic pentameters. After that the study of law held no terrors for me – not even the rule against perpetuities.

THE TREE THAT IS WILLING TO BEND

The second passage which I would like to talk about is at line 710 and following, where Haemon is arguing with his father Creon. He urges his father to be willing to listen to others and change his mind. In the Loeb translation the passage is as follows:

> It is not shameful for a man, even if he is wise, often to learn things and not to resist too much. You see how when rivers are swollen in winter those trees that yield to the flood retain their branches, but those that offer resistance perish, trunk and all. Just so whoever in command of a ship keeps the sheet taut, and never slackens it, is overturned and thereafter sails with his oarsmen's benches upside down. No, retreat from your anger and allow yourself to change; for if I too, young as I am, have some judgement, I say that it is best by far if a man is altogether full of knowledge; but that, since things are not accustomed to go that way, it is also good to learn from those who give good counsel.

In that passage I think Sophocles was appealing to the good sense of his fellow citizens of Athens. This was after all the birthplace of democracy. Democracy rests on discussion and a willingness to listen to others and to change one's mind. Professor Edith Hall, in her commentary on the *Antigone*, says that the

> setting in Thebes is highly significant: in reality this city was anti-democratic and hostile to Athens, which was the democratic home of Sophocles, his audience and most of his performers. The patriotic Athenian dramatists consequently often displaced enactments of political strife, tyranny and domestic chaos onto legendary Thebes rather than legendary Athens.

A HIGHER LAW

But the third passage is the one that I want to focus on in particular this evening. This is in the exchange between Creon and Antigone, when she readily admits that she was the person who gave a burial to Polyneices and that she knew that this was contrary to his decree. She is defiant in her explanation for disobeying Creon's proclamation.

This appears from line 450 and is translated as follows in the Loeb edition:

> Yes, for it was not Zeus who made this proclamation, nor was it Justice who lives with the gods below that established such laws among men, nor did I think your proclamations strong enough to have power to overrule, mortal as they were, the unwritten and unfailing ordinances of the gods. For these have life, not simply today and yesterday, but forever, and no-one knows how long ago they were revealed. For this I did not intend to pay the penalty among the gods for fear of any man's pride. I knew that I would die, of course I knew, even if you had made no proclamation. But if I die before my time, I account that gain. ... [I]f I had endured that the son of my own mother should die and remain unburied, that would have given me pain, but this gives me none.

So far as I have been able to discover, that passage contains the first reference in western thought to a higher law, which overrides the laws laid down by man.

CIVIL DISOBEDIENCE

Antigone can be regarded as a person who chooses to obey her own conscience rather than the law of the state where she lives. In that respect she provides an early example of someone who engages in civil disobedience.

At first sight, one might think that the law would have no place for a person who engages in civil disobedience. After all that person has broken that very law. However, the law in this country has come to acknowledge that a person may have broken the law out of conscience, as an act of civil disobedience. In *R v Jones (Margaret)*,[1] at paragraph 89, Lord Hoffmann said that:

> Civil disobedience on conscientious grounds has a long and honourable history in this country. People who break the law to affirm their belief in the injustice of a law or Government action are sometimes vindicated by history. The suffragettes are an example which comes immediately to mind. It is the mark of a civilised community that it can accommodate protests and demonstrations of this kind. But there are conventions which are generally accepted by the law-breakers on one side and the law-enforcers on the other. The protestors behave with a sense of proportion and do not cause excessive damage or inconvenience. And they vouch the sincerity of their beliefs by accepting the penalties imposed by the law. The police and prosecutors, on the other hand, behave with restraint and the Magistrates impose sentences which take the conscientious motives of the protestors into account.

---

[1] [2007] 1 AC 161.

In *R v Roberts*,[2] the Lord Chief Justice confirmed that approach when considering how protestors against fracking should be sentenced for the offence of public nuisance. Lord Burnett of Maldon CJ said:

> When sentencing an offender, the value of the right to freedom of expression finds its voice in the approach to sentencing.

However, he continued, public nuisance is a serious offence and there is no bright line between custody and non-custody in such cases. There is no rule that a person in such cases will not be sent to prison. But, he continued:

> particular caution attaches to immediate custodial sentences.

NATURAL LAW VERSUS POSITIVE LAW

The unwillingness of Antigone to obey the law of the state because she felt an obligation to a 'higher law' provides an early illustration of what in subsequent centuries came to be known as the distinction between natural law theories and positive law. Positive law is the law laid down by the state in any given community at any given time. Natural law is particularly associated with the medieval scholar, Thomas Aquinas. It continues to find modern echoes, for example in the writings of Professor John Finnis of Oxford University, who wrote a book called *Natural Law and Natural Rights*, which was first published in 1980.

The belief that there can be a higher law over and above ordinary law influenced the American revolutionaries who drafted the Constitution of the United States and the American Bill of Rights. Not only is the Constitution and the Bill of Rights regarded as a higher law, breach of which will render legislation passed by Congress or by the individual states to be unconstitutional and invalid, but there is this provision in the Ninth Amendment:

> The enumeration in the Constitution, of certain rights, shall not be construed to deny or disparage others retained by the people.

However, one does not necessarily have to believe in natural law theories to see modern echoes of the concept of a 'higher law'. In modern times there is not only the law laid down by each state but there is also recognised international law.

In *Oppenheimer v Cattermole*,[3] Lord Cross of Chelsea was considering a German law of 1941 which deprived Jewish émigrés of their status as German nationals. Further, this discriminatory withdrawal of their citizenship was used as a peg upon which to hang a discriminatory confiscation of their property. Lord Cross said that a judge should be very slow to refuse to give effect to the

---

[2] [2018] EWCA Crim 2739.
[3] [1976] AC 249, at 277.

legislation of a foreign state in any sphere in which, according to accepted principles of international law, the foreign state has jurisdiction. However, he continued at page 278:

> What we are concerned with here is legislation which takes away without compensation from a section of the citizen body singled out on racial grounds all their property on which the state passing the legislation can lay its hands and, in addition, deprives them of their citizenship. To my mind a law of this sort constitutes so grave an infringement of human rights that the courts of this country ought to refuse to recognise it as a law at all.

More recently, the principle in *Oppenheimer* was applied by the House of Lords outside the context of fundamental human rights in *Kuwait Airways v Iraqi Airways*.[4] That case arose out of the first Gulf War of 1991. Iraq had invaded Kuwait in breach of the basic norms of international law, including the prohibition on the use of force against another state in Article 2(4) of the UN Charter. It had confiscated aeroplanes belonging to Kuwait Airways. The issue in the litigation in this country was who owned those planes. The House of Lords held that the principle of public policy in *Oppenheimer v Cattermole* was not confined to cases about human rights. They held that the norms of international law which had been breached by Iraq were so fundamental that they form part of what is called *ius cogens*, that is peremptory norms of international law which permit of no derogation. Accordingly, the courts of this country would not recognise and give effect to Iraq's confiscation of Kuwaiti property. At paragraph 18 Lord Nicholls of Birkenhead said:

> the courts of this country must have a residual power ... to disregard a provision in the foreign law when to do otherwise would affront basic principles of justice and fairness which the courts seek to apply in the administration of justice in this country.

Another example of a norm which is part of the *ius cogens* is the absolute prohibition on the use of torture. Although that prohibition is set out in various treaties, including Article 3 of the European Convention on Human Rights and the UN Convention on Torture, it is also a norm of customary international law, in other words that part of international law which is not based on treaties. Not only is it part of customary international law, it is so fundamental that it is a part of the *ius cogens* and permits of no derogation even in time of war or national emergency.

THE LAW OF HUMANITY

But it is not only in international law that one can find such echoes of a 'higher law'. In English law consider this statement by Lord Ellenborough CJ in *R v Inhabitants of Eastbourne*:[5]

> As to there being no obligation for maintaining poor foreigners before the statutes ascertaining the different methods of acquiring settlements, the law of humanity, which is anterior to all positive laws, obliges us to afford them relief, to save them from starving; ...

---

[4] [2002] 2 AC 883.
[5] (1803) 4 East 103, at p 107.

And that statement is not merely of historical interest. It was cited some 20 years ago by Simon Brown LJ in the Court of Appeal, in *R v Secretary of State for Social Security, ex parte Joint Council for the Welfare of Immigrants*.[6] Simon Brown LJ said that:

> So basic are the human rights here at issue that it cannot be necessary to resort to the European Convention on Human Rights to take note of their violation.

The reason why he said that was because the case predated the Human Rights Act 1998.

In the *JCWI* case the Court of Appeal was able to strike down regulations which had been made under an apparently broad power enabling regulations to be made by the Secretary of State but which were held to be *ultra vires*. This was because they would have had the effect of driving asylum claimants to 'penury', so as to require them either to leave the country before the determination of their claim for asylum or render them unable to prosecute their claim effectively. Simon Brown LJ concluded, at p 293:

> Some basic provision should be made, sufficient for genuine claimants to survive and pursue their claims.

The question of course which then arises is what would happen if legislation of that kind were set out not in secondary legislation but in primary legislation, in other words Acts of the United Kingdom Parliament itself.

Even in that context, at least so long as the UK is in the European Union, the concept of a higher law is not alien to us now. Courts in this country have become used in the last 45 years or so to the concept of the supremacy of EU law and this may require the disapplication even of primary legislation enacted by our own Parliament if there is an incompatibility. In *R (Miller) v Secretary of State for Exiting the European Union*[7] (the case concerning whether the Government could give notice under Article 50 without the authority of Parliament) the Supreme Court described the European Communities Act 1972 as a 'constitutional' statute. At paragraph 67 the majority judgment summarised the relationship between the law of this country and European Union law as a result of the 1972 Act as follows:

> the normal rule is that any domestic legislation must be consistent with EU law. In such cases, EU law has primacy as a matter of domestic law, and legislation which is inconsistent with EU law from time to time is to that extent ineffective in law.

As is well known, the Human Rights Act 1998 (HRA) does not enable courts in this country to 'strike down' or even disapply Acts of Parliament even if they are incompatible with fundamental human rights as set out in the European Convention on Human Rights. However, under section 4 of the HRA, what the higher courts in this country do have power to do is to make a 'declaration of incompatibility'. That in one sense is again a recognition that the positive law of a state may be incompatible with a 'higher law' protecting fundamental human rights.

---

[6] [1997] 1 WLR 275, at p 292.
[7] [2018] AC 61.

AFTER *ANTIGONE*

The power of the *Antigone* has continued to appeal to writers and audiences ever since it was first produced. There was a French adaptation by Anouilh. A German one by Brecht, in 1948, about Nazism. A Polish one by Andrzej Wajda, in 1984, protesting against martial law in Poland. More recently, Wajda made a film about the massacre of Polish officers by Soviet forces in the Second World War, called *Katyn*. That massacre was falsely attributed to the Germans for many decades afterwards, until the collapse of the USSR. The film concerns a woman who wants to give a proper burial to her husband. In the background there is a version of the *Antigone* being performed at the local theatre.

The *Antigone* has been turned into operas: one version (by Traetta) even has a happy ending, in which Creon sees the error of his ways in good time and Antigone is saved.

Seamus Heaney wrote a brilliant adaptation of the play in verse called *Burial at Thebes*.

Recently Kamila Shamsie wrote a novel which has been described as a 'contemporary reimagining' of the *Antigone*, called *Home Fire*, which won the Women's Prize for Fiction in 2018. In that novel, Antigone has become Aneeka; Creon is a Muslim Home Secretary called Karamat Lone; and his son is now Eamonn. Aneeka's brother, Parvaiz, has gone abroad to become a jihadist and is killed overseas. The Home Secretary will not allow his body to be brought back to the UK for burial.

So the story of *Antigone* continues to have resonance in literature and the arts more generally. What I have tried to suggest in this talk is that *Antigone* also has relevance for the law. Antigone's appeal to a higher law than Creon's decree has echoed down through the centuries. Antigone conceived of the higher law in explicitly religious terms and many people around the world continue to see things in that way. However, since at least the Enlightenment it has been possible to believe in a higher law, for example a law which protects fundamental human rights, which does not depend on any religious faith.

Note the contrast between the opening words of the American Declaration of Independence in 1776 and the Universal Declaration of Human Rights in 1948. Jefferson, in the Declaration of Independence, said that 'all men are created equal' and that they are endowed by their Creator with certain inalienable rights. However, Article 1 of the Universal Declaration no longer refers to a creator but simply states that: 'All human beings are born free and equal in dignity and rights'.

In conclusion, I would suggest that such talk of higher law, which does not depend on the positive law as laid down by any particular state, can be traced back to what I have called in this talk 'Antigone's law'.

Public Law

Judicial Review and the Rule of Law

Judicial review, administrative law or public law as it is usually called nowadays, has been the mainstay of my work, both as a barrister and as a judge. It is integral to maintenance of the rule of law in this country. I gave this talk in Bristol to the South West Administrative Lawyers Association in the summer of 2017, towards the end of my time as a High Court judge. One very important case which was decided after this lecture was given was the second Miller *case:* R (on the application of Miller) v Prime Minister [2019] UKSC 41; [2020] AC 373 – *I referred in this lecture to the first* Miller *case:* R (on the application of Miller) v Secretary of State for Exiting the European Union [2017] UKSC 5; [2018] AC 61. *The second one, decided in September 2019, was even more important, concerning as it did the prorogation of Parliament. If anything, that decision underlines even more powerfully the theme of this lecture: that no one is above the law and that judicial review is important to maintain the rule of law even if the context is political. Even in that context, the task of independent courts is to decide questions of law, no more and no less.*

THANK YOU FOR inviting me to give this year's SWALA lecture. It is a genuine pleasure to be here. I am honoured to be the Liaison Judge for the Administrative Court on the Western Circuit and proud to return to the great city of Bristol.

Lord Diplock once commented that the development of judicial review had been the most significant development in the law of this country in his professional lifetime. That was in the early 1980s. If that was true then it is even more so now. Although judicial review has historic origins going back many centuries, there can be no doubt about two things.

First there has been a remarkable increase in the volume of litigation, particularly in what is now called the Administrative Court, in the last 40 years or so. When the predecessor to the Administrative Court, the Crown Office List, was created in 1980, there were only a few hundred cases brought each year in that jurisdiction. Just a few years earlier, following the recommendations of the Law Commission, the rules relating to the old prerogative orders had been reformed. In 1977, under what was then called the 'new' Order 53 of the Rules of the Supreme Court, a procedure known as the application for judicial review was first created.

Today many thousands of cases are started in the Administrative Court every year, even though there has been a dramatic reduction in the number in the last few years, as the majority of immigration judicial review cases are now heard in the

Upper Tribunal. Recent figures published by the Ministry of Justice show that, last year (2016), there were 1,832 claims for judicial review brought against the Home Office, which was the government department facing the largest number of such claims, and that was an increase of 18 per cent on the previous year.

In 1980 there were just four High Court judges nominated to sit in the Crown Office List. Today almost all the judges of the Queen's Bench Division sit in the Administrative Court, as do several judges of the Family and Chancery Divisions. Many others sit in the Administrative Court as additional or deputy High Court judges, including here in Bristol.

The second point is this. It is arguable that the substantive law of judicial review represents the greatest contribution which the common law has made in the last 50 or 60 years. It is still a body of law which remains essentially the creation of the judges. In that sense it is reminiscent of the development of commercial law by the common law courts in the eighteenth century and the development of the law of negligence in the first half of the twentieth century. Parliament has intervened in this area of law to a limited extent but has done so not so much to amend the substantive content of public law; rather to regulate procedure and remedies and to deal with ancillary matters such as costs. I will return to that later.

Two further but fundamental comments can perhaps be made. The first is that judicial review of the lawfulness of the actions of the Executive is vital to maintenance of the rule of law. As Lord Denning was fond of saying, citing Dr Thomas Fuller: 'Be you never so high, the Law is above you'.[1] Judicial review is the practical, day-to-day manifestation of this country's commitment to the rule of law. That is the idea that even the government is subject to the law.

One aspect of this is that the law protects everyone, not just saints but sinners as well. Every judge on appointment takes an oath or makes an affirmation to 'do right to all manner of people … without fear or favour, affection or ill-will'. Last year I decided an application for judicial review brought by Joanne Dennehy, a notorious murderer of three men, who is one of only two women in this country currently serving a whole life order. Her claim for judicial review failed save on one ground which was conceded by the defendants in the light of a decision of the Supreme Court. In that judgment I said:

> It is important to recall that everyone within the jurisdiction is entitled to the protection of the law, including the protection of their human rights. That includes even someone who has committed the most serious crimes. This is because ours is a society governed by the rule of law.[2]

The second fundamental point is this. There is no contradiction between democracy and judicial review. As Lord Bingham famously remarked in the Belmarsh case (2004),[3] the enforcement of the law by an independent judiciary is now regarded as a cornerstone of a democratic society. This has particular relevance in the context

---

[1] See, for the origins of this phrase, Tom Bingham, *The Rule of Law* (London, Allen Lane, 2010), 4 and fn 8.

[2] *R (Dennehy) v Secretary of State for Justice* [2016] EWHC 1219 (Admin), at para 178.

[3] *A v Secretary of State for the Home Department* [2005] 2 AC 68, at para 42.

of judicial review. This is because the purpose of judicial review is primarily to give effect to the will of Parliament. Usually there will be legislation which governs the powers and duties of a public authority. The function of the court is to ensure that the authority acts in accordance with that legislation: that it does not exceed its powers or abuse them and that it complies with its duties.

In doing so the courts are not usurping the function of the democratically accountable legislature. Far from it, they support it and implement what Parliament has required of the Executive. In that context, it is important to bear in mind that there is a separation of powers between the Executive and the legislature. Although it is well known that there is no separation of *persons* between those two institutions, nevertheless there is an important distinction between their respective *functions*.

Although there is a constitutional convention that Ministers of the Crown should always be members of one or other of the Houses of Parliament, there is a vital distinction in law between the Queen in Parliament (which is the legislature) and Her Majesty's Government (which is the Executive). One case in which this fundamental distinction had apparently been forgotten by the government concerned an application for judicial review brought by the Child Poverty Action Group and which I decided in 2012.[4] In that case the incoming coalition government had decided not to establish the Child Poverty Commission which was required by the Child Poverty Act 2010. In admirable compliance with the duty of candour, which rests on public authorities in judicial review proceedings, a witness statement was filed on behalf of the Secretary of State, which explained that a ministerial meeting had been held, at which it was decided that the Commission would not be established because new legislation would be drafted with a view to setting up an alternative body.

In granting the application for judicial review, I noted the eloquent words of Lord Bridge in *X Ltd v Morgan Grampian Ltd*:

> The maintenance of the rule of law is in every way as important in a free society as the democratic franchise. In our society the rule of law rests upon twin foundations, the sovereignty of the Queen in Parliament in making the law and the sovereignty of the Queen's courts in interpreting and applying the law.[5]

It follows from that dual sovereignty of Parliament and the courts that the Executive as such enjoys no sovereignty. It is accountable to Parliament for the wisdom of its policies and accountable to the courts for the legality of its actions. As Lord Diplock put it in the *National Federation* case:

> It is not … a sufficient answer to say that judicial review of the actions of officers or departments of central government is unnecessary because they are accountable to Parliament for the way in which they carry out their functions. They are accountable to Parliament for what they do so far as regards efficiency and policy, and of that Parliament is the only judge; they are responsible to a court of justice for the lawfulness of what they do, and of that the court is the only judge.[6]

---

[4] *R (Child Poverty Action Group) v Secretary of State for Work and Pensions* [2012] EWHC 2579.
[5] [1991] 1 AC 1, at 48.
[6] *R v Inland Revenue Commissioners, ex parte National Federation of Self-employed and Small Businesses* [1982] AC 617, at 644.

In the *CPAG* case I said (at paragraph 31) that:

> the executive enjoys no power to amend or repeal primary legislation in the absence of delegation by Parliament itself.

I went on to say that:

> In the present context, however meritorious the new Government in 2010 may have thought its proposed replacement commission might be, it was not entitled ... to pre-empt any primary legislation that Parliament might or might not pass in the future if so invited. ... The new Government may have had good reason to adopt a different policy from that of the previous government. However ... they were not entitled as a matter of law to ignore, or to fail to comply with, primary legislation as laid down by Parliament itself.

Although, as I have said, the vast majority of judicial review cases concern the implementation of the will of Parliament as expressed in legislation governing the powers and duties of the Executive, there are occasions when judicial review will involve controlling the Royal Prerogative. This was most notably seen earlier this year in the decision of the Supreme Court in the *Miller* case,[7] which of course concerned the question whether the Government would be entitled to invoke Article 50 of the Treaty on European Union without express authorisation by Parliament. As is well known the Supreme Court held that the Royal Prerogative did not confer such a power and that an Act of Parliament was indeed required. That Act has now been passed and Article 50 has now been triggered, starting the process of the United Kingdom's departure from the European Union (or 'Brexit'). Although the legal nature of prerogative powers is still controversial, it is arguable that it simply represents the residual body of powers which are conferred upon the Crown not by Parliament but by the general law of this country, in other words by the common law.

As most law students will know, the fundamental principles of modern administrative law were established by the House of Lords in a small but important series of cases in the 1960s. The principal cases were *Ridge v Baldwin*;[8] *Padfield*;[9] and *Anisminic*.[10]

In *Ridge v Baldwin* (1962) Lord Reid observed that:

> We do not have a developed system of administrative law – perhaps because until fairly recently we did not need it.[11]

Just 20 years later, Lord Diplock was able to comment in *O'Reilly v Mackman*,[12] that:

> We did [by 1977] have ... a developed system of administrative law, to the development of which Lord Reid himself ... had made an outstanding contribution.

The importance of the decisions in *Padfield* and *Anisminic* cannot be overstated. They provide the jurisprudential foundations for modern administrative law.

---

[7] *R (Miller) v Secretary of State for Exiting the European Union* [2017] UKSC 5 [2017] 2 WLR 583.
[8] [1964] AC 40.
[9] *Padfield v Minister of Agriculture, Fisheries and Food* [1968] AC 997.
[10] *Anisminic Ltd v Foreign Compensation Commission* [1969] 2 AC 147.
[11] p 72.
[12] [1983] 2 AC 237, at 279–80.

In *Padfield* the House of Lords made it clear that there is no such thing as an unfettered discretion: however broadly a discretionary power may be worded, that power must always be exercised so as to promote the policy and objects of the Act of Parliament which conferred it. In *Anisminic* the House of Lords removed the distinction between errors of law within the jurisdiction and jurisdictional errors.[13] That means in practice that the Executive and inferior bodies have no power to get the law wrong. It is always for the courts to say what the law is. That is fundamental to the rule of law in this country.

The common law continues to retain its ability to create new concepts of public law. I will give examples from three contexts.

The first is the development of the doctrine of legitimate expectation. This phrase was first used in the courts of this country, as far as I have been able to discover, in 1969 by Lord Denning in *Schmidt v Secretary of State for Home Affairs*.[14] At first it was thought to give rise only to procedural rights of fairness. In other words, even though a person did not have a legal right which was being taken away, if he or she had a legitimate expectation, then the rules of natural justice or, as we more commonly say today, the duty to act fairly or the right to procedural fairness would apply. In due course the courts began to develop a doctrine of substantive legitimate expectation, particularly in the context of tax cases: see the classic decision of the Divisional Court in *MFK Underwriting Agents* (1990).[15] That developed into a general doctrine, applicable across the whole range of public law, in the Court of Appeal decision in *Coughlan* (1999).[16]

The second main development to which I would point is even more recent. This concerns the relevance of policies to the making of public decisions. The conventional view used to be that, since discretionary powers can never be fettered, a failure to act in accordance with a policy was not a ground for judicial review. There was no obligation to adopt a policy. There was no obligation to publish any policy that there was. If there was a policy, there was no obligation to act in accordance with it. The highest that it was sometimes put was that the policy was a relevant consideration which should be taken into account. All that has changed.

The leading authority now is the decision of the Supreme Court in *Lumba* (2011).[17] It now appears to be the case that policies must be adopted, at least in cases where Convention rights are affected, because of the requirement that an interference with those rights must be in accordance with law. If a policy is adopted, it should normally be published. There may of course be good reason not to do so, for example in the interests of national security. Furthermore, it will normally be a requirement of public law that a discretionary decision is taken in accordance with whatever policy the public authority concerned has at that time. Merely taking it into account will no longer suffice. And if there is to be a departure from the policy there will have to be a good reason for doing so, which will be scrutinised by the court.

---

[13] See further *R (Cart) v Upper Tribunal* [2012] 1 AC 663, at para 18 (Baroness Hale of Richmond JSC).
[14] [1969] 2 Ch 149.
[15] *R v Inland Revenue Commissioners, ex p. MFK Underwriting Agents Ltd* [1990] 1 WLR 1545.
[16] *R v North and East Devon Health Authority, ex p. Coughlan* [2001] QB 213.
[17] *R (Lumba) v Secretary of State for the Health Department* [2012] 1 AC 245.

Finally, and very importantly, it has now been clearly established by the Supreme Court, in the case of *Tesco Stores v Dundee* (2012),[18] that the interpretation of a policy is a question of law for the court to determine; it will not suffice that an interpretation has been adopted by a public authority which was reasonably open to it. That said, it is still important to bear in mind that a policy is precisely that; it is not legislation and should not be interpreted as if it were. This point was made in *Tesco Stores* itself and was reiterated by the Supreme Court last month in *Hopkins Homes*.[19] In *Hopkins Homes* the Supreme Court also stressed that it is only the question of interpretation of a policy which is a question of law for the court to determine; when it comes to the application of a policy (correctly interpreted), that is a matter for the decision-maker, not for the court. It is important not to elide the two.[20]

The third area of law in which the common law continues to develop is the duty to give reasons for administrative decisions. This is particularly interesting because there are many pieces of legislation which impose an express statutory duty to give reasons on a public authority. It might be thought, at first sight, that, in those situations where there is no legislation imposing a duty to give reasons, no such duty will arise at all. However, that would be too simplistic an approach.

As Elias LJ put it in the recent case of *Oakley*: 'It is firmly established that there is no general obligation to give reasons at common law …'.[21] This was confirmed by the House of Lords more than 20 years ago in *Doody*.[22]

However, as was illustrated by the facts of *Doody* itself, there are a number of exceptions to the general principle.

The first is where, as in *Doody*, the nature of the decision requires disclosure of reasons to be given on grounds of fairness.

The second exception is where there was something 'aberrant' in the particular decision which calls out for explanation: see *R v Higher Education Funding Council, ex p. Institute of Dental Surgery*.[23] An example of such an aberrant decision is provided by the Court of Appeal decision in *R v Civil Service Appeal Board, ex p. Cunningham*.[24]

Thirdly a duty to give reasons has been imposed where failure to do so may frustrate a right of appeal, because without reasons a party will not know whether there is an appealable ground or not: see eg *Norton Tool Company Ltd v Tewson*.[25]

Fourthly there may be a legitimate expectation that reasons will be given: an example of this, again cited by Elias LJ, is *Martin v Secretary of State for Communities and Local Government*,[26] in which it was held by Lindblom LJ that there was a legitimate expectation that inspectors would give reasons in a written representations planning

---

[18] *Tesco Stores Ltd v Dundee City Council* [2012] UKSC 13 [2012] 2 P & CR 9.
[19] *Hopkins Homes Ltd v Secretary of State for Communities and Local Government* [2017] 1 WLR 1865, paras 22–25 (Lord Carnwath JSC); and para 74 (Lord Gill).
[20] ibid, para 26 (Lord Carnwath JSC); and paras 72–73 (Lord Gill).
[21] *Oakley v South Cambridgeshire District Council* [2017] EWCA Civ 71, at para 29.
[22] *R v Secretary of State for the Home Department, ex p. Doody* [1994] AC 531.
[23] [1994] 1 WLR 242 (Sedley J, as he then was).
[24] [1999] 4 All ER 300.
[25] [1973] 1 WLR 45, cited by Elias LJ in *Oakley* at para 31.
[26] [2015] EWHC 3435 (Admin).

appeal which was generated by the Secretary of State's long established practice of giving reasons in such cases. This is a good example of where the concept of legitimate expectation can arise without there being any need for a promise; a past practice will suffice.

Fifthly there may be cases in which, if no reasons are given by a public authority, the court may infer that the decision is irrational: see the decision of the House of Lords in *Padfield*. However, as Elias LJ explained in *Oakley* at paragraph 33:

> Even then ... the applicant may not be given full reasons, merely such explanation of the reasoning as meets the particular ground of challenge. Moreover, if the basis of the claim is too speculative – as it may well be when no reasons are available – the application is likely to fail at the leave stage.

The existence of so many exceptions to the apparently general principle that there is no general obligation to give reasons at common law led Lord Clyde to express the opinion, almost 20 years ago, in *Stefan v General Medical Council* that:

> There is certainly a strong argument for the view that what was once seen as exceptions to a rule may now be becoming examples of the law, and the cases where reasons are not required may be taking on the appearance of exceptions.[27]

As Elias LJ observed in the *Oakley* case, there are powerful reasons why it is desirable for administrative bodies to give reasons for their decisions. They include improving the quality of decisions by focussing the mind of the decision-maker and so increasing the likelihood that the decision will be lawfully made. I would add to that that it is to be hoped that that process of focussing the mind will lead to decisions that are quite simply better decisions and not only ones that are lawful. Secondly to promote public confidence in the decision making process. Thirdly by providing, or at least facilitating, the opportunity for those affected to consider whether the decision was lawfully reached, so that for example they may be able to exercise any right of appeal or challenge a decision by way of judicial review if there are grounds for doing so. In this way the giving of reasons helps to promote the rule of law. Finally, the giving of reasons helps to respect the individual's interest in understanding – and perhaps therefore more readily accepting – why a decision has been made.

On the other hand, there are, as Elias LJ also recognised in *Oakley*, potential disadvantages in imposing a duty to give reasons. They include the possible undue burden, especially if there are many decisions of a routine kind which have to be taken by a public authority. They also include, exceptionally, 'some powerful public interests, such as national security, which could justify withholding reasons'.[28]

Oakley itself was a planning case. As is well known, there are many circumstances in which there is a statutory duty to give reasons in the context of planning law: for example where planning permission is refused or where it is granted but only subject to conditions. However, for a long time there used to be no statutory duty to give reasons where permission was granted. This was only introduced by a legislative amendment to the relevant regulations with effect from 2003 and was then removed 10 years later, in 2013.

---

[27] [1999] 1 WLR 1293, at p 1300.
[28] See para 27.

In *Oakley* itself, the result was that, despite the removal of that statutory duty, the Court of Appeal imposed a duty to give reasons – as a matter of common law – in the circumstances of that particular case. Elias LJ was of the view that the abrogation of the express duty to give reasons in such cases was not inconsistent with that outcome.[29] This was because, he said, the abrogation of that duty was not intended to reduce transparency. However, the Court of Appeal did not decide the case ultimately on the broad grounds which were advanced before it. Rather it decided the case on the narrower argument presented before it and having regard to the particular circumstances of that case. That was the view clearly expressed by Sales LJ, in his concurring judgment, and also the view of Elias LJ, with whose judgment Patten LJ agreed. As Elias LJ said, 'the courts develop the common law on a case by case basis ...'.[30]

The *Oakley* case, which was decided as recently as February this year, provides a good illustration of the continuing ability of the common law to develop in a creative way in the area of administrative law.

As I have mentioned, Parliament has on the whole been content to leave the development of the substantive grounds for judicial review to the courts. It can reasonably be presumed that Parliament has not wished to reverse the developments to which I have referred because it has not taken the opportunity to pass legislation altering the content of public law.

Nevertheless, there have been some pieces of legislation which have introduced new substantive obligations on public authorities. The main one to which I would draw attention here is the public sector equality duty, now contained in section 149 of the Equality Act 2010. Originally this was enacted in the context of racial equality by an amendment to the Race Relations Act 1976, made by Parliament in the year 2000 in order to implement one of the main recommendations of Sir William Macpherson in the Stephen Lawrence Public Inquiry.

One case I would mention in particular in this context is the decision of the Court of Appeal in *Elias*.[31] In that case (in which I appeared for the Claimant, when I was still at the Bar) it was held that there had been a breach of what was then section 71 of the Race Relations Act, since the Secretary of State had failed to have due regard to the matters set out in that section *before* the policy under challenge had been arrived at. As Arden LJ put it (at paragraph 274):

> It is the clear purpose of section 71 to require public bodies to whom that provision applies to give advance consideration to issues of race discrimination before making any policy decision that may be affected by them. This is a salutary requirement, and this provision must be seen as an integral and important part of the mechanisms for ensuring the fulfilment of the aims of anti-discrimination legislation.

Earlier in her judgment Arden LJ set out what those aims of anti-discrimination legislation are, in terms that are relevant to the maintenance of equality of all persons before the law, which is a facet of the rule of law itself:

> The adverse effects of unlawful discrimination are manifold. Discrimination can have a severe negative psychological effect on the individual involved, as well as a loss of dignity

[29] See para 54.
[30] At para 55.
[31] R (Elias) v Secretary of State for Defence [2006] 1 WLR 3213.

and self-esteem, and induce a sense of alienation. This sense of alienation can lead to a mistrust of institutions, such as the police or the justice system. This mistrust is detrimental to social cohesion. The co-operation of minority groups is particularly important in the fight against crime and terrorism.[32]

More usually Parliament has legislated in the field of administrative law to make changes to matters of procedure, remedies and costs. This is true for example of the amendments made by the Criminal Justice and Courts Act 2015 to the Senior Courts Act 1981, in particular section 31. The court may be required to refuse permission or, at the substantive stage, any remedy if it is highly likely that the outcome for the applicant would not have been substantially different even if the conduct complained of had not occurred.[33] However, the court may disregard those requirements if it considers that it is appropriate to do so 'for reasons of exceptional public interest'.[34] This perhaps underlines the fundamental difference between judicial review proceedings and ordinary civil litigation. At the end of the day, judicial review is not just about the vindication of the private rights of a particular applicant; it is about upholding the rule of law in the public interest.[35]

Before I leave matters of practice and procedure I should mention two important relatively recent innovations. The first is the publication of the Administrative Court Guide in 2016. This has quickly become established as a vital tool for everyone involved in the work of that court. Particular gratitude is owed to David Gardner, the lawyer based in Cardiff who has done a lot of the work which went into production of that Guide, with Mrs Justice Whipple and Mr Justice Lewis. A revised edition of that Guide is due out shortly.

The second important development is the creation in 2014 of the Planning Court as a distinct, specialist part of the Administrative Court. As you will know the Planning Court sits in court centres such as Bristol as well as in London. It has its own procedures, which are set out in Part 54 and the Practice Directions relating to it. Generally speaking the Planning Court aims to and does achieve a more rapid resolution of disputes than is the case more generally, even in the Administrative Court.

Finally, I want to say a few words about the importance of the Administrative Court in Bristol and more generally on the Western Circuit. It is very important that, so far as possible, administrative law work which concerns the West country should be issued and heard here. That means hearings taking place not necessarily only in Bristol but in other parts of the South West too.

Not only are there good local solicitors and barristers able and willing to do the work; the judges are here too. In particular I would like to mention that the new Designated Civil Judge for this area, Judge Barry Cotter QC, sits regularly in the Administrative Court and is authorised to sit in the Planning Court.

I will do everything that I can, as the liaison judge, in order to support and reinforce that process. The trend is in the right direction. More claims for judicial

---

[32] Para 269.

[33] Section 31(2A) and (2D) of the Senior Courts Act 1981.

[34] Section 31(2B) and (2E).

[35] See eg *R v Secretary of State for the Environment, ex p. Kirkstall Valley Campaign Ltd* [1996] 3 All ER, at 325 (Sedley J).

review which relate to the West Country are now being issued here than ever before. I would urge you to issue claims for judicial review here if you can. Even if they are not issued here, it may well be that they will be suitable for transfer here. The lawyers in the Administrative Court Office will be alert to look out for cases that are potential candidates for transfer and have recently been given delegated powers to make a 'minded to transfer' order. If necessary, I consider representations as to venue as the Liaison Judge. Of course there may be good reasons why a case should be heard in London even though it has a close connection with this region. However, in suitable cases a transfer order will be made. In that context please bear in mind that cases can often be listed for hearing much more quickly here than in London, even without an order for expedition.

Before I conclude I should return to the main theme of my lecture, that is the link between judicial review and the rule of law. There is no better guide to the many meanings of the phrase 'the rule of law' than the wonderful book which bears that title which was published by Lord Bingham in the last year of his life, seven years ago. The aspect of the rule of law on which I have focussed in this lecture was the subject of chapter 6 of his book, on 'The Exercise of Power', in which he suggested that judicial review is the exercise of a constitutional power which the rule of law requires. Lord Bingham recognised that this does not always endear itself to those in power, of whatever political persuasion. However, he ended with these salutary words:

> There are countries in the world where all judicial decisions find favour with the powers that be, but they are probably not places where any of us would wish to live.

Divided by a Common Language: American and British Perspectives on Constitutional Law

This was the Sir David Williams lecture of 2017 at the University of Cambridge, given at a time when I was a High Court judge. Sir David had been Rouse Ball Professor of English Law at the university. I attended his lectures on constitutional law in the first year of my undergraduate degree and on administrative law in my second year. He was a very kind man, who encouraged me to study in the USA, as he himself had done, on a Harkness Fellowship, and, like him, to go to Berkeley. He told me that, when he was a student there in the 1950s, he met Hans Kelsen, the great legal theorist, who had been an academic and judge in Austria before going into exile as a result of the rise of Nazism, and was for many years a professor at Berkeley. In this lecture, which was first published in [2017] Judicial Review 165, I was able to explore one of the enduring themes of my legal career, a comparison between the constitutions of the UK and the USA.

I T IS A great honour and pleasure to be asked to deliver this year's Sir David Williams lecture. The first time that I saw Sir David was on my first day of lectures as an 18 year old undergraduate, when he gave the first lecture I attended on constitutional law at the lecture theatre at Mill Lane. At that time, according to our timetable, he was known as Mr DGT Williams. From that moment on his qualities became quickly apparent. He was not only a wise teacher but also a modest man. In my second year I had the privilege of being lectured by Sir David on administrative law. Towards the end of my undergraduate career here, I also had the benefit of advice from him as to the future. In particular he was one of those teachers who encouraged me to go to the USA. I followed in his footsteps in the sense that, like him, I was a Harkness Fellow and, like him, I studied at the University of California. I have therefore taken as my subject for this year's lecture what I think would have been one of Sir David's interests: that is a comparison between American and British perspectives on constitutional law. Inevitably these reflections will be selective, since the topic is so vast that it could easily take many years of study.

In this lecture I will focus on four topics. First, by way of introduction, I will outline some of the key differences between the constitutions of the US and the UK.

* I would like to thank Jeff Minear for help with research for this lecture. All errors are mine.

Secondly, I will look at some history relating to the drafting of the US Constitution and the American Bill of Rights. Thirdly, I will look, by way of example, at a particular right: the right to freedom of speech. Fourthly, I will consider the process for appointment of judges in the two countries.

INTRODUCTION

The United States and the United Kingdom clearly have many things in common. Both our countries are stable democracies and have been for a long time. The franchise was extended beyond a privileged elite at different times in their histories but both became full democracies, with universal suffrage, around the same time just under a hundred years ago. Both countries have a longstanding commitment to the rule of law. Both countries have a commitment to the protection of civil liberties. Accordingly, although the language used in the two countries may sometimes differ, we recognise that both are countries in which the people have the power to choose their own government at regular elections; the government is subject to the law; and individual liberty is protected by the law, if necessary by resort to the courts. Let me turn to some of the main differences between the two constitutions.

First, as is well known, the US has a written constitution, which is set out in a short document and which can be carried around by citizens, whereas the UK does not. In the recent case concerning the invocation of Article 50 of the Treaty on European Union (the Brexit case), Lord Neuberger put it this way:

> Unlike most countries, the United Kingdom does not have a constitution in the sense of a single coherent code of fundamental law which prevails over all other sources of law. Our constitutional arrangements have developed over time in a pragmatic as much as in a principled way, through a combination of statutes, events, conventions, academic writings and judicial decisions. Reflecting its development and its contents, the UK constitution was described by the constitutional scholar, Professor A V Dicey, as 'the most flexible polity in existence' – *Introduction to the Study of the Law of the Constitution* (8th ed, 1915), p 87.[1]

As that quotation makes clear, unlike the constitution of the US, our own constitution (i) is not codified in a single document; (ii) is to be found in the ordinary law of the land rather than a fundamental law; and (iii) is flexible because it can be changed in the same way that other laws can be, rather than requiring a special procedure for amendment.

The second main difference is that the US is a republic whereas the UK is a monarchy. But it has been a constitutional monarchy for many centuries, since the Glorious Revolution of 1688. It became clear, after the Great Reform Act of 1832, limited though that measure was, that the monarch would no longer be able to insist

---

[1] *R (Miller) v Secretary of State for Exiting the European Union* [2017] UKSC 5 [2017] 2 WLR 583, para 40.

on a government being formed which did not have the confidence of the House of Commons. In the century which followed, the UK became a representative democracy.

The third main difference between the constitutions of the two countries is that, although we both use the term 'separation of powers', and Montesquieu famously misunderstood the English constitution in this regard, the US draws a sharp distinction between the executive branch and the legislature. The President is elected separately from members of the two houses of Congress. In contrast, in the UK the Prime Minister is not directly elected but is usually the leader of the political party which can command a majority in the House of Commons. And all ministers are expected by convention to be a member of one or other of the Houses of Parliament, at least after their appointment if not before.

Although the legislative power of the United States is expressly vested by the Constitution in Congress, it is clear that the President enjoys some rule-making power in the form of Executive Orders. To be clear – this is not delegated legislation, although that concept exists in the US as it does in the UK. Executive Orders are not rules made under powers delegated by Congress but are inherent in the executive function, which is assigned by the Constitution to the President. The concept of Executive Orders has assumed particular prominence in recent weeks, as Donald Trump has issued a number of such orders on becoming President last month. It is only rarely that the US Supreme Court has held that an Executive Order was outside the President's powers on the ground that it violated the doctrine of separation of powers and purported to enact what was in substance legislation, which is a matter exclusively for Congress. The most famous example of that was in 1952, when the Court struck down President Truman's Executive Order which had seized the country's steel mills at a time of industrial dispute.[2]

In the UK there is very limited scope for the executive to make rules which are tantamount to legislation unless there has been delegated power to do so given by Parliament, although there are some areas of the Royal Prerogative where there remains a residual legislative power. In the Brexit case, Lord Neuberger said, at paragraph 44:

> In the early 17th century *Case of Proclamations* (1610) 12 Co Rep 74, Sir Edward Coke CJ said that 'the King by his proclamation or other ways cannot change any part of the common law, or statute law, or the customs of the realm'. Although this statement may have been controversial at the time, it had become firmly established by the end of that century.

I turn to the fourth main difference between the two countries. Although we rightly regard both countries as democracies, the UK still has one part of its legislature which is not elected: the House of Lords. In contrast the US Senate comprises two senators each, who are elected by the voters of each state, however large or small. However, it should be noted that this is a relatively recent development in American history. The original Constitution, in section 3, stipulated that the senators should be chosen by the legislature of each state. This was altered by the 17th Amendment,

---

[2] *Youngstown Sheet & Tube Co. v Sawyer* 343 US 579 (1952).

which was ratified in 1913, during a time known in American history as the Progressive era. Since then US senators have been directly elected by the people.

The fifth main difference lies in the concept of federalism, a fundamental feature of the US Constitution, which necessarily means that the powers of the national or 'federal' government are limited. Recent developments in the UK have led to devolution to the constituent nations of the UK, in particular to Scotland; to a lesser extent to Wales; and in a different way to Northern Ireland (which had its own 'Home Rule' from 1920 until direct rule was imposed in 1972). Devolution was, of course, a subject close to Sir David Williams' heart. These developments, important though they are, have still not introduced a federal structure to the distribution of powers in the UK. First, England – the largest part of the union – remains without its own Parliament, although recent changes have been introduced to the procedures of the House of Commons in relation to legislation that affects only England ('English Votes for English Laws' as it is sometimes called).[3] Secondly, a fundamental feature of our constitution remains the supremacy of the Westminster Parliament. The US Congress has no such supremacy even in theory.

SOME HISTORY

I will now turn to some history. Although the Revolutionary War, as it tends to be called in America, or the American War of Independence, as it tends to be called in this country, marked an obvious rupture in the constitutional arrangements for what had until then been English colonies in North America, it is important to note that, at the time, the founders of the American Republic believed that they were (in the words of Gordon Wood): 'Englishmen with a strong sense that they were heirs of the English tradition of freedom'.[4] There had been, and continued to be even after the war, considerable movement between America and Britain, both physical travel of people; and metaphorical travel in the sense of exchange of ideas. As Jonathan Clark puts it in his study of political discourse in the Anglo-American world between 1660 and 1832: 'The Revolution of 1776 was slow to happen because Englishmen on both sides of the Atlantic were locked into the belief that they were already living in a libertarian polity'.[5] Clark goes on to suggest that:

> From the middle of the eighteenth century in both England and America, it began to be re-emphasised that William I had corrupted the Saxon constitution by imposing the 'Norman Yoke'; that its restoration had been alternatively the work of the barons who drafted Magna Carta; or of sixteenth century Protestant reformers; or of Civil War heroes; or of Glorious Revolution patricians; or, most radical of all, that it remained to be accomplished.

[3] For a more detailed description of how the concept works see the Report of the House of Lords Select Committee on the Constitution, 'English votes for English laws', HL Paper 61 (2016).

[4] Gordon S Wood, *The Idea of America: Reflections on the Birth of the United States* (New York, Penguin, 2011) 173.

[5] JCD Clark, *The Language of Liberty 1660–1832: Political Discourse and Social Dynamics in the Anglo-American World* (Cambridge, Cambridge University Press, 1994) 7.

Clark attributes this view in particular to a Welsh Dissenting minister who, as it happens, was also called David Williams, who lived from 1738 to 1816 and who was a '[f]riend of Benjamin Franklin, libertine and would-be liturgical reformer'.[6]

Even the most obvious difference between the new republic and the 'Mother country' from which it had just broken away, namely its written constitution, was not necessarily perceived at the time to represent such a great change from what had happened in the past. Many of the colonies had been established by Crown Charters. As Wood puts it:

> The whole of the colonial past was littered with such charters and other written documents of various sorts to which the colonial assemblies repeatedly appealed in their squabbles with Royal power.[7]

This was regarded as a continuation of an earlier English tradition, of putting rights down in a written document: the best known of these of course was the Magna Carta. It is perhaps no surprise that Magna Carta is still revered today, arguably more in the United States than it is in this country.

Nonetheless, despite their common origins, there can be no doubt that the two countries quickly diverged in a radical way. Over the two centuries after the American colonies had become independent, the principal concern in Britain became how to make Parliament more democratic and therefore more representative of the people. Parliament was perceived as the guarantor of the liberties of the people and the principal threat to those liberties was perceived to come from the Crown. The fundamental doctrine of constitutional law in this country became the doctrine of Parliamentary Sovereignty, particularly as set out by Blackstone in the eighteenth century and Dicey in the nineteenth. In contrast, in the American colonies even before independence and more particularly, after 1787, in what became known as the United States, the idea took hold that there should be a higher form of law, set out in a written constitution, which would be the fundamental law of the land and to which even legislatures would be subject. In fact many Americans believed that they were drawing on an earlier tradition in England, illustrated by *Dr Bonham's case*,[8] in which Coke CJ suggested that even an Act of Parliament might be held to be void by the courts if it were 'against common right and reason, or repugnant, or impossible to be performed'.[9]

As is well known, there was no express provision set out in the Constitution of 1787 itself to provide for the judicial review, let alone nullification or striking down, of Acts of Congress. The doctrine which Americans call 'judicial review', in other words the power of the courts to review the constitutionality of Acts of Congress, was only made explicit by a decision of the US Supreme Court: *Marbury v Madison*.[10] Although the doctrine of judicial review was never expressly set out in the Constitution of the United States, it has become an accepted and fundamental

[6] ibid, 18.
[7] ibid, 175.
[8] (1610) 8 Co Rep 114.
[9] For the early history of the American tradition drawing on *Dr Bonham's case*, in particular in the colonies before the Revolutionary war, see B Schwarz, *A History of the Supreme Court* (Oxford, Oxford University Press, 1993) 3–11.
[10] 5 US (1 Cranch) 137 (1803).

feature of that constitution. It has never been seriously attempted to repeal that doctrine, for example by constitutional amendment. For good or ill, therefore, the power of the courts, in particular that of the US Supreme Court, to strike down even Acts of the elected Congress for their inconsistency with the Constitution, has become embedded in American life and culture.

Of course we have no such concept in this country. We still have no fundamental law in the sense of the written constitution which Americans have. Even what are sometimes described as 'constitutional statutes', such as the European Communities Act 1972 and the Human Rights Act 1998, are still ordinary Acts of the Westminster Parliament. They were not enacted by any special procedure being required. In principle, they can be repealed by another ordinary Act of Parliament.

Nevertheless, so long as the European Communities Act remains in force, we have had something similar to the American doctrine of judicial review whenever an issue has arisen which fell within the scope of European Community (now European Union) law. To that extent it has been possible for, indeed the duty of, courts in this country to disapply even provisions in an Act of the Westminster Parliament if and to the extent that they are incompatible with a provision of European Union law which has direct affect. This of course is now subject to the decision of the people of this country to leave the European Union in the referendum on 23 June 2016. However, as I have said, unless and until the Westminster Parliament repeals the European Communities Act 1972, the duty of the courts of this country remains clear. Indeed, in the *Miller* case the Supreme Court has held that even the start of the process of leaving, by invoking Article 50, must be authorised by Act of Parliament rather than being a matter for the Royal Prerogative. A bill to obtain that authority for the government is currently before Parliament.

So far as the protection of human rights is concerned, as is well known, the structure which was adopted by the Human Rights Act is somewhat different. Parliament was careful not to give the courts the power to strike down Acts of Parliament on the ground that they are incompatible with human rights. However, Parliament did place what is in substance responsibility for judicial review of Acts of Parliament with the courts by enacting the Human Rights Act. In particular Parliament gave the higher courts (that is, in England and Wales, the High Court and above) the power to make a declaration of incompatibility in respect of primary legislation. This power has been exercised, although not on a large number of occasions, since 2000, when the Human Rights Act came into full force. About 20 declarations of incompatibility have been made. Conor Gearty has described this novel kind of court order in characteristically provocative terms: 'They are grand announcements of judicial distaste but no more than that – shouts of antipathy dressed up as legal remedies but without the usual enforceability that we take for granted comes with victory in court'.[11]

Perhaps most importantly this power was exercised by the House of Lords in the Belmarsh case: *A v Secretary of State for the Home Department* (2004).[12] In that case the House of Lords made a declaration that Part 4 of the Anti-terrorism, Crime and

---

[11] CA Gearty, *On Fantasy Island: Britain, Europe and Human Rights* (Oxford, Oxford University Press, 2016) 69.
[12] [2005] 2 AC 68.

Security Act 2001 was incompatible with fundamental rights as set out in Schedule 1 to the Human Rights Act, in particular the right to personal liberty in Article 5 and the right to equality in the enjoyment of other Convention rights in Article 14. Although a controversial decision, it is notable that the response of both the Government of the day and Parliament was to accept that declaration of incompatibility. The incompatible provisions of primary legislation were repealed by Parliament. This is despite the fact that a declaration of incompatibility is expressly not made binding.

The American Bill of Rights, which comprises the first 10 amendments to the US Constitution, has much in it that we would recognise, even if the language now seems a little archaic. Freedom of speech, freedom of religion, the right to a fair trial and the right to property are all there. This is hardly surprising, since the founders were drawing on what they perceived to be their heritage from the English common law. They were also in some instances drawing on the express language of the English Bill of Rights of 1689, for example the prohibition on 'cruel and unusual punishments' in the Eighth Amendment. Although at one time, in the 1970s, it appeared that this might be interpreted in such a way as to prohibit the death penalty, that has not occurred. In contrast the UK has now accepted the abolition of the death penalty in all circumstances, including wartime, by ratifying the 13th Protocol to the European Convention on Human Rights. There are some rights in the American Bill of Rights that have no counterpart at all in our understanding of fundamental rights, in particular the right to bear arms in the Second Amendment.

The American Bill of Rights originally applied only to the federal government and not to the states. This should not come as any surprise. After all the original structure of the constitution of 1787 was one in which the several states, which had recently become independent from Great Britain, convened in order to create what they called 'a more perfect union', following the unsatisfactory experience of the Articles of Confederation of 1781. The founders of the American republic, who had met in Philadelphia in 1787, generally speaking regarded the Federal Government as at best a necessary evil. Some indeed feared that it might become as tyrannical as the British Government was perceived to have been in the years leading up to the War of Independence. Consideration was given to enacting a Bill of Rights at the Philadelphia convention. However, the delegates decided not to proceed in that way at that time.

One of the founders of the American republic, Alexander Hamilton, was opposed to the idea of a bill of rights. As Carol Berkin puts it in her recent history of the drafting process:

> Hamilton insisted that [it] was redundant in a Lockean republic. Guarantees of rights, he declared, might be valuable as stipulations between kings and their subjects. But in a constitution 'founded upon the power of the people, and executed by their immediate representatives and servants … the people surrender nothing, and as they retain everything they have no need of particular reservations.'[13]

Nevertheless it soon became apparent to the supporters of the new federal government that, in order to assist in the ratification process, it was going to be necessary to introduce amendments to the Constitution by enacting what became the Bill of

[13] C Berkin, *The Bill of Rights* (New York, Simon & Schuster, 2015) 26.

Rights. This was what James Madison then achieved and the first 10 amendments were ratified by 1791.

Some had a concern that setting out certain rights expressly in a bill of rights might be taken to imply that they were the only rights which people have. That would have been contrary to the natural rights theory in which they believed as heirs to John Locke. It was for this reason that the final two amendments were included in the Bill of Rights. They are relatively unknown provisions and are rarely referred to in the jurisprudence of the Supreme Court. The Ninth Amendment states: 'The enumeration, in the Constitution, of certain rights, shall not be construed to deny or disparage others retained by the people'. The Tenth Amendment states: 'The powers not delegated to the United States by the Constitution, nor prohibited by it to the states, are reserved to the states respectively, or to the people'.

THE RIGHT TO FREEDOM OF SPEECH

As a major example of the way in which American constitutional law protects fundamental rights, I now intend to consider the right to freedom of speech. This is one of the rights contained in the First Amendment. That amendment has attained an almost mythical status not only in American law but in American culture. Even the fact that it is numbered the First Amendment has had some significance attached to it. In fact, as it happens, in the original draft Bill of Rights, the rights which are now contained in the First Amendment were to have been in a clause numbered four. Madison's original proposal would have made textual amendments to the main body of the Constitution.[14] It was only later that it was decided to set out the amendments separately, in effect as an addendum to the Constitution. Even in the version which was eventually passed by both Houses of Congress and sent to the states for ratification, freedom of speech was mentioned in the third proposed amendment. Since the first was never ratified and the second had to wait another 200 years before it was ratified in 1992, the famous clause concerning freedom of speech and religion became the First Amendment.[15]

The second point to make about the express language of the First Amendment is that, on its face, it applies only to the federal government and not to the states. In fact, if read literally, it applies only to one branch even of the federal government, namely Congress. So far as relevant it provides that Congress shall make no law abridging the freedom of speech. There was in Madison's original proposal an amendment, in the then clause 5, which would have included a prohibition on violation of 'the freedom of the press' against the states but this was not enacted in the final version of the Bill of Rights.[16]

The jurisprudence of the US Supreme Court only established that the right to freedom of speech applied to the states indirectly in the early part of the twentieth century.

---

[14] The text of the original amendments proposed by Madison to Congress on 8 June 1789 is set out in Berkin, ibid, 149–52.

[15] For more detail about the drafting and ratification process, see Richard Lubanski, *James Madison and the Struggle for the Bill of Rights* (Oxford, Oxford University Press, 2007), in particular Appendix V, which sets out the amendments as sent by Congress to the states on 25 September 1789.

[16] ibid, 151.

This was achieved through the 'due process' clause of the Fourteenth Amendment, which prohibits the states from depriving any person of life, liberty or property without due process of law. The Fourteenth Amendment was one of the amendments passed after the American Civil War in the late 1860s. To a lawyer in this country it might seem surprising at first sight that a clause which appears to deal with 'due process' has been interpreted by the US Supreme Court to include substantive guarantees as well. However, in American law it is now well established that this is the case. Americans refer to this doctrine as 'substantive due process'. This is the vehicle by which the Bill of Rights has been held to bind the states as well as the federal government.[17]

Despite the rhetoric which surrounds the First Amendment, and indeed the Bill of Rights more generally, it took a long time for the Supreme Court to establish the modern principles on freedom of speech. As Eric Foner puts it:

> Today, the liberties enshrined in the Bill of Rights are central to Americans' conception of freedom. This has not always been the case; indeed, at many moments in our history, from the suppression of abolitionist meetings in the 1830s to the Red Scare after World War I and the depredations of McCarthyism during the Cold War, individual rights have been seriously curtailed – often in the name of freedom. The growth of civil liberties in this country is not a story of linear progress or simply a series of Supreme Court decisions, but a highly uneven and bitterly contested part of the story of American freedom.[18]

Samuel Walker, in his history of the American Civil Liberties Union, suggests that:

> There was no tradition of free speech before World War I, in either legal doctrine or public tolerance for unpopular views. The glittering phrases of the First Amendment were an empty promise to the labor movement, immigrants, unorthodox religious sects, and political radicals. Intolerance began with the first English settlers who attempted to suppress religious heresy. The Puritans may have come to the new world seeking religious freedom for themselves, but they had no intention of granting it to others in their own communities. Through the end of the nineteenth century, American society was a set of 'island communities', each a 'closed enclave', intolerant of the ideas or behavior it disliked.

Indeed, Walker suggests that in the nineteenth century 'the courts scarcely functioned in many frontier communities. The majority imposed swift and certain justice through vigilante action'.[19]

There is a well-established distinction in American constitutional law between the restriction of the 'content' of speech and the regulation of the time, place and manner of the exercise of the right to freedom of speech. It is conventionally thought that regulation of time, place and manner is permissible as long as it is reasonable.

When it comes to the content of speech, the generally received wisdom is that Americans will not tolerate any restriction of what they can say at all. However,

---

[17] Cf the situation where some rights on their face bind only the states, eg the Fourteenth Amendment, which guarantees the equal protection of the laws. It was held in *Bolling v Sharpe* 347 US 497 (1954) that this indirectly binds the Federal government through the Due Process clause of the Fifth Amendment. By this means the US Supreme Court was able to hold that racial segregation in the schools of Washington DC was unconstitutional, even though the Equal Protection clause on its face only applies to the states.

[18] E Foner, *The Story of American Freedom* (New York, Picador, 1998) xvii.

[19] S Walker, *In Defense of American Liberties: A History of the ACLU* (Oxford, Oxford University Press, 1990) 28–29.

this has never been the law. Historically the way in which the US Supreme Court addressed the problem was by recognising that there were certain categories of speech which were outside the protection of the First Amendment. Traditionally obscenity was such a category, although in practice today this will hardly apply in the case of adults. Child pornography is an entirely different matter. Another famous category of unprotected speech relates to what Americans call 'fighting words'. Even defamation, although the doctrines have been different in our two countries, is not protected speech under the First Amendment. It has also long been recognised in American law that the state is entitled to criminalise incitement to commit criminal acts. However, as a result of what was originally called the 'clear and present danger' test, it has been established that there has to be a close nexus between the words used and the likelihood of a criminal offence in fact occurring.[20]

The problems with which both our countries are grappling today are not new ones. A hundred years ago, shortly after the First World War and the Russian Revolution, America had to address the question of what, if any, restrictions could be placed on 'extremist' speech. At that time the fear was of violent revolution along the lines of what had just happened in Russia.

One of the most famous such cases was *Whitney v California* (1927).[21] Anita Whitney was a member of the Socialist Party who was arrested after giving a speech called 'The Negro Question', in which she protested about race riots and lynching. She was convicted under a California law which prohibited 'criminal syndicalism'. She was convicted of assisting in organising an association to advocate terrorism. Although the US Supreme Court upheld that conviction, Justice Brandeis concurred rather than dissented. However, his concurring judgment is usually regarded as being tantamount to a dissenting one. It has also been described by his recent biographer, Jeffrey Rosen, as 'a kind of constitutional poetry'.[22]

In *Whitney* Brandeis said:

> Those who won our independence believed that the final end of the state was to make men free to develop their faculties, and that in its government the deliberative forces should prevail over the arbitrary. They valued liberty both as an end and as a means. They believed liberty to be the secret of happiness and courage to be the secret of liberty. They believed that freedom to think as you will and to speak as you think are means indispensable to the discovery and spread of political truth; that without free speech and assembly discussion would be futile; that with them, discussion affords ordinarily adequate protection against the dissemination of noxious doctrine; that the greatest menace to freedom is an inert people; that public discussion is a political duty; and that this should be a fundamental principle of the American government.

As Rosen observes, Brandeis clearly had in mind the words of President Jefferson in his first inaugural address in 1801:

> That though the will of the majority is in all cases to prevail, that will to be rightful must be reasonable; that the minority possess their equal rights, which equal law must protect, and to violate would be oppression.

---

[20] *Brandenburg v Ohio* 395 US 444 (1969).
[21] 274 US 357 (1927).
[22] J Rosen, *Louis D. Brandeis: American Prophet* (London, Yale University Press, 2016) 128.

Brandeis echoed those words when he said that:

> Recognising the occasional tyrannies of governing majorities, they [ie the Founders] amended the Constitution so that free speech and assembly should be guaranteed.

In *A v Secretary of State for the Home Department* Lady Hale expressly quoted the same passage from Jefferson's inaugural and said, at paragraph 237:

> Democracy values each person equally. In most respects, this means that the will of the majority must prevail. But valuing each person equally also means that the will of the majority cannot prevail if it is inconsistent with the equal rights of minorities.

In fact, as we have seen, Anita Whitney's conviction was upheld by the Supreme Court and Brandeis' opinion was a concurring one, even if it reads like a dissent. A month after the court's decision, the Governor of California pardoned her, saying that freedom of speech is the 'indispensable birthright of every free American'. She was soon to be back before the courts, for violating a state statute which made it a crime to display a red flag. In 1931 the US Supreme Court held that that law was 'repugnant to the guaranty of liberty contained in the Fourteenth Amendment'.[23]

In the last 25 years the US Supreme Court has come to recognise that there are no categories of speech which are in principle unprotected by the First Amendment. On the other hand, the Court has also come to recognise that it may be possible in principle for the state to regulate even the content of speech where a law is narrowly tailored to serve a compelling state interest. This is sometimes called 'strict scrutiny'. In this way, although Americans would not necessarily use the same terminology as we use in Europe, there is in practice a doctrine similar to our own principle of proportionality.

Accordingly, I would suggest that, although at first sight the experiences of the US and the UK appear to be very different in the context of freedom of expression, in fact there are many similarities too. A major exception to this is in relation to the concept of 'hate speech'. The US Supreme Court has taken a fundamentally different approach to 'hate speech' from that taken in many other democratic societies, including the United Kingdom: see its decision in *RAV v City of St Paul, Minnesota*.[24] Whereas, like many countries, we have laws which prohibit (for example) incitement to racial hatred, such laws have not survived scrutiny in the US.

Although the law in the United Kingdom has not had, until relatively recently, a positive right to freedom of expression, the values underlying it were embedded in the culture of this country and in the common law for many centuries. In particular the marketplace of ideas theory can be found in the writings of John Stuart Mill in the nineteenth century. They were clearly influential on the jurisprudence of the US Supreme Court in the early part of the twentieth century, eg *Abrams v United States* (1919).[25]

More recently, it is clear that the flow of ideas has also come in the other direction: American law has influenced our law, even before the Human Rights Act came into

---

[23] Foner (n 19) 185. The case was known as *Stromberg v California* 283 US 359 (1931).
[24] 505 US 377 (1992).
[25] 250 US 616 (1919).

force. Most notable was the decision of the House of Lords in *R v Secretary of State for the Home Department, ex parte Simms* (1999).[26] Lord Steyn said:

> Freedom of expression is, of course, intrinsically important: it is valued for its own sake. But it is well recognised that it is also instrumentally important. It serves a number of broad objectives. First, it promotes the self-fulfilment of individuals in society. Secondly, in the famous words of Holmes J (echoing John Stuart Mill), 'the best test of truth is the power of the thought to get itself accepted in the competition of the market': *Abrams v United States* (1919) 250 US 616, 630 per Holmes J (dissenting). Thirdly, freedom of speech is the lifeblood of democracy. The free flow of information and ideas informs political debate. It is a safety valve: people are more ready to accept decisions that go against them if they can in principle seek to influence them. It acts as a brake on the abuse of power by public officials. It facilitates the exposure of errors in the government and administration of justice of the country.[27]

Another example of American 'constitutional poetry' can be found in a freedom of religion case: *West Virginia State Board of Education v Barnette*.[28] At page 642 Jackson J said:

> If there is any fixed star in our constitutional constellation, it is that no official, high or petty, can prescribe what shall be orthodox in politics, nationalism, religion or other matters of opinion, or force citizens to confess by word or act their faith therein.

Note even the use of alliteration in that passage. That case concerned whether the state could compel school children to salute the American flag. Although that practice is often thought to be one of the most fundamental features of American culture, the US Supreme Court held that Jehovah's witnesses could not be compelled to do so. It is also notable that the decision, which reversed the court's own earlier decision of just three years before, was made at the height of the Second World War. It perhaps provided an indication of what Americans thought they were fighting for against the totalitarian regimes, in particular Nazi Germany.

As the Divisional Court (of which I was a member) said, after citing these authorities, in *R (BBC) v Secretary of State for Justice*: 'History has taught us that, in fields as diverse as politics, religion, science and the law, what starts as a heresy may well end up as the orthodxy'.[29]

Furthermore, as the European Court of Human Rights has often said in its jurisprudence on Article 10, freedom of expression constitutes one of the essential foundations of a democratic society. Accordingly 'it is applicable not only to information or ideas that are favourably received or regarded as inoffensive or as a matter of indifference, but also to those that offend, shock or disturb the state or any sector of the population'.[30] The jurisprudence of the European Court has frequently stressed that the hallmarks of a democratic society are not simply that the will of the majority must prevail. Rather a democratic society is characterised by pluralism, tolerance and broad-mindedness.[31]

---

[26] [2000] 2 AC 115.
[27] ibid, p.126.
[28] 319 US 264 (1943).
[29] [2013] 1 WLR 964, para 41.
[30] *Sunday Times v United Kingdom* (1979) 2 EHRR 245, para 65.
[31] *Handyside v United Kingdom* (1976) 1 EHRR 737, para 49.

In this context I would recall again what was said by the Divisional Court in the *BBC* case, at paragraph 49:

> these words, which appear in many of the articles of the Convention, are not superfluous. The framers of the Convention, arising as it did out of the ashes of European conflict in the 1930's and 1940's, recognised that not everything that the state asserts to be necessary will be acceptable in a democratic society.

JUDICIAL APPOINTMENTS AND INDEPENDENCE

As I said at the outset of this lecture, both the United States and the United Kingdom have mature legal systems, with a strong tradition of judicial independence and respect for the rule of law. In this context, judicial independence is a particular aspect of the separation of powers.

It is often thought that in the US judges are elected. In fact the picture is much more complicated. There is an important distinction between the federal judiciary and judges in each of the states. It is in the nature of American federalism that there will be different systems for the appointment of judges in each state.

The federal judiciary are not elected at all. The Constitution created the Supreme Court, although its composition was not spelt out in the Constitution itself and has been affected by Congressional legislation since 1789. Over time the number of judges on the Supreme Court has been increased to its current number of nine, including the Chief Justice. The power to appoint judges to the Supreme Court is vested by the Constitution in the President, with the 'advice and consent' of the Senate. A similar appointment process is used for the District Bench and the US Court of Appeals, which is divided into various circuits, covering the vast geographical area of the United States' territory.

Presidential appointments, in particular to the Supreme Court, can be the subject of intense public debate. There are confirmation hearings before the US Senate. Some see this as an unfortunate introduction of partisanship into what should be an independent process; others regard it as an important, democratic check on what is otherwise the great power vested in the Supreme Court. Although judicial interpretations of the Constitution can be reversed by constitutional amendment, the system for amendment of the Constitution was deliberately made difficult by the Founders, and in practice, it is rare for a decision of the US Supreme Court to be overturned in this manner. That means that the prospect of having well-established judicial decisions of that court overturned can be the subject of intense political controversy: in particular the decision of the US Supreme Court in *Roe v Wade* (1973), which decided that the Constitution confers the right to choose to have an abortion.[32] Since February last year there has been a vacancy on the US Supreme Court, arising from the death of Justice Scalia. President Obama nominated Merrick Garland for the appointment but the Senate declined to consider the nomination before the outcome of the Presidential election was known in November. At the end of January this year the new President,

[32] 410 US 113 (1973).

Donald Trump, nominated another judge to fill the same vacancy: Neil Gorsuch. It will now be for the US Senate to decide whether to confirm that appointment.

So far as state courts are concerned, the practice relating to judicial appointments varies enormously. Originally each of the 13 states after the War of Independence selected its judges through either executive or legislative appointment. There were at that time no elections for the state judiciary. However, in the first half of the nineteenth century there was a democratic movement associated with the presidency of Andrew Jackson, often referred to as 'Jacksonian democracy'. As it has been put by Rachel Paine Caufield: 'states began to move away from appointive selection methods in the mid-eighteen hundreds with the rise of Jacksonian democracy and its emphasis on democratic accountability, individual equality, and direct voter participation in governmental decision-making'.[33] By the time of the American Civil War the vast majority of states had changed their method of judicial selection to direct election by the voters.

However, a contrary trend began to emerge in the first half of the twentieth century. This was initially associated with the Progressive era. A movement began for what Americans call a 'merit system'. The first state to adopt the merit system was Missouri in 1940. Since then a large number of states have adopted such a system, in particular for the highest court in each state. In fact 24 of the states and the District of Columbia have adopted some form of merit system, 'making it the most prevalent system of judicial selection in use in the United States today'.[34] As Brian Fitzpatrick explains, although there are differences among these various systems, they have two common features. First, with regard to initial selection, judges are not elected but are appointed by the Governor of the state, from a list of names submitted by a nominating commission. Secondly, at some point after appointment in most of the systems, state judges must come before the public in a referendum (albeit an uncontested one), through which voters can remove a judge from the bench.

Even in those states where there is no election for the initial appointment of a state judge, and for this purpose I will confine myself to the highest court in the state, the general practice tends to be that a judge must then face a 'retention' election. I will describe the practice in the state with which I am most familiar, that is California. According to the constitution of the State of California, judges for the Supreme Court must be nominated by the Governor and confirmed by the Commission on Judicial Appointments, which consists of the Chief Justice, the Attorney General, and the Presiding Justice of the Court of Appeals. Since 1979 it has been required that the State Bar commission on judicial nominees' evaluation should conduct a thorough investigation of the background and qualifications of prospective nominees. However, the Governor is not bound by that commission's recommendations. Once appointed, judges must stand for retention at the time of the next gubernatorial election after their appointment. Appellate judges serve twelve-year terms.

[33] 'However pickers pick: finding a set of best practices for judicial nominating commissions' (2007) 34 *Fordham Urb LJ* 163, 167.
[34] Brian T Fitzpatrick, 'The Politics of Merit Selection' (2009) 74 *Missouri Law Review* 676, 678.

Although, in many states, judicial retention elections are low key affairs, in the state of California they have often been controversial. I remember that, while I was a student in California in 1986, there was a well-organised campaign against some members of the state Supreme Court, including the Chief Justice, Rose Elizabeth Bird. The particular reason why they were unpopular with many electors was their perceived antipathy to use of the death penalty. A total of $11.5 million was spent on campaigning both for and against the judges, setting what was at that time a record for spending in a judicial election. They were voted off the state Supreme Court.

In this country, of course, we have no election for judges, not even what the Americans call a 'retention' election. There was a time, around the turn of the nineteenth and twentieth centuries, when Lord Halsbury was Lord Chancellor in the Salisbury governments, when party affiliation does appear to have played a part in judicial appointments. However, that has long since passed. In any event, today we have the Judicial Appointments Commission (in England and Wales). That commission was created by Parliament in the Constitutional Reform Act 2005, with the express purpose of placing it at arm's length from the government of the day. There are similar appointment bodies in Scotland and Northern Ireland. When it comes to the Supreme Court of the UK, appointees are selected by a panel which includes representatives of the JAC and its counterparts in the other parts of the UK. The sole criterion for judicial appointments is merit: that is now a statutory requirement in the 2005 Act.

In the past it was not uncommon for judges in this country to have had party political careers. Some of our best judges had such a background:[35] for example, Lord Reid, who served with great distinction on our highest court, the House of Lords, between 1949 and 1975, had been a Conservative MP. Another Law Lord, Lord Simon of Glaisdale, was appointed straight to become President of the old Probate, Admiralty and Divorce Division of the High Court in 1962. Before his appointment he was a Conservative MP and Solicitor General in Harold Macmillan's government.

There was until well into the twentieth century a practice by which, if the post of Lord Chief Justice became vacant, the Attorney General of the day had the right of first refusal upon it. Sir Rufus Isaacs became Lord Reading CJ in that way, having been a Liberal MP and a member of the Asquith Government. Indeed our modern sensibilities about the separation of powers may be quite recent. While Lord Reading was a serving Chief Justice, he was also appointed to be this country's ambassador to the United States. The last such appointment was that of Lord Hewart CJ, who had been a Liberal MP and Attorney General in the National government of the 1930s.

In the United States, one former President became Chief Justice of the US Supreme Court (William Howard Taft). One of the most successful Chief Justices in American history, Earl Warren, had been a Republican Governor of California and only just lost out to Eisenhower for the Republican nomination for the presidency in 1952. It is often reported that, when President Eisenhower left the White House, he was asked

---

[35] In the more distant past other examples include Coke CJ, Lord Camden and Lord Mansfield, all of whom had served as Attorneys General.

whether he had made any mistakes during his presidency. He replied 'only two: and they are both sitting on the Supreme Court'. He was thinking of Chief Justice Warren and Justice Brennan.

There can be no doubt that some great American judges have previously held high political office. For example Justice Robert Jackson had been Attorney General in the administration of President Franklin Roosevelt and served with great distinction both on the US Supreme Court and as the Chief Prosecutor at the Nuremberg War Crimes Tribunal after the Second World War. More recently, one of the current justices of the Supreme Court, Elena Kegan, was Solicitor General in President Obama's administration, having previously been Dean of Harvard law school.

In this country also we have experience of such appointments, indeed quite recently. Lord Mackay of Clashfern was a highly regarded Lord Chancellor and Law Lord, having previously been Lord Advocate in Margaret Thatcher's government. More recently still, Lord Rodger of Earlsferry was a highly regarded Law Lord and then Justice of the Supreme Court, having previously been Lord Advocate in the John Major administration.

Indeed some commentators would suggest that it can be desirable for the senior judiciary to include at least some judges who have previous experience of government and the legislature, in the light of the important constitutional questions which judges sometimes have to decide. This does not compromise the principle of independence, provided there is a separation of powers at the time when they are serving judges. Judges must relinquish any links they may have had with a political party on their appointment to the bench.

CONCLUDING REMARKS

I would like to end with a few concluding remarks. Clearly the United States and the United Kingdom have a long and shared commitment to constitutionalism. However, the structural differences between the two constitutional systems mean that it is difficult to prune principles from one legal system and simply transplant them to the very different soil of the other. Sometimes we use the same phrases, such as 'separation of powers' and 'due process' but these can be false friends, as their meaning may be quite different in the two countries. Having said that, the two systems have clearly influenced each other too and continue to do so, as in the field of freedom of speech. Looking at the jurisprudence of the US can be helpful in providing useful insights into the way in which a problem is analysed, even if the answer would not necessarily be the same. It can also, quite simply, be enjoyable for the 'constitutional poetry' one can find there.

Interpreting Bills of Rights[†]

In 2007 (at a time when I was still a barrister) I gave the annual Statute Law Society lecture, which was first published in [2008] Statute Law Review 82. My subject was the interpretation of bills of rights and how this is not the same as the interpretation of ordinary legislation. The UK's Human Rights Act is in substance a bill of rights although it is an Act of Parliament. It is regarded by the courts as a constitutional statute. In this lecture I looked at comparative experience of interpreting bills of rights in various democratic countries. I also looked specifically at the way in which the HRA had been interpreted by the courts of this country in its early years, in particular the obligation in section 2, to take into account the jurisprudence from Strasbourg when interpreting the Convention rights.

INTRODUCTION

I N HIS RECENT book, *Interpreting Constitutions* Jeffrey Goldsworthy has written that '[C]onstitutional interpretation is an extraordinarily difficult enterprise, which requires striking an appropriate balance between competing, weighty considerations'.[1] My talk today focuses on one aspect of this difficult enterprise, namely, the interpretation of Bills of rights.

An initial question is why the interpretation of human rights instruments is thought to require special attention. Why should this topic not be subsumed into general discussions about statutory interpretation? What is distinctive about constitutions and Bills of rights in particular? And is it possible to extract principles of interpretation that have application generally, and not only in particular jurisdictions? These are the concerns of the first part of this talk, where I explore these questions in the light of comparative law. I should say at once that I do not claim to be an expert on other jurisdictions and hope I shall be forgiven for what will no doubt be errors or oversimplifications. Nevertheless comparative experience is, I hope, of interest in this field as in others. Those who seek more profound scholarship should consult the book edited by Professor Goldsworthy.

Unlike these other jurisdictions, it is trite that the United Kingdom does not have a written constitution, in the sense of a single document setting out the basic powers

---

[†] I am extremely grateful to Max du Plessis for his research assistance. All errors are mine.
[1] 'Conclusions' in *Interpreting Constitutions: A Comparative Study* (Oxford, Oxford University Press, 2006) 324.

and duties of the three branches of the state. However, the United Kingdom does have the Human Rights Act (HRA), a statute that gives effect in domestic law to most of the rights in the European Convention on Human Rights and which-by virtue of obliging judges to consider whether legislation, the common law, and the conduct of public authorities are compatible with the Convention rights-would seem to require judges in this country to engage in something very much like the enterprise of constitutional interpretation. It is well known that under the HRA, our courts do not have the power to strike down primary legislation but, save for that important limitation on the remedy which can be granted, as a matter of substantive law, the HRA does require courts to engage in a form of constitutional review quite unlike anything they have had to do before.[2] In a recent case, brought by the Countryside Alliance, Baroness Hale of Richmond summarised the position as follows:

> the purpose of such human rights instruments is to place some limits upon what a democratically elected Parliament may do: to protect the rights and freedoms of individuals and minorities against the will of those who are taken to represent the majority. Democracy is the will of the people, but the people may not will to invade those rights and freedoms which are fundamental to democracy itself.[3]

COMPARATIVE PERSPECTIVES

At the outset, it will be useful to distinguish between different approaches that can be taken to the interpretation of a Bill of rights. First, a distinction can be drawn between 'positivism' and 'normativism'.[4] Let me explain what I mean. The former conceives of a constitution as a set of discrete written provisions whose authority derives from having been formally enacted. Positivism can include literalism but also permits purposive approaches, provided that words are not overridden or supplemented.[5] Normativism, on the other hand, conceives of a constitution in holistic terms. On this view, a constitution consists of more than the sum of its written provisions. Instead, it has a normative structure rooted in principles of political morality – this is not the same as personal or subjective morality but is used rather in the sense of the values which are inherent in the structure of government which an organised community has created for itself. Ultimately, this is the source of its authority. Furthermore, in order for these principles to be realised, enacted words may be stretched, compressed, read in, or read down.[6]

---

[2] For example, *R (Countryside Alliance) v Attorney General* [2007] UKHL 52, para 113 (Baroness Hale of Richmond).

[3] ibid, para 114.

[4] Goldsworthy (n 1) 322.

[5] The claim that legal positivism entails a particular theory of interpretation is controversial. John Gardner, for instance, regards this as a 'myth'. See 'Legal Positivism: 5 ½ Myths' (2001) 46 *American Journal of Jurisprudence*, 199. However, this issue is too complex to explore here. A further difficulty is to arrive at a suitable alternative term. As discussed, literalism is inappropriate because 'positivism' can include a purposive approach. For these reasons, I have opted to retain the term 'positivism' to describe the interpretative approach under discussion.

[6] Goldsworthy (n 1) 322.

The experience of the Indian Supreme Court provides a striking example of the contrast between positivist and normative approaches to interpretation. In its early days, the pervasive influence of English law meant that the Indian Supreme Court adopted a positivist approach to constitutional interpretation. In *AK Gopalan v India*, a case dealing with provisions allowing for preventive detention without trial, Kania CJ held that '[t]he courts are not at liberty to declare an Act void because in their opinion it is opposed to a spirit supposed to pervade the Constitution but not expressed in words'.[7] In time, however, the Court adopted an increasingly normative approach to constitutional interpretation, culminating in the judgment of *Golaknath v Punjab*,[8] in which the Court held that the power to amend the Constitution does not extend to abrogation of any of the Fundamental Rights, notwithstanding the fact that the Indian Constitution mentions no such limitation. In effect, the Court found that the words 'the Constitution' refer not merely to a document but to a basic structure of checks and balances intended to sustain certain enduring values – a highly normative approach.[9]

Perhaps the most famous example of such an approach being taken in history is provided by the seminal American decision in *Marbury v Madison*,[10] in which the US Supreme Court asserted for itself the power to strike down legislation which is inconsistent with the Constitution even though there is no express provision conferring that power of what Americans call 'judicial review' in the text itself.

Even in the United Kingdom, it has been suggested at the highest judicial level that our constitution too rests on fundamental principles which may not be confined (as traditionally thought) to the doctrine of Parliamentary sovereignty. In *Jackson*,[11] the House of Lords held that the Parliament Act 1949 and, by consequence, the Hunting Act 2004 were valid Acts of Parliament. It rejected the submission that legislation made under the Parliament Act 1911 was subordinate, rather than primary legislation.

It had been submitted that the scope of section 2(1) of the 1911 Act was not unlimited and had to be read with qualifications which prevented it from having unreasonable consequences which Parliament had not intended. A narrow interpretation had to be employed so that the section did not read as modifying the identity of the sovereign Parliament. The House of Lords held that the use of the word 'any' in the 1911 Act should be taken to mean what it did in ordinary language, the result being that any Bill – apart from those falling under express exceptions – could be subject to the provisions of the Parliament Act. Historical record and the language of the section both showed that Parliament had not intended section 2(1) to be incapable of amendment using the procedure under the Parliament Act itself. The House of Lords also rejected the suggestion made by the Court of Appeal that the Parliament

---

[7] AIR 1950 SC 27, 42.

[8] AIR 1967 SC 1643.

[9] SP Sathe, 'India: From Positivism to Structuralism', in Goldsworthy (n 1) 226, 244. For an excellent example of a clash between positivist and normative approaches to constitutional interpretation in the South African context, see *S v Mhlungu* (1995) 3 SA 867 (CC).

[10] 1 Cranch 137 (1803).

[11] *R (Jackson) v Attorney General* [2006] 1 AC 262.

Act procedure could not be used to amend certain legislation of a constitutional or fundamental character: it was observed that the Parliament Act had been enacted with the very purpose of permitting the Irish Home Rule Bill to be passed in spite of decades of opposition from the upper House, that being a Bill which was clearly of a constitutional character.

However, what is likely to be of more enduring interest in the future are the dicta in some of the opinions in the House of Lords which suggest that the powers of Parliament to enact primary legislation are not unlimited. Lord Steyn said:

> We do not in the United Kingdom have an uncontrolled constitution as the Attorney General implausibly asserts. In the European context the second *Factortame* decision [1991] 2 AC 603 made that clear. The settlement contained in the Scotland Act 1998 also points to a divided sovereignty. Moreover, the European Convention on Human Rights as incorporated into our law by the Human Rights Act 1998 created a new legal order. ... The classic account given by Dicey of the supremacy of Parliament, pure and absolute as it was, can now be seen to be out of place in the modern United Kingdom. Nevertheless, the supremacy of Parliament is still the *general* principle of our constitution. It is a construct of the common law. The judges created this principle. If that is so, it is not unthinkable that circumstances could arise where the courts may have to qualify a principle established on a different hypothesis of constitutionalism.[12]

Lord Hope of Craighead said:

> Our constitution is dominated by the sovereignty of Parliament. But Parliamentary sovereignty is not, if it ever was, absolute. ... It is no longer right to say that its freedom to legislate admits of no qualification whatsoever. Step by step, gradually but surely, the English principle of the absolute legislative sovereignty of Parliament which Dicey derived from Coke and Blackstone is being qualified.[13]

After noting that the doctrine of the sovereignty of the Westminster Parliament has never been fully accepted in Scotland in view of the arguably fundamental character of the Act of Union of 1707, Lord Hope continued:

> Nor should we overlook the fact that one of the guiding principles that were identified by Dicey ... was the universal rule or supremacy throughout the constitution of ordinary law. Owen Dixon ... was making the same point when he said that it is of the essence of supremacy of the law that the courts shall disregard as unauthorised and void the acts of any organ of government, whether legislative or administrative, which exceed the limits of the power that organ derives from the law. In its modern form, now reinforced by the European Convention on Human Rights and the enactment by Parliament of the Human Rights Act 1998, this principle protects the individual from arbitrary government. The rule of law enforced by the courts is the ultimate controlling factor on which our constitution is based.[14]

At paragraph 159, Baroness Hale of Richmond said:

> The concept of Parliamentary sovereignty which has been fundamental to the constitution of England and Wales since the 17th century (I appreciate that Scotland may have

---

[12] Para 102 (emphasis in original).
[13] Para 104.
[14] Para 107.

taken a different view) means that Parliament can do anything. The courts will, of course, decline to hold that Parliament has interfered with fundamental rights unless it has made its intentions crystal clear. The courts will treat with particular suspicion (and might even reject) any attempt to subvert the rule of law by removing governmental action affecting the rights of the individual from all judicial scrutiny. Parliament has also, for the time being at least, limited its own powers by the European Communities Act 1972 and, in a different way, by the Human Rights Act 1998. It is possible that other qualifications may emerge in due course.[15]

I would also note that Parliament itself has recently recognised that the rule of law is an 'existing constitutional principle', in section 1(a) of the Constitutional Reform Act 2005.[16] It may be therefore that we are witnessing the beginning of a new era in constitutional thinking in this country, which views our system of government as resting not on the absolute and unfettered power of one branch of the state, but rather a new constitutionalism which requires each branch of the state carefully to respect the province of the other branches, and which recognises that Parliament's authority comes from the democratic will of the people but that it may not be open to Parliament to do whatever it may wish to do at a given moment in time, even at the expense of undermining the enduring values of this country, such as democracy and the rule of law themselves. If that turns out to be right, it may come to be thought that we have a balanced constitution, like that of other democracies governed by the rule of law, and not a lop-sided one.

For now, however, I will return to constitutional interpretation more generally. A further distinction can be drawn between 'originalism' and 'non-originalism'.[17] Originalism describes the view that the content of a constitution is determined by the intentions or purposes of its founders or at least the understandings of the founding generation. Non-originalism, on the other hand, treats these considerations as irrelevant or of little weight. Instead, judges should interpret the text according to the meanings, values or understandings of contemporary society.

With this background in mind, how should Bills of rights be interpreted? Obviously, much depends upon factors specific to particular jurisdictions. In Germany, for example, the *Grundgesetz* (or Basic Law) can be amended with relative ease. This results in a judicial reluctance to bring about substantial changes through interpretation. From a German perspective, it has been said by one commentator that: 'any judicially imposed remodelling of the Basic Law ... would diminish the clarity, precision, and predictability of the constitutional *Rechtsstaat* [state governed by law]'.[18] In the United States, by way of contrast, the Constitution is very difficult to amend and the political culture is averse to formal amendments. In Mark Tushnet's view, the Supreme Court has therefore felt compelled to make adaptations through creative

---

[15] Para 109.
[16] For further discussion of *Jackson* and analysis of potential future developments, see J Jowell, 'Parliamentary Sovereignty under the New Constitutional Hypothesis' [2006] *Public Law* 562. On the principle of the rule of law, see Lord Bingham of Cornhill's lecture 'The Rule of Law' [2007] *Cambridge Law Journal* 67.
[17] Goldsworthy (n 1) 322.
[18] D Kommers, 'Germany: Balancing Rights and Duties', in Goldsworthy (n 1) 171.

interpretation and the American public appears to have accepted this as the appropriate method of updating the Constitution.[19] Very few of the amendments to the Constitution have been passed to reverse a decision of the US Supreme Court. The first Ten Amendments of course constitute the original Bill of Rights and additional rights have been added from time to time, in particular the important amendments passed after the Civil War in 1865, to abolish slavery and to guarantee the right to vote and the equal protection of the laws.

Still, I would suggest that certain general observations can be made. An initial question is why the interpretation of constitutions, and human rights instruments in particular, is thought to require special attention. Put differently, why should this issue not be subsumed into a general discussion of statutory interpretation?

On this point, there is a great deal of authority, from numerous jurisdictions, emphasising that constitutions and Bills of rights stand apart from (or above) ordinary statutes. In the US Supreme Court, for example, Marshall CJ famously declared in *McCulloch v Maryland* that 'we must never forget, that *it is a constitution we are expounding*'.[20] In *Fisher*, Lord Wilberforce in the Privy Council held that a constitutional instrument, giving effect to fundamental rights, is 'sui generis, calling for principles of interpretation of its own, suitable to its character ... without necessary acceptance of all the presumptions that are relevant to legislation or private law'.[21] The Supreme Court of Canada has likewise emphasised that the 'task of expounding a constitution is crucially different from that of construing a statute'.[22]

However, in what respects do constitutions and Bills of rights differ from statutes and what are the consequences of this for their interpretation? In the view of Marshall CJ, constitutions cannot deal in detail with everything the governments they created would do: 'A Constitution, to contain an accurate detail of all the subdivisions of which its great powers will admit, and of all the means by which they may be carried into execution, would partake of the prolixity of a legal code, and could scarcely be embraced by the human mind. It would probably never be understood by the public'.[23] Therefore, 'only its great outlines should be marked, its important objects designated, and the minor ingredients that compose those objects be deduced from the nature of the objects themselves'.[24] Marshall CJ observed further that a constitution is 'intended to endure for ages to come, and, consequently, to be adapted to the various crises of human affairs'.[25]

There are a number of points being made here. The *first* is that constitutions are invariably cast in broad, vague and open-textured terms. This means that a purely literal approach to interpretation is difficult to sustain. The text simply provides insufficient guidance. For this reason, even those of positivist inclination concede that a generous or purposive approach to constitutional interpretation is necessary but stress that it should not override the enacted words. Thus Sir Sydney Kentridge,

---

[19] 'The United States: Eclecticism in Service of Pragmatism' in Goldsworthy (n 1) 7, 15–17.
[20] *McCulloch v Maryland* (1819) 17 US 316, 414.
[21] *Minister of Home Affairs (Bermuda) v Fisher* [1980] AC 319, 328–29.
[22] *Hunter v Southam* [1984] 2 SCR 145, 155.
[23] *McCulloch v Maryland* (n 20) 407.
[24] ibid.
[25] ibid.

sitting as an Acting Judge of the South African Constitutional Court in its early days, held that:

> While we must always be conscious of the values underlying the Constitution, it is nonetheless our task to interpret a written instrument ... I would say that a constitution embodying fundamental principles should *as far as its language permits* be given a broad construction.[26]

In the same case he said: 'If the language used by the lawgiver is ignored in favour of a general resort to "values" the result is not interpretation but divination'. This was quoted by Lord Hoffmann in a Privy Council case called *Matadeen v Pointu*.[27] Lord Hoffmann then continued in his own words:

> The background of a constitution is an attempt, at a particular moment in history, to lay down an enduring scheme of government in accordance with certain moral and political values. ... It is however a mistake to suppose that these considerations release judges from the task of interpreting the statutory language and enable them to give free rein to whatever they consider should have been the moral and political views of the framers of the constitution.

To return to my quotation from Marshall CJ, the *second* point made by him was that constitutions differ from statutes because they are 'intended to endure for ages to come, and, consequently, to be adapted to the various crises of human affairs'.[28] In his discussion of constitutional interpretation, the American judge Benjamin Cardozo elaborated this point as follows:

> Statutes are designed to meet the fugitive exigencies of the hour. Amendment is easy as the exigencies change. In such cases, the meaning, once constructed, tends legitimately to stereotype itself in the form first cast. A constitution states or ought to state not rules for the passing hour, but principles for an expanding future.[29]

This observation has a number of consequences. One is that the abstract and open-textured nature of constitutions is unavoidable. Cardozo explains further that, as a constitution 'descends into details and particulars, it loses its flexibility, the scope of interpretation contracts, the meaning hardens. While it is true to its function, it maintains its power of adaptation, its suppleness, its play'.[30] Another consequence is that originalist approaches to constitutional interpretation are, like literal approaches to constitutional construction, difficult to sustain. The fact that constitutions are enacted in broad terms, meant to be applied to unforeseen scenarios in a distant future, means that judicial adaptation is unavoidable. As Tushnet notes, somehow the founders of the American Constitution were able to see in its words a charter for liberty from the British and yet were unable to see in those same words a condemnation of slavery – a position that is not only implausible today but would be regarded as grotesque.[31]

---

[26] *S v Zuma* 1995 (2) SA 642 (CC) para 17.
[27] [1999] 1 AC 98, 108.
[28] *McCulloch v Maryland* (n 20).
[29] 'The Nature of the Judicial Process' (New Haven and London, Yale University Press, 1921) 83–84.
[30] ibid, 84.
[31] Tushnet (n 19) 36.

The European Court of Human Rights has long taken this dynamic approach to interpretation, holding that the European Convention on Human Rights is a living instrument that 'must be interpreted in light of present-day conditions'.[32] The Court must therefore have regard to the 'changing conditions in contracting states'.[33]

However, does this mean that evidence of original intent should never be taken into account? This question was considered by the South African Constitutional Court in *State v Makwanyane*,[34] where the Court sought to determine why the Interim Constitution had not dealt specifically with the issue of the death penalty. The Court noted that, while legislative history is generally excluded, in 'countries in which the Constitution is similarly the supreme law, it is not unusual for the courts to have regard to the circumstances existing at the time the constitution was adopted, including the debates and writings which formed part of the process'.[35] The Court cautioned against placing undue reliance on the comments of individual participants given that the Constitution is the product of a multiplicity of persons. The Court nonetheless held that legislative history may provide a useful context within which to understand the relevant human rights guarantee. In the context of the European Convention on Human Rights, since it is a treaty, it is well-established that the *travaux* (or drafting history) may be used as a supplementary aid to its interpretation, as Article 32 of the Vienna Convention on the Law of Treaties expressly provides. This does not mean, as we have seen, that the European Convention is to be regarded as having been fossilised in 1950: far from it.

A sterile, backward-looking approach to constitutional interpretation would put the entire constitutional project at risk. Justice Kirby of the High Court of Australia reminds us: 'As one anonymous sage once put it: if you construe a constitution like a last will and testament, that is what it will become'.[36]

A *third* point flowing from Marshall CJ's exposition of constitutional interpretation is that a constitution is said to differ from ordinary statutes simply by virtue of its subject matter. In the famous words of Lord Wilberforce in *Fisher*, the fact that constitutions deal with basic rights means that they should be given 'a generous interpretation ... suitable to give to individuals the full measure of the fundamental rights and freedoms referred to' and avoiding what Professor de Smith called 'the austerity of tabulated legalism'[37] – a view that has been endorsed by the Supreme Court of Canada[38] and the South African Constitutional Court.[39]

It is often assumed that generous and purposive interpretations are synonymous. The Supreme Court of Canada, for example, asserts that the interpretation of rights should be a 'generous rather than a legalistic one, aimed at fulfilling the purpose of

---

[32] *Tyrer v United Kingdom* (1979–80) 2 EHRR 1, para 31.
[33] *Stafford v United Kingdom* (2002) 35 EHRR 32, para 68.
[34] 1995 (3) SA 391.
[35] ibid, para 16.
[36] The Hamlyn Lectures, *Judicial Activism, By The Hon. Justice Michael Kirby AC CMG, Justice of the High Court of Australia*, (2004), 40.
[37] *Fisher* (n 21). The quotation is from SA de Smith, *Laws of the Commonwealth* (London, Stevens & Sons, 1964).
[38] *Big M Drug Mart Ltd* (n 21).
[39] *Makwanyane* (n 34) para 9.

the guarantee'.[40] However, the leading scholar of the Canadian constitution, Peter Hogg, warns that this is not necessarily the case. He argues that the widest possible interpretation of the language may 'overshoot' the purpose of the right by including behaviour that is outside the purpose and unworthy of constitutional protection.[41] This can be illustrated by the Canadian case of *B (R) v Children's Aid Society of Metropolitan Toronto*,[42] in which B, a child of Jehovah's Witnesses in urgent need of a blood transfusion, had been made a ward of the Children's Society. In the Supreme Court, the parents argued that the wardship provisions were contrary to section 7 of the Charter, the right to life, liberty, and security of the person. La Forest J gave section 7 a generous interpretation, concluding that the scope of the liberty interests it protected included a large degree of personal autonomy, which extended to decisions about how to raise children. Lamer CJC, in contrast, adopted a purposive approach. After contextual analysis of section 7, its structure, its relationship to other provisions of the Charter and its history, he concluded that the purpose of section 7 was limited to the protection of physical liberty. The interpretation favoured by La Forest J was therefore overbroad.

Finally, although not a necessary component of constitutional interpretation, it is noteworthy that courts are increasingly turning to comparative jurisprudence to better understand the content of human rights provisions, leading some commentators to speculate about the emergence of a transnational 'common law' of human rights.[43] Human rights lend themselves to this approach, given that they are frequently cast in universalist terms, and very often in a form similar to corresponding provisions in other jurisdictions. The South African Constitutional Court is a leading exponent of the use of foreign authority, in part because section 39(1)(c) of the Constitution expressly declares that '[w]hen interpreting the Bill of Rights, a court, tribunal or forum may consider foreign law', and section 39(1)(b) provides that the Court 'must' consider international law. Commenting on its use of comparative material, the Court has stated that:

> Comparative research is generally valuable, and is all the more so when dealing with problems new to our jurisprudence but well developed in mature constitutional democracies ... Nevertheless the use of foreign precedent requires circumspection and acknowledgment that transplants require careful management.[44]

In a recent case in this country called *Gillan* Lord Bingham warned that it was 'perilous ... to seek to transpose the outcome of Canadian cases decided under a significantly different legislative regime'.[45] I will return to this later but it leads into the second part of my talk, which is about the HRA itself.

---

[40] *Big M Drug Mart Ltd* (n 38).

[41] 'Canada: From Privy Council to Supreme Court' in Goldsworthy (n 1) 55, 89.

[42] [1995] 1 SCR 315. See the discussion in RA Edwards 'Generosity and the Human Rights Act: The Right Interpretation?' [1999] *Public Law* 400.

[43] C McCrudden, 'Common Law of Human Rights? Transnational Judicial Conversations on Human Rights' (2000) 20 *Oxford Journal of Legal Studies* 499. See also C Booth QC and M du Plessis 'Home Alone? The US Supreme Court and International and Transnational Judicial Learning' [2005] *European Human Rights Law Review* 127.

[44] *Sanderson v Attorney-General, Eastern Cape* 1998 (2) SA 38 (CC).

[45] *R (Gillan) v Commissioner of Police for the Metropolis* [2006] 2 AC 307, para 23.

THE HRA 1998

Unlike the other jurisdictions to which I have referred, the United Kingdom does not have a Bill of Rights in the classic mode. Instead, it has the HRA, a statute that (in a loose but not entirely accurate sense) incorporates the European Convention on Human Rights into domestic law.

In theory, the HRA can be amended or repealed through an ordinary act of Parliament. However, it would be a mistake to assume that the Act is therefore an ordinary statute. As Laws LJ has emphasised, it is, in fact, a 'constitutional statute'. It enjoys an elevated status because, first, it governs the legal relationship between the individual and the state and does so in a general overarching manner; and, secondly, it enlarges the scope of what are now regarded as fundamental constitutional rights.[46] An indication of the status enjoyed by the HRA is that, unlike ordinary statutes, it is, according to Laws LJ, not subject to the doctrine of implied repeal. Instead, it can only be repealed through express words in a later statute. In part, this is the consequence of section 3 of the HRA itself, which requires even a later statute to be read, so far as possible, to be compatible with the HRA. Where that is impossible, even a later statute can be the subject of a declaration of incompatibility; whereas received constitutional theory before the HRA would have suggested that a later statute which is inconsistent with the HRA by implication repeals it to the extent of that inconsistency.

The 'constitutional' nature of the HRA has led some commentators to assert that it should not be subject to ordinary norms of statutory interpretation. Instead, it should be approached in the same manner as a Bill of rights, in accordance with the principles of interpretation I have outlined earlier. Thus David Pannick has quoted Lord Wilberforce in *Fisher* in suggesting that the HRA should be interpreted in a manner that avoids 'the austerity of tabulated legalism' and ensures that individuals are afforded the full measure of the fundamental rights and freedoms referred to.[47] The courts initially at least appeared to accept the correctness of this proposition and in cases such as *Kebilene*[48] and *Brown v Stott*[49] echoed the language of the Canadian and South African courts by endorsing a 'generous and purposive' approach to the interpretation of Convention rights. In *Kebilene*, Lord Hope of Craighead cited Privy Council cases such as *Fisher* and said:

> The same approach will now have to be applied in this country when issues are raised under the Act of 1998 about the compatibility of domestic legislation and of acts of public authorities with the fundamental rights and freedoms which are enshrined in the Convention.

---

[46] *Thoburn v Sunderland City Council* [2002] 1 CMLR 50.

[47] D Pannick QC, 'Principles of Interpretation of Convention Rights under the Human Rights Act and the Discretionary Area of Judgment' [1998] *Public Law* 545.

[48] *R v DPP, ex parte Kebilene* [2000] 2 AC 326, 375.

[49] *Brown v Stott* [2003] 1 AC 681, 703.

In *Brown* Lord Bingham of Cornhill appeared to equate the HRA to a constitutional Bill of rights when he said:

> In interpreting the Convention, as any other treaty, it is generally to be assumed that the parties have included the terms which they wished to include and on which they were able to agree, omitting other terms which they did not wish to include or on which they were not able to agree. ... This does not mean that nothing can be implied into the Convention. The language of the Convention is for the most part so general that some implication of terms is necessary ... But the process of implication is one to be carried out with caution, if the risk is to be averted that the contracting parties may, by judicial interpretation, become bound by obligations which they did not expressly accept and might not have been willing to accept. As an important constitutional instrument the Convention is to be seen as a 'living tree capable of growth and expansion within its natural limits' (*Edwards v Attorney General for Canada* [1930] AC 124, 136 per Lord Sankey LC), but those limits will often call for very careful consideration.

> In interpreting the rights set out in the HRA, a key question for English courts is the weight that should be accorded to Strasbourg jurisprudence. Should domestic courts treat this authority as binding or merely persuasive? This issue is important because the European Court of Human Rights recognizes a 'margin of appreciation'. This is a doctrine of international law, not domestic law.[50] This doctrine concerns the European Court's reluctance to substitute its judgment for that of the national authorities, including domestic courts. The justification for this approach is that '[b]y reason of their direct and continuous contact with the vital forces of their countries, the national authorities are in principle better placed than an international court to evaluate local needs and conditions'.[51]

Clearly, the margin of appreciation does not apply when a national court is considering the application of the Convention rights within domestic law.[52] Under the HRA, this issue is dealt with under section 2(1) which provides that a court or tribunal determining a question which has arisen in connection with a Convention right must 'take into account' any relevant judgment, decision, declaration, or opinion emanating from the European Court of Human Rights or the former Commission. At face value, the HRA would therefore seem to be alive to the danger outlined earlier. It would appear that Strasbourg jurisprudence is not binding but merely persuasive. In practice, it is difficult to envisage how domestic courts could provide a level of protection below the minimum standard stipulated by the Strasbourg institutions. That would simply necessitate an application to Strasbourg, where it would be highly likely to succeed. However, as Grosz, Beatson and Duffy wrote in 2000, it would seem to 'be open to national courts to develop a domestic jurisprudence under the Convention which may be more generous to applicants than that dispensed at Strasbourg, while remaining broadly consistent with it'.[53] In other words, before the Act came into force, it was widely thought that

[50] *R v DPP, ex p Kebilene*, above n 48, 326, 380 (Lord Hope of Craighead).

[51] *Buckley v United Kingdom* (1996) 23 EHRR 101, 129.

[52] Pannick (n 47) 548; also R Singh, M Hunt, and M Demetriou, 'Is There a Role for the "Margin of Appreciation" in National Law After the Human Rights Act?' [1999] *European Human Rights Law Review* 15. But now cf. *R (Countryside Alliance) v Attorney General* (n 2) para 126.

[53] *Human Rights: The 1998 Act and the European Convention* (London, Sweet & Maxwell, 2000) 20.

national courts would be authorised to develop a distinctively British human rights law. In this sense, it was commonly predicted that the HRA would provide a 'floor' rather than a 'ceiling'.

How then has section 2(1) been interpreted? Domestic courts have increasingly adopted what Lady Justice Arden recently described as a 'self-denying ordinance':[54] subject to certain narrow exceptions, our courts appear to regard themselves as tethered to and constrained by Strasbourg jurisprudence so that the scope and content attributed by domestic courts to municipal rights under the HRA correspond to that attributed to Convention rights by the European Court of Human Rights-no less but no more.[55]

The first explicit statement of this approach was found in the opinion of Lord Slynn of Hadley in *Alconbury*.[56] This approach was subsequently endorsed by Lord Bingham of Cornhill in the *Anderson* case, where he stated that 'the House will not without good reason depart from the principles laid down in a carefully considered judgment of the Court sitting as a Grand Chamber';[57] and in *Ullah* where he held that the 'duty of national courts is to keep pace with the Strasbourg jurisprudence as it evolves over time: no more but certainly no less'.[58]

The principle has now been applied by the House of Lords in many other cases. In *Clift*, Lord Hope of Craighead cautioned that '[a] measure of self-restraint is needed, lest we stretch our jurisprudence beyond that which is shared by all the States parties to the Convention'.[59] In *Quark Fishing*, Lord Bingham held that a party unable to mount a successful claim in Strasbourg can never mount a successful claim under the HRA,[60] while in *Al-Skeini*, Lord Brown went so far as to suggest that Lord Bingham's phrase 'no more, but certainly no less' in *Ullah* should be rewritten to read 'no less, but certainly no more'.[61] The Court of Appeal has, of course, found itself bound by this approach.[62]

In practice, it would seem that English courts, for all intents and purposes, regard themselves as bound by Strasbourg case law.[63] And, where Strasbourg has not yet spoken with a direct answer, our courts appear unwilling to step into the vacuum and will await an answer from Strasbourg.[64]

---

[54] Dame Mary Arden, 'The Changing Role of the Judiciary: Human Rights, Community Law and the Intention of Parliament', ALBA Annual Lecture, 26 November 2007: www.adminlaw.org.uk/library/publi-cations.php.

[55] See J Lewis, 'The European Ceiling on Human Rights' [2007] *Public Law* 720 for a thorough analysis of the development of the case law.

[56] *R (Alconbury Developments Ltd) v Secretary of State for the Environment, Transport and the Regions,* [2002] 2 AC 295, para 26.

[57] *R (on the application of Anderson) v Secretary of State for the Home Department,* [2003] 1 AC 837, para 18.

[58] *R (on the application of Ullah) v Special Adjudicator,* [2004] 2 AC 323 at para 20.

[59] *R (on the application of Clift) v Secretary of State for the Home Department,* [2007] 1 C 484.

[60] *R (on the application of Quark Fishing Ltd) v Secretary of State for Foreign and Commonwealth Affairs,* [2006] 1 AC 529 at para 25.

[61] *R (Al-Skeini) v Secretary of State for Defence,* [2007] 3 WLR 33 at para 106.

[62] For example, *Secretary of State for the Home Department v JJ,* [2007] QB 446 at para 20 and *R (on the application of Countryside Alliance) v Attorney-General,* [2007] QB 305 at para 80.

[63] Lewis (n 55) 731.

[64] See above n 2, para 126. This appears to have been the view of the House of Lords in *R (Al-Skeini) v Secretary of State for Defence* [2007] 3 WLR 33 in relation to the meaning and scope of the concept of

A further issue raised by section 2(1) is the use of foreign case law, an issue I touched on in the first part of this presentation. As it stands, section 2(1) clearly does not preclude the use of foreign authority. Recognising this, in early cases the domestic courts showed themselves willing to make use of Commonwealth jurisprudence. For instance, in *Brown v Stott* Lord Bingham and Lord Hope of Craighead made reference to Canadian jurisprudence on the right against self-incrimination. Similarly, in *R v A (No 2)*[65] Lord Hope analysed rape shield provisions in the United States, Australia, Canada and Scotland. However, it seems that recently there has been a narrowing of this approach.[66] In *Sheldrake v DPP*, Lord Bingham noted that even though the House of Lords has on a number of occasions 'gained valuable insights from the reasoning of Commonwealth judges deciding issues under different human rights instruments ... the United Kingdom courts must take their lead from Strasbourg'.[67]

It is worth examining the justifications that national courts have advanced for the 'self-denying' approach that they have adopted.

First, the English courts have stressed that the Convention must be uniformly understood by all contracting states.[68] Lord Hoffmann has stated that there should be no divergence between domestic and Strasbourg jurisprudence,[69] while Lord Nicholls of Birkenhead has said that: '[i]t goes without saying that that it would be highly undesirable for the courts of this country, when giving effect to Convention rights, to be out of step with the Strasbourg interpretation of the relevant Convention article'.[70]

However, the Convention system is intended to ensure a minimum, rather than a uniform, standard of compliance with human rights. As Judge Martens, formerly of the European Court of Human Rights, states, the role of the domestic judiciary under the Convention system 'goes further than seeing to it that the minimum standards in the ECHR are maintained. That is because the ECHR's injunction to further realise human rights and fundamental freedoms contained in the preamble is also addressed to domestic courts'.[71] There is therefore no bar to individual states adopting more generous interpretations of Convention rights. Indeed, this is implicit in the very notion of the margin of appreciation.

Furthermore, as discussed in the first part of my talk, the European Court of Human Rights has held on numerous occasions that the Convention is a living instrument which 'must be interpreted in light of present-day conditions'.[72] For the European Court, an important source of information in this regard are the decisions of domestic courts. This is likewise implicit in the Court's statement in *Handyside*

'jurisdiction' in Art 1 of the European Convention on Human Rights in the light of the Grand Chamber decision in *Bankovic v Belgium* (2001) 11 BHRC 435.

[65] [2002] 1 AC 45.

[66] 'Section 2(1) of the Human Rights Act 1998: Binding Domestic Courts to Strasbourg' [2004] *Public Law* 725, 726.

[67] [2005] 1 AC 264 at para 33.

[68] *Kay v Lambeth LBC* [2006] UKHL 10, [2006] 2 AC 465 at para 44.

[69] *R v Lyons*, [2003] 1 AC 976 at para 46.

[70] *M v Secretary of State for Work and Pensions*, [2006] 2 AC 91 at para 29.

[71] 'Incorporating the European Convention: The Role of the Judiciary' (1998) *European Human Rights Law Review* 5, 14.

[72] *Tyrer* (n 32).

that domestic authorities are in 'direct and continuous contact with the vital forces of their countries'.[73] This observation sits uneasily with the view of the Court of Appeal in *Anderson* that it is the European Court, a supra-national institution, that better understands the 'ambit and reach'[74] of Convention rights and which brings to its task 'a range of knowledge and principle that a national court cannot aspire to'.[75]

Secondly, it has been argued that departing from Strasbourg jurisprudence raises the spectre of 'appeal' by dissatisfied litigants to the European Court of Human Rights, where the decision of the national court would surely be reversed. In *Alconbury*, Lord Slynn indicated that if domestic courts do not follow Strasbourg jurisprudence, 'there is at least a possibility that the case will go to that court, which is likely in the ordinary case to follow its own constant jurisprudence'.[76] Similarly, in *Amin* Lord Bingham warned that if Strasbourg jurisprudence was not followed, the dissatisfied litigant would have a right to go to Strasbourg where existing jurisprudence is likely to be followed.[77] Again, with respect, this point (although undoubtedly correct) does not lead to the conclusion that the Strasbourg case law should be regarded as imposing a ceiling and not simply laying down a floor. A litigant would only be likely to take a case to Strasbourg where domestic law affords *less* generous protection.[78] The European Court of Human Rights is unlikely to reprimand states for generous rights protection. Instead, it would simply employ the 'margin of appreciation' doctrine, appreciating, in the positive sense of that word, the state's concern to accord generous human rights protections to those within its jurisdiction.

Thirdly, more persuasively in my view, it has been observed that, if the domestic courts go too far and give too generous an interpretation to the Convention rights, there is no opportunity for the Government to 'appeal' to Strasbourg.[79] Nor is there any mechanism similar to the procedure for a reference to the European Court of Justice in Luxembourg. This might not matter if the HRA is viewed as a purely domestic Bill of rights. After all, many European states have both incorporated the ECHR and have their own domestic Bill of rights: in interpreting the latter, their courts would not be bound to treat the case law of the Strasbourg Court as being decisive, while they would have to ensure that the bare minimum required by the former was complied with. But whether the HRA is to be regarded in that way leads me to the fourth point.

Fourthly and most fundamentally, the English courts' reluctance to accord a broad interpretation to section 2(1) appears to be rooted in a perception about the nature of the HRA itself. There has always been a certain ambiguity in the character of the HRA. Is it a domestic Bill of rights at all or is it merely machinery

---

[73] *Handyside v. United Kingdom* 1 EHRR 737, at para 48.

[74] *Anderson* (n 57) at para 65.

[75] ibid, para 91.

[76] *Alconbury* (n 56) at para 26.

[77] *R (on the application of Amin) v Secretary of State for the Home Department*, [2004] 1 AC 653 at para 44.

[78] Lewis (n 55) 737.

[79] *R (Al-Skeini) v Secretary of State for Defence* [2007] 3 WLR 33, para 106 (Lord Brown of Eaton-under-Heywood). See also *Secretary of State for the Home Department v JJ* [2007] 3 WLR 642, para 106 (Lord Brown of Eaton-under-Heywood).

for the incorporation of an international treaty, which enables a person to enforce Convention rights in domestic law? I myself agree with Francesca Klug both that the HRA is a Bill of rights and not merely an incorporating measure but that it has not been accepted as such by the British public. As she puts it in a recent article in *Public Law*: 'The reality is that the Act has never been sufficiently "owned" by British people as "*their* bill of rights"'.[80]

The idea has gained currency that the purpose of the HRA was essentially practical: a response to the reality that the process whereby British litigants were previously expected to enforce their rights claims in Strasbourg took too long and was too expensive. In this sense, the HRA might be understood as simply making it easier for people to access rights that they *already* had but not as creating new rights in domestic law.

This is a potentially cogent argument because it throws into question whether the HRA should be approached in a manner akin to a Bill of rights, as my talk has so far suggested. If the purpose of the HRA is simply to facilitate access to rights that existed anyway, it might be that the principles of interpretation outlined in the first part of this presentation should not apply – or should be applied only selectively. But this approach does not sit altogether comfortably with the reasoning of the House of Lords in cases such as *R v Lyons* and *McKerr*,[81] to the effect that the HRA creates new rights in municipal law and does not merely provide a mechanism for enforcement of the Convention rights, which continue to exist on the plane of international law, thus maintaining the traditional dualist approach which English law takes to treaties.

Lord Bingham has said that the purpose of the HRA 'was not to enlarge the rights or remedies of those in the United Kingdom whose Convention rights have been violated but to enable those rights and remedies to be asserted and enforced by the domestic courts of this country and not only by recourse to Strasbourg'.[82] He has also held that 'the purpose of incorporating the Convention in domestic law through the 1998 Act was not to give victims better remedies at home than they could recover in Strasbourg but to give them the same remedies without the delay and expense of resort to Strasbourg'.[83] Lord Nicholls too has stated that the purpose of the HRA is to 'provide a means whereby persons whose rights under the Convention were infringed by the United Kingdom could, in future, have an appropriate remedy available to them in the courts of this country'.[84]

It is important not to lose sight of the fact that this attitude, which has been called the 'mirror principle',[85] is not inherently a conservative one and has in fact led to decisions of the courts of which progressives would approve. It is to their credit that the

---

[80] F Klug, 'A Bill of Rights: Do We Need One or Do We Already Have One?' [2007] *Public Law* 701, 713.

[81] *R v Lyons* (n 69), para 27 (Lord Hoffmann); *In re McKerr* [2004] 1 WLR 807, para 25 (Lord Nicholls of Birkenhead); cf. *R (S & Marper) v Chief Constable* [2004] 1 WLR 2196, para 66 (Lord Rodger of Earlsferry).

[82] *R (on the application of SB) v Denbigh High School*, [2007] 1 AC 100 at para 29.

[83] *R (on the application of Greenfield) v Secretary of State for the Home Department*, [2005] 1 WLR 673 at para 19.

[84] *Quark Fishing* (n 60) at para 33.

[85] Lewis (n 55).

judiciary of this country, whom many used to criticise as being inherently unsuited to the task of enforcing human rights because of their innate conservatism, have risen to the task given them by Parliament – indeed, in the view of some have been altogether too successful in the enterprise. They have also loyally sought to follow the lead taken by the Strasbourg Court even in cases that have not made their decisions popular, for example, in the *Belmarsh* case,[86] and in cases about whether people who are a threat to the national security of this country may be deported to countries where they face a real risk of torture. Furthermore, it was in effect the 'mirror principle' which led the majority of the House of Lords in *Al-Skeini* to conclude that the HRA does in principle apply to British forces outside the territory of the United Kingdom, for example in Iraq, when they exercise 'jurisdiction' over individuals within the meaning of Article 1 of the ECHR, an article which is not itself set out in the HRA at all. The submission for the Secretary of State was that some individuals such as the father of Baha Mousa, who was brutally ill-treated and died in British custody near Basra, could complain of breach of the ECHR in Strasbourg but not in the courts of this country. In rejecting that submission, Lord Rodger of Earlsferry said:

> It involves reading into sections 6 and 7 a qualification which the words do not contain and which runs counter to the central purpose of the Act. That would be to offend against the most elementary canons of construction which indicate that, in case of doubt, the Act should be read so as to promote, not so as to defeat or impair, its central purpose. If anything, this approach is even more desirable in interpreting human rights legislation. As Lord Brown of Eaton-under-Heywood points out, this interpretation also ensures that, in these exceptional cases, the United Kingdom is not in breach of its Article 13 obligation to afford an effective remedy before its courts to anyone whose human rights have been violated within its jurisdiction.[87]

There is no doubt that the primary purpose of the HRA was to 'bring rights home', as the title of the government's White Paper suggested.[88] However, to characterise this as the *sole* purpose of the HRA, in my view, is inaccurate. In order to understand why, we need to make reference to the HRA's legislative history. I do so for reasons of exposition, not necessarily because this would be admissible under the rule in *Pepper v Hart*.[89]

An examination of Hansard reveals that the purpose of the HRA was not solely to facilitate access to rights that would have existed at a supra-national level in any event. As Francesca Klug, who was in many ways the inspiration behind the HRA, notes the Act was also designed to modernise and democratise the political system.[90] Jack Straw, introducing the Bill in the House of Commons as Home Secretary, said it was intended to bring about 'a better balance between rights and responsibilities,

---

[86] *A v Secretary of State for the Home Department* [2005] 1 AC 68.

[87] *R (Al-Skeini) v Secretary of State for Defence* [2007] 3 WLR 33, para 57.

[88] *Rights Brought Home: The Human Rights Bill* (1997). See also the Labour party's consultation paper *Bringing Rights Home* (1996), issued a few months before the party won the general election of May 1997.

[89] [1993] AC 593.

[90] 'The Human Rights Act 1998, *Pepper v Hart* and All That' [1999] *Public Law* 246. See too by the same author: above n 80, 701.

between the powers of the state and the freedom of the individual'.[91] According to Francesca Klug, the Act was also intended to give rise to a culture of human rights awareness.[92] The Home Office Minister, the late Lord Williams, said that the Act was much more than a practical measure: 'Every public authority will know that its behaviour, its structure, its conclusions and its executive actions will be subject to this culture'.[93]

More importantly, there is ample evidence that the wording of section 2(1) was chosen deliberately to ensure that Strasbourg jurisprudence would not restrict the development of domestic human rights law. The White Paper is, for instance, quite clear that 'our courts will only be required to take account of relevant decisions of the European Commission and Court of Rights (although these will not be binding)'.[94] Furthermore, objections to section 2(1) were raised on at least two occasions. In the House of Lords at Committee Stage, Lord Kingsland (the Shadow Lord Chancellor) voiced his concern that: 'if our judges only take account of the jurisprudence of the European Court of Human Rights, we cast them adrift from their international moorings'.[95] An Opposition amendment to replace the words 'must take into account' with the words 'shall be bound by' was also rejected. The Lord Chancellor, Lord Irvine of Lairg, stated that 'the word "binding" is the language of precedent but the Convention is the ultimate source of law … I think that "binding" certainly goes further … than the Convention itself requires'.[96]

Furthermore, Lord Irvine insisted that 'our courts should be free to try to give a lead to Europe as well as to be led'[97] – a very clear statement that, in developing the meaning of the Convention rights, domestic courts should not take their cue solely from Strasbourg.

In the *Countryside Alliance* case, the House of Lords upheld the compatibility of the Hunting Act with the Convention. However, in a minority opinion Lord Brown of Eaton-under-Heywood made no secret of the fact that he would have preferred to be able to go further than Strasbourg case law currently permits had he been free to do so. If he had been free to do so, he would have held that the Hunting Act did interfere with the right to respect for private life in Article 8 of the Convention. As the law currently stands, that course was not open.

Not all judges in this country have subscribed to the current position of the House of Lords about the way in which section 2 of the HRA should be interpreted. There have been other views along the way. In *ProLife Alliance*, for example, Laws LJ commented that:

'The English court is not a Strasbourg surrogate … our duty is to develop by the common law's incremental method, a coherent and principled domestic law of human rights …

---

[91] *Hansard*, HL vol 306, col 781 (16 February 1998).
[92] Klug (n 80) 247.
[93] *Hansard*, HL vol 582, col 1308 (3 November 1997).
[94] *Rights Brought Home* (n 88), para 2.4.
[95] *Hansard*, HL vol 583, col 514 (18 November 1997).
[96] *Hansard*, HL, col 514 (18 November 1997).
[97] *Hansard*, HL vol 583, col 514 (18 November 1997).

[T]reating the ECHR text as a template for our own law runs the risk of an over-rigid approach'.[98]

But, for now, it is clear that the HRA is a hybrid. It is the nearest thing to a Bill of rights that we have in this country and has served us well, as a recent report by Justice notes,[99] but the interpretation of the substantive rights set out in it is now firmly anchored to what Lord Kingsland called the 'international moorings'[100] of the jurisprudence of the European Court of Human Rights. Some have concluded from this development that this should lead this country now to proceed to enact its own British Bill of rights. But, tempting though it would be to embark on that debate now, that is a matter for another day.

---

[98] *R (on the Application of ProLife Alliance) v British Broadcasting Association*, [2004] AC 185, at para 33 of the Court of Appeal judgment.
[99] Report of the Justice constitution committee, 'A British Bill of Rights: Informing the Debate' (2007) 15.
[100] n 97.

Tribute for Lord Steyn

Lord Steyn (1932–2017) was not only a great judge but a kind and humane person, as I tried to show in this tribute given at his memorial service in 2017 at Lincoln's Inn. In this tribute, which was first published in [2018] JR 102, I also summarised some of his immense contribution to public law in this country.

WHEN I FIRST met Lord Steyn in the mid-1990s he was already a Law Lord and I was a relatively junior member of the Bar. He told me that he would refuse to speak to me unless I called him by his first name 'Johan'. It is often said that the test of a person's character is how they treat someone who is not important. Anyone can be nice to someone they think is important. Johan Steyn treated everyone around him with humanity and respect.

Many of you will know Johan Steyn from his excellent commercial law practice and his judgments as a commercial judge. But his interests in the law were varied and wide-ranging. That was true when he was a practitioner in South Africa before he came to this country in 1973. Those interests included criminal law. After he became a High Court judge in this country in 1985 he served for several years as a Presiding Judge of the Northern Circuit, when he tried many criminal cases in the Crown Court.

However, Johan Steyn came to make a unique contribution to public law and human rights law in this country, particularly after he was appointed to the Court of Appeal in 1992. In 1994 he was a member of that court when he gave a judgment in *Secretary of State for the Home Department v Abdi and Gawe.*[1] He began his judgment in the following way:

> The lot of refugees is often a desperate one. The spectre of torture or death, or both, often haunt them. The Amnesty International reports graphically document the scale of the inhumanity of man to man. That is why it is right to treat the rights of asylum seekers as fundamental rights. In a European democracy founded on values of liberty and human-ity, such as ours, our law accords special protection to such fundamental rights. Everybody should know this. Parliament certainly does. The Courts can therefore accept as a work-ing assumption that Parliament would not curtail such rights by a side-wind but only by the clearest provision in the plainest English if it considered that such fundamental rights of refugees should be sacrificed in aid of the economic prosperity of the citizens of this country.

[1] [1994] Imm AR 402.

In that passage we can see so many aspects of the person that Johan Steyn was. The language is elegant and concise. Johan Steyn's humanity shines through. His commitment to fundamental human rights is obvious. But he was also well aware of the reality of life for many people around the world. There can be no doubt that this must have been in large part the consequence of his experiences of living and working in South Africa before his self-imposed exile, at a time when the system of apartheid represented the negation of everything that Johan Steyn believed in and felt as a human being.

But, although Johan Steyn took his work and his principles seriously, he never took himself too seriously. He was a man with a mischievous sense of humour. He was fond of telling the story about the case in which the court had to decide whether a person could have a fair trial even though the trial judge had fallen asleep. The outcome of the appeal was apparently that it was possible to have a fair trial so long as the jury were awake even if the judge was not.

In 2001 Johan Steyn gave a lecture called 'Human Rights: The Legacy of Mrs Roosevelt'.[2] He began that lecture by recounting the story of the Kilikov trial. There was a town called Kilikov in which, during the Polish Wars, a man had killed his friend. The man was arrested and convicted of the murder. But when the time came to carry out the sentence of death, somebody remembered that the man was a blacksmith by profession and that in all of Kilikov there was no other blacksmith. Enquiries were made and it was discovered that in the town there were two tailors but that they could make do with just one. The judges reconvened and said that, instead of the blacksmith, one of the tailors should be hanged instead, for the city could not manage without a blacksmith but one tailor would suffice. As Johan Steyn put it: 'The wisdom of the judges became legendary'.

Later in the same lecture Johan Steyn said this:

> It is a fundamental tenet of democracy that both law and Government accord every individual equal concern and respect for their welfare and dignity. Everyone is entitled to equal protection of the law, which should be applied without fear or favour. Law's necessary distinctions must be justified but must never be made on the grounds of race, colour, belief, gender or any other irrational ground.

These were the values and principles which animated everything that Lord Steyn said in his judgments in the House of Lords, where he served from 1995 for a decade.

Time does not permit me to go through all of the important judgments that Johan Steyn gave while he was in the House of Lords. However, it would be remiss of me not to mention three, which have become classic statements of the law and will be read for many years to come.

The first is *R v Secretary of State for the Home Department ex p. Simms*,[3] which was a case decided in 1999, when the Human Rights Act had been enacted but was not yet in full force, so the case was decided on principles of domestic public law, in particular the principle of legality. In his opinion Johan Steyn set out in the most eloquent terms the rationale for protecting freedom of expression in a democratic

---

[2] [2002] Public Law 473.
[3] [2000] 2 AC 115.

society. He drew on the writings of John Stuart Mill and the judgments of Oliver Wendell Holmes in the Supreme Court of the United States. He said that:

> Freedom of speech is the lifeblood of democracy. The free flow of information and ideas informs political debate. It is a safety valve: people are more ready to accept decisions that go against them if they can in principle seek to influence them. It acts as a brake on the abuse of power by public officials. It facilitates the exposure of errors in the governance and administration of justice of the country.

The second case is *R (Daly) v Secretary of State for the Home Department*,[4] in which Johan Steyn analysed the difference between the doctrine of *Wednesbury* unreasonableness in domestic public law and the human rights concept of proportionality. He was sure that the principle of proportionality, while requiring a more intensive scrutiny by the court, would not lead to a merits-based approach. He ended his judgment with this famous aphorism: 'In law context is everything'.

The last of the trilogy of cases I will mention is *Ghaidan v Godin-Mendoza*[5] (in particular at paragraphs 39 and 41). That decision has become the *locus classicus* on the strong obligation of interpretation in section 3 of the Human Rights Act. As Johan Steyn said in his opinion, section 3 is the 'principal remedial measure, and … the making of a declaration of incompatibility is a measure of last resort'. He continued:

> Nowhere in our legal system is a literalistic approach more inappropriate than when considering whether a breach of a Convention right may be removed by interpretation under section 3. Section 3 requires a broad approach concentrating, amongst other things, in a purposive way on the importance of the fundamental right involved.

It was not only through his judgments that Johan Steyn influenced the development of modern constitutional law. His lectures outside court helped to shape informed public opinion about constitutional reform. In particular he was a strong advocate of the separation of powers. As early as 1996, when he gave the annual ALBA lecture, he began, I think, the process that culminated with the Constitutional Reform Act 2005 and saw the replacement of the Lord Chancellor by the Lord Chief Justice as head of the judiciary in England and Wales. In his lecture Johan Steyn said: 'For my part the proposition that a Cabinet member must be the head of our judiciary … is no longer sustainable on either constitutional or pragmatic grounds'.[6]

Johan Steyn also favoured the creation of a Supreme Court for the United Kingdom, which was clearly separate from Parliament.

In his ALBA lecture, which he called 'The Weakest and Least Dangerous Department of Government' (echoing the words of Alexander Hamilton in the *Federalist Papers*) Johan Steyn suggested that an independent and impartial judiciary is an indispensable part of our democratic system. He noted that:

> Uniquely in our society, the judges seem to be the only public servants who do all their own work. … The parties, and the public, can be confident that the decision has been taken not in a secret cabal but wholly and exclusively by the judge or judges who heard the evidence

---

[4] [2001] 2 AC 532 at [24]–[28].
[5] [2004] 2 AC 557.
[6] 'The Weakest and Least Dangerous Department of Government' [1997] *Public Law* 84 at 91.

and the arguments. ... Generally judges hear cases in open court in the searchlight of public opinion. This principle ensures, as Bentham observed, that the judge is constantly on trial.[7]

In the same lecture Johan Steyn also said that the idea underlying the human rights movement is a simple one. To make his point accessible to non-lawyers as well as to lawyers he quoted JB Priestley, who, during the Great Depression, set out on a journey around England and wrote up what he had observed in a book called *English Journey*. In that book, in words that Johan Steyn clearly found moving, JB Priestley said:

> Let us be too proud ... to refuse shelter to exiled foreigners, too proud to do dirty little tricks because other people can stoop to them, too proud to lose an inch of our freedom, too proud, even if it beggars us, to tolerate social injustice here, too proud to suffer anywhere in this country an ugly mean way of living.[8]

Today we pay tribute to the memory of Lord Steyn. He was not only a great judge. Perhaps more importantly, he was a good person.

[7] ibid, 84–85.
[8] ibid, 93–94.

Human Rights

The Development of Human Rights Thought from Magna Carta to the Universal Declaration of Human Rights

2015 marked the 800th anniversary of Magna Carta (the Great Charter), which was signed by King John in his truce with the barons, and has come to symbolise many things, some of which are not in fact in it like the concept of democracy. Among the many events held in this country and elsewhere to commemorate this anniversary was a conference held at the Temple Church in London, which has associations with both the Knights Templar and the legal profession. The theme of the conference was in very broad terms about religion and Magna Carta. In my lecture I traced the development of human rights thought from Magna Carta to the Universal Declaration of Human Rights, which was adopted by the General Assembly of the United Nations in 1948. At the time of this lecture I was a High Court judge. It was first published in a book edited by Robin Griffith-Jones and Mark Hill QC: Magna Carta, Religion and the Rule of Law *(Cambridge, Cambridge University Press, 2015).*

I N THE OPENING section of this chapter, I trace the development of human rights thought from the time of Magna Carta to the Universal Declaration of Human Rights of 1948. In the second part, I proceed to discuss the relationship between that development and religious thought. When I visited Runnymede some years ago, I bought a souvenir postcard which reminded me that it is regarded as the 'birthplace of democracy'. This may be bad history but, as Professor Linda Colley has observed, there is a 'cult and mode of memory' which rests on bad history and which includes Magna Carta as the most important text in stories of liberty.[1] On reflection I would suggest that there are three fundamental ideas which can be traced back, at least so far as the United Kingdom is concerned, to the drafting of what later became known as the Great Charter in June 1215. They are three related ideas but are in fact distinct.

First is the idea that even the king was subject to the law. This is what has evolved into the concept of the rule of law, a concept which was so elegantly and comprehensively analysed by the late Lord Bingham in his Sir David Williams lecture on that subject in 2006 and his later book with that title in 2010.[2] At the heart of this concept is the idea that the government itself, and not only those who are governed by it, is subject to the law. As is well known, the symbolic importance of Magna

---

[1] L Colley, *Acts of Union and Disunion* (London, Profile Books, 2014), 35–36.
[2] T Bingham, *The Rule of Law* (London, Penguin, 2010).

Carta has always been greater than the precise provisions it actually contained. It has been argued about and reinterpreted ever since. As Professor Elizabeth Wicks has explained in her account of key moments in British constitutional history:

> Even though it originated as merely an attempt to protect baronial interests, by establishing the principles inherent in the Rule of Law, the Magna Carta left a legacy for individuals of future ages to ensure that their governments acted according to the law and legal processes.[3]

The second idea is that the legitimate basis of all government is the consent of the governed. It could not be said that the United Kingdom was anything approaching a democracy in the thirteenth century or at any time until the extensions of the franchise in the various reform acts of the nineteenth century. It did not become a full democracy until 1928, when the franchise was extended to all women on an equal basis to men. Much of the endeavour, both philosophical and practical, in which many people engaged over the centuries in between, was devoted to making the king subject to the will of his subjects in this sense, in other words to transform the government of this country into a representative democracy. It would be a truism of our modern constitutional arrangements that Her Majesty's Government (or, if you will, the Crown) depends for its legitimacy on the support of a majority in the House of Commons, the elected chamber of Parliament, that is on the consent of the governed.

The writings of John Locke, in particular his *Second Treatise on Civil Government* in 1690,[4] addressed this subject, the consent of the governed as the basis of legitimate government, even though he would not have regarded himself as a democrat. His main practical objective was to provide a philosophical justification for the Glorious Revolution of 1688–89, when Parliament finally secured its ascendancy over the Crown. The Crown was offered to William and Mary on conditions which were set out in the Bill of Rights of 1689. The Bill of Rights, important though it remains as a constitutional document, was concerned primarily with the powers of Parliament vis-á-vis the executive and not so much with what we would today call a bill of rights.

Even Thomas Paine, when writing *The Rights of Man* in 1792, his provocative defence of the French Revolution, was focusing primarily on the right of the people to select their own government, not human rights in the modern sense. In the ensuing century the two concepts, of democracy and fundamental rights, were of course thought to be related: that the rights of the people were best secured from tyranny if they had a say in the choice of their government. However, most people were not yet concerned about the possible tyranny of the majority, at a time when the majority did not have a vote. Their primary objective was to extend the franchise, at least to all men: the best example of this is the Chartist movement, referring, perhaps in an echo of Magna Carta, to a charter, this time the People's Charter of the 1830s and 1840s. Famously, of course, John Stuart Mill *was* concerned about the possible tyranny of the majority, in his work *On Liberty*, published in 1859.

---

[3] E Wicks, *The Evolution of a Constitution* (Oxford, Hart Publishing, 2006) 6.
[4] J Locke, *Two Treatises of Civil Government* (London, JM Dent/EP Dutton, 1924; first published 1690) 117ff.

It is the third idea which can be traced back to Runnymede in 1215 that I want to focus on in this chapter. That is the idea of fundamental human rights. It was certainly not at the forefront of the Great Charter. As Lord Bingham explained in one of his last public lectures in 2010, it would be a travesty to regard the barons who met King John at Runnymede as a thirteenth-century precursor to Charter 88, the constitutional reform group. He continued: 'They were driven, not by an altruistic concern for the future of the country, but by an intention to protect their own particular interests. Establishment of a charter of human rights in the sense understood today was not among their objectives'.[5] Nevertheless the germ of the idea can be found there, in particular in chapters 39 and 40, which Lord Bingham described as still having the power to make the blood race. The idea of fundamental rights which could be asserted even against state power never went away. It had to be developed and continues to be developed.

In human rights thought there are usually taken to have been three stages of development, often referred to as the three 'generations' of rights. The first generation is the one that will be familiar to most of us from such instruments as the European Convention on Human Rights (ECHR), the main rights in which are now set out in schedule 1 to the Human Rights Act 1998. This first generation consists of civil and political rights.

This brings me to the Universal Declaration of Human Rights, which took the form of a resolution passed by the General Assembly of the United Nations on 10 December 1948. It is not surprising that Eleanor Roosevelt, the chair of the drafting committee, compared the Declaration to an 'international Magna Carta for all men everywhere'. It is also important to note that the Universal Declaration was truly universal in the sense that it had almost unanimous support in the General Assembly. Of course the membership of the UN was much smaller then than it is now but no state voted against the resolution and there were just eight abstentions, from the Soviet bloc, Saudi Arabia and South Africa. Even the abstaining states had participated in the drafting process.[6] The drafting committee included members from different regions of the world and different religious and cultural traditions.

Article 1 of the Declaration proudly announced that: 'Everyone is born free and equal in dignity and rights'. Many of the rights in the Universal Declaration will be familiar to us as they are also reflected in the ECHR, which followed just two years after the Declaration and expressly referred to it in its preamble. This list of rights would be recognised by many people in most democracies ranging from the USA, which enacted its constitutional bill of rights in 1791, in the form of the first ten Amendments to the Constitution, to India, whose constitution of 1950 created a parliamentary system of government based on the Westminster model but with an American-style bill of rights.

The catalogue of rights varies from charter to charter but most modern democracies have such a list of fundamental rights and would certainly recognise it. The right to liberty and security of the person; the right to freedom of expression, the right to

---

[5] T Bingham, *Lives of the Law* (Oxford, Oxford University Press, 2010) 5.

[6] J Morsink, *The Universal Declaration of Human Rights: Origins, Drafting, and Intent* (Philadelphia PA, University of Pennsylvania Press, 1999) 21.

freedom of religion and the right to a fair trial will be among this basic catalogue of civil and political rights. The right to property will often be included but not necessarily so. It is not to be found in the Canadian Charter of Fundamental Rights and Freedoms of 1982. It was not in the original text of the ECHR but was immediately added in Article 1 of the First Protocol, although the structure of that provision is quite different from that of the other qualified rights in the ECHR, such as the right to freedom of expression. This is because it is generally recognised that state regulation of private property, or even the taking of property (most obviously in the form of taxes), may be required in a modern society so as to enable human beings to flourish and indeed to make a reality of other fundamental rights.

The Universal Declaration did not stop at civil and political rights. It also included the second generation of human rights: social, economic and cultural rights. The list of such rights would include the right to education, the right to housing, the right to healthcare and the right to social security. It would also include cultural rights, such as the right to have access to the arts. The preamble to the Universal Declaration made express reference to the war aims of the Allies, in particular the USA, in which President Franklin D Roosevelt had set out the Four Freedoms: freedom of speech and freedom of religion but also freedom from want and freedom from fear. These were carried over from his own domestic programme of the 1930s known as the New Deal. They were very much the flavour of the age in the years immediately after the Second World War. In the United Kingdom the Beveridge Report of 1942 had laid the groundwork for the social reforms of the Attlee government elected in 1945, which established the welfare state and the National Health Service.

One of the striking and important features of the Universal Declaration of Human Rights is that it included both first-generation and second-generation human rights in the same document. The longer-term aim was then to place both generations of rights on a secure legal footing in international law by drafting a treaty. However, the ideological differences of the cold war era meant that it was not possible to put them in a single treaty and so they were eventually the subject of two treaties drafted under the auspices of the UN and opened for signature in 1966. One was the International Covenant on Civil and Political Rights; the other was the International Covenant on Economic, Social and Cultural Rights. The United Kingdom ratified both treaties in 1976. Although neither has been incorporated into domestic law by Act of Parliament (in contrast to the ECHR), both are international treaties and are legally binding on the UK as a matter of international law. However, even today the question whether such rights are fundamental human rights at all continues to be the subject of some controversy.

The third generation of human rights is more controversial still. This is said to include such rights as the right to a healthy environment, and reflects concerns which perhaps have become more prominent since the end of the Second World War and were not set out in the Universal Declaration, in 1948. Such concerns have become more pronounced in the last 25 years as the impact of human activities on the natural environment, and in particular the phenomenon of climate change, has received much wider recognition. For example, the Aarhus Convention of 1998 refers, in Article 1, to 'the right, of every person, of present and future generations to live in an environment adequate to his or her health and well-being'.

Although the origin of human rights can certainly be detected in Magna Carta, and in particular the early seeds of what would today be called civil and political rights can be seen, the scope of modern human rights is clearly much wider. But it is not only the scope which has changed and expanded so much in the intervening centuries. It is also our understanding of who should be the bearer of rights; in other words, who is entitled to assert fundamental rights even against the power of the state. This has been much contested through the intervening centuries and people have often fought, sometimes literally, over it.

Let us consider again the opening words of Article 1 of the Universal Declaration: 'Everyone is born free and equal in dignity and rights'. Note that word 'everyone': I would suggest that it may be the most important word in human rights charters: it is easy to say but difficult to implement in practice. In truth most legal systems have differentiated between human beings and accorded them rights by reference to their status. Certainly at the time of the Great Charter it would have been unthinkable that everyone was entitled to certain basic rights. They belonged to certain persons by virtue of their status, in particular as a freeman. Serfdom still existed. Women would have been excluded, as they have been from many basic rights in most societies until relatively recently. Others have been excluded because of their race or religion or other similar reason. Today we would regard this as a basic denial of human rights, but it has for much of history been regarded as the natural order of things. Two clauses of Magna Carta itself, chapters 10 and 11, contained provisions which were on their face discriminatory against Jews. In the late thirteenth century Jews were expelled from England in the reign of Edward I. They were not permitted to return until the time of Oliver Cromwell.

The American historian Eric Foner has written a fascinating account of the development of fundamental rights in his book *The Story of American Freedom*, which of course he traces back to ideas which had originated in the Old World. But he says:

> British freedom was anything but universal. Nationalist, often xenophobic, it viewed nearly every other nation on earth as 'enslaved' – to popery, tyranny or barbarism … British freedom was the linear descendant of an understanding of liberty derived from the Middle Ages, when 'liberties' meant formal privileges such as self-government or exemption from taxation granted to particular groups by contract, charter, or royal decree … The medieval understanding of liberty assumed a hierarchical world in which individual rights in a modern sense barely existed, and political and economic entitlements were enjoyed by some social classes and denied to others.[7]

Even Jefferson's eloquent drafting of the American Declaration of Independence in 1776 referred to all men as being created equal. It was no accident that he did not include women. It is also notorious that most of the men who created the United States of America were themselves slave-owners, including Jefferson himself. The Constitution of the new republic in 1787 did not confer rights on slaves but had to recognise their presence in order to calculate the population of each state for the purpose of allocation of political representation in Congress. This led to the infamous provision that a member of the slave population of a state would count as

---

[7] E Foner, *The Story of American Freedom* (London, W.W. Norton & Co, 1998) 6.

three-fifths of a person.[8] Even after the end of the American Civil War, when slavery was abolished by the Thirteenth Amendment, and the right to vote and equal protection of the laws were conferred upon former slaves by the Fourteenth and Fifteenth Amendments, the reality fell far short of the rhetoric for a century or more. As President Obama said in his inaugural speech when he became President in 2009, 50 years earlier it would have been impossible for his father to be served at a lunch counter in Washington, DC. That is why a million people marched on Washington in 1963 to hear Martin Luther King give his 'I have a dream' speech on the centenary of Lincoln's Emancipation Proclamation, at the height of the civil rights movement.

So the message of the Universal Declaration is something quite new and, despite its simplicity, profoundly radical in human history. It is the idea that all of us have certain rights simply because of our common humanity. They are not acquired by birth or some other status. They do not even have to be earned. They simply are, because we are all born human.

One of the inspirational figures behind the enactment of the Human Rights Act 1998 was Francesca Klug, then an academic at King's College London and now at the London School of Economics. In 2000, the year when the Act came into full force, she published a book telling the story of the United Kingdom's new Bill of Rights, as she called it. The title of her book was *Values for a Godless Age*. In the introduction, she said that human rights are best understood as part law, part philosophy and part political movement. She suggested that the values which drive the idea of human rights owe almost as much to poetry and music as they do to legal principles. They owe nearly as much to the spirituality of all the great religions and to the eternal quest for righteousness as they do to revolution and the demand for freedom from state tyranny. She continued:

> human rights are now probably as significant as the Bible has been in shaping modern, Western values. With the coming into force of the Human Rights Act their influence in Britain is set to expand significantly. In a country where there is no one unifying religious or ethical world-view, human rights values have an as yet untapped potential to bind and cement a diverse society. They are, I suggest, values for a 'godless age'. It is in these terms that they must be understood and judged.[9]

While I would not disagree with Professor Klug's central thesis, I would slightly quibble with the phrase 'godless age'. I would prefer to use the phrase 'secular age'. It is certainly the case that it is possible to believe in human rights values without subscribing to any faith system. It is also to be hoped that human rights values have the potential to provide modern societies with a set of values on which they can agree and join together as communities, irrespective of any individual's own faith or lack of it. Nevertheless it is also apparent that throughout history the concept of human rights has owed much to religious belief.

The shift in human rights thinking can perhaps be illustrated by comparing the text of the American Declaration of independence in 1776 with the Universal Declaration of Human Rights in 1948. When Jefferson drafted the American Declaration of

---

[8] Constitution of the United States, Art 1, s 2.
[9] F Klug, *Values for a Godless Age* (London, Penguin, 2000) 18.

Independence, he referred in its famous opening words to the fact that all men are *created* equal and that they are endowed by their creator with certain inalienable rights, among which are the right to life, liberty and the pursuit of happiness. By the time that the General Assembly of the United Nations adopted the Universal Declaration in 1948, it proclaimed, in Article 1, that all human beings are *born* free and equal in dignity and rights. There is no longer any reference to a divine creator, although it is worth noting that the next sentence of Article 1 refers to human beings being endowed with reason and that they should live in a spirit of brotherhood, phrases that have spiritual undertones. The drafting of the Universal Declaration in this way was the result of considered reflection and not accident. During the drafting process, it was proposed by some delegations that there should be overt reference made in Article 1 to God, but this was rejected, on the ground that the Declaration was intended for mankind as a whole, whether believers or not.[10]

However in the course of human history it is clear that different faith systems have undoubtedly played their part in shaping human rights thinking. To take one obvious example, two of the Ten Commandments, thou shall not kill and thou shall not steal, are widely acknowledged to correspond to the basic rights that everyone has to life and to property.

As already stated above, one of the most important contributions which Magna Carta has made to legal and political thinking around the world is the idea that even the King is subject to the law. This idea was not new even in 1215. It goes back in Western thought at least to the time of classical Athens in the fifth century BC. In Sophocles' play *Antigone*, Creon, the King of Thebes, demands to know why Antigone has disobeyed the law of the state, which prohibited her from giving a burial to her brother, who had fought in a campaign against his own country. She replies that she was obeying a higher law, and for this defiance she is prepared to face her own death. In the verse translation by Sir George Young, Antigone tells the king:

> Because it was not Zeus who ordered it,
>
> Nor Justice, dweller with the Nether gods,
>
> Gave such a law to men; nor did I deem
>
> Your ordinance of so much binding force,
>
> As that a mortal man could overbear
>
> The unchangeable unwritten code of Heaven;
>
> This is not of today and yesterday,
>
> But lives forever, having origin
>
> Whence no man knows ...[11]

What is of interest for present purposes is that, when Antigone appeals to a higher law, she clearly regards it as having been laid down by the gods. That idea, that the law laid down by human beings in any state is subject to the higher law of God, is one that

---

[10] For a more detailed discussion of the drafting process on this issue, see Morsink, *Universal Declaration of Human Rights* (n 6) 284–90.

[11] G Young (trans), *Sophocles' Dramas* (London, 1906) 14–15.

can be found in many belief systems around the world and continues to inspire many people today. In Catholic thinking about law and justice, what we would today call human rights have clearly played an important part. From Thomas Aquinas through to the contemporary legal philosopher John Finnis, there has been a strong belief in natural law and natural rights.

One of the founders of international law, Grotius, wrote on the laws of war and peace in 1625. He expressed the view that the source of law is the free will of God. He noted that the Stoics used to say that the origin of law should be sought in no other source than Jupiter himself; and from the name Jupiter the Latin word for law (*ius*) was probably derived. From that word was also derived the Latin word *iustitia*, from which we have inherited our own word 'justice'.

It is right to acknowledge that over the millennia many terrible things have been done in the name of religion. This is a phenomenon which is not confined to any one faith group. One example is the way in which European empires treated the indigenous communities which they encountered in the New World in the sixteenth century. In modern parlance, many human rights abuses were committed and have been committed in the name of religion. However, even, in the sixteenth century, alternative voices were to be heard. Bartolomé de las Casas wrote (in defence of the Indian) to the King of Spain that:

> from Christ, the eternal truth, we have the command 'you must love your neighbour as yourself' … He who wants a large part of mankind to be such that … he may act like a ferocious executioner towards them, press them into slavery, and through them grow rich, is a despotic master, not a Christian; a son of Satan, not of God; a plunderer, not a shepherd; a person who is led by the spirit of the devil, not heaven.[12]

Nor has this phenomenon been confined to religions. After all, some of the worst atrocities of the twentieth century were committed in the name of two secular ideologies: fascism and communism.

I mentioned earlier the concept of social and economic rights. I would suggest that this too has been influenced by religious thought. Although social and economic rights remain controversial as a matter of philosophy and their status remains far from certain in law, public opinion often regards these as truly fundamental human rights. In particular the ethical basis of the NHS remains profoundly popular right across society: that a person who is ill or injured should be treated according to medical need, not his or her ability to pay.

How did this development in the concept of human rights come about? British liberalism had set about reforming the state in the nineteenth century so as to increase access to the franchise and to remove restrictions on basic freedoms like freedom of religion; in other words, by extending civil and political rights. Many of the disabilities and restrictions which applied to Nonconformists, Catholics and Jews were removed, such as the ability to stand for Parliament and attend one of the ancient universities. But the economic philosophy of the time was laissez-faire. The state was regarded as the enemy of liberty and it was certainly not regarded as having a positive

[12] Quoted in M Ishay, *The Human Rights Reader* (London, Routledge, 1997) 69.

role to play in economic affairs. However, by the late Victorian period liberalism itself was undergoing change and in part this was attributable to the influence of Thomas Hill Green. In his 'Lecture on liberal legislation and freedom of contract' Green sought to explain how a commitment to liberalism could include state intervention with concepts like freedom of contract when that was necessary to protect (for example) workers from working in dangerous conditions. He said:

> We shall probably all agree that freedom, rightly understood, is the greatest of blessings; that its attainment is the true end of all our efforts as citizens ... We do not mean a freedom that can be enjoyed by one man or one set of men at the cost of loss of freedom to others. When we speak of freedom as something to be so highly prized, we mean a positive power or capacity of doing or enjoying something worth doing or enjoying, and that, too, something that we do or enjoy in common with others. We mean by it a power which each man exercises through the help or security given him by his fellow-men, and which he in turn helps to secure for them.[13]

It is no accident, I think, that TH Green was a devout Christian.

Green's influence was felt particularly after 1906, in the governments of Campbell-Bannerman and Asquith, which introduced reforms such as old age pensions and national insurance, under the banner of 'New Liberalism'. A prominent member of the government was Lloyd George, who is reputed to have said that, while Man cannot live by bread alone, he needs bread if he is to be able to worship at the temple of liberty (again note the use of religious language). In other words, it is all very well saying that people should have the right to freedom of expression and belief but this will be of little practical use to them if they are hungry or sick and left to fend for themselves. The point was made by Owen Jones more recently as follows:

> the individual needs to be defended from more than the state. Poverty strips individuals of their freedom, imposing limitations on every aspect of their lives, from what they can eat to how they spend their leisure time. To provide for themselves and their families, workers are compelled to work some of the longest hours in Europe, losing time that could be spent on more fulfilling activities. Hence the need to limit the working day and crack down on unpaid overtime. Freed from financial hardship, excessive work and the constant fear of job and housing insecurity, the individual can prosper and fulfil his or her potential.[14]

While the status of social and economic rights may remain controversial as a matter of law, they come as no surprise to anyone with an interest in ethics or religion. As every law student knows, the law of negligence was described in explicitly biblical terms by Lord Atkin in *Donoghue v Stevenson*.[15] However, the way in which Lord Atkin referred to the premise that one should love one's neighbour was relatively minimalist: that one should not harm one's neighbour or at least not negligently. He said

> The rule that you are to love your neighbour becomes in law, you must not injure your neighbour; and the lawyer's question, Who is my neighbour? receives a restricted reply You must take

---

[13] T Green, 'Liber legislation and freedom of contract' in P Harris and J Morrow (eds), *Lectures on the Principles of the Political Obligation* (Cambridge, Cambridge University Press, 1986) 199.

[14] O Jones, 'Who really wants to roll back the state? Not the right', *The Guardian*, 12, 2014.

[15] [1932] AC 562 at 580.

reasonable care to avoid acts or omissions which you can reasonably foresee would be likely
to injure your neighbour.

A fuller understanding of the moral precept might suggest that one should do more:
for example, if the neighbour is hungry one should feed him and if he is ill one should
help him to become better.

Many religions understand this. At the heart of Sikhism is the concept of service
to others around you. This is given practical effect in the gurdwara where any person
who comes will be fed for free from the common kitchen irrespective of their own
faith or background. The food is cooked and served by volunteers. It is no accident
that the Golden Temple, Sikhs' holiest shrine, in Amritsar, has four doors, which are
to open the corners of the world: it is because everyone is welcome, no matter what
their own faith or background. This is the message of universal love and equality
which lies at the core of most faith traditions and, I would suggest at the root of the
concept of human rights too.

Nevertheless, as I have mentioned, it can be seen that, from the time of the
Enlightenment in the mid-eighteenth century, a divergence began to emerge between
religion and human rights thinking. Sometimes there was even hostility, in particular
in the form of anti-clericalism after the French Revolution. Many of the philosophers
associated with the Enlightenment such as Kant, were themselves believers. However,
others such as Thomas Paine were certainly not adherents of any conventional religion, Paine regarding himself as a deist rather than an atheist. Deists believed in a
universal God existing outside the institutions of formal religions. Eve Darian-Smith
has suggested that deism was attractive to many in prerevolutionary America and had
a particular influence on the founders of the American republic, such as Franklin,
Washington and Jefferson.[16]

In one sense, it could be said that human rights no longer needed religion but religion still needed human rights. One of the basic rights which is usually to be found in
any charter of human rights is the right to freedom of religion. This is to be found in
Article 9 of the ECHR. Much earlier it can be found in the First Amendment to the
US Constitution as part of the American Bill of Rights, which was enacted shortly
after the original Constitution, in 1791. Even before that time, in Virginia, Jefferson
had helped to draft a statute for religious freedom. It was in many ways because the
founders of the new American Republic were believers that they wished to create a
strict wall of separation between Church and state, turning their back on the notion
of established churches which had prevailed in the Old World in Europe. Even today it
could be said that the United States is a secular state but far more religious as a society
than perhaps the United Kingdom is.

It would be wrong to assume that the association between faith and human rights
thinking is to be found only in the Judaeo-Christian tradition or in the West. So far
as 1 am aware, in most if not all of the great faith systems of the world, certainly as
they exist today, there can be found basic values and principles of ethical living which
in our terminology could be regarded as human rights thinking. Senator Robert
Kennedy, who was himself a Catholic, gave a famous speech in Cape Town in 1966, in

[16] E Darian-Smith, *Religion, Race, Rights* (Oxford, Hart Publishing, 2010) 95, 110–11.

which he said that the essence of human rights thinking is that each human being is the precious child of God. He said:

> At the heart of ... Western freedom and democracy is the belief that the individual man, the child of God, is the touchstone of value and all society, groups, the state exist for his benefit. Therefore the enlargement of liberty for individual human beings must be the supreme goal and the abiding practice of any Western society.[17]

Many faith groups around the world would agree.

Once one accepts that every human being is the individual child of God, each unique and precious in his or her own right, and not to be used for any utilitarian purpose, it is but a short step to conclude that every human being is my brother or a sister. From that basic belief many people have derived the notion that ethical living requires universal love towards others. From a similar starting point human rights thinking has developed the notion that every human being is a member of the human family, born free and equal in dignity and rights, as the Universal Declaration proclaimed in 1948.

I therefore venture a couple of general concluding remarks. First, the concept of human rights is not primarily a legal one; it is a moral concept, it is about how human beings ought to live in relation to each other, a relationship of mutual dignity and respect. Sometimes human rights have been recognised and given effect in law, often not. But they have still been there even when violated or denied in the most grotesque form. René Cassin was a French Jew who was a member of the drafting committee of the Universal Declaration. The René Cassin Centre continues to honour his memory through its work for human rights. It recently suggested that the best way to remember the Holocaust through a lasting memorial would be to reaffirm our commitment to the cause of human rights.

Second, throughout history the concept of human rights has been shaped and influenced by those who believed in God and belonged to a faith tradition. This was true of the early origins of human rights thought. It has also been true of the more recent development of social and economic rights as human rights. It has certainly been true of the notion of the equality of all human beings. For many people this has flowed from their belief, rooted in their faith, that we are all the children of God and members of one human family.

However, belief in human rights does not have to depend on having faith or belonging to any faith system. Particularly since the Enlightenment it has been possible to have a secular belief in human rights. This is one of the things that everyone can agree upon, whether or not they belong to any faith. It has even been suggested by some that belief in human rights has become, or could be, a secular religion, setting out fundamental values which could unite a society which has very little else that people agree about.

---

[17] Robert Kennedy, quoted in B MacArthur, *Penguin Book of Twentieth-century Speeches* (London, Penguin, 1992) 367.

The Moral Force of the United Kingdom's Human Rights Act

In 2011 New Zealand celebrated the 21st birthday of its Bill of Rights Act 1990. I was asked to take part in a conference to mark that birthday at Victoria University of Wellington. As part of that event I gave this lecture, in which I suggested that human rights instruments such as the UK's Human Rights Act are not simply pieces of legislation but carry a moral force. I also tried, by reference to some of the major decisions of the UK courts in the first decade of the operation of the HRA, to illustrate the rhetorical force of many of the judicial statements of principle which have been made about it. At the time of this lecture, I was a barrister and was just about to be sworn in as a High Court judge. It was first published in (2013) 11 New Zealand Journal of Public and International Law 39.

T HE HUMAN RIGHTS Act 1998 (UK) is the nearest thing that the United Kingdom has to a bill of rights. Some have suggested that it should be repealed and replaced by what they call a British bill of rights, and a commission has been established by the coalition government in the United Kingdom to inquire into that possibility, which is due to report by the end of 2012.[1]

Others have expressed surprise at that suggestion, as they thought that the United Kingdom already had one – and that the Human Rights Act is that bill of rights.[2]

As you might imagine, the Human Rights Act did not emerge out of the blue in 1998, when it was passed by the United Kingdom Parliament. It has a history and a pedigree, a lineage in human rights thinking which goes back hundreds and perhaps thousands of years, in both religious and secular thought. It belongs as much to the moral realm as to the legal.

In *R (Daly) v Secretary of State for the Home Department* that great New Zealand judge, Lord Cooke, when sitting in the House of Lords, said:[3]

> The truth is, I think, that some rights are inherent and fundamental to democratic civilised society. Conventions, constitutions, bills of rights and the like respond by recognising rather than creating them.

---

[1] Commission on a Bill of Rights *Discussion Paper: Do we need a UK Bill of Rights?* (United Kingdom, August 2011).

[2] See for example Francesca Klug, 'A Bill of Rights: Do We Need One or Do We Already Have One?' [2007] *PL* 701. This was published before the general election of 2010 (which produced a coalition between the Conservatives and Liberal Democrats) in response to the suggestion by some that the Human Rights Act 1998 (UK) should be replaced by a British bill of rights.

[3] *R (Daly) v Secretary of State for the Home Department* [2001] UKHL 26, [2001] 2 AC 132 (HL) at [30].

In *R (European Roma Rights Centre) v Immigration Officer at Prague Airport* Lord Steyn said that: 'The Universal Declaration of Human Rights (1948) was a proclamation of ethical values rather than legal norms'.[4] Later in the same paragraph he said that: 'The moral force of this instrument was enormous'.[5] It is that moral force of the Human Rights Act which will be the theme of this paper.

The words of article 1 of the Universal Declaration of Human Rights pronounce to the world that: 'All human beings are born free and equal in dignity and rights'.[6]

At first sight this statement may seem to us today to be obvious, perhaps even trite. But it is a remarkably modern view. First, note that it does not say, as Rousseau did in the opening line of *The Social Contract*, only that 'Man is born free'.[7] Here we have equality too. True it is that the United States Declaration of Independence did refer to equality but Thomas Jefferson's words started with the proclamation that: 'all men are created equal', not all human beings.[8]

It is also worth noting that the Universal Declaration of Human Rights refers to all human beings being 'born' with certain rights, not that they are created or, as the United States Declaration of Independence went on to say, that they are 'endowed by their Creator with certain inalienable rights' and that 'among these are the right to life, liberty and the pursuit of happiness'. This reflects the secularisation of human rights. This is not to deny the importance of religious thought in the origins and development of human rights. To the contrary, it is clear that all the major faiths (and many minor ones) have emphasised the sanctity and dignity of human life; that each human being is the individual child of God. As Robert Kennedy put it in 1966 in his famous 'tiny ripple of hope' speech, delivered in Cape Town, at the height of apartheid in South Africa:[9]

> At the heart of ... Western freedom and democracy is the belief that the individual man, the child of God, is the touchstone of value, and all society, groups, the state, exist for his benefit.

Nevertheless, what has become apparent since the Enlightenment is that it is no longer necessary to believe in a divine creator to believe in human rights. Many people who are atheists, in particular humanists, do so because they cherish the individual human being. As William Shakespeare put it in *Hamlet*: 'What a piece of work is a man, how noble in reason, how infinite in faculties'.[10] Hamlet himself may have questioned the value of what he called 'this quintessence of dust', but many would still marvel at what the individual human being is capable of at his or her best.[11]

The philosopher of the Enlightenment who has perhaps had the most lasting influence on human rights thought is Immanuel Kant. In particular the principle of

---

[4] *R (European Roma Rights Centre) v Immigration Officer at Prague Airport* [2004] UKHL 55, [2005] 2 AC 1 (HL) at [46].

[5] At [46].

[6] Universal Declaration of Human Rights GA Res 217, III (1948), art 1.

[7] Jean-Jacques Rousseau, *The Social Contract and Discourses* (London, Dent, 1913).

[8] Declaration of Independence (1776).

[9] Robert F Kennedy, 'Day of Affirmation Speech' (University of Capetown, South Africa, 6 June 1966).

[10] William Shakespeare *Hamlet* (London, Dent, 1934) at Act II, Scene II.

[11] At Act II, Scene II.

universalisability or the categorical imperative: that a human person is an end and not a means, and that we should treat others as we would have them treat us.[12] Two hundred years later, much in Ronald Dworkin's writing, in particular, the principle of equal concern and respect, is derived from Kantian ethics.[13] This strand in moral philosophy is fundamentally inconsistent with the other great strand handed down to us from Enlightenment thinking, the philosophy of utilitarianism associated with Jeremy Bentham. He famously said that talk of rights was nonsense and talk of natural rights was 'nonsense upon stilts'.[14] Going back to Kantian ethics, there is no great mystery about this. Most children understand the concept. And I believe it gives us a great insight into the fundamental values of human rights.

One of those values is mutual respect. What does that mean? I think the key is the notion of empathy – that you should put yourself in someone else's shoes. Can you see the world from his or her point of view? Sometimes people suggest that talk of rights is selfish. It is all about 'me me me'. I do not share that view. I do not think it is about me. I think it is about you, her, him – the network of people in our community. I will return to this theme of the importance of community to a proper understanding of human rights later.

Another key idea is the principle of equality. That all human beings are equal – no matter what their colour, religion, gender, wealth, education or any other status. This is again about mutual respect. It is about caring about another person even if he or she is not like us.

Perhaps he or she believes in things or says things which we totally disagree with. But the human rights response is not to silence him or her. Our response is to allow people to have their say, even those we regard as misguided or just plain wrong.

There is one other thing I would like to add here. Mutual respect is not the same thing as mutuality. Some people suggest that the basis of human rights is mutuality, in other words that we should treat others as they would treat us. I do not think that is right. I think the basis of human rights is that we should treat others as we would want them to treat us – not how they would treat us. Even if we know that, given half the chance, they would bully us or hate us or mistreat us, we should not respond in kind. We should not stoop to the level of others – instead we should stick to our own values.

It is arguable that the most important word in the European Convention on Human Rights (the European Convention) is 'everyone'.[15] Each of the main articles in the European Convention begins with the word 'everyone'. So, quite apart from article 14, which prohibits discrimination in the enjoyment of rights, the rights in the European Convention belong to everyone. That is the fundamental premise of human rights thought: that we are all entitled to some basic rights because of our

[12] Immanuel Kant, *Groundwork for the Metaphysics of Morals* (Peterborough, Broadview Press, 2005) at 87.

[13] See Ronald Dworkin, *Taking Rights Seriously* (Cambridge, Harvard University Press, 1977); Ronald Dworkin, *Sovereign Virtue* (Cambridge, Harvard University Press, 2000).

[14] Jeremy Bentham, 'Anarchical Fallacies' in *The Works of Jeremy Bentham* (Edinburgh, William Tait, 1843) vol 2, 489 at 501.

[15] Convention for the Protection of Human Rights and Fundamental Freedoms 213 UNTS 222 (opened for signature 4 November 1950, entered into force 3 September 1953) [ECHR].

common humanity, not because they have been conferred or earned. Nor can they be lost or given away: for example, no one can sell himself or herself into slavery. That was the original meaning of the word 'inalienable', which is to be found in the opening words of the United States Declaration of Independence: rights which cannot be alienated are rights which cannot be given away or sold.

This basic insight into the nature and source of human rights leads to a realisation that there is no inconsistency between the notion of democracy and a belief in human rights. It is sometimes suggested that there is. But I would suggest that the notion of democracy itself rests on this more basic value of human equality, that everyone counts but no one counts more than anyone else. That is why everyone has a vote but no one has more than one vote. Whatever the differences in our wealth, background or education, we are all equal at the ballot box. That is a profoundly moving and noble idea.

As Lady Hale put it in the leading case on gay rights under the Human Rights Act, *Ghaidan v Godin-Mendoza*:

> Democracy is founded on the principle that each individual has equal value. Treating some as automatically having less value than others not only causes pain and distress to that person but also violates his or her dignity as a human being. The essence of the Convention ... is respect for human dignity and human freedom ... Second, such treatment is damaging to society as a whole. Wrongly to assume that some people have talent and others do not is a huge waste of human resources. ... Third, it is the reverse of the rational behaviour we now expect of government and the state. Power must not be exercised arbitrarily. If distinctions are to be drawn, particularly upon a group basis, it is an important discipline to look for a rational basis for those distinctions. Finally, it is a purpose of all human rights instruments to secure the protection of the essential rights of members of minority groups, even when they are unpopular with the majority. Democracy values everyone equally even if the majority does not.[16]

To that eloquent summary I would add one further rationale for why equality is so important as an underlying value of human rights. Experience around the world, both from history and from recent times, has shown that respect for equality is essential for the maintenance of social peace. Conversely, when some groups in society feel that they are systematically excluded from the benefits of membership of that society, whether in the form of legal rights, or social and financial benefits, particularly if they perceive that there is discrimination against them on the basis of race or some similar status, these people may well resort to violence. This is not to excuse such violence; but it would be unrealistic to ignore the danger to peace and social stability which may result from systematic discrimination.

Another insight as to the importance of equality was provided in *A v Secretary of State for the Home Department* (*Belmarsh*) by Lord Bingham when he quoted Sir Hersch Lauterpacht's seminal work from 1945, where he suggested that the claim to equality 'is in a substantial sense the most fundamental of the rights of man'.[17]

---

[16] *Ghaidan v Godin-Mendoza* [2004] UKHL 30, [2004] 2 AC 557 (HL) at [132].

[17] Hersch Lauterpacht, *An International Bill of the Rights of Man* (New York, Columbia University Press, 1945) at 115 as quoted by Lord Bingham in *A v Secretary of State for the Home Department* [2004] UKHL 56, [2005] 2 AC 68 (HL) [*Belmarsh*] at [46].

Lord Bingham then expressly approved the following passage from Jackson J in a United States case, *Railway Express Agency Inc v New York*:

> The framers of the Constitution knew, and we should not forget today, that there is no more effective practical guaranty against arbitrary and unreasonable government, than to require that the principles of law which officials would impose upon a minority must be imposed generally. Conversely, nothing opens the door to arbitrary action so effectively as to allow those officials to pick and choose only a few to whom they will apply legislation and thus to escape the political retribution that might be visited upon them if larger numbers were affected. Courts can take no better measure to assure that laws will be just than to require that laws be equal in operation.[18]

Belmarsh concerned the Anti-terrorism, Crime and Security Act 2001 (UK), which was enacted by the United Kingdom Parliament within weeks of the terrible events of '9/11'. Part 4 of that Act conferred a power on the Secretary of State for the Home Department to authorise the detention of certain persons who were suspected of international terrorism. Such persons had to be foreign nationals and there had to be a legal obstacle to their deportation: usually this would be where they could not be returned to their own country as there was a real risk of torture or other ill-treatment, so that there would be a breach of article 3 of the European Convention if they were to be deported.[19] Around 14 such individuals were detained in Belmarsh, a high security prison in south-east London. As it turned out, they were held there without charge or trial for several years.

In order to avoid a possible breach of the European Convention, the United Kingdom Government lodged a formal derogation from article 5 (the right to liberty and security) with the Secretary-General of the Council of Europe.[20] Such a derogation is in principle permitted under article 15 where there is a public emergency threatening the life of the nation and where it is strictly required by the exigencies of the situation. The House of Lords held in *Belmarsh* that this derogation had not been lawfully made and so the legislation was contrary to the European Convention. However, since the offending provisions were in primary legislation, the courts had no power to strike them down, as they might in a constitution such as that of the United States. Instead, as is well known, the scheme of the Human Rights Act empowers the higher courts in the United Kingdom to make a declaration of incompatibility[21] and that is what the House of Lords did in respect of Part 4 of the Anti-terrorism, Crime and Security Act.

The principle of equality was important to the decision in *Belmarsh* in two ways. First, the House of Lords held, by a large majority, that the discrimination between British citizens and foreign nationals in the context of a power of executive detention was unjustified and a breach of article 14 of the European Convention.[22] Although

---

[18] *Railway Express Agency Inc v New York* 336 US 106 (1949) at 112–13 as quoted by Lord Bingham at [46].

[19] Article 3 of the European Convention provides: 'No one shall be subjected to torture or to inhuman or degrading treatment or punishment'.

[20] Human Rights Act 1998 (Designated Derogation) Order 2001 (UK).

[21] Section 4.

[22] *Belmarsh*, above n 17, at [50]–[70] per Lord Bingham, [138] per Lord Hope, [157] per Lord Scott and [234]–[236] per Lady Hale.

the Government had derogated from article 5, it had not sought to derogate from article 14. But, secondly, the discrimination in issue had a more profound consequence. This is because it tended to undermine the justification put forward by the Government as to why the power of executive detention was needed at all – in other words the justification for the derogation even from article 5 did not make sense. Quite simply, the House of Lords could not understand what reason there could be for wishing to detain some, but not all, terrorist suspects without trial after 9/11. They therefore could see no rational connection between the aim of the legislation and the means chosen.[23] This need for a rational connection is one of the classic ingredients of the principle of proportionality, which is a critical tool of analysis and adjudication in human rights law.

It was also in *Belmarsh* that Lord Bingham met head-on the suggestion that there is anything undemocratic about the courts enforcing human rights. He was addressing an argument that had been made at the hearing by the Attorney-General and said:

> I do not ... accept the distinction he drew between democratic institutions and the courts. It is of course true that the judges in this country are not elected and are not answerable to Parliament. ... But the function of independent judges charged to interpret and apply the law is universally recognised as a cardinal feature of the modern democratic state, a cornerstone of the rule of law itself. The Attorney General is fully entitled to insist on the proper limits of judicial authority, but he is wrong to stigmatise judicial decision-making as in some way undemocratic. It is particularly inappropriate in a case such as the present in which Parliament has expressly legislated in section 6 of the [Human Rights Act] to render unlawful any act of a public authority, including a court, incompatible with a Convention right, has required courts (in section 2) to take account of relevant Strasbourg jurisprudence, has (in section 3) required courts, so far as possible, to give effect to Convention rights and has conferred a right of appeal on derogation issues [the issue in the case itself concerned the legality of the Government's derogation from the right to liberty in art 5 purportedly made under art 15 of the European Convention]. The effect is not, of course, to override the sovereign legislative authority of the Queen in Parliament, since if primary legislation is declared to be incompatible [as happened in *Belmarsh* itself] the validity of the legislation is unaffected (section 4(6)) and the remedy lies with the appropriate minister (section 10), who is answerable to Parliament. The [Human Rights Act] gives the courts a very specific, wholly democratic, mandate.[24]

I would add only that the remedy in practice very often lies with Parliament itself, as occurred in response to the judgment in *Belmarsh*, when primary legislation was quickly introduced to repeal Part 4 of the Anti-terrorism, Crime and Security Act, which had been declared by the House of Lords to be incompatible with human rights.

To this, one can also add the observations of Lady Hale in *R (Countryside Alliance) v Attorney General*, which concerned the compatibility of the Hunting Act 2004 (UK). This Act bans the hunting of wild mammals by chasing them with dogs, a controversial measure which was enacted by the House of Commons without

---

[23] *Belmarsh*, above n 17, at [43] per Lord Bingham, [132]–[133] per Lord Hope, [158] per Lord Scott, [188]–[189] per Lord Rodger and [231] per Lady Hale.
[24] At [42].

the consent of the unelected upper House using the procedure in the Parliament Act 1949 (UK):

> [113] The Human Rights Act 1998 has for the first time (outside the particular territory of European Community law …) given us all rights against the state. … If Parliament makes laws which might be incompatible with our Convention rights, the courts and others applying those laws must, so far as possible, read and give effect to them in a way which is compatible with the Convention rights: s 3(1). If Parliament makes a law which cannot be read compatibly with the Convention rights, the courts and others must still give effect to it, but the higher courts may declare that it is incompatible: … s 4. Such declarations have proved powerful incentives to Government and Parliament to put the matter right: for if the court is right, the United Kingdom is in breach of its international obligations in maintaining such a law on the statute book.

> [114] … the purpose of … human rights instruments is to place some limits upon what a democratically elected Parliament may do: to protect the rights and freedoms of individuals and minorities against the will of those who are taken to represent the majority. Democracy is the will of the people but the people may not will to invade those rights and freedoms which are fundamental to democracy itself.[25]

But she ended that passage with this important caveat: 'To qualify as such a fundamental right, a freedom must be something more than the freedom to do as we please, whether alone or in company with others'.[26]

This accords with another fundamental doctrine in the jurisprudence of the European Court of Human Rights, which has always emphasised that, while the only system of government which is compatible with the European Convention is a democratic one, a democratic society is not one which is simply a majoritarian one. Rather the Court has repeatedly stressed that a democratic society is one which is characterised by tolerance, pluralism and broad-mindedness.[27] It is that word 'pluralism' which is of particular interest in this context. It suggests not only different points of view but also strong civil society institutions which stand between the individual and the state, such as charities, trade unions, faith groups and other voluntary associations. It also suggests a society which is not afraid to have vigorous debate, in which important issues are discussed in an open and respectful way, where sometimes we may have to agree to differ rather than always impose our own view through the force of law, still less the coercion of the criminal law.

I am now coming to the end of my career at the Bar. It has been my privilege to have acted as an advocate in many interesting cases which have arisen under the Human Rights Act in its first 11 years of operation in the United Kingdom. I have appeared on behalf of the government and other public authorities as well as on behalf of individuals and non-governmental organisations. My personal view is that the Human Rights Act has had a humanising influence on our society and in particular our legal system. I have already mentioned *Belmarsh*, regarded by many people as the most important case decided in the United Kingdom since the Second World War.

---

[25] Parliament Act 1949 (UK), s 1; *R (Countryside Alliance) v Attorney General* [2007] UKHL 52, [2008] AC 719 (HL).
[26] At [114].
[27] See for example *Handyside v United Kingdom* (1976) 1 EHRR 737 (ECHR) at [49].

If that case had been decided the other way by the House of Lords, as it was by the Court of Appeal, there might still be some terrorist suspects languishing in prison in the United Kingdom without charge or trial.

I have also mentioned the *Ghaidan* case, which powerfully demonstrated the capacity of the Human Rights Act to advance the rights of same-sex couples even before the Civil Partnerships Act 2004 (UK) came into force.[28] In that case the House of Lords in effect departed from its own decision of just five years earlier, in which it had held that the succession rights given to the spouse of a deceased tenant by the Rent Act 1977 (UK), as amended, did not extend to a same-sex partner.[29] In *Ghaidan*, the House of Lords held unanimously that such an interpretation would violate article 14 of the European Convention, which prohibits discrimination in the enjoyment of the other rights in the European Convention – in that case the right to respect for the home in art 8. More controversially, the House of Lords also held, by a majority, that the relevant legislation could and therefore must be read as if the definition of spouse does include a same-sex partner. This was because of the strong interpretative obligation in section 3 of the Human Rights Act.[30]

I am aware that the Supreme Court of New Zealand has not felt able to follow a similar approach in the context of the interpretation provision in section 6 of the New Zealand Bill of Rights Act 1990.[31] It would not be appropriate for me to comment on whether that is right or desirable since that is a matter of New Zealand law. What I can say is that the outcome in *Ghaidan* can perhaps be understood in the particular context of the United Kingdom: I refer not only to the text of section 3 of the Human Rights Act but also the potential consequences if a compatible interpretation had not been possible in that case. There would almost certainly then have been issued a declaration of incompatibility under section 4. It would also probably have resulted in the government of the United Kingdom being found to be in breach of its international obligations under the European Convention by the European Court of Human Rights in Strasbourg. Compensation claims might then have been expected against the state rather than private landlords. As we shall see, the international legal framework which binds the United Kingdom in Europe has exercised a strong influence on the way in which the domestic courts have tended to interpret the Human Rights Act. This is what sometimes has been called the mirror principle, in other words the notion that the domestic statute should, so far as possible, reflect the position in Strasbourg.[32] It is not always possible to respect the mirror principle. However, my opinion is that the domestic courts in the United Kingdom strive to do so whenever they can.

An example is provided by the case of *R (Al-Skeini) v Secretary of State for Defence*, in which the House of Lords held, by a majority, that the Human Rights Act applied to British forces outside the territory of the United Kingdom in those

---

[28] *Ghaidan*, above n 16.

[29] *Fitzpatrick v Sterling Housing Association Ltd* [2001] 1 AC 27 (HL).

[30] This section requires that: 'So far as it is possible to do so, primary legislation and subordinate legislation must be read and given effect in a way which is compatible with Convention rights'.

[31] *Hansen v R* [2007] NZSC 7, [2007] 3 NZLR 1. See also Claudia Geiringer, 'The Principle of Legality and the Bill of Rights Act: A Critical Examination of *R v Hansen*' (2008) 6 *NZJPIL* 59.

[32] See *R (Ullah) v Special Adjudicator* [2004] UKHL 26, [2004] 2 AC 323 at [20] per Lord Bingham.

exceptional circumstances where a person fell within the jurisdiction of the United Kingdom within the meaning of article 1 of the European Convention, even though the events took place outside the territory of the United Kingdom.[33] It rejected the argument that, even in cases that fell within the jurisdiction of the United Kingdom and therefore could be actionable in the European Court of Human Rights, the Human Rights Act should be interpreted as having no application because it did not have any extra-territorial effect. Lord Rodger took the view that that argument would defeat the 'central purpose' of the Human Rights Act, which was to provide a remedial structure in domestic law for the rights guaranteed by the European Convention, as it would leave a victim without a remedy in the courts of the United Kingdom where they would have a remedy in Strasbourg.[34]

This had the important practical consequence that the case of Baha Mousa, who died in British custody in Iraq in September 2003, not only fell within the United Kingdom's jurisdiction under article 1 of the European Convention but was also one which was justiciable in the English courts. Eventually the Secretary of State for Defence established an independent public inquiry into the Baha Mousa incident. Sir William Gage, a retired Court of Appeal judge, conducted that inquiry in 2009–2010 and he is due to publish his report on 8 September 2011.[35] Sir William examined not only the individual circumstances which led up to the death of Baha Mousa and the ill-treatment of other detainees at the time but wider systemic issues about how certain techniques, which were prohibited and unlawful, had come to be used in Iraq. These techniques included hooding detainees and forcing them to adopt what are called 'stress positions'.[36] We await Sir William's report with interest but there can be little doubt that it will have a profound impact on the further development of moral standards in the United Kingdom's armed forces and perhaps on British society more generally.

Before I leave the case of *Al-Skeini* I should mention that the cases which were unsuccessful in the House of Lords proceeded to the European Court of Human Rights, where the Grand Chamber gave a unanimous judgment in favour of the applicants on 7 July 2011.[37] All of the victims who had died in that case were held to fall within the jurisdiction of the United Kingdom. There was held to have been a violation of the right to an effective and independent investigation of their deaths under article 2 of the European Convention.

Of course, it is important to appreciate that the United Kingdom was a free society committed to human rights even before the Human Rights Act. Many of the rights in the European Convention are based on concepts which were and remain embedded in the common law, such as personal liberty and the abhorrence of torture. However, the common law was not always up to the task of protecting human rights to the full extent required by modern international standards. The change effected

---

[33] *R (Al-Skeini) v Secretary of State for Defence* [2007] UKHL 26, [2008] AC 153 at [56].
[34] At [56].
[35] This paper is based on a lecture that was delivered shortly before the report of the Baha Mousa Public Inquiry by Sir William Gage was published on 8 September 2011: William Gage, *The Report of the Baha Mousa Public Inquiry* (HC 2010-12, 1452).
[36] See Gage, ibid, at [1.11].
[37] *Al-Skeini v United Kingdom* (2011) 53 EHRR 18 (Grand Chamber, ECHR).

by the Human Rights Act was clearly enunciated in the decision of the House of Lords in *R (Laporte) v Chief Constable of Gloucestershire*, a case about the freedom to demonstrate peacefully arising from an attempt to protest against the Iraq war at a United States airforce base at Fairford in England.[38] In a case decided by the Divisional Court in 1935, Lord Hewart CJ had observed that, although there had been much talk during the hearing of the right to protest, the common law did not know of such a right. He said that: 'English law does not recognise any special right of public meeting for political or other purposes'.[39] In 2006, with the Human Rights Act now firmly in place, Lord Bingham was able to refer to a 'constitutional shift' which had taken place, so that there certainly was a right to peaceful assembly in article 11 of the European Convention, which is one of the rights set out in Schedule 1 to the Human Rights Act.[40]

The case of *R (Limbuela) v Secretary of State for the Home Department* provides an important illustration not only of the potential of the Human Rights Act to have a humanising effect on society but also the subtle relationship between Parliament and the courts which has resulted from the Human Rights Act.[41] This case concerned the provisions of section 55 of the Nationality, Immigration and Asylum Act 2002 (UK). Section 55(1) was on its face a draconian measure, which prohibited the Secretary of State for the Home Department from giving any support to a person who had not claimed asylum as soon as reasonably practicable after arriving in the United Kingdom. In practice this had the consequence that many asylum claimants were refused any support in circumstances where they had sought to claim asylum a few days after arrival in the United Kingdom but not at the port of arrival, which may have been because of linguistic, cultural or other understandable difficulties. They could not be given any accommodation, food or washing facilities. And they could not lawfully work since they were not permitted to do so. It was difficult to see what they could do to support themselves except resort to begging, crime or prostitution.

But section 55 contained a curious provision which in the end proved to be its own undoing. Section 55(5) provided an exception to the apparently draconian effect of section 55(1) to the extent necessary for the purpose of avoiding a breach of a person's rights under the Human Rights Act. Although the precise extent of this obligation was left uncertain by Parliament, this left the way open to the House of Lords to hold that, in many cases, it would be necessary to provide certain basic support to an asylum claimant since otherwise he or she would be subjected to inhuman or degrading treatment, which is in breach of article 3 of the European Convention. As Lady Hale put it:

> It might be possible to endure rooflessness for some time without degradation if one had enough to eat and somewhere to wash oneself and one's clothing. It might be possible to endure cashlessness for some time if one had a roof and basic meals and hygiene facilities provided. But to have to endure the indefinite prospect of both, unless one is in a place where it is both possible and legal to live off the land, is in today's society both inhuman and degrading.[42]

---

[38] *R (Laporte) v Chief Constable of Gloucestershire* [2006] UKHL 55, [2007] 2 AC 105.
[39] *Duncan v Jones* [1936] 1 KB 218 at 222.
[40] *Laporte*, above n 38, at [34].
[41] *R (Limbuela) v Secretary of State for the Home Department* [2005] UKHL 66, [2006] 1 AC 396.
[42] At [78].

And Lady Hale went on to provide an important insight into the practical effect of the legislation on women in particular when she said:

> If a woman … had been expected to live indefinitely in a London car park, without access to the basic sanitary products which any woman of that age needs and exposed to the risks which any defenceless woman faces on the streets at night, would we have been in any doubt that her suffering would very soon reach the minimum degree of severity required under Article 3? I think not.[43]

As I have mentioned, the drafting of the legislation which was considered in *Limbuela* was influenced by the moral force exerted by human rights principles. This is a good example of the impact which the Human Rights Act has had, not just in the court-room, but in the wider sphere of policy-making. This impact can also be seen in the important work done by the Joint Committee on Human Rights. This is a joint committee of both Houses of Parliament, which has a legal adviser. Among its functions is the task of advising Parliament on draft Bills as they go through the legislative process and, in particular, to assess their compatibility with human rights.[44] This is important in a democracy: human rights should not be regarded as being relevant only, or even primarily, to litigation. They belong to all of us and those of us who are fortunate to live in democracies can feel some pride that our elected parliaments take human rights seriously.

The understandable question that is often raised when a person, especially an unappealing one like a convicted criminal or a terrorist suspect, relies on human rights is: 'what about your duties? What about responsibilities?' In the United Kingdom, the Labour Government of Tony Blair which introduced the Human Rights Act felt it necessary to use the phrase 'rights and responsibilities' almost as a mantra. In the Australian state of Victoria, when a Labor government introduced the Charter of Human Rights and Responsibilities Act 2006 (Vic) in 2006, it was felt important that its title should include the word 'responsibilities' as well as the word 'rights'. The traditional answer to this question which is given by supporters of human rights is the one given by Tom Paine when the question was raised in the National Assembly after the French Revolution, when it was debating the Declaration of the Rights of Man and the Citizen. Paine said that there was no need to spell out the citizen's duties since rights belong to each one of us and so inevitably, if we have rights, we also have a duty to respect the rights of others.[45] As has sometimes been noted, my freedom to swing my arm ends where your nose begins.

In my view, while that answer is a good one, it is not by itself sufficient. The problem is that the concept of reciprocity, while it is an important moral principle, is not the basis of a legal obligation. The legal obligation in the Human Rights Act to act in a way which is compatible with the rights in Schedule 1 is not imposed on private individuals or corporations. It is imposed by section 6 only on public authorities. There is a similar provision in section 3 of the New Zealand Bill of Rights Act 1990. This reflects the position in international law generally, that human rights

---

[43] At [78].
[44] Standing Orders of the House of Commons 2012, SO 152B.
[45] Thomas Paine, *Rights of Man* (Peterborough, Broadview Press, 2011) at 147.

obligations are imposed on states and not on individuals or corporations. Time does not permit me to deal here with the important topic of positive obligations, which can sometimes arise under the European Convention and other treaties. However, the significant point for present purposes is to note that such positive obligations, when they do arise under treaties, are still imposed on the state. They are not imposed directly on private individuals or entities. The state may be in breach of its positive obligations if it fails to put in place measures to protect one individual from another, but the individual affected will still not be able to take legal action against the other individual. In that sense, neither the European Convention nor the Human Rights Act has horizontal effect.

It seems to me that several more answers need to be given as to why a human rights charter like the Human Rights Act does not set out a list of duties and responsibilities as well. The first answer is that actually to some extent it does. For example, the text of article 10(2) of the European Convention expressly refers to the 'duties and responsibilities' which accompany the right to freedom of expression. There is a deeper point here. As I mentioned at the outset, the European Convention is descended from the Universal Declaration of Human Rights, to which it refers in its preamble. Article 29(1) of the Declaration provides that: 'Everyone has duties to the community in which alone the free and full development of his personality is possible'.

The whole of the law of human rights is infused with notions of balance between the rights of the individual and the general interest. It is untrue and alarmist when it is suggested that human rights law allows criminals to escape detection or punishment or that the rights of a wrongdoer can never be limited or curtailed. Very few rights are absolute. The one major exception is the rule against torture. Most rights can be restricted provided this is done in accordance with law, for a legitimate purpose such as the prevention of crime or disorder or for the protection of the rights of others and (most importantly) provided a fair balance is struck in accordance with the principle of proportionality.

The second part of the answer, it seems to me, is that in fact the whole of the rest of the law sets out a person's duties. If you go just to the criminal law part of any series of statutes, you will see laws that now run into thousands. And of course in England, many criminal offences are still offences at common law and have not been codified in legislation. And then there are all the duties imposed by the civil law. The whole point of a bill of rights is to have a short, simple statement of a person's basic rights which can be relied upon as an enclave or oasis within the vast framework of the rest of the legal system.

The third part of the answer that can be given, it seems to me, is that if the law were to attempt to set out a person's duties and responsibilities, they would either be repetitive and superfluous, as in stating that a person has a duty to obey the criminal law or to pay such taxes as are lawfully due, or (worse) would be vacuous as they would be unenforceable as a matter of legal obligation. There has already been a tendency in recent times for legislation to be enacted not because it is needed or is even intended to have any practical effect but in order to make some gesture.

Having said all of that, I am not opposed to the concept that in principle there should be responsibilities set out in a basic charter, for example to serve on a jury, a general anti-avoidance tax law, perhaps even to vote, as there is in Australia but not in the United Kingdom or New Zealand. It is arguable that such a statement of the basic duties of the citizen can have a useful educational role to play, just as one of the purposes of a bill of rights is to educate the public as to everyone's fundamental rights in a free and democratic society.

In conclusion, the Human Rights Act is currently the United Kingdom's bill of rights. Like all such charters of fundamental human rights, it is more than an ordinary law: its influence ranges beyond the courtroom to Parliament, the executive, the media and to the public generally. It is intended to lay down fundamental values for society and not detailed rules of law. The Human Rights Act also has important rhetorical force and has generated some eloquent prose from some of the most senior judges in the United Kingdom such as the late Lord Bingham, Lord Steyn and Lady Hale. They have reminded us of the moral force of the Human Rights Act and its fundamental values such as liberty, equality and the rule of law.

However, in the words of the famous Chinese curse, we live in 'interesting times'. In the last decade we have witnessed not only the terrible events of 9/11 and the London bombings of '7/7', but also the worst economic crisis since the 1930s and widespread public disorder. This is a troubled world and I wish I could pretend otherwise. But things have been bad before, much worse. Those who came before us and handed down to us the Universal Declaration of Human Rights and the European Convention did not flinch even in the most dangerous period of the twentieth century. Modern human rights law was born out of the ashes of the atrocities of the Second World War. It must fall to us to keep those values alive in the twenty-first century when they are under challenge from so many different angles.

The Place of the Human Rights Act in a Democratic Society

I gave this talk in 2000 (at a time when I was still a barrister) at University College London, around the time when the Human Rights Act was about to come into full force. It was first published in a book edited by Jeffrey Jowell QC and Jonathan Cooper, Understanding Human Rights Principles *(Oxford, Hart Publishing, 2001). I traced the history of the HRA and sought to place it in its context. I suggested that it was to be a democratic bill of rights for the UK, in particular because of the unique way in which it seeks to reconcile the legislative supremacy of Parliament with the protection of fundamental human rights. The HRA does not enable the courts to strike down primary legislation but it does give them the function of assessing the compatibility of primary legislation with the Convention rights and gives them the power to make a declaration of incompatibility.*

This paper will look at three topics:

- the political and philosophical background to the relationship between fundamental human rights and democracy;
- the principles developed in the case law of the European Court of Human Rights on that relationship; and
- the features of the Human Rights Act 1998 which make it a democratic Bill of Rights.

THE POLITICAL AND PHILOSOPHICAL BACKGROUND TO THE RELATIONSHIP BETWEEN FUNDAMENTAL HUMAN RIGHTS AND DEMOCRACY

ALTHOUGH THE PHILOSOPHICAL origins of human rights go back to ancient times, the modern idea of human rights burst onto the political stage in the eighteenth century. At that time there was in the minds of its proponents a congruence between popular government (or at least a limited form of it, usually confined to white men who had some property) and fundamental rights. When Paine talked of the 'rights of man' he was writing in the main about the right of the people to self-government.[1] When the Second Continental Congress adopted the American

---

[1] T Paine, *The Rights of Man* (original 1791–92) (Harmondsworth, Penguin, 1984).

Declaration of Independence, its famous second paragraph[2] was as much about the legitimate basis of government – the consent of the governed – as it was about the fundamental rights which it announced to be self-evidently the endowments of all 'men'. The revolutionaries in the United States and France fairly early on decided to impose legal limits on the powers of the new, republican governments they were creating. In 1789 the National Assembly issued the Declaration of the Rights of Man and the Citizen, which in some form has remained a part of the French republican constitutions until today. The US Constitution of 1787 did not originally contain a list of fundamental human rights, although the individual states did usually include such a declaration in their constitutions, most famously Virginia and Massachusetts, which both played a crucial role in the revolution, through such figures as Jefferson, Madison and the 'Adams family', Samuel and John. But the Constitution quickly acquired a Bill of Rights in 1791, in the form of the first ten Amendments. Those amendments, together with the important amendments passed after the Civil War, in particular the Fourteenth Amendment, which guarantees due process and the equal protection of the laws against the state governments, became the modem American Bill of Rights. The American system is one that combines commitment to democracy with a profound belief in fundamental rights. As the US Supreme Court judge, Justice Jackson, put it in *West Virginia State Board of Education v Barnette*:

> The very purpose of a Bill of Rights was to withdraw certain subjects from the vicissitudes of political controversy, to place them beyond the reach of majorities and officials and to establish them as legal principles to be applied by the courts. One's right to life, liberty, and property, to free speech, a free press, freedom of worship and assembly, and other fundamental rights may not be submitted to vote; they depend on the outcome of no elections.[3]

The revolutionary tradition which was started in the eighteenth century carried on in the nineteenth and twentieth centuries, as former colonies of the European powers became independent. They usually created a constitution which was based on the Westminster form of parliamentary government, but with an American style Bill of Rights attached to it: the best example is perhaps India, which became a republic in 1950 (a plaque commemorating Dr Ambedkar, the architect of that constitution, can be found in the garden of Gray's Inn, of which he was a member). And in more recent times, as the former Communist countries of the Eastern bloc have become democracies, they have not rushed to adopt a Westminster style of constitution but rather have joined the family of those democratic nations which recognise that it is essential to have a Bill of Rights for a proper democracy to function (a theme to which I return later).

In contrast, Britain, which had had its revolution earlier than the rest of the world, has for the last two centuries travelled a different path. Its revolution had in a sense occurred a century too soon. The Glorious Revolution of 1688 was concerned with a different problem – wresting power from the Crown and vesting it in the legislature.

---

[2] The second paragraph reads: 'We hold these truths to be self-evident; that all men are created equal; that they are endowed by their Creator with certain unalienable rights; that among these are life, liberty and the pursuit of happiness; that to secure these rights governments are instituted among men, deriving their just powers from the consent of the governed'. See further P Maier, *American Scripture: How America Declared its Independence from Britain* (London, Pimlico, 1999).

[3] 319 US 624 (1943) at 638.

So in Britain we talk about parliamentary sovereignty rather than the sovereignty of the people. In contrast, the American War of Independence was fought about the limits of Parliamentary power: the Americans did not accept Parliaments assertion in the Declaratory Act 1766 that it had power to make laws for the colonies 'in all cases whatsoever'.[4]

This was not because Britain has not been a free country for the last two centuries. To the contrary, liberalism 'with a small l' has been a powerful creed and for much of the time between 1830 and 1915 the Liberal Party 'with a big L' was in power. The economic philosophy of the age was *laissez faire* at home and free trade abroad and much of what governments did was about removing legal barriers to individual achievement, such as religious qualifications for admission to the ancient universities and paper duties, a 'tax on public knowledge' the removal of which led to a big increase in the circulation of newspapers.[5] On the political front, although democracy was not fully achieved until after the First World War, the main campaign for reform for a century was for the extension of the franchise, to working class men and to women. Even the People's Charter of 1838, which set out the demands of the Chartists, was not a Bill of Rights: its six points all related to the democratisation of Parliament – all but one of the six points (that there should be annual Parliaments) have been achieved.

The attainment of universal suffrage was a big achievement and its importance should not be underestimated. But the dominant strand in British liberalism was utilitarianism. This fitted in well with the general *Zeitgeist* in the economic sphere, it was suited to the creation of free markets, in which the individual would decide what ought to be produced through consumer demand and, in the political sphere, it made sense of the extension of the franchise, which was the equivalent of the free market in that it allowed everyone to have a say and the majority would prevail. When the Labour Party took over from the Liberals as the main party opposed to the forces of conservatism after the First World War, the utilitarians had a new home. Fabian socialism was not particularly concerned about the rights of the individual: it was concerned about improving the general welfare of society and to use parliamentary power once captured through the democratic franchise to effect that improvement. So the dominant creed, although it was progressive, was at best neutral and at worst hostile to the notion of human rights. As Tony Wright MP – the intellectual voice of new Labour – puts it:

> If British socialism was about using the state to achieve social and economic objectives, then the British constitution seemed to put the state at the disposal of majority parties. The left was instrumental in defining a twentieth-century theory and practice of the constitution that sustained this view, and in defending it against those who hankered after something else. ... Dicey may not have liked socialism ... but socialists have nevertheless liked Dicey's constitution. Its doctrine of sovereignty, once rooted in an enfranchised people, enabled a parliamentary majority to get its way.[6]

---

[4] Maier (n 2) 77.
[5] See R Jenkins, *Gladstone* (London, Macmillan, 1995) 225.
[6] T Wright, *Citizens and Subjects* (London, Routledge, 1994) 59–60.

And yet the tension between the majority and the rights of individuals or minorities never went away. The most famous expression of the concern for protection from the tyranny of the majority came in John Stuart Mill's famous essay *On Liberty*.[7] Now, more than two centuries after Paine was convicted in his absence for seditious libel in publishing the second part of *The Rights of Man* we have come to realise that a modem democracy does after all need a Bill of Rights. And in so doing we have re-joined the mainstream of democratic societies.

How is the concept of fundamental human rights to be reconciled with democracy? At first sight it seems obvious that the two are irreconcilable. Democracy seems to fit well with utilitarianism. If one believes that there is no particular view of life which is better than others and the correct course to take is what the majority want, it can be said that this will maximise the greatest happiness of the greatest number. On that view, it does not matter that the opinions of others, however deeply held as a matter of conscience they may be, are crushed on the way.

However, experience has taught us that this is a shortsighted view of democracy. For one thing, if the people are to make informed decisions as they exercise their vote, they must have freedom to receive and impart ideas. So immediately a fundamental right to freedom of expression becomes an integral component in the machinery of democracy. Furthermore, history has also taught us that the views of the eccentric and the heretic sometimes end up becoming the orthodoxy of the majority: Galileo and Darwin provide obvious examples. So the right to freedom of thought and freedom of expression has to be given time to flourish. When experiments are being conducted, no one knows at the outset how things are going to turn out. This gives us the insight that democracy, if it is good thing, is something we should want to continue. In other words, democracy is entitled to protect itself. Oliver Wendell Holmes famously put it this way in *Abrams v United States*:

> Persecution for the expression of opinions seems to me perfectly logical. If you have no doubt of your premises or your power and want a certain result with all your heart you naturally express your wishes in law and sweep away all opposition. ... But when men have realized that time has upset many fighting faiths, they may come to believe even more than they believe the very foundations of their own conduct that the ultimate good desired is better reached in free trade in ideas – that the best test of truth is the power of the thought to get itself accepted in the competition of the market ... Every year if not every day we have to wager our salvation upon some prophecy based upon imperfect knowledge. While that experiment is part of our system I think that we should be eternally vigilant against attempts to check the expression of opinions that we loathe and believe to be fraught with death, unless they so imminently threaten immediate interference with the lawful and pressing purposes of the law that an immediate check is required to save the country.[8]

But this still leaves a problem. We know from human rights jurisprudence that what it requires is more than just the protection of freedom of expression. How, for example,

---

[7] JS Mill, *On Liberty* (original 1859) in JS Mill, *Utilitarianism* (London, Collins, 1979).
[8] 250 US 616 (1919) at 630. Holmes J (with whom Brandeis J concurred) dissented but his views have become the orthodoxy in American First Amendment jurisprudence.

is the decision that gay people have the right to serve in the armed forces to be reconciled with an apparent decision by the majority that they do not want homosexuals in those forces? In my view, the link is provided by the concept of equality. Democracy is a wonderful thing because it treats everyone as an equal. No matter what your social background or education, when it comes to the ballot box you have one vote – like everyone else. There is no *a priori* reason why this should be so. We could have a rule that the more money a person earns or the more tax they pay (which is not necessarily the same thing) the more votes they should have. But no one would seriously suggest such changes to the franchise today.

This suggests that underlying democracy are more basic notions. Those notions are that legitimate government rests on the consent of the governed and that everyone is equal – we all count but no one counts any more than anyone else. This is reflected in Article 1 of the Universal Declaration of Human Rights, which announces that all human beings are born free *and equal* in dignity and rights. The right to vote in Article 21(3) of the Declaration also refers to the right to universal and equal suffrage. Democracy should therefore be seen as a community of free and equal participants.[9] If the majority from time to time could simply use their power to attack the minority it would be to treat them as not equal or free at all but subjects whose survival depends on the good will of the majority. That cannot be right.

On the other hand, the majority have to be able to get things done. After all, the purpose of government is to govern. This is where the concept of 'necessity' comes in. To recognise that a person has a fundamental right is not to say that it must always prevail. Other interests are also important but the fundamental human rights should be curtailed only where there is a need to do so and even then only to the extent that it is necessary to do so. Putting it the other way, why should someone's private life be interfered with unnecessarily? Everyone of the majority who say that they do not want gays in the armed forces would say that their own (heterosexual) private lives are their business and no one else's. So why should others be sacrificed on the altar of popular demand simply because they do not have the numerical strength to protect themselves? We know from common sense that, if the tables were turned and we were at risk of interference with our privacy by others – whether those of a different religion, a different race or a different political grouping – we would not think it right that their will could prevail simply because they had strength of numbers on their side. We should be willing to give others the same concern and respect. This common sense insight is what Kant meant when he referred to the principle of universalisability or, even more obscurely, the categorical imperative: we should treat others as we would have them treat us.

The concept of equality also underlies many of the substantive rights which are found in charters of rights such as the European Convention on Human Rights. For example, freedom of expression and freedom of religion are both based on the fundamental notion that it is not the business of the State to choose between

---

[9] See Immanuel Kant, *Political Writings* (ed H Reiss) (Cambridge, Cambridge University Press, 1991) 73; Ronald Dworkin, *A Bill of Rights for Britain* (London, Chatto & Windus, 1990) 35.

different doctrines or ideologies and impose them on individuals. As Justice Jackson once said:

> If there is any fixed star in our constitutional constellation, it is that no official, high or petty, can prescribe what shall be orthodox in politics, nationalism, religion or other matters of opinion to force citizens to confess by word or act their faith therein.[10]

The concept of equality could and should play a greater part in human rights juris-prudence after incorporation than it has necessarily done in the case-law of the European Court of Human Rights. For example, in *Wingrove v United Kingdom*,[11] the Court held, by a majority, that the refusal of a classification certificate for the video 'Visions of Ecstasy' on the ground that it was blasphemous was permissible under Article 10(2) of the ECHR, having regard to the wide margin of apprecia-tion afforded to Contracting States in the field of morals. However, Judge Loehmus perceptively pointed out in dissent that, although it may be possible to justify such a ban in a democratic society, the justification itself should not be discriminatory:[12] the English law of blasphemy is discriminatory, because it protects Christianity but not other religions.

It remains to be seen whether such discrimination will survive the incorporation of the Convention rights into domestic law.

THE PRINCIPLES IN THE CASE-LAW OF THE EUROPEAN COURT OF HUMAN RIGHTS ON THE RELATIONSHIP BETWEEN DEMOCRACY AND HUMAN RIGHTS

The European Court of Human Rights has long recognised that the rights in the European Convention on Human Rights (ECHR) are essential features of a demo-cratic society. It has placed particular stress on the role of freedom expression, including freedom of the press, in a democracy. In *Lingens v Austria*[13] the Court said:

> Freedom of the press ... affords the public one of the best means of discovering and form-ing an opinion of the ideas and attitudes of political leaders. More generally, freedom of political debate is at the very core of the concept of a democratic society which prevails throughout the Convention.

The Court has also stressed the important link between freedom of expression and the right in Article 3 Protocol 1 to take part in free elections. In *Bowman v United Kingdom*[14] it said:

> Free elections and freedom of expression, particularly freedom of political debate, together form the bedrock of any democratic system. ... For this reason it is particularly important

---

[10] *West Virginia State Board of Education v Barnette* 319 US 624 (1943) at 642. The Supreme Court held in that case that children who were Jehovah's Witnesses could not be compelled to salute the US flag at school. Contrast the decision of the European Court of Human Rights in *Valsamis v Greece* (1997) 24 EHRR 294.
[11] (1997) 24 EHRR 1.
[12] ibid p 38, para 4.
[13] (1986) 8 EHRR 407, para 42.
[14] (1988) 26 EHRR 1, para 42.

in the period preceding an election that opinions and information of all kinds are permitted to circulate freely.

But the Court tends to use the phrase 'a democratic society' in a wider sense than just the political system we would call a democracy. It regards the substantive rights in the ECHR as being inherent in the concept of a democratic society. For example, in *Kokkinakis v Greece*[15] the Court said:

> As enshrined in Article 9, freedom of thought, conscience and religion is one of the foundations of a 'democratic society' *within the meaning of the Convention* … The pluralism indissociable from a democratic society, which has been dearly won over the centuries, depends on it.

Even rights such as the right to a fair hearing in Article 6 of the ECHR, which might be thought to be rights associated with the legal system rather than the political system, are regarded by the European Court of Human Rights as defining the concept of a democratic society envisaged by the ECHR. For example, in *Delcourt v Belgium*[16] the Court said:

> In a democratic society within the meaning of the Convention, the right to the fair administration of justice holds such a prominent place that a restrictive interpretation of Article 6(1) would not correspond to the aim and the purpose of that provision.

When it comes to restrictions on the rights in the ECHR, the concept of a democratic society again plays a vital role. There are three kinds of rights in the ECHR:

(1) absolute and unqualified rights;
(2) rights where an interference is permitted where it is 'necessary in a democratic society'; and
(3) rights where interference is permitted where some other interest outweighs the right in question.

In category (1) no balancing is required or permitted. Indeed, some of these rights are so important in the Convention system that they cannot be derogated from even in time of war or national emergency.[17] The rights which fall into this category are the right to life in Article 2, the right to be free from torture and inhuman or degrading treatment in article 3, the right to be free from slavery in Article 4(1) and the freedom from retrospective criminal penalties in Article 7. It might be said that, in a democracy, even these rights ought in principle to be capable of being overridden when necessary in a national emergency. However, the view taken by the framers of the ECHR was that they should be non-derogable as well as absolute and all the countries which have accepted the obligations in the ECHR are democracies that did so willingly.

The second category contains the rights which are expressly qualified in the text of the ECHR: the right to respect for private and family life, the home and correspondence in Article 8; the right to freedom to manifest one's religion in Article 9 (though note that the right to freedom of conscience in the same article is unqualified,

---

[15] (1994) 17 EHRR 397, para 31 (emphasis added).
[16] (1979–80) 1 BHRK 355, para 26.
[17] Article 15 of the ECHR.

so making a distinction between what is internal to one's heart and mind and what is manifested externally, because the latter may have an impact on others); the right to freedom of expression in Article 10 and the right to freedom of peaceful assembly and association in Article 11. As is well known, these rights may be interfered with but only if the interference is 'prescribed by law'/'in accordance with the law'; where the interference has a legitimate aim; where there is a pressing social need and where the interference meets the test of proportionality. In *Sunday Times v United Kingdom*,[18] the Court said that what is necessary is more than what is 'desirable' or 'reasonable', although it need not be indispensable. Clearly the more important the right in the scheme of the ECHR, the more convincing the reasons required to justify a restriction on them.

Even in the context of freedom of expression, however, the European Court of Human Rights in fact takes a flexible approach. The right to freedom of expression is given greatest protection in the case of political speech: this is consistent with the view that freedom of expression is essential for the healthy functioning of a democratic society. Other kinds of speech, such as commercial advertising, are less likely to contribute to the democratic process and are given less protection.[19] In any event, those who are regulated by restrictions on commercial speech, such as tobacco companies, can be expected to have the opportunity to lobby politicians and exercise their influence through the democratic process. Commercial speech is, therefore, an area in which the Court tends to take the view that restrictions are best left to the margin of appreciation afforded to Contracting States.[20] More controversially, the Court has not been particularly astute to protect artistic speech, as in *Mueller v Switzerland*[21] (which concerned an exhibition of pictures which were said to be obscene) and *Wingrove v United Kingdom*[22] (which, as mentioned above, concerned the ban on the video 'Visions of Ecstasy'). It may well be that the courts of this country, when they come to consider similar cases after incorporation, will take a more rigorous approach to the protection of artistic speech. After all, it is difficult to distinguish between art and politics; so much of what people believe comes from habits of mind created over many years through cultural influences. And it is precisely in the context of artistic speech that there is the greatest danger that the lone voice of dissent will be silenced simply because the majority do not like what is said, rather than because it is necessary to meet some pressing social need.

Also in the second category are rights which are not qualified in express terms but which the European Court of Human Rights has held are subject to implied limitations. One of these is the right to a fair hearing in Article 6(1) of the ECHR: for example in *Osman v United Kingdom*[23] the Court engaged in an assessment of proportionality in deciding whether an apparently general immunity conferred on the police from actions for negligence was compatible with the right to a fair hearing

---

[18] (1979–80) 2 BHRK 245, para 59.
[19] See eg *Casado Coca v Spain* (1994) 18 EHRR 1, which concerned regulation of professional advertising.
[20] See eg *Marki Intern and Beermann v Germany* (1990) 12 EHRR 161, para 32, which concerned statements made for the purposes of competition.
[21] (1991) 13 EHRR 212.
[22] (1996) 24 EHRR 1.
[23] (2000) 29 EHRR 245.

of such claims. Another, more controversial, example is the presumption of innocence in article 6(2). On the face of it that provision is entirely unqualified. Yet the Court has held that it is subject to reasonable limitations which maintain the rights of the defence: see *Salabiaku v France*.[24] The case-law on this is relatively under-developed in Strasbourg and the exact scope of the 'reasonable limitations' will need to be worked out after incorporation, but the concept of implied qualifications does reflect the common sense view that there will be exceptions to the normal rule that the prosecution should bear the burden of proof on every issue. There are well-known exceptions in English law, for example where a defendant claims the advantage of an exception or an excuse conferred by the statute which creates an offence.[25]

The third category of rights is those which may be qualified but where the test of necessity is not applied. The best example of this is the right to property (or peaceful enjoyment of possessions, as it is put in Article 1 of Protocol 1). This article does not require either the deprivation of property or control of its use to be 'necessary in a democratic society'. It uses the more flexible phrases 'in the public interest' and 'in accordance with the general interest'. The European Court of Human Rights has made it clear that the question of whether there is a public purpose for which property should be taken or regulated is one for the national authorities and that the Court will interfere only if that judgment is manifestly devoid of reasonable foundation.[26] Likewise, although the test of proportionality is not entirely absent from the case-law on Article 1, the Court has stressed that it will give a wide margin of appreciation to national authorities in this context.

Moreover, it is worth noting two further features of the case-law on the right to property. The first is that the Court has stressed not only the margin of appreciation, in the more general sense that delineates the respective responsibilities of national authorities and the supranational court, but also the special place enjoyed by the legislature in this context.[27] The second point to note is that the Court has also stressed that the Convention does not impose any particular political philosophy on Contracting States. The Court is clearly aware of the controversial nature of the right to property and that decisions about the control of its use are the stuff of democratic debate. It is in that context that most questions arising under Article 1 of Protocol 1 should be resolved.

Although the concept of margin of appreciation is not one which should be imported into national law after incorporation,[28] this is one context in which the alternative concept of 'due deference' to the democratically accountable parts of the state should play a prominent role. Otherwise there is a real risk that the courts will be drawn into areas where they are relatively unqualified to tread, as happened in the United States in the early part of the twentieth century, when the Supreme Court

---

[24] (1991) 13 EHRR 379. See further *R v Director of Public Prosecutions, ex p Kebilene* [1993] 3 WLR 972, especially the opinion of Lord Hope of Craighead.

[25] See eg *R v Hunt (Richard)* [1987] AC 352.

[26] See eg *James v United Kingdom* (1986) 8 EHRR 123.

[27] ibid.

[28] See eg R Singh, M Hunt and M Demetriou, 'Is there a role for the "margin of appreciation" in national kw after the Human Rights Act?' [1999] *EHRLR* 15; and *R v Director of Public Prosecutions, ex p Kebilene* [1999] 3 WLR 972 at 993–94 (Lord Hope of Craighead on the 'discretionary area of judgment').

struck down state welfare laws such as those which sought to regulate the number of hours that children could work: *Lochner v New York*.[29] As Oliver Wendell Holmes said in dissent in that case, the economic theories of Herbert Spencer are not part of the US Constitution. It would be better if our courts took the same position on which the US Supreme Court settled from the late 1930s that it would jealously guard certain rights such as freedom of speech and the rights of 'discrete and insular minorities'[30] but that questions of economic regulation would be left to the democratic organs of the State, provided they had a rational basis.

It is important to note that the phrase 'in a democratic society' has substantive content and is not mere verbiage. The European Court of Human Rights has stressed that the concept of a democratic society which is reflected in the ECHR is not one in which the majority as it is from time to time simply has its way. Rather it is characterised by pluralism, tolerance and brand-mindedness: the classic exposition of this was in *Handyside v United Kingdom*.[31] It is worth dwelling on what a pluralist society is. It is one in which there are fluctuating groups which overlap and which may come together from time to time to form a majority. For example, a person may be wealthy or poor, unemployed or in work, male or female, a trade union member or not, of a particular religion or of no religion, gay or straight, black or white. Most of the time the democratic process should allow people to decide for themselves how they want their political representatives to coalesce around these various interests. The main political parties are coalitions, sometimes uneasy ones, of all these groups and others. Most of the time, at least in theory it should possible for today's minorities to become tomorrow's majority by joining forces with others around a common programme. But sometimes there is a systemic failure. There may be no conventional political party that has much interest in representing the interest of a particular group or it may take their support for granted. They may not have the vote at all. It is in such circumstances that the ordinary give and take of the democratic process is unlikely to protect the rights of a vulnerable and unpopular minority.

To make the point less abstract, look at the groups of people who have been 'clients' of the European Court of Human Rights from this country. The United Kingdom accepted the right of individual petition under the ECHR in 1966. Most people rightly believe that they have since that time – and before – been living in a free country. They have not needed to trouble themselves with the ECHR or what it said. But consider the people who have had to take the long and hard road to Strasbourg to vindicate their rights.

The first main group comprised immigrants or potential immigrants. In the notorious *East African Asians case*[32] the European Commission of Human Rights found that the Commonwealth Immigrants Act 1968, passed in a hurry by a Labour Government to stop British passport holders in East Africa from coming to the United Kingdom as they faced persecution in their home countries, was motivated by racism.

---

[29] 198 US 45 (1905).

[30] See the famous dicta of Stone J in *United states v Caroline Products Co*. 304 US 144 (1938) at 152–53, n 4.

[31] (1979–80) 1 EHRR 737, para 49.

[32] (1981) 3 EHRR 76. The Commission considered the case in 1973.

It held that in such circumstances racial discrimination could amount to degrading treatment contrary to Article 3 of the ECHR. The case was the subject of a 'friendly settlement' and did not proceed to the court. Other famous cases about immigration have included *Abdulaziz, Cabales and Balkandali v United Kingdom*[33] (on the splitting up of families in a way which was discriminatory against women) and *Chahal v United Kingdom*[34] (which concerned among other things, the absence of effective judicial scrutiny of deportation orders made on the grounds of national security).

The second main group of people who have had to go to Strasbourg were gay men and lesbians: the two famous cases are *Dudgeon v United Kingdom*[35] and the recent one of *Lustig-Prean v United Kingdom*,[36] to which I will return in more detail. Another sexual minority have been transsexuals: four of the five major cases in the Court involving transsexuals have been brought against the United Kingdom: *Rees*,[37] *Cossey*,[38] *X, Y and Z*[39] and *Sheffield and Horsham*.[40] Each time the Court of Human Rights has suggested that in time it might come to view the position of English law, that a person's gender fixed for all time at birth, as conflicting with the right to respect for private life. The Court has held that Article 8 of the ECHR does not require the English legal system to recognise a change effected by gender re-assignment surgery but the votes in favour of these judgments have been going down with every case: in *Sheffield and Horsham*, the majority was only 11 judges to nine. Since the decisions have rested on the Strasbourg concept of the margin of appreciation, and since the rule of English law is a judge-made one (first laid down in *Corbett v Corbett*)[41] rather than a statutory one, there is every chance that, after incorporation, the courts will reconsider it. Other groups of people that have had to go to Strasbourg include mental patients,[42] travellers[43] and prisoners, particularly in cases involving executive decisions in the field of sentencing.[44]

All of these groups had to go to Strasbourg because they had nowhere else to go for legal remedies. English law had failed them. A good example of the European Court approach to the issues in this paper, and how it differs from the traditional English law approach, is provided by the gays in the military case.

In *Lusting-Prean v United Kingdom*[45] the applicants had been compulsorily discharged from the armed forces, after enquiries about their private lives, on the ground that they were homosexuals. The applicants sought judicial review of the ban in the domestic courts. The Divisional Court (Simon Brown LJ and Curtis J) refused the applications because the ban was not irrational or *Wednesbury* unreasonable.[46]

---

[33] (1987) 7 EHRR 471.
[34] (1996) 23 EHRR 413.
[35] (1981) 4 EHRR 149.
[36] (2000) 29 EHRR 548.
[37] (1987) 9 EHRR 56.
[38] (1991) 3 EHRR 622.
[39] (1998) 24 EHRR 143.
[40] (1999) 27 EHRR 163.
[41] (1971) P 83.
[42] Eg *X v United Kingdom* (1981) 4 EHRR 188.
[43] Eg *Buckley v United Kingdom* (1997) 23 EHRR 101.
[44] Eg *Hussain v United Kingdom* (1996) 23 EHRR 1.
[45] (2000) 29 EHRR 548.
[46] (1996) QB 517.

Simon Brown LJ did express the view that the ban was not likely to survive scrutiny in the European Court of Human Rights. The applicants' appeal to the Court of Appeal was dismissed on essentially the same grounds, although all the members of that court, like Simon Brown LJ, had sympathy for the applicants but felt it inappropriate to speculate on how the European Court might view the ban.

The applicants' petition for leave to appeal to the House of Lords was dismissed. Having exhausted their domestic remedies the applicants then took their case to Strasbourg. The judgment of the Court is a landmark one, not only for its result (that the applicants' rights had been violated) but because the Court's analysis provides a textbook example of human rights reasoning. The Court accepted that the ban on homosexuals in the armed forces, although it constituted an interference with the right to respect for private life in Article 8, was 'in accordance with the law' and had a legitimate aim (to ensure the operational effectiveness of the armed forces). The crucial question was whether the interference was 'necessary in a democratic society'.

The Court reminded itself that the characteristics of a democratic society are pluralism, tolerance and broad-mindedness.[47] It also noted that, in the intimate context with which it was dealing, the requirements of proportionality required 'particularly weighty and convincing reasons' to be demonstrated in justification of the ban.[48] The Court then assessed the reasons advanced by the Government and found them to be less than impressive. In substance what they amounted to was the assertion that the dislike and unwillingness of others to serve with homosexuals would undermine their morale and so the operational effectiveness of the armed forces. The Court said that the perceived problems 'were founded solely upon the negative attitudes of heterosexual personnel towards those of homosexual orientation'.[49] The Court rejected such reasoning. As the Court said:

> To the extent that they represent a predisposition on the part of a heterosexual majority against a homosexual minority, these negative attitudes cannot, of themselves, be considered by the Court to amount to sufficient justification for the interferences with the applicants' rights ... any more than similar negative attitudes towards those of a different race, origin or colour.[50]

For good measure, in the related case of *Smith v United Kingdom*[51] the Court also held that the applicants' right to an effective remedy for breach of their Convention rights – in Article 13 – had been violated. The Court considered that the principle on which the English courts could interfere with the policy banning homosexuals from the armed forces (irrationality) was, even when applied in a heightened manner in human rights cases, inadequate to provide the protection required by Article 13. The Court said:

> In such circumstances, the Court considers it clear that, even assuming that the essential complaints of the applicants before this Court were before and considered by the domestic courts, the threshold at which the High Court and the Court of Appeal could find Ministry of Defence policy irrational was placed so high that it effectively excluded any

---

[47] Paragraph 80.
[48] Paragraph 87.
[49] Paragraph 89.
[50] Paragraph 90.
[51] (2000)29 EHRR 493.

consideration by the domestic courts of the question of whether the interference with the applicants' rights answered a pressing social need or was proportionate to the national security and public order aims pursued, principles which lie at the heart of the Court's analysis of complaints under Article 8 of the Convention.[52]

There could be no better reason for incorporation of the ECHR than this ruling that, despite the advances made by English law in the last decade, it is still doctrinally incapable of engaging in the kind of reasoning which human rights jurisprudence requires.

THE HUMAN RIGHTS ACT: A DEMOCRATIC BILL OF RIGHTS

The first thing to note about the Human Rights Act is that it did not come suddenly, fully formed from the head of some Olympian god. It did not even happen primarily or even largely because the Government wanted it to. The Humans Rights Act came about because a progressive coalition had come together over a sustained period to press for a number of constitutional reforms of which it was only one. Although the structural problems in the constitution of the United Kingdom had long been present, they were only really noticed once the Conservative Party had managed to win four elections in a row between 1979 and 1992. The traditional swing of the pendulum, which had tended to ensure that both main parties could expect to be in office every five or ten years, could no longer be relied on. This highlighted the main defects of the constitution. One party could win a majority (often a large majority) of seats in the House of Commons on approximately 43 per cent of the vote. This in turn gave that party access to unlimited power since Parliament may do anything it likes. In reality the sovereignty of Parliament means the sovereignty of the executive. Parliament is dominated by the government through the whip system and by the promise or expectation of ministerial office. The Conservative Government did not have to share power on a regional basis, even though Scotland and Wales consistently voted for Labour. When local government became a nuisance, it could simply be abolished, as happened to the Greater London Council and the other metropolitan councils in 1986. The House of Lords (which had a large Conservative majority) could not stop legislation for long even if it wanted to (on the poll tax it did not even try, as hereditary peers turned out in force to push it through). And, of course, there was no Bill of Rights which could be enforced by the courts, although they did their best to curb the excesses of the government through judicial review, but that (as *Smith* shows) was insufficient to protect human rights.

It was against that background that non-governmental organisations like Charter 88, Liberty, JUSTICE and the Constitution Unit began to create a new climate of opinion on the centre left. In particular the influence of Charter 88, and the *New Statesman* to which it was linked through the editorship of Stuart Weir, cannot be over-estimated. It was no accident that it was at a Charter 88 conference in 1993 that the late John Smith committed the Labour Party to incorporation of the ECHR.

---

[52] Paragraph 138.

His shadow Home Secretary then was one Tony Blair, who has carried through the party's promise in government. As the Prime Minister put it in his preface to the White Paper which accompanied the Human Rights Bill when it was introduced in the House of Lords in October 1997:

> We are committed to a comprehensive programme of constitutional reform. We believe it is right to increase individual rights, to decentralise power, to open up government and to reform Parliament.[53]

To see the significance of the Human Rights Act as part of this comprehensive programme of reform, it may be instructive to start with Scotland, which can be seen now to have become a modern country, like many others in the liberal democratic world. First it has its own Parliament, which is elected on an additional member system, which ensures proportional representation overall while retaining constituency MSPs. This has had the result that the Labour Party, which won the vast majority of seats from Scotland at Westminster on 42 per cent of the vote, had to form a coalition government in Edinburgh on the same share of the vote. Secondly, the powers of the Scottish Parliament and Executive are limited by the Convention rights, which are entrenched:[54] in that sense the Human Rights Act is already deemed to have effect in Scotland.[55] Thirdly the courts are given the power of judicial review to strike down acts of the Scottish parliament which are incompatible with the Convention rights. The question many may be left asking is: if these arrangements are good enough for Scotland, why are they not good enough for the rest of the United Kingdom?

From Scotland it is worth visiting Northern Ireland, where the Good Friday peace agreement included a commitment to human rights which went beyond incorporation of the ECHR. The Northern Ireland Act 1998 too makes the Human Rights Act an entrenched Act, so that the Northern Ireland Assembly may not infringe the Convention rights and may not modify or repeal the Human Rights Act.

Both Scotland and Northern Ireland give an insight into the relationship between democracy and the Human Rights Act in the new United Kingdom which has been created before our eyes in the last three years. It cannot be democracy based simply on numbers. If numbers were all that mattered, the electorate of England could, if it wished, simply ignore the interests of Scotland – as many people there think it did during the long Conservative Government between 1979 and 1997. Yet devolution has forever ended that concept of democracy. The Northern Ireland Act is based on an even subtler notion of democracy which recognises that there are two minorities in Ulster: the Unionists are a permanent minority within the United Kingdom and could be expelled from the United Kingdom if that is what Great Britain wanted. But they are a permanent majority within Ulster. This is why the Good Friday agreement seeks to accommodate their interests as well as those of the Nationalist minority. The notion of power-sharing in the Executive and cross-community voting on crucial issues in the Assembly is based on a much more sophisticated kind of democracy than one in which sheer strength of numbers would prevail. And the reason, of course, is a

---

[53] *Rights Brought Home: the Human Rights Bill*, Cm 3782.
[54] Section 29(1) and (4)(d) of the Scotland Act 1998.
[55] Section 129(2) of the Scotland Act 1998.

good one: the experience of simple majority rule, where the human rights of a minority are consistently infringed without any realistic prospect of redress through the ballot box leads to violence, which in the end threatens democracy itself.

In an important essay Jeremy Waldron has pointed out that a concern for fundamental human rights need not entail a Bill of Rights which is enforceable by unelected judges.[56] He recalls that, in the US Constitution as originally adopted, James Madison thought it better to protect rights through structural arrangements: the famous 'checks and balances'. But, of course, a particular country may choose to have more than one approach to the protection of rights. One can have checks and balances and as a last resort one can have a Bill of Rights as well. This was the view to which Madison came after 1787 and, with the zeal of a convert, he then drafted the American Bill of Rights, which was ratified in 1791. And there can be variants on the Bill of Rights model. Contrary to popular belief, a Bill of Rights does not have to entail the power of judicial review or the power to strike down legislation.[57]

In the restructuring of the United Kingdom which is currently taking place checks and balances are introduced through devolution, proportional representation in Scotland, Wales and Northern Ireland and for the European Parliament elections, and through possible further reform of the House of Lords and of the electoral system for the House of Commons. But the Human Rights Act introduces a new element: a Bill of Rights. This is not, however, to be enforced only by the courts.

Section 19 of the Human Rights Act, which was brought into force almost two years before most of the Act was due to be brought into force, ordinarily requires ministers to give a statement of compatibility when they introduce a Bill into Parliament. Some have suggested that this is mere 'window dressing'. I hope they are not proved right. It was certainly intended to be a serious obligation to hold the executive to account in Parliament. If it works it should have two consequences. First, the Government will have had to go through a human rights reasoning process before it introduces legislation: for example, it will have had to assess the proportionality of any measure which appears to infringe a Convention right. Secondly, Members of Parliament will be able to scrutinise legislation and probe the executive if they are not satisfied about compatibility. Whichever way they answer the question, at least they have to ask the question. Of course, one can be cynical and say that MPs will not take the trouble to scrutinise legislation carefully. But there is reason to be more hopeful. Non-governmental organisations like JUSTICE and Liberty will produce the valuable briefing papers for which they are renowned, which will in turn prompt MPs and members of the House of Lords to ask the right questions. The Joint Parliamentary Committee on human rights should be more than a rubber-stamping body. And there will be the House of Lords. Even if, as seems likely, its powers are not increased after its reform, it can continue to perform its historic function: to scrutinise legislation with care and to send a Bill back to the House of Commons. It can delay legislation under the Parliament Acts 1911 and 1949: this could be a valuable power if it is not satisfied that a Bill is compatible with the Convention rights.

[56] J Waldron, 'Rights and Majorities: Rousseau Revisited' in *Liberal Rights: Collected Papers 1981–1991* (Cambridge, Cambridge University Press, 1993).
[57] P Craig, 'Constitutionalism, Regulation and Review' in R Hazell (ed), *Constitutional Futures* (Oxford, Oxford University Press, 1999) ch 5, 67–68.

So the Human Rights Act consciously builds into our constitutional arrangements a democratic scrutiny of the compatibility of legislation with human rights. This reflects what Jeremy Waldron would call a 'Rousseauan' model of democracy: one where the legislature asks not only what would be in the interests of the majority but what would be in the general interest (including a consideration of the fundamental rights of minorities):

> we should revise the way we think about rights to accommodate the prospect that voters and representatives in a democratic system will approach their responsibilities in a Rousseauan spirit. If we accept that as a possibility, we should recognize that rights may already be weighed in majoritarian decision-making. If so, the standard opposition between the democratic process and rights as external constitutional constraints would have to be discarded.[58]

But there is no need for the concept of rights as external constraints to be discarded altogether. Of course, Waldron is right to point out that we must admit the possibility that a majority may act in a Rousseauan way because we need it to adopt a Bill of Rights in the first place. But that proves only that a majority at a given point in history takes that view. That same majority could take the view that, as a last resort, a judicially enforceable Bill of Rights should be adopted. If future governments comply there will be no need to resort to it. If they do not, because – as Madison put it – men may not always behave as angels, the Bill of Rights will be there.

Even then it is not a necessary feature of a Bill of Rights that the courts should be able to strike down primary legislation. After incorporation our courts will have to read and give effect to all legislation, whether primary or secondary and whether enacted in the past or in the future, in a way which is compatible with Convention rights, so far as it is possible to do so.[59] It remains to be seen how imaginative an approach to interpretation this may require: the various members of the House of Lords in *Kebilene*[60] suggested that it might be more or less radical. But everyone accepts that, in principle, there may be legislation which cannot be interpreted in a way which is compatible with Convention rights. When that occurs, the Human Rights Act gives the higher courts the power to make a declaration of that incompatibility: they can declare but they cannot make a coercive order.

But in substance the courts would do what the European Court of Human Rights does when it finds that a breach of an applicant's rights has occurred as a result of an Act of Parliament. The Court does not strike down the legislation. It does not declare it void within the national legal system. It expects the respondent state to remedy the breach by amending the legislation accordingly. This process is, if anything, improved by the scheme of the Human Rights Act. This is because a minister has the power to make a remedial order under section 10 of the Human Rights Act to amend an Act of Parliament to bring it into line with a judgment of the European Court of Human Rights and not only to comply with a declaration of incompatibility made by a court in the United Kingdom.

---

[58] Waldron (n 56) 420.
[59] Section 3 of the Human Rights Act.
[60] *R v Director of Public Prosecutions, ex p. Kebilene* [1999] 3 WLR 972.

As is well-known the only legal effect of a declaration of incompatibility will be to permit (but not oblige) a minister to amend the offending Act by a 'remedial order' under section 10 and Schedule 2. This will only be used where there are 'compelling' reasons to do so.[61] If the declaration of incompatibility is not accepted by the government of the day, and assuming that there is no parliamentary pressure to change the law in the meantime, the applicant will still be able to take the case to Strasbourg. If the European Court of Human Rights takes the same view as the domestic court, which it may not do given the doctrine of the margin of appreciation applied by that Court, precedent suggests that the Government of the United Kingdom would comply at that stage with the Court's judgment.

So the scheme of the Human Rights Act is to establish a relationship of balance between Parliament, the courts of this country and the European Court of Human Rights. But in practice it may well introduce a further, very important player into this relationship: the people. A declaration of incompatibility is likely to be made only in relation to the most controversial and sensitive types of legislation: abortion or terrorism may well be the subject-matter. Once a declaration is made, there is likely to be public debate about it. If the government of the day decides not to implement the declaration normal politics can be expected to play their part. Opposition parties and non-governmental organisations will campaign on one side of the issue or the other. There may well be a general election in which the issue registers with the electorate precisely because it has been the subject of a formal declaration by the highest court in the land In this way, and in others, the Human Rights Act may bind all of us together in support of human rights.[62]

Some commentators have suggested, with apparent relief, that the scheme of the Human Rights Act preserves Parliamentary sovereignty.[63] So it does in a formal sense, although it is hard to see how, after the major reforms of recent years, the constitution can plausibly be said now to rest on the doctrine of Parliamentary sovereignty. But in any event, for me there is no virtue in parliamentary sovereignty as such. Parliamentary democracy is another matter. In a modern constitution there should be no one person or body which enjoys absolute power. This is particularly true when one recalls that Parliament is very largely controlled by the executive. That is simply the modern reincarnation of the old divine right of kings.

As I have suggested, the Human Rights Act, especially when placed in the context of the other reforms which are modernising the United Kingdom, is part of a new constitutionalism in this country, where power is dispersed among regions and shared among institutions. The Human Rights Act is an experiment. It represents a vision that human rights will best be protected when everyone in society is bound into a common enterprise rather than engaged in conflict.[64] It is a democratic Bill of Rights.

---

[61] Section 10(2) of the Human Rights Act.

[62] This is an example of what Francesca Klug has called the 'third wave' of human rights: see F Klug, *Values in a Godless Age* (Harmondsworth, Penguin, 2000) Chs 5–6.

[63] See eg K Ewing, 'The Human Rights Act and Parliamentary Democracy' [1999] *MLR* 79.

[64] See further M Hunt, 'The Human Rights Act and Legal Culture: the Judicial and the Legal Profession' (1999) 26 *Journal of Law and Society* 86 at 89, where Murray Hunt says that: '[the Human Rights Act] is designed to institutionalize a creative tension between the judiciary on the one hand and Parliament and the executive on the other'.

What is a 'Democratic Society'?

This was the Chevrette-Marx lecture, given in 2018 at the University of Montréal and was first published in 2019 under the auspices of that university. Professors François Chevrette and Herbert Marx were distinguished members of the law faculty there and authors of a treatise on Canadian constitutional law. This lecture gave me the opportunity to explore the meaning of a 'democratic society', a concept which appears in both the Canadian Charter of Fundamental Rights and Freedoms and the European Convention on Human Rights. In particular I suggested that a democratic society in this context is not simply a majoritarian one but one in which the fundamental rights of minorities are protected.

INTRODUCTION

MESDAMES ET MESSIEURS. Bonsoir et merci beaucoup. C'est un grand plaisir de donner cette conférence en l'honneur de François Chevrette et Herbert Marx. Ils étaient tous les deux des savants distingués. Malheureusement, je ne parle pas bien français et je vais donc donner ma conférence en anglais.

Section 1 of the Canadian Charter of Rights and Freedoms guarantees the rights and freedoms set out in it subject only to such reasonable limits prescribed by law as can be demonstrably justified in 'a free and democratic society'. The European Convention on Human Rights ('ECHR'), many of whose rights have been given effect in domestic law in the United Kingdom ('UK') by the Human Rights Act 1998[1] ('HRA'), does not have a similar general limitation provision like section 1 of the Canadian Charter. However, most of the rights set out in the ECHR can in principle be limited. The only one which is truly absolute is the prohibition on torture and inhuman or degrading treatment in Article 3.

A good example of a limited right in the ECHR can be seen in Article 10, which guarantees the right to freedom of expression, and provides that limitations can be placed on that right where this is prescribed by law (again echoing – or perhaps anticipating – the language of section 1 of the Charter) and is 'necessary in a democratic society' to achieve one or more of the express aims set out in it, for example the protection of the rights of others. Both the Canadian Charter and the ECHR make reference therefore to the concept of 'a democratic society'. The question which I want to try to address in my lecture is: what is a democratic society for this purpose?

* Lord Justice of Appeal, Court of Appeal of England and Wales.
[1] (UK), c 42.

There is a textual difference which exists on the face of section 1 of the Canadian Charter (which refers to 'a free and democratic society') and the ECHR (which refers only to a 'democratic society'). I will suggest in this lecture that in fact that textual difference in language between the two documents does not make a material difference. The jurisprudence of the European Court of Human Rights has made it clear that it too envisages a democratic society which is also a free society.

In *R v Oakes*[2] [*Oakes*], Dickson CJ famously set out the requirements which must be satisfied before a restriction on a fundamental right in the Charter will be regarded as being reasonable and demonstrably justified. First, the objective of the measure must be sufficiently important to warrant overriding a constitutionally protected right or freedom. Secondly, the measure must satisfy the test of proportionality, which in turn requires an answer to three questions: (i) there must be a rational connection between the measure and its objective; (ii) the means used should impair the right as little as possible; and (iii) there must be a proportionality between the effects of the measure on the right in question and the objective which has been identified as of sufficient importance.

The principle of proportionality is also very familiar to us in Europe as it is at the heart of the jurisprudence of the European Court of Human Rights. The questions set out in *Oakes* are very similar to the ones that courts in the UK have formulated for use under the HRA. Indeed the decision in *Oakes* was very influential in helping us to settle what the relevant questions are for deciding whether a restriction on a fundamental right satisfies the principle of proportionality: see, in particular, the decision of the House of Lords in *Huang v Secretary of State for the Home Department*.[3]

In *Oakes*, at 136, Dickson CJ also emphasised the importance of that phrase in section 1 of the Charter: 'a free and democratic society'. He said:

> The Court must be guided by the values and principles essential to a free and democratic society which I believe embody, to name but a few, respect for the inherent dignity of the human person, commitment to social justice and equality, accommodation of a wide variety of beliefs, respect for cultural and group identity, and faith in social and political institutions which enhance the participation of individuals and groups in society. The underlying values and principles of a free and democratic society are the genesis of the rights and freedom guaranteed by the *Charter* and the ultimate standard against which a limit on a right or freedom must be shown, despite its effect, to be reasonable and demonstrably justified.

Similarly, in its seminal jurisprudence of the 1970s, the European Court of Human Rights made it clear that its vision of a democratic society is not simply one in which the majority will must prevail. Rather it is one which is characterised by 'pluralism, tolerance and broad-mindedness'. In *Handyside v United Kingdom*[4] the Court said at paragraph 49:

> Freedom of expression constitutes one of the essential fecundations of such a society [ie a democratic society], one of the basic conditions for its progress and for the development of every man. Subject to [Article 10(2)], it is applicable not only to 'information' or 'ideas'

---

[2] [1986] 1 SCR 103 at 138–39, 26 DLR (4th) 200.
[3] [2007] 2 UKHL 11, [2007] 2 AC 167.
[4] (1976), I EHRR 737, [1976] ECHR 5.

that are favourably received or regarded as inoffensive or as a matter of indifference, but also those that offend, shock, or disturb the Slate or any sector of the population. Such are the demands of that pluralism, tolerance and broadmindedness without which there is no 'democratic society'.

In 2012, in giving judgment in a freedom of expression case brought by the BBC in the High Court of England and Wales, I suggested that the words 'in a democratic society' in the ECHR are not superfluous:

[T]he framers of the Convention, arising as it did out of the ashes of European conflict in the 1930s and 1940s, recognised that not everything that the state asserts to be necessary will be acceptable in a democratic society.[2]

Let me explain what I will endeavour to do in this lecture. I am not a historian, philosopher or political scientist. I am a lawyer by background and now a judge. The concept of a democratic society is one which is no doubt of interest to historians, philosophers and political scientists. But they will have a potentially different understanding depending on their discipline.

For example, the historian may be interested in the difference between a modern representative democracy and direct democracy, such as that in classical Athens in the age of Pericles, with all its limitations, which are well known: the right to participate in the affairs of the *polis* (city-state) was limited to adult male citizens and so it excluded women, slaves and others. It was a very different kind of democracy from what we know of in the modern era because the citizens of Athens all met in the ekklesia (assembly) to take the most important decisions facing the state. We have become used to the idea of a representative democracy rather than direct participation in the affairs of the state.[5]

The philosopher will be interested in what the underlying justification for a democracy is, for example whether it is based on the principle of the consent of the governed.

The political scientist may question whether it is strictly accurate to conceive of a democratic society as including other elements such as liberty and equality. In a very interesting and provocative book published earlier this year, *The People vs. Democracy*,[6] a scholar at Harvard University (Yascha Mount) has suggested that we should no longer necessarily speak of a 'liberal democratic society' because it is possible for there to be a society which is democratic and yet illiberal. Although he does not approve of the idea, he suggests that it is possible to conceive of a 'democracy without rights' (Ch. 1).

It may be that the world is now seeing something very different from what it has seen in the past. For example, in the 1920s and 1930s there was a clear and obvious distinction between what were called democracies and what were called dictatorships. Some twentieth century dictators came to power in part by using the ballot box but then got rid of the institutions of democracy. Today it is not impossible for

---

[5] R *(British Broadcasting Corporation) v Secretary of State for Justice* [2012] EWHC 13 (Admin) at para 49: [2013] 1 WLR 964 (Singh J, giving the judgment of the Divisional Court, which also included Hooper LJ).
[6] See Paul Cartledge, *Democracy: A Life* (Oxford, Oxford University Press, 2016).

a leader to win an election and continue to subject himself to further elections. They do not necessarily want to abolish democracy in the basic sense of having elections but they may be hostile to the concept of human rights, particularly if those rights are conferred on unpopular minorities.

The intellectual historian, Professor Sir Larry Siedentop, has suggested in his stimulating book *Inventing The Individual: The Origins of Western Liberalism*[7] that the origins of our modern conception of democracy lie in the Christian belief in the 'equality of all souls'. He suggests that in western philosophy it was not until Christianity came on the scene that it was considered that all human beings were inherently equal. Before that time, and in particular in classical thinking in ancient Greece and Rome, society was founded on the inherent inequality of human beings, based on social status.

All of these are valid and interesting viewpoints but the theme of my lecture will be to ask the question what is a democratic society from a legal viewpoint. Both the Canadian Charter and the ECHR are legal instruments. It is therefore appropriate to ask what they mean by a 'democratic society' understood as a legal concept.

I will start with something which may be regarded as lying close to the heart of a democracy: that is the right to vote. Universal adult suffrage was the result of long and sometimes bitter struggle. In the UK this year we have celebrated the centenary of the extension of the franchise to women although not all women were given the vote until 1928. In Canada I understand that women were able to vote in federal elections from 1918 although they had been able to vote in the province of Manitoba from 1916.

THE RIGHT TO VOTE

The right of every Canadian citizen to vote is now guaranteed by section 3 of the charter and was described by McLachlin CJ in *Sauvé v Canada (Chief Electoral Officer)*,[8] as a right which 'lies at the heart of Canadian democracy'.

Curiously the ECHR does not contain an express right to vote which is conferred on individuals as such. However that individual right has been held to be implicit in Article 3 of the First protocol, which provides:

> The High contracting Parties undertake to hold free elections at reasonable intervals by secret ballot, under conditions which will ensure the free expression of the opinion of the people in the choice of the legislature.

Because the right to vote lies at the heart of democracy, it might be thought that particularly close scrutiny should be required of any law which denies the right to vote to a certain class of people. In both Canada and the UK there was at one time legislation which denied the right to vote to all serving prisoners. In Canada that was held to be unconstitutional by the Supreme Court in *Sauvé v Canada (Attorney*

---

[7] 2002 CSC 68 at paragraph 1, [2002] 3 SCR 519 *Sauvé* (No 2).
[8] Yasha Mounk, *The People vs Democracy: Why Our Freedom Is in Danger and How to Save it* (Cambridge, MA, Harvard University Press, 2018).

General).[9] The legislation was then amended, to disenfranchise only prisoners serving a sentence of two years or longer. The amended legislation, set out in section 51(e) of the Canada Elections Act 1985, as amended, was in turn held to be constitutional in *Sauvé (No 2)*.

In the meantime, in some of the first cases that were brought under the Human Rights Act[10] in 2000, the English courts had held, in a group of cases which included *Hirst*,[11] that the UK legislation, contained in section 3 of the Representation of the People Act 1983[12] was compatible with the rights in the HRA. In part this was because the English courts followed what at that time was the decision of the Federal Court of Appeal in *Sauvé (No 2)*[13] which was later reversed by a narrow majority of five to four in the Supreme Court of Canada.

The case of *Hirst* then proceeded to the European Court of Human Rights in Strasbourg. In *Hirst (No 2) v United Kingdom*,[14] the European Court held (by a majority of 12 to five, the minority including the then President of the Court, Judge Wildhaber) that the UK legislation was incompatible with Article 3 of the First Protocol. This was essentially because the legislation contained a complete ban which applied to all serving prisoners irrespective of the length of sentence or any other characteristic of the individual prisoner. This was therefore held to be disproportionate. At paragraph 80 of its judgment, the Court noted that the decision in *Sauvé (No 2)* of the Federal Court of Appeal had later been overturned by the Canadian Supreme Court. At paragraph 82, the Court stated that, although the margin of appreciation afforded to Contracting States in this field is wide, it is not all-embracing:

> Such a general, automatic and indiscriminate restriction on a vitally important Convention right must be seen as falling outside any acceptable margin of appreciation, however wide that margin might be ...

The decision in *Hirst* has proved extremely controversial, particularly in British society and in Parliament. Uniquely in my experience (and I should say that I acted as counsel for the Government of the *Hirst*), the judgment in Court was not implemented quickly. In fact it has taken over a decade for the practice in the UK to be amended. A number of later court cases have been brought both in the domestic courts of the UK and in Strasbourg.

Finally, in December 2017, the UK Government published proposals which the Council of Europe has said that, if implemented, would be sufficient to signify compliance with the judgment in *Hirst* in 2005. Even now, the proposed changes are administrative only and not legislative. They were announced by the Secretary of State for Justice to the House of Commons on 2 November 2017 (UK HC, Debates, vol 630, col 1007). He said that, first, the Government would work with the judiciary to make it clear to criminals when they are sentenced that when they are in prison they will lose the right to vote. That directly addresses a specific concern of the judgment

---

[9] [1993] 2 SCR 4.38, [1993] SCJ No, 59 [*Sauvé (No I)*].
[10] (London, Penguin UK, 2015).
[11] *Supra* note 1.
[12] *R (Pearson) v Home Secretary* [2001] EWHC Admin 239, (2001) HRLR 39.
[13] (UK), c 2.
[14] (2006), 42 EHRR 41, [2005] ECHR 681.

in *Hirst* that there was not sufficient clarity in confirming to offenders that they could not vote whilst in prison. Secondly, the Government would amend guidance to address an anomaly where offenders who are released back in the community on licence using an electronic tag under the Home Detention Curfew Scheme can vote but those in the community on temporary licence cannot vote. Release on temporary licence would not be granted in order to enable a prisoner to vote.

In its meeting of 5–7 December 2017 the Committee of Ministers of the Council of Europe, which is the body charged with the function of supervising the compliance by Contracting States with judgments of the European Court of Human Rights, concluded that, overall, these measures 'are an effective package to ensure compliance with *Hirst* group of judgments'. The Government of the UK intends to implement the proposed changes by the end of 2018 and has agreed to report back to the Committee of Ministers this month, September 2018.

THE RIGHT TO FREEDOM OF EXPRESSION

My next suggestion will be that, apart from the right to vote, there are other rights which are essential to the healthy functioning of a democratic society. The most important of these is the right to freedom of expression. As Lord Steyn put it in *R v Secretary of State for the Home Department, ex parte Simms*:[15] 'In a democracy it is the primary right: without it an effective rule of law is not possible'.

He went on, at 126, to describe freedom of speech as:

> The lifeblood of democracy. The free flow of information and ideas informs political debate … It acts as a brake on the abuse of power by public officials. It facilitates the exposure of errors in the governance and administration of justice of the country.

However, as Lord Steyn went on to say in *Simms* itself, at 127:

> Not all types of speech have an equal value. For example, no prisoner would ever be permitted to have interviews with a journalist to publish pornographic material or to give vent to so-called hate speech.

Simms was decided just before the HRA came into force in the UK. Now the right to freedom of expression is guaranteed by Article 10 of the ECHR through the HRA.

In Canada the right to freedom of expression is guaranteed by section 2(b) of the Charter, However, it is also to be noted that there is an equality provision in section 15(1) of the Charter, which provides that:

> Every individual is equal before and under the law and has the right to the equal production and equal benefit of the law without discrimination and, in particular, without discrimination based on race, national and ethnic origin, colour, religion, sex, age or mental or physical disability.

Furthermore, section 27 of the *Charter* provides that it: 'shall be interpreted in a manner consistent with the preservation and enhancement of the multicultural heritage of Canadians'.

---

[15] [1999] UKHL 33, [2000] 2 AC 115 at 125 *[Simms]*.

In the UK we do not have any statutory provision like Article 27 of the Charter. We do have an equality provision, in Article 14 of the ECHR. Although Article 14 is not a freestanding provision, like section 15 of the Canadian Charter, it does guarantee equal treatment in the enjoyment of other Convention rights. The Twelfth Protocol to the ECHR does contain a freestanding right to equal treatment but it has not been signed by the UK.

In both Canada and the UK there are criminal laws prohibiting the propagation of hate speech, particularly speech which is directed at certain groups in society defined by reference to race or religion. In the UK at least, such laws had their origins in concern about public disorder, for example the Public Order Act 1936,[16] enacted at a time when the British Union of Fascists was active; that Act later being amended to include incitement to racial hatred by the Race Relations Act 1976.[17] More recently, in 2006, Parliament has prohibited speech which is likely to incite religious hatred.[18]

In Canada the compatibility of legislation prohibiting hate speech (section 319 of the Criminal Code) was considered by the Supreme Court in *R v Keegstra*.[19] The law was upheld by a majority of four to three. The majority judgment was given by Dickson CJ. The Supreme Court considered that in principle section 319(2) of the Criminal Code did constitute an infringement of the character guarantee of freedom of expression. Accordingly the crucial question was whether that infringement could be justified under section 1 of the character as a reasonable limit in a free and democratic society. At 736, Dickson CJ said:

> [A] practical application of s. I requires more than an incantation of the words 'free and democratic society'. These words require some definition, an elucidation as to the values that they invoke. To a large extent, a free and democratic society embraces the very values and principles which Canadians have sought to protect and further by entrenching specific rights and freedoms in the Constitution, although the balancing exercise in s. 1 is not restricted to values expressly set out in the Charter.

Dickson CJ identified two sorts of injury which are caused by hate propaganda. This went beyond mere offensiveness. As I have mentioned, the European Court of Human Rights has frequently said that the right to freedom of expression includes the right not only to express ideas which are found to be acceptable by others in society but also to say things which may cause offence. However, as Dickson CJ said in *Keegstra*, hate propaganda goes beyond mere giving of offence and causes real harm. First, there is harm done to members of the target group:

> It is indisputable that the emotional damage caused by words may be of grave psychological and social consequence. In the context of sexual harassment ... this Court has found that words can in themselves constitute harassment ... In a similar manner, words and writings that wilfully promote hatred can constitute a serious attack on persons belonging to a racial or religious group, and in this regard the Cohen Committee noted that these persons are humiliated and degraded ... In my opinion, a response of humiliation and degradation from an individual targeted by hate propaganda is to be expected. A person's sense of

---

[16] [2000] 2 PC 117, ISO DLR (4th) 385.
[17] (UK), c 6.
[18] (UK), c 74.
[19] [1990] 3 SCR 697, 1 DLR (4th) 129 [*Keegstra*].

human dignity and belonging to the community at large is closely linked to the concern and respect accorded the groups to which he or she belongs ... The derision, hostility and abuse encouraged by hate propaganda therefore have a severely negative impact on the individual's sense of self-worth and acceptance. ... Such consequences bear heavily in a nation that prides itself on tolerance and the fostering of human dignity through, among other things, respect for the many racial, religious and cultural groups in our society.[20]

Dickson CJ said that a second harmful effect of hate propaganda is its influence upon society at large. After referring to the experience of the twentieth century, which had shaken faith in earlier Enlightenment views about the rationality of humankind, he said at 747: 'It is thus not inconceivable that the active dissemination of hate propaganda can attract individuals to its cause, and in the process serious discord between various cultural groups in society'.

He went on to say, at 748:

The threat to the self-dignity of target group members is thus matched by the possibility that prejudiced messages will gain some credence, with the attendant result of discrimination, and perhaps even violence, against minority groups in Canadian society.

Dickson CJ also noted that international human rights instruments support Canadian (and I would suggest British) policy in this context. Article 4 of the international Convention on the Elimination of All Forms of Racial Discrimination, 21 December 1965, 660 UNTS 1995 (entered into force 4 January 1969) is of special interest, providing that:

States Parties condemn all propaganda and all organizations which are based on ideas or theories of superiority of one race or group of persons of one colour or ethnic origin, or which attempt to justify or promote racial hatred and discrimination in any form, and undertake to adopt immediate and positive measures designed to eradicate all incitement to, or acts of, such discrimination and, to this end ...

(a) [s]hall declare an offence punishable by law all dissemination of ideas based on racial superiority or hatred, incitement to racial discrimination, as well as all acts of violence or incitement to such acts against any race or group of persons of another colour or ethnic origin.

Dickson CJ also noted that the International Covenant on Civil and Political Rights, 19 December 1966, 999 UNTS 171, which guarantees the right to freedom of expression in Article 19, goes on, in Article 20(2), to state that: 'Any advocacy of national, racial or religious hatred that constitutes incitement to discrimination, hostility or violence shall be prohibited by law'.

At 763–65 Dickson CJ turned to the heart of the dispute in *Keegstra* itself. He noted the particular link with the 'political' rationale for protection of freedom of expression in a democracy. He said at 764:

Freedom of expression is a crucial aspect of the democratic commitment, not merely because it permits the best policies to be chosen from among a wide array of proffered options, but additionally because it helps to ensure that participation in the political process is open to all persons. Such open participation must involve to a substantial degree the notion that all persons are equally deserving of respect and dignity.

---

[20] Racial and Religious Hatred Act 2006 (UK).

Dickson CJ recognised that suppression of hate propaganda undeniably muzzles the participation of a few individuals in the democratic process but he considered the degree of that limitation 'not substantial'. He went on to say at 769 that hate propaganda can work to undermine our commitment to democracy when employed to propagate ideas 'anathemic' to democratic values:

> Hate propaganda works in just such a way, arguing as it does for a society in which the democratic process is subverted and individuals are denied respect and dignity simply because of racial or religious characteristics. This brand of expressive activity is thus wholly inimical to the democratic aspirations of the free expression guarantee.

In a very important passage, in my view, Dickson CJ went on to state at 765:

> I am very reluctant to attach anything but the highest importance to expression relevant to political matters. But given the unparalleled vigour with which hate propaganda repudiates and undermines democratic values, and in particular its condemnation of the view that all citizens need to be treated with equal respect and dignity so as to make participation in the political process meaningful, I am unable to see the protection of such expression as integral to the democratic ideal so central to the s. 2(b) rationale.

In the context of the ECHR it is worth noting that Article 17 of the Convention itself contains a provision designed to prevent abuse of the rights set out in it:

> Nothing in this Convention may be interpreted as implying for any State, group or person any right to engage in any activity or perform any act aimed at the destruction of any of the rights and freedoms set for herein or at their limitation to a greater extent than is provided for in the Convention.

The position in both Canada and the UK can be contrasted with the starkly different approach which has been taken by the Supreme Court of the United States, for example in *RAV v City of St. Paul*,[21] where a city ordinance prohibiting certain forms of hate propaganda was invalidated. This is no doubt because of the very strict nature of the First Amendment guarantee of free speech in the US.

I would suggest, as Dickson CJ did in *Keegstra*, that the underlying value which is protected by laws against hate speech is the right to equality. In *A v Secretary of State for the Home Department*,[22] (often known in the UK as the '*Belmarsh case*'), at para 46, Lord Bingham quoted Professor (later Sir) Hersch Lauterpacht: 'The claim to equality before the law is in a substantial sense the most fundamental of the rights of man'.[23]

Lord Bingham then went on to observe that, in the Privy Council, in *Matadeen v Pointu*,[24] Lord Hoffmann had said, with reference to the principle of equality: '[S]uch a principle is one of the building blocks of democracy and necessarily permeates any democratic constitution'.

---

[21] 505 US 377 (1992).
[22] [2004] UKHL 56, [2005] 2 AC 68.
[23] *Keegstra*, at 746–47.
[24] [1998] UKPC 9, [1999] I AC 98 at 109.

In *Ghaidan v Godin-Mendoza*,[25] at paragraph 132, Baroness Hale said:

> Such a guarantee of equal treatment is also essential to democracy. Democracy is founded on the principle that each individual has equal value. ... [I]t is a purpose of all human rights instruments to secure the protection of the essential rights of members of minority groups even when they are unpopular with the majority. Democracy values everyone equally even if the majority does not.

In that important passage I would suggest lies the key to an understanding of the legal concept of a democratic society. The reason why we value democracy is precisely because it is founded on the inherent equality of every participant in it. This is why everyone in a democracy has the right to vote but no one has more than one vote. That was not always the case in the UK. At one time, until as recently as the end of the Second World War, people who were graduates of one of the so-called ancient universities could vote more than once, both in the constituency where they lived and secondly for a Member of Parliament who represented their former university. In theory at least it is not impossible to conceive of a society in which it might be said that someone who pays more in taxation should have more votes than a person who pays little into the state's coffers. Such ideas seem fanciful and indeed wrong to us now. This is because, I would suggest, at its root democracy is properly considered to be a system in which everyone counts but no one counts more than anyone else. This is the fundamental idea of equality.

When therefore one member of society abuses their right to freedom of expression to deny the right of another member of society to participate on an equal basis in a democracy, as in the case of hate speech, this could regarded as striking at the very heart of what a democracy is.

THE RIGHTS OF MINORITIES – AND THE RIGHTS OF A MINORITY WITHIN A MINORITY

In the *Belmarsh case*, at paragraph 237, Baroness Hale (who is now the President of the Supreme Court of the UK) quoted Thomas Jefferson in his inaugural address on becoming President of the United States in 1801:

> Though the will of the majority is in all cases to prevail, that will to be rightful must be reasonable ... The minority possess their equal rights, which equal law must protect, and to violate would be oppression.

She added, in her own words:

> Democracy values each person equally. In most respects, this means that the will of the majority must prevail. But valuing each person equally also means that the will of the majority cannot prevail if it is inconsistent with the equal rights of minorities.

In the last year I have sat in two cases as a judge in which this issue of the protection of the rights of minorities has arisen in a stark way. The first case was in the Divisional Court, which is part of the High Court of England and Wales, in which I

---

[25] [2004] UKHL 30, [2004] 2 AC 557.

sat with Whipple J: *R (Adath Yisroel Burial Society) v HM Coroner for Inner North London.*[26] That case concerned a policy which was adopted by a coroner not to take into account the religious views (for example of Jewish or Muslim people) that their cases should be dealt with urgently because they felt there was a need to bury a loved one quickly and, if possible, on the day of death. The policy was described as a 'cab rank' principle, in other words that every case would be dealt with in the order in which it was notified to the coroner's office. We held that the policy was unlawful on a number of grounds, including a breach of the right to freedom of religion in Article 9 of the ECHR and the right to equal treatment in Article 14. That did not mean that members of a religious minority such as Jewish or Muslim people always had to be given priority, because there may be other legitimate demands on a coroner's time and resources; but it did mean that there could not be a policy that their needs would never be taken into account. The principle of proportionality had to be complied with.

At paragraph 115 we quoted Lord Steyn from a paper he gave in 2001:

> It is a fundamental tenet of democracy that both law and Government accord every individual equal concern and respect for their welfare and dignity.

That phrase, 'equal concern and respect' echoes the central thesis in the writings of the laic Professor Ronald Dworkin.[27,28]

In our judgment we added at paragraph 115 that:

> The kind of society which is envisaged by the Convention and the HRA is one which is based on respect for everyone's fundamental rights, on an equal basis ... It regards democracy as being a community of equals.

We observed that it would be a mistake to think that having a "cab rank" policy will always lead to everyone being treated equally. At paragraph 111, we said:

> What on its face looks like a general policy which applies to everyone equally may in fact have an unequal impact on a minority. In other words, to treat everyone in the same way is not necessarily to treat them equally. Uniformity is not the same thing as equality.

The second case that I would like to mention in this context is *In re A (Children) (Contact: Ultra-Orthodox Judaism: Transgender Parent)*,[29] which was decided by the Court of Appeal of England and Wales last December. I was a member of the Court, which included Arden LJ and was presided over by Sir James Munby, the then President of the Family Division, who gave the judgment of the Court. That case concerned the right of a male to female transgender person to have direct contact with her children in circumstances when the family's community (which was an ultra-Orthodox Jewish community) said that it would ostracise the entire family if there was such contact. Such ostracism would have had a detrimental effect on the welfare of the children. But the consequence of the alternative course of action was that the children would no longer have direct contact with their natural father. We allowed the

---

[26] [2018] EWHC 969 (Admin) [2018] 3 WLR 1354.
[27] *An International Bill of the Rights of Man* (New York, Columbia University Press, 1945) at 115.
[28] *Taking Rights Seriously* (Cambridge, MA, Harvard University Press, 1977).
[29] [2017] EWCA Civ 2164, (2018) 4 WLR 60.

appeal and remitted the case to the High Court for further consideration to be given to whether it was possible to promote contact, judging the children's welfare by the contemporary standards of society.

At paragraph 60, the Court said:

> [T]he function of the judge in a case like this is to act as the 'judicial reasonable parent', judging the child's welfare by the standards of reasonable men and women today ... having regard to the ever changing nature of our world including ... *changes in social attitudes*, and always remembering that the reasonable man or woman is receptive to change, broad-minded, tolerant, easy-going and slow to condemn. ... We live in a democratic society subject to the rule of law. We live in a society whose law requires people to be treated equally and where their human rights are respected. We live in a plural society, in which the family takes many forms, some of which would have been thought inconceivable well within living memory. [emphasis in original]

We were acutely conscious that the case concerned not only the rights of the children or the rights of a transgender person hut also the rights of a religious minority to live their lives in accordance with their sincerely held beliefs. However, at paragraph 95, we recalled that:

> It is well-established on authority that discrimination which is motivated by a religious belief (however sincerely held and even if the discrimination is mandated by that religious belief) does not make discrimination under the Equality Act [2010] lawful.

Both of the recent cases I have mentioned raise in an acute way sensitive issues about the balance which needs to be struck in a democratic society between the rights of individuals and minority groups on the one hand and the rights of the majority on the other. There may indeed also be a tension between the rights of an individual *within* a religious minority group, such as a transgender person, and the rights of others in that group. The courts in both Canada and the UK have no choice but to grapple with such sensitive issues when they are brought before them by litigants.

This leads me on to my final point, the relationship between the elected institutions in a democracy and the courts. This was addressed by Lord Bingham in the *Belmarsh case*, at paragraph 42, as follows:

> I do not accept the full breadth of the Attorney General's submissions. I do not in particular accept the distinction, which he drew between democratic institutions and the courts. It is of course true that the judges in this country are not elected and are not answerable to Parliament. It is also of course true ... that Parliament, the executive and the courts have different functions. But the function of independent judges charged to interpret and apply the law is universally recognised as a cardinal feature of the modern democratic state, a cornerstone of the rule of law itself. The Attorney General is fully entitled to insist on the proper limits of judicial authority, but he is wrong to stigmatise judicial decision-making as in some way undemocratic. ... The [HRA] gives the courts a very specific, wholly democratic, mandate.

CONCLUSION

By way of conclusion let me try to draw together the threads of my theme in this lecture.

I would suggest that the sort of democratic society which is envisaged by a human rights charter is not one which can be based simply on the notion of majority rule but rather is one which is based on the three fundamentals of liberty, equality and fraternity, the last of those perhaps now better expressed as community. We no longer conceive of fundamental rights as belonging to atomised individuals living in a state of nature. Rather they exist within the framework of an organised community. Indeed they often depend on the community for their protection and full enjoyment. This is one reason why there can be limitations placed on a fundamental right, provided the limitation is objectively justified and satisfies the principle of proportionality.

But I would suggest that a democratic society is a community of equals. The concept of democracy itself is founded on the basic value of human equality.

Finally, a democratic society is one in which there are independent courts entrusted with the task of the protection of fundamental tights, including the rights of individuals and minority groups even if they are unpopular with the majority. In the words of the oath of office which every judge in England and Wales has to take, the courts will protect those rights 'without fear or favour, affection or ill-will'.

What all of this indicates is that a democratic society is not only one in which the people elect their government. It is also a community in which everyone enjoys fundamental human rights on an equal basis and in which those rights are enforceable in independent courts.

Equality

Equality: The Neglected Virtue

This was the Administrative Law Bar Association lecture for 2003, given at the London School of Economics, where I was a visiting professor at the time (as well as being a practising barrister). It was first published in [2004] EHRLR 141. I examined the importance of equality as a constitutional principle, drawing on American constitutional thinking, and tried to apply that to practical situations in the UK. In particular I considered the decision of the Court of Appeal in the 'Belmarsh' case, which had decided that the legislation under challenge in that case, which permitted the detention without charge of suspected international terrorists but only if they were foreign nationals, was compatible with the Human Rights Act. That decision was later reversed by the House of Lords in 2004: A v Secretary of State for the Home Department [2005] 2 AC 68. *This lecture was cited with approval by Lord Steyn in* R (European Roma Rights Centre) v Immigration Officer at Prague Airport [2004] UKHL 55; [2005] 2 AC 1, *at paragraph 37.*

A RTICLE 1 OF the Universal Declaration of Human Rights proudly proclaims that all human beings are born free and equal in dignity and rights. Not only born free, as Rousseau had said in the first sentence of *The Social Contract*, but equal. And not, as the American Declaration of Independence had asserted, only men but all human beings.

It is easy to under-estimate how profound a development this is in human history. The idea that all human beings are equal is a very recent notion. For most of history people have been divided precisely in accordance with notions of inequality. Privilege, not equality, has been the guiding principle. It is often suggested that democracy was born in Athens of the fifth century BC – but political rights were denied to slaves and women and foreigners, 'hoi barbaroi' as the Greeks called them, from which we derive the word 'barbarians'. As the Roman Empire grew from a city-state on the Tiber to a huge empire, more and more people were granted Roman citizenship – but it still meant something to say anywhere in the Empire *civis Romanus sum* ('I am a Roman citizen'). Many other societies have been built on rigid social strata – not least the Indian caste system. In more recent times, the European empires which lasted well into the second half of the twentieth century could only be justified on the basis of white superiority – to recognise that subjects were equals to their masters would have spelt – as it did in the end – the death of those empires.

In this country the struggle for women's equality was at first the struggle for civil rights in the strict sense, the right to own property, the right to enter into contracts, the right to practise a profession, indeed the right to be recognised as a legal person at all. So deeply embedded was the notion of inequality that, as recently as 1909, the courts could not accept that the gender-neutral word 'person' could include women: that was the conclusion reached by the House of Lords in *Nairn v University of St Andrews*,[1] a case about whether women could vote for the old university seats in Parliament. The Lord Chancellor said this:

> It is incomprehensible to me that any one acquainted with our laws or the methods by which they are ascertained can think, if, indeed, any one does think, there is room for argument on such a point. It is notorious that this right of voting has, in fact, been confined to men.[2]

Lord Robertson added:

> I think that a judgment is wholesome and of good example which puts forward subject-matter and fundamental constitutional law as guides of construction never to be neglected in favour of verbal possibilities.[3]

In principle it is possible for a legal system to have a principle of equality at two levels: the constitutional level and the ordinary level. To some extent this corresponds to the distinction between public law and private law but by no means exactly. For example, a public authority may well be subjected to obligations (usually in a statute) to refrain from discrimination in its employment functions. However, that would not be at the constitutional level. There would be no prohibition on discrimination on the legislature itself, or even on the executive when performing core state functions such as immigration control, policing and taxation.

The law of the United States can be taken by way of example. The original Constitution did not include an equality provision even in the Bill of Rights, ie the first 10 amendments. The famous equal protection clause was included at the end of the Civil War as part of the 14th Amendment. At around the same time Congress enacted a series of statutes, the first Civil Rights Acts, which were designed to confer legal rights on former slaves. They were largely emasculated by the courts and ignored in practice by a society which had legally enforced segregation from about 1890 to the 1960s. Eventually Congress passed the Civil Rights Act 1964, which prohibited discrimination in the provision of employment, housing and other facilities. In the meantime the US Supreme Court had begun in 1954 its long-neglected duty of dismantling state-imposed segregation. In other words discrimination was prohibited in relations between individuals by statute; and prohibited as between the state and the individual by the constitution.

In this country we had no developed principle against discrimination in the common law. In consequence Parliament had to fill the void and did so, at first with weak legislation passed in 1965 and 1968, and eventually with stronger legislation in

---

[1] [1909] AC 147 (HL); cf. *Edwards v Attorney General of Canada* [1930] AC 124 (PC).
[2] At 160.
[3] At 165–66.

the form of the Sex Discrimination Act 1975 and the Race Relations Act 1976, which, despite the imperfections which have become clear since then, have stood the test of time remarkably well, surviving the long period of Conservative government from 1979 to 1997, and remain our main equality laws in those respective fields. Further reform has arrived or is coming soon in the shape of regulations to implement EU directives extending protection against discrimination to cover religion, sexual orientation and age.

What we have not had for so long is a constitutional guarantee of equality. There were hints of it in the common law. Indeed the common law principle can be seen as long ago as *Kruse v Johnson* in 1898,[4] when Lord Russell CJ referred to the possibility that bye-laws might be struck down as being unreasonable if 'they were found to be partial and unequal in their operation as between different classes'.

In a seminal article in 1994, Professor Jeffrey Jowell put the justification for recognition of a common law/constitutional principle of equality like this:

> Just like free speech it is a principle that derives from democracy itself. Basic to democracy is the requirement that every citizen has an equal vote, and therefore an equal opportunity to influence the composition of the government. The notion of equal worth is thus a fundamental precept of our constitution. It gains its ultimate justification from a notion of the way individuals should be treated in a democracy. It is constitutive of democracy.[5]

Later in the same article Professor Jowell said this:

> Our constitution rests upon an assumption that government should not impose upon any citizen any burden that depends upon an argument that ultimately forces the citizen to relinquish her or his sense of equal worth. This principle is deeply embedded in our law, although it is rarely made explicit.[6]

I agree with much of what Professor Jowell says but note that, whether deliberately or not, he moves between references to 'citizens' and references to 'individuals'.

Similarly, in a lecture given in Australia in April 2003 entitled 'Human Rights and Minorities' Lord Woolf, the Lord Chief Justice, said this:

> Just as it is the essence of democracy that every individual has an equal right to vote, so each individual has the right to expect that a democratically elected government will regard it as its responsibility to protect each of its citizen's human rights. Human rights come with true democracy whether the government wants them or not.

One of the major problems that our legal system has to grapple with is how to deal with discrimination against non-citizens. They may well not have the vote; they may not even have any lawful entitlement to be here. But the premise of human rights is that fundamental rights flow from our common humanity, not from legal concepts such as nationality. This is how the point was put in *Andrews*, an early and important

---

[4] [1898] 2 QB 91, at p.99.
[5] J Jowell, 'Equality as a Constitutional Principle' (1994) 7 *CLP* 1, at 7.
[6] ibid, 18.

case on section 15 of the Canadian Charter of Fundamental Rights and Freedoms, by Justice McIntyre in the Supreme Court of Canada:

> It is clear that the purpose of section 15 is to insure equality in the formulation and application of the law. The promotion of equality entails the promotion of a society in which all are secure in the knowledge that they are recognised at law as human beings equally deserving of concern, respect and consideration.[7]

Nor is this some strange foreign notion which has only recently arrived in this country. As the Court of Appeal noted in *Abbasi*, the principle which protects personal liberty at common law is one 'which applies to every person, British citizen or not, who finds himself within the jurisdiction of the court',[8] quoting Lord Scarman's famous speech in *Khawaja* that: 'He who is subject to English law is entitled to its protection'.[9]

This is a problem to which I will return later in this talk.

The authority which is often cited these days for the proposition that there is a common law principle of equality is the decision of the Privy Council in *Matadeen v Pointu* in which Lord Hoffmann said this:

> Their Lordships do not doubt that such a principle is one of the building blocks of democracy and necessarily permeates any democratic constitution. Indeed, their Lordships would go further and say that treating like cases alike and unlike cases differently is a general axiom of rational behaviour. It is, for example, frequently invoked by the courts in proceedings for judicial review as a ground for holding some administrative act to have been irrational ...

> But [Lord Hoffmann continued] the very banality of the principle must suggest a doubt as to whether merely to state it can provide an answer to the kind of problem which arises in this case. Of course persons should be uniformly treated, unless there is some valid reason to treat them differently. But what counts as a valid reason for treating them differently? And, perhaps more important, who is to decide whether the reason is valid or not? Must it always be the courts? ... The fact that equality of treatment is a general principle of rational behaviour does not entail that it should necessarily be a justiciable principle – that it should always be the judges who have the last word on whether the principle has been observed. In this, as in other areas of constitutional law, sonorous judicial statements of uncontroversial principle often conceal the real problem, which is to mark out the boundary between the powers of the judiciary, the legislature and the executive in deciding how that principle is to be applied.[10]

It is open to argument whether judicial review cases in which the principle of equality has been successful are 'frequent' but nevertheless it has long been established that some considerations are simply irrelevant to a decision and therefore should not be taken into account, for example the colour of a person's hair in the famous example about a teacher given *obiter* in *Short v Poole Corporation*.[11] But what is less

---

[7] *Andrews v Law Society of British Columbia* [1989] 1 SCR 143, at 171. Justice McIntyre wrote the judgment for the majority of the Court.

[8] *R (Abbasi) v Secretary of State for Foreign and Commonwealth Affairs* [2002] EWCA Civ 1598 [2003] UKHRR 76, at para 60 (Lord Phillips of Worth Matravers MR, giving the judgment of the Court).

[9] *Khawaja v Secretary of State for the Home Department* [1984] AC 74, at 111.

[10] [1999] AC 98, at 109. See also *R (Gurung) v Ministry of Defence* [2002] EWHC 2463 Admin (27 November 2002, McCombe J), in which discrimination on racial grounds was held to be irrational.

[11] [1926] KB 66, at 91 (Warrington LJ).

well-known is that, on the facts of that case, the Court of Appeal held that it was lawful for a local education authority to dismiss a teacher on the ground that she was a married woman. It is worth reading the decision letter in that case:

> Town Clerk's Office, Poole, 19th May, 1924. Dear Sir, Married Women Teachers. The Education Committee have had under consideration the desirability of continuing the employment, in the public elementary schools in the Borough, of married women teachers, and they have decided that, so far as the Council schools are concerned, the engagement of all such teachers will be terminated unless in any particular case some sufficient reason exists for the engagement being continued ... The Committee were led to this decision for the following reasons: (1.) They consider the duty of the married woman is primarily to look after her domestic concerns and they regard it as impossible for her to do so and to effectively and satisfactorily act as a teacher at the same time; (2.) That it is unfair to the large number of young unmarried teachers who are at present seeking situations that the positions should be occupied by married women, who presumably have husbands capable of maintaining them.

Even today, the problem with the common law principle of equality is that it really does nothing to move forward the debate from traditional grounds of administrative law, e.g. that irrelevant considerations should not be taken into account and that a decision should not be irrational in the sense that no reasonable body could have reached it. It is rarely the case that a public body will do that, although last year the Ministry of Defence was held to have done so in *Gurung*, in which discrimination was held to have been on purely racial grounds and therefore irrational.

The weakness of irrationality as a ground for protecting people against discrimination can be demonstrated by the well-known litigation concerning the blanket ban on homosexuals in the armed forces. That was an application for judicial review brought before the Human Rights Act was enacted. In the domestic legal system, both the Divisional Court and the Court of Appeal felt unable to grant the application.[12] There was evidence before the courts that the view of senior members of the armed forces was that the ban was needed for reasons of military effectiveness. Even though the courts recognised the human rights background they felt unable to hold that the ban was irrational and so the applicants had to follow the well-trodden path to Strasbourg. There they were successful. The European Court of Human Rights held that not only had there been a violation of Article 8 (the right to respect for private life) because the ban was excessive and disproportionate, but also that there had been a violation of the right to an effective remedy in Article 13, because the standard of review applied by the domestic courts was too low to give the protection to Convention rights which is required. Although the Court did not find a violation of Article 14, the non-discrimination provision in the Convention, this was only because it did not need to address it in the light of its other findings.[13] It is clear that otherwise the Court would have found a breach of Article 14 because there was clearly discrimination which the Court did not think was objectively justified and proportionate. If there was any single case which demonstrated the need for the Human Rights Act it was that one.

---

[12] *R v Ministry of Defence, ex p. Smith* [1996] QB 517.
[13] *Smith and Grady v United Kingdom* (2000) 29 EHRR 493, paras 115–16.

I therefore turn to the Human Rights Act and the European Convention on Human Rights to which it gives effect in domestic law. This does operate at the constitutional level. As Lord Steyn and others have observed, it is a constitutional statute, not an ordinary one, not least because it provides for judicial review of Acts of Parliament albeit it does not permit the courts to strike them down but only to issue a declaration of incompatibility.

In many ways the most important word in the European Convention on Human Rights is 'everyone'. Most of the substantive articles of the Convention begin with the word 'everyone'. The real challenge is to take that word seriously and accept that it means what it says. Many of the articles of the Convention are inherently based on the idea of human equality: that each one of us is entitled to express a view however much others may disagree with it; to have a religious belief of our choice or to have none; to organise our private life as we see fit. This reflects a concept of human happiness in which it is not for the state to impose a particular view or belief or lifestyle on any person. In that sense, one can say that the Convention treats us all equally, without descending into the bankruptcy of moral relativism. The Convention is not saying that every view is as good as any other; merely that the state should treat us as mature human beings who can work out the answers for ourselves without imposing a view from on high. And, of course, there is Article 14, which guarantees equality in the enjoyment of other Convention rights.

I have already mentioned the equal protection clause in the 14th Amendment to the US Constitution and I would like to express my debt to a highly instructive article on that clause published by Tussman and tenBroek in the California Law Review as long ago as 1949.[14] Although written before the classic jurisprudence of the US Supreme Court on the equal protection clause emerged from 1954 onwards, when *Brown v Board of Education*[15] was decided, this seminal article deserves careful consideration by those who are interested in developing a constitutional law of equality in this country. It is impossible to do justice to the article here but I will seek to summarise its main points.

The equal protection of the laws requires more than merely the equal application of the laws. This is because otherwise the content of the law itself may be unequal. A discriminatory law may be applied equally to all who fall within its scope. So, early on in the history of the 14th Amendment, Justice Matthews said in 1886 that: 'The equal protection of the laws is a pledge of the protection of equal laws'.[16]

All legislation necessarily places persons into classes and therefore classification by itself cannot be a sound basis for regarding the legislation as unequal. As the Constitutional Court of South Africa put it in relation to the equality guarantee in the Interim Constitution:

> in order to govern a modern country efficiently and to harmonise the interests of all of its people for the common good, it is essential to regulate the affairs of its inhabitants extensively. It is impossible to do so without differentiation and without classifications which

---

[14] J Tussman and J tenBroek, 'The Equal Protection of the Laws' (1949) 37 *Calif LR* 341.
[15] (1954) 347 US 483.
[16] *Yick Wo v Hopkins* (1886) 118 US 356, at 369.

treat people differently and which impact on people differently. ... In regard to [such] mere differentiation the constitutional state is expected to act in a rational manner. It should not regulate in an arbitrary manner or manifest 'naked preferences' that serve no legitimate governmental purpose, for that would be inconsistent with the rule of law and the fundamental premises of the constitutional state.[17]

Accordingly, as in American law, the courts will give considerable deference to the other parts of the state when they seek to regulate economic matters and will be reluctant to infer that a line which has been drawn between two classes of persons has been drawn in the wrong place.

However, some classifications are so invidious that they are 'suspect' and so will be subjected to strict scrutiny, requiring much more than mere rationality. Indeed, in practice, it may be impossible to justify certain kinds of discrimination, such as discrimination on the ground of colour. The test which has subsequently been developed in US constitutional law is that the law must be narrowly tailored to meet a compelling state interest.

In principle there are five different possible relationships between the scope of the mischief aimed at by legislation, its purpose, and the scope of the class actually caught by it.

The first is where there is a perfect fit between the purpose to be achieved and the means used to achieve it: this is the ideal to be sought but may be very difficult to achieve in practice.

The second is where there is no fit at all: this kind of measure could be said to lack even a rational connection between the aim sought to be achieved and the means used.

The third type is where the law hits more than the class aimed at. For example, if the aim of the law is to prevent acts of disloyalty by US citizens, but all citizens of Japanese ancestry are detained, the law is overbroad, or over-inclusive:[18] this is known as the doctrine of overbreadth and we would recognise it as a classic example of a law which is disproportionate because it goes further than is necessary to achieve its aim.

However, there is a fourth type of law, which is less familiar to us. This is where the law hits some of its target but not all of it. At first sight this seems not to raise any problem about proportionality at all. It does not go further than is necessary. But it penalises some people and leaves others alone. From an equal treatment perspective, this should raise alarm bells: how have the two pools of people been defined? Why is the state not prepared to go as far as its stated purpose would dictate it should go? Are there objective and compelling reasons or is it that some are more popular than others? In the example I gave earlier, the law did not extend to US citizens of German or Italian origin: yet they too could have been said to have a potential conflict of loyalty in the Second World War. It was only citizens of Japanese origin who were detained without trial.

---

[17] *Prinsloo v Van Der Linde* (1997) 3 SA 1012, paras 24–25 (Ackermann, O'Regan and Sachs JJ).

[18] This provided the background to *Korematsu v United States* (1944) 323 US 214. The challenge in fact failed in the US Supreme Court. See further Lord Bingham, 'Personal Freedom and the Dilemma of Democracies' (2003) 52 *ICLQ* 841, at 856–58.

The final type of law is one which appears to be at first sight a contradiction in terms but is in fact fairly common. It is the law which is both over-inclusive and under-inclusive. The example from the Second World War again illustrates this type: the law was both overbroad because it treated the loyal and the disloyal person of Japanese ancestry in the same way; and it was under-inclusive because it did not apply to others who might have been disloyal as well.

Where a law uses a suspect classification the courts should be astute to see that there is as tight a fit as possible between the scope of the legislation and the scope of the professed purpose. Otherwise there is a danger that, however much it acts in good faith and even if discrimination is subconscious, the state will sacrifice an unpopular minority for the perceived good of the majority.

The discipline of equality analysis is important for two main reasons. First, it provides a rigorous analytical framework for what might otherwise be perceived to be simply political decisions not suitable for judicial interference. As so often in the law, getting the right answer is difficult but it helps to ask the right questions. Secondly, the discipline of equality is consistent with the democratic structure of our society. It gives the courts a useful role in protecting fundamental rights without encroaching on the purely political function which is the province of the government and of Parliament. This is because, when the court finds that a decision or even a piece of legislation violates the right to equal treatment it does not prescribe the only response available to the state. What the other branches of the state may then do is respond by levelling down or levelling up. But the 'political price' for levelling down has to be paid. This is morally right as well because it means that, in difficult areas such as the allocation of resources, the state is entitled to a wide latitude of judgment on the underlying question but when it comes to the discriminatory allocation of benefits or burdens, there is no reason why the state should be given much, if any, deference. Indeed it is in this perpetual struggle between minorities and the majority that the court should play the most vigilant role. It should always be vigorous in acting as the guardian of minority rights. This is because the majority can usually be expected to use their superior political power through the ballot box to achieve the outcomes which they perceive to be in their interests. If the majority abuse their power (even unwittingly) and impose burdens on the minority which are not necessary and objectively justified, the democratic system suffers a systemic failure. It is in danger of eating itself up. What the courts can and should do is stand up for the enduring values of our society, which include the principle of equality. As Lord Steyn said in his lecture on 2 October 2003 in memory of Chief Justice Dickson in Canada:

> A core characteristic of a constitutional democracy is the protection it offers to the rights of individuals against the majority view as reflected by an elected government. In our new constitutional order Parliament itself has placed this duty on the courts. It permits judicial review of Acts of Parliament. … The courts may not abdicate their responsibilities by developing self-denying constitutional limitations on their powers.

Against that background I would like to turn to the decision of the Court of Appeal in *A v Secretary of State for the Home Department*,[19] which concerned detention

---

[19] [2002] EWCA Civ 1502 [2003] 2 WLR 564, at para 7.

without trial of suspected international terrorists. The Court had to consider the legality of the UK's derogation from Article 5 of the ECHR under Article 15, which permits derogation in time of war or other public emergency threatening the life of the nation. In relation to the discrimination part of the challenge, Lord Woolf CJ started off well by referring to an important American case from 1949:

> The vice involved in discrimination was well identified by Jackson J of the United States Supreme Court in 1949:
>
> 'equality is not merely abstract justice. The framers of the Constitution knew, and we should not forget today, that there is no more effective practical guaranty against arbitrary and unreasonable government than to require that the principles of law which officials would impose upon a minority must be imposed generally. Conversely, nothing opens the door to arbitrary action so effectively as to allow those officials to pick and choose only a few to whom they will apply legislation and thus to escape the political retribution that might be visited upon them if larger numbers were affected. Courts can take no better measure to assure that laws will be just than to require that laws be equal in operation.'
> *Railway Express Agency Inc v New York* (1949) 336 US 106, 112–113.

However, when he came to analyse the discrimination part of the argument in the case of *A* itself, Lord Woolf held that Special Immigration Appeals Commission had erred in concluding that there was discrimination as between British citizens, who cannot be detained on the certificate of the Secretary of State, and foreign nationals, who can be under the conditions laid down in section 23 of the Anti-terrorism, Crime and Security Act 2001.

> 47 ... the position here is that the Secretary of State has come to the conclusion that he can achieve what is necessary by either detaining or deporting only the terrorists who are aliens. If the Secretary of State has come to that conclusion, then the critical question is: are there objective, justifiable and relevant grounds for selecting only the alien terrorists, or is the discrimination on the grounds of nationality? As to this critical question, I have come to the conclusion that there are objectively justifiable and relevant grounds which do not involve impermissible discrimination. The grounds are the fact that the aliens who cannot be deported have, unlike nationals, no right to remain, only a right not to be removed, which means legally that they come into a different class from those who have a right of abode.

This reasoning is remarkable. It amounts to saying that foreigners can not only be regulated in the context of immigration control but also outside that context because they have no right to be here in the first place. But Article 5 provides that 'everyone' has the right to liberty. If that had not been so, there would have been no need for the derogation anyway. Suppose Parliament enacted a law which abrogated the right to a fair trial for offences generally (including murder or theft) but did so only in relation to foreign nationals. Lord Woolf's reasoning appears to suggest that that would be permissible because a foreign national has no right to be here, so while they are here, they cannot complain that their Convention rights are being interfered with in a discriminatory way.

Brooke LJ set out an extensive discussion about international law and the detention of foreign nationals, concluding that both customary international law and multilateral treaties had recognised that states are entitled to detain foreign nationals without trial in times of war or other emergencies even if they do not detain their own citizens. This argument again misses the point and proves too much. The question is not what international law generally permits but whether the criteria for a lawful derogation under Article 15 of the ECHR are met. Those criteria include the important requirement that the measures taken should be 'strictly required' to meet the needs of an emergency. It is difficult to see how a discriminatory measure can be regarded as strictly required. Moreover, the argument simply fails to address the point that what needs to be justified is not just the underlying measure but the discrimination. The point can be tested in this way. Suppose the Government had expressly derogated from Article 14 of the ECHR and not only from Article 5. It would then have had to show that the discrimination involved in its measures was strictly required. That would have been an uphill struggle to say the least. But the implication of the Court of Appeal's judgments is that the Government has somehow improved its legal position by not derogating from Article 14 and so it does not need to justify the discrimination inherent in its measures. It is interesting to note that at first instance the Government argued that it had impliedly derogated from Article 14 and from Article 26 of the International Covenant on Civil and Political Rights. That argument, which was a bold one, was rejected by SIAC and not revived in the Court of Appeal. But the Court of Appeal seems to have concluded that it did not matter. The result of cases in such a fundamental area should not depend on procedural or tactical points.

Chadwick LJ agreed with the other members of the Court and added:

> 153 … The decision to confine the measures to be taken to the detention of those who are subject to deportation, but who cannot (for the time being) be removed, is not a decision to discriminate against that class on the grounds of nationality. It is a decision that it is only persons who fall within that class who need to be detained in order to meet the emergency. What would be discriminatory would be to decide that all suspected international terrorists needed to be detained in order to meet the emergency; but to confine the power to detain to those who, because they were foreign nationals, were subject to immigration control. If that were what the Secretary of State had done, then it would be right to quash the Derogation Order.

But, on an objective scrutiny, that is precisely what Parliament has done. The professed purpose of the derogation is to deal with international terrorism as a direct result of September 11. But the means chosen to achieve that aim are under-inclusive and discriminate on the ground of citizenship.

In the *A* case the Secretary of State was represented by Lord Goldsmith, the Attorney General. The Attorney General recently gave an interesting lecture to the International Bar Association in San Francisco on 18 September 2003. There is much with which I am sure many here would agree. He said, for example, this in relation to balancing security and fundamental rights:

> I do not believe that this can be a simple utilitarian calculation of balancing the right to security of the many against the legal rights of the few. That would be to ignore the values on which our democratic society is built. For in the war on terrorism we are fighting for more than the safety of our citizens … We are fighting for the preservation of our democratic way of life, our right to freedom of thought and expression and our commitment

to the rule of law ... These are the very liberties and values which the terrorists seek to destroy.[20]

The Attorney General referred in passing to the decision in *A*. He mentioned that the Government had lost on one point in SIAC but that the Court of Appeal had reversed SIAC. He said that the ground could be described as follows: 'that the powers were not wide enough'. I have to say that I fundamentally disagree with the Attorney General on this point. The difficulty with that approach is that it could be used to undermine any equality argument. Whenever a person argues that a measure is discriminatory the state could always caricature the argument as an argument that the state has not gone far enough.

To take an extreme example which one hopes would never happen in this country: suppose the state announces that there is an economic crisis and that it is necessary in the public interest that property should be seized without compensation. It seeks to derogate from Article 1 of the First Protocol. But then suppose that the state announces that the only property which is to be seized is that belonging to Jewish people. Immediately the question of discrimination arises. In one sense it could be said that the state has acted more proportionately by drafting its measure in a narrow way rather than by hitting everyone in society. But no one could seriously suggest that such a measure was compatible with human rights principles, because it would constitute the most offensive kind of discrimination. In the context of the case of *A*, there is nothing surprising about a civil liberties organisation like Liberty arguing both that the power to detain without trial is unnecessary in general and that it is discriminatory in particular. Of course Liberty and many others would prefer to see there being no power to detain without trial at all. But if there is to be such a power it should include everyone equally. By imposing the discipline of equality on the state, the law would compel the state to face up to the full gravity of what it is doing. It would truly have to be a national emergency to justify such legislation. It is also consistent with democratic principle, because the court's decision that there has been a breach of the principle of equality forces the issue back to the democratic arena.

The fact that the Government is reluctant to ask Parliament to pass wider legislation suggests that in fact it is not 'strictly required' to meet the exigencies of the situation. In any event, one has to be careful to appreciate what has to be justified as being objectively necessary. It is not just the underlying measure – that would be true in any event because of the requirements of Article 15. What has to be justified is the *discrimination*. In *Gaygusuz v Austria*[21] the Court of Human Rights said that 'very weighty reasons would have to be put forward before the Court could regard a difference based exclusively on the ground of nationality as compatible with the Convention'.

And the test under Article 15 is even harder to satisfy than the normal test of proportionality. The measure used has to be strictly necessary to meet the exigencies

---

[20] In similar vein, Lord Woolf CJ put it pithily in his lecture (above): 'In defending democracy, we must not forget the need to observe the values which make democracy worth defending'.

[21] (1996) 23 EHRR 364, at para 42.

of the emergency. Far from being strictly necessary, discrimination means that the measure is less effective. How can it be necessary to discriminate when it would assist the fight against terrorism if there were no discrimination? And if the state is not prepared to go that far, it should not pick on a small unpopular minority.

I would like to turn next to the *European Roma Rights* case.[22] This was a claim for judicial review brought by an NGO based in Budapest devoted to the protection of the rights of Roma people in Europe and by individuals who were refused leave to enter the UK by immigration officers at Prague Airport. For present purposes the only relevant ground of challenge was based on section 19B of the Race Relations Act 1976, as inserted by the Race Relations (Amendment) Act 2000. As is well-known the 2000 Act was passed to implement many of the recommendations made by the Stephen Lawrence Inquiry Report. It is designed to extend to various public functions the duty not to discriminate on racial grounds which had previously only applied to a limited range of functions, such as employment, housing, education and goods and services. Services in this context had been interpreted in the past to exclude statutory functions such as immigration functions because they were not analogous to what a private person can do in the provision of services.[23] That restriction has now been swept away by the 2000 Act. Accordingly, it could be said that the 2000 Act is part of the constitutionalisation of discrimination law, just as the Human Rights Act is.

Section 19B makes it unlawful for a public authority in carrying out any functions of the authority to do an act which constitutes discrimination under section 1. Section 19D provides an exception in certain circumstances, including where there has been a ministerial authorisation in the fields of immigration and nationality. On 23 April 2001 a ministerial authorisation had been made which, under the heading 'Examination of passengers', permitted an immigration officer, by reason of a person's ethnic or national origin, to subject that person to a more rigorous examination than other persons in the same circumstances. In a schedule, this authorisation was made applicable to Roma people. However, the evidence filed on behalf of the Secretary of State was that the authorisation had not in fact been relied on to discriminate against Roma applicants at Prague airport. The argument was rather that the actions of immigration officers had complied with the 1976 Act in full and there had been no discrimination. The appellants alleged that there had been direct discrimination in that, for example, there was longer and more intrusive questioning of Roma than non-Roma; the treatment of them with greater suspicion; and a requirement of a higher standard of proof before leave to enter the UK would be granted. They placed what Simon Brown LJ called 'striking figures' before the Court of Appeal. These showed that, in a three month period in early 2002, of 6,170 passengers recorded as Czech nationals but not Roma, only 14 were refused (that was 0.2 per cent); whereas, of 78 applicants who were apparently Roma, 68 were refused (that was 87 per cent).

Simon Brown LJ, who gave the main judgment for the majority, said that:

> The question is this: what is the position in law if, as seems to the court wholly inevitable, immigration officers, aware of the fact that the overwhelming majority of those seeking

---

[22] *R (European Roma Rights Centre) v Immigration Officer, Prague Airport* [2003] EWCA Civ 666 [2003] 4 All ER 247.
[23] *In re Amin* [1983] AC 818.

asylum from the Czech Republic are Roma (it may be doubted, indeed, whether any such are non-Roma), bring a greater degree of scepticism to bear on a Roma's application for leave to enter for some permitted purpose than upon an apparently comparable application by a Czech non-Roma?[24]

In answering that question, Simon Brown LJ said:

> because of the greater degree of scepticism with which Roma applicants will inevitably be treated, they are more likely to be refused leave to enter than non-Roma applicants. But this is because they are less well placed to persuade the immigration officer that they are not lying in order to seek asylum. That is not to say, however, that they are being stereotyped. Rather it is to acknowledge the undoubtedly disadvantaged position of many Roma in the Czech Republic. Of course it would be wrong in any individual case to assume that the Roma applicant is lying, but I decline to hold that the immigration officer cannot properly be warier of that possibility in a Roma's case than in the case of a non-Roma applicant. If a terrorist outrage were committed on our streets today, would the police not be entitled to question more suspiciously those in the vicinity appearing to come from an Islamic background?[25]

Laws LJ dissented:

> when a Roma and non-Roma both present themselves at the desk at Prague airport and state they wish to visit London for the weekend, the immigration officer at that stage knows nothing of their personal circumstances. He has not seen what evidence they have to support their applications for leave to enter as visitors. All he knows, from their appearance, is that one is Roma and the other is not. He treats the Roma less favourably, by subjecting him or her to a more intrusive enquiry with a lesser prospect of leave to enter being granted. One asks ... why did he treat the Roma less favourably? It may be said there are two possible answers: (1) because he is Roma: (2) because he is more likely to be advancing a false application for leave to enter as a visitor. But it seems to me inescapable that the reality is that the officer treated the Roma less favourably *because* Roma are (for very well understood reasons) more likely to wish to seek asylum and thus more likely to put forward a false claim to enter as a visitor. The officer has applied a stereotype; though one which may very likely be true. That is not permissible. More pointedly, he has an entirely proper reason (or motive) for treating the Roma less favourably on racial grounds: his duty to refuse those without a claim under the Rules, manifestly including covert asylum-seekers, and his knowledge that the Roma is more likely to be a covert asylum-seeker. But that is irrelevant.[26]

It seems to me that Laws LJ must be right. It is clear that there was less favourable treatment. It is also clear that it was on racial grounds. As all the judges acknowledged, the reason for the discrimination is immaterial: in particular, the absence of a hostile intent or the presence of a benign motive is immaterial. What the majority view amounts to is, on analysis, an attempt to introduce into the law of direct discrimination the possibility of justification. But Parliament could have provided for that possibility – as it has done in the context of allegations of indirect discrimination – and has chosen not to do so. In so far as the fields of immigration and nationality

---

[24] At para 66.
[25] At para 86.
[26] At para 109.

may be thought to require special treatment, permitting discrimination on certain grounds (ethnic or national origins) but not others (such as colour), again Parliament has catered for that possibility in enabling a minister to give an authorisation. The Government did not want to rely on the authorisation in the *Roma* case: that was a matter for its tactical choice but the courts should not bend over backwards to save the executive from what may have been its own folly. Their duty, as Laws LJ said, is to apply the will of Parliament as enacted in its laws. Moreover, the danger in the majority's reasoning is that it is capable of application outside the limited areas with which the Court was concerned. For example, it could be applied in the context of police stop and search powers. Simon Brown LJ expressly gives an example from just that context. This is potentially very damaging to race relations law going beyond what may have been perceived to be the problem in the *Roma* case itself.

In case it be thought that I am unduly gloomy, there is one beacon of hope in the early case law on Article 14 and it is the *Ghaidan* case.[27] At first sight that case might not appear to be a constitutional case at all. It was a landlord and tenant dispute between two individuals, about whether the defendant could succeed to a statutory tenancy under the Rent Act 1977. But, because the case turned on the meaning of an Act of Parliament, it was a constitutional law case. The question arose whether Parliament had discriminated in a way which was incompatible with Article 14 of the ECHR. The Rent Act had been amended in 1988 to give the right of succession to a statutory tenancy to the surviving partner in an unmarried relationship as well as to the surviving partner in a married one. The question was whether the right was available in a same-sex relationship or whether it was confined to a heterosexual one. The Court of Appeal held unanimously that it was available to same-sex partners as well. In a text-book example of the generous and progressive spirit with which the Human Rights Act should work, the Court took the following innovative steps:

1. It was prepared to depart from a decision of the House of Lords, in *Fitzpatrick v. Sterling Housing Association*,[28] decided in 1999, just a year before the Human Rights Act came into full force.
2. It was prepared to depart from earlier case law of the European Commission of Human Rights which was directly in point on the ground that the court's task is to interpret the ECHR as a 'living instrument' and it is required by section 2 of the HRA only to take such case law into account and is not bound by it.
3. It was prepared to use section 3 of the HRA to give the Rent Act a meaning which was not its ordinary meaning, as the House of Lords had held in *Fitzpatrick*, but a meaning which was 'possible'. As Buxton LJ put it:

> Th[e] duty in section 3 of the HRA] can be properly discharged by reading the words 'as his or her wife or husband' to mean 'as *if they were* his or her wife or husband'.
>
> ... It is quite true ... that the words 'husband' and 'wife' are in their natural meaning gender-specific. They are also, however, in their natural meaning limited to persons who are party to a lawful marriage. ... And, Parliament having swallowed the camel of including unmarried partners within the protection given to married couples, it is

---

[27] *Ghaidan v Godin-Mendoza* [2002] EWCA Civ 1533 [2003] 2 WLR 478.
[28] [2001] 1 AC 27.

not for this court to strain at the gnat of including such partners who are of the same sex as each other.[29]

4.   Perhaps most importantly, when it came to assessing whether there was an objective and reasonable justification for the discrimination between heterosexual couples and same-sex couples, the Court was not prepared to give much deference to Parliament. As Buxton LJ said:

> The general organisation of housing policy, and in particular of public housing … clearly involves complex questions of social or economic policy that the courts should only enter with trepidation. But I have no hesitation in saying that issues of discrimination, which it is conceded we are concerned with in this case, do have high constitutional importance, and are issues that the courts should not shrink from. In such cases deference has only a minor role to play.

> 20 … once it is accepted that we are not simply bound by whatever Parliament has decided … then we need to see whether the steps taken in implementation of the supposed policy are, not merely reasonable and proportionate, but also logically explicable as forwarding that policy. If it is accepted for the moment that Parliament seeks by the Schedule to promote the interests of landlords, flexibility in the housing market and the protection of the family, how is any of that significantly forwarded by depriving the survivors of same-sex partnerships of statutory but not of assured tenancies? Since this part of the argument rested simply on assertion, no actual facts or evidence were available to assist us; so the court has to fall back on common sense.

Keene LJ added:

> 43 As for proportionality, one accepts that in a number of areas of social and economic policy-making the courts should grant a generous degree of deference to Parliament when it comes to striking the balance between the individual and the community. But this depends crucially on the context. The issue here is one of discrimination between two groups on the basis of their sexual orientation, rather than one of housing policy.

> 44 Where discrimination against a minority is concerned, amounting on the face of it to a breach of article 14 rights, the courts are entitled to require to be satisfied that a proper and rational justification for the difference in treatment has been made out. It is, as Buxton LJ has emphasised, a matter involving rights of high constitutional importance where the courts are equipped to arrive at a judgment. It is indeed a classic role of the courts to be concerned with the protection of such minority rights.

Although it is difficult to speculate, it may be that the reasons which explain why the courts were prepared to be so much more intrusive in *Ghaidan* than in *A* or in the *Roma* case are not so much legal as subconscious:

1.   There seems to remain the residual but instinctive feeling that equality is about equality as between citizens. Foreign nationals are not regarded as analogous because foreigners are 'different'.
2.   The contexts of the first two cases are politically more controversial (terrorism and asylum), where the courts would be taking on the Government directly and doing so in areas where the Government may well have many people, perhaps the

---

[29] At para 35.

majority of people in society, on its side. But, of course, one should recall that, when an equality argument is made, the court does not have to enter the merits of national security or asylum policy; rather it is concerned with whether there is an objective and pressing justification for the discrimination involved.

3.   In contrast, in the *Ghaidan* case, the parties were private litigants, and the Government was not represented even as an intervenor. Furthermore, the Court may well have felt, from its own reading of the social and political context, that the tide of opinion is moving in favour of equalisation of rights in the field of sexual orientation, for example, the Government is proposing to introduce civil partnerships for same-sex couples.

Whatever the reasons, it seems to me that equality has been for too long a neglected virtue in our constitutional law. But it could not be more important as a symbol of the kind of society we are. As Lord Woolf put it eloquently in his recent lecture in Australia:

> The real test of the [Human Rights Act] arises when individuals or minorities attract the antagonism of the majority of the public. When the tabloids are in full cry. Then, the courts must, without regard to their own interests, make the difficult decisions that ensure that those under attack have the benefit of the rule of law. At the heart of the HRA is the need to respect the dignity of every individual by ensuring that he or she is not subject to discrimination.

These are important statements of the right approach but the time has come to turn the rhetoric into reality. The tabloids are indeed in 'full cry' on the issues of asylum-seekers and terrorist suspects. It is important to recall that, when Lord Scarman used his Hamlyn Lectures nearly 30 years ago to advocate incorporation of the ECHR, one of the main reasons he gave was that it is when fear stalks the land that unpopular minorities most need protection. And if one thing is certain after September 11, it is that people are more afraid of terrorist attack. It is precisely in that climate of opinion that the courts have to step in and protect not only minorities but the enduring values of our society.

Racial Equality and the Law

Sir Mota Singh QC was the first person of colour to become a judge in this country: he became a Circuit Judge in 1982. He retired in 2002 and was knighted in 2010. He passed away in 2016. In 2018 a lecture series was established in his memory at Lincoln's Inn (of which he had been a Bencher). I gave the inaugural lecture and chose as my theme racial equality and the law. I examined in particular the development of the law in the USA and, more recently, the UK. This lecture was first published in [2019] EHRLR 598.

INTRODUCTION

I T WAS EXACTLY two years ago, on 13 November 2016, that sadly Sir Mota Singh passed away. It is an honour to give the inaugural lecture in his memory at Lincoln's Inn, of which he was a Bencher. It is a particular pleasure for us to welcome Swaran Kaur (Lady Singh) and other members of his family to be with us this evening. Mota Singh was not only a wise judge but a much loved person, amongst his colleagues, amongst practitioners and with the staff at Southwark Crown Court, where he sat for some 20 years after his appointment as a Circuit Judge in 1982. I know that because, having myself sat at Southwark when I was a Presiding Judge on the South Eastern Circuit, I found that, more than a decade after his retirement, Mota Singh was still remembered with great affection by the judges and staff there.

Having grown up in Kenya, Mota Singh came to this country initially in the 1950s to complete his education. He then settled in this country in the 1960s in order to practise law at the Bar. He took Silk in 1978 and was appointed to the Circuit bench in 1982. He was an inspiration to many of us. It is difficult for us to imagine today what the environment must have been like for a person of colour when he was first beginning to establish himself both as a practitioner and later to become a judge in this country. It is no exaggeration I think to say that Sir Mota Singh opened doors which enabled others like me to come through in a way which would have been very difficult if not impossible to imagine previously. And he did so not by banging on those doors in any aggressive way. Far from it. That was not his character. He was a quiet and gentle person.

I have called my lecture 'Racial Equality and the Law' but I want to make one thing clear at the outset: there is only one race, the human race. Race is not a scientific concept. The law in this area makes this clear, for example in the preamble to the EU Race Directive of 2000,[1] recital (6) of which states that:

> The European Union rejects theories which attempt to determine the existence of separate human races. The use of the term 'racial origin' in this Directive does not imply an acceptance of such theories.

That this had to be said at the beginning of the EU Directive on racial discrimination is perhaps understandable in view of the history of Europe in the twentieth century. The law as it has developed in this area emerged in order to counteract the pernicious effects of racism and the spurious pseudo-scientific theories on which it was sometimes based. Robert Wald Sussman, Professor of Physical Anthropology at Washington University in St. Louis, has written a comprehensive book entitled *The Myth of Race*,[2] in which he demolishes the unscientific idea of race but also addresses why the notion still persists. He points out that in 1950 UNESCO issued a statement that the human race is one species and that the concept of race has no basis in biological fact. Race is a social construct, intertwined with history, geography, language, religion and most of all with culture. But the fact that race does not exist does not mean that racism does not.

In the preface to his book *Black and British* the historian David Olusoga describes his own experience of growing up on a council estate in the north-east of England in the 1980s in the following way:

> Almost every black or mixed-race person of my generation has a story of racial violence to tell ... In 1984 my family ... were driven out of our home by a sustained campaign of almost nightly attacks ... We lived in darkness, as the windows of our home were broken one by one, smashed by bricks and rocks thrown from ... across the street. As replacing the glass merely invited further attacks the windows were boarded up and we slowly disappeared into the gloom, quarantined together behind a screen of plywood.[3]

In her book *Brit(ish)* Afua Hirsch, who is a barrister of this Inn and a journalist, describes this incident when she was growing up in a more affluent area in the 1990s:

> The harshest lessons came in my late teens, visiting my best friend at work at a boutique in Wimbledon Village. The manager told her I could not come in: 'It's off-putting to the other customers,' she said 'and the black girls are thieves. Tell her she is not welcome.' ... The sense that I was not welcome in my own local shops, in the place I had lived since childhood, had a profound effect.[4]

CONSTANTINE v IMPERIAL HOTELS LTD

I want to start with a story about cricket, or at least a famous cricketer. I hope Sir Mota would have approved. As many of you will know one of Mota Singh's loves

---

[1] Directive 2000/43.
[2] (Cambridge MA, Harvard University Press, 2014).
[3] *Black and British: A Forgotten History* (London, Pan Books, 2016) xvii.
[4] *Brit(ish): On Race, Identity and Belonging* (London, Jonathan Cape, 2018) 11.

was cricket. In fact he was widely regarded as having the potential to play for the Kenyan national team.

On 30 July 1943 the famous cricketer from the West Indies, Learie Constantine (later Lord Constantine) thought that he had booked himself and his wife a room at the Imperial Hotel in London. However, when they arrived at the hotel they were informed that there was, as it were, no room at the inn for them. It would appear that the underlying reason why they were turned away was that there were American soldiers stationed at the hotel who objected to their presence on racial grounds. At that time the armed forces of the United States were still subject to racial segregation. Mr Constantine and his wife went under protest to the Bedford Hotel instead.

Mr Constantine brought an action against Imperial Hotels which came before Mr Justice Birkett as he then was.[5] Mr Constantine was represented by one of the foremost advocates of his day: Sir Patrick Hastings KC, leading Rose Heilbron, who would later become one of the first two women silks in this country and a High Court judge. The cause of action relied upon was a breach of an innkeeper's duty to receive a traveller. After lengthy consideration of the authorities, Mr Justice Birkett held that this cause of action did not require proof of special damage. He considered that the principles of the decision in *Ashby v White*[6] applied to this context. Therefore judgment was given for the plaintiff and damages awarded of five guineas.

The decision in *Constantine* is of interest not only for historical reasons but because it illustrates the capacity of the common law to develop from time to time in order to remedy an injustice. However, Mr Constantine might not have been so fortunate if he had for example been subjected to racial discrimination not when seeking accommodation from an innkeeper but applying for a job or to rent accommodation. As is well known, right up to the 1960s, there was openly practised racial discrimination in this country in fields such as employment, housing and the provision of goods and services to members of the public. It is possible that the common law might have developed in such a way as to control racial discrimination even in those contexts. It is certainly possible to conceive that implied terms could have been inserted into many contracts or leases to that effect. However, it would have been much more difficult if not impossible for the common law to deal with the very common situation where a person was discriminated against on racial grounds without there ever being a contract or other relevant legal relationship already in existence, typically where they applied for a job or for housing and were turned down.

Before I turn to the development of the law in this area it is worth recalling the reasons why racial equality is important. As various courts have said over the years, there are four main reasons why it is important.[7]

First, it follows from the fundamental principle that each individual should be treated on their own merits and not for some irrelevant reason, especially if that reason is immutable and something over which a person has no control, such as their colour or ethnic or national origins. In a modern democracy we consider that every human being has equal worth and should be afforded equal concern and respect.

---

[5] [1944] 1 KB 693.

[6] 2 Lord Raymond 938; 3 Howell's State Trials Volume XIV, Lord Raymond 320.

[7] *Ghaidan v Godin-Mendoza* [2004] 2 AC 557, at paras 131–32 (Baroness Hale of Richmond); and *R (Elias) v Secretary of State for Defence* [2006] 1 WLR 3213, at paras 269–71 (Arden LJ).

As Article 1 of the Universal Declaration of Human Rights puts it: 'Every human being is born free and equal in dignity and rights'. As a devout Sikh, Mota Singh would have recognised this, since it is a fundamental tenet of the Sikh faith that every human being is equal. Sikhism rejects notions such as race and caste.

Secondly, the law in this area recognises the harm that is done to an individual who is the victim of racial discrimination. This can be financial harm, as when a person is refused a job or a promotion which they deserve on their merits, but it can also include injury to feelings. Anyone who has suffered discrimination will know that it can cause embarrassment, humiliation and self-doubt: a questioning of a person's self-worth.

Thirdly, there is a utilitarian justification. Society generally benefits when a person is treated on their individual merits, not just that person. This is because, for example, society will then have the best person appointed for the job in question. This can be illustrated by the film *Hidden Figures*, made in 2017, which was based on the true story of Katherine Goble Johnson and her colleagues at NASA in the 1960's. They were known as the 'computers', at a time when human beings rather than machines still had to do the maths that would enable astronauts to go into orbit and eventually reach the moon. Katherine Johnson was employed in what was called the 'colored computers' section of NASA. She and her colleagues suffered dual discrimination, as they were women and they were African-Americans. In the film there is a scene when Katherine Johnson points out to her white colleagues that they are prepared to use her calculations but they are not prepared to drink from the same coffee jug as her: she has to drink from a separate jug marked 'colored'. Yet she and others persevered. Eventually, Katherine Johnson's contribution to the American space programme was recognised by President Obama when she was awarded the Presidential Medal of Freedom (the highest civilian honour in the US) in 2015.

Fourthly, there is also this utilitarian justification for promoting racial equality: the maintenance of social harmony and cohesion. History teaches that, in a society in which a racial minority – or perhaps even a majority, as in South Africa during *apartheid* – is systematically discriminated against, there is likely to be public disorder and violence. Racial discrimination is not good for the health of society.

At this stage of my lecture I want to go back in time to look at the history of racial discrimination and the law in the United States because in that country we see that the first attempts were being made to use the law to prohibit racial discrimination as early as the 1860s after the American Civil War. There are two reasons for looking at the American experience. First, it is intrinsically interesting in showing us both the limits of law and also its potential in combatting racial discrimination. Secondly, American law has influenced the development of the law in this country too.

THE AMERICAN EXPERIENCE

I have suggested elsewhere that the approach of the law to issues of racial discrimination can be viewed at two different levels.[8] The first level is the constitutional level.

---

[8] R Singh, 'Equality: the Neglected Virtue' [2004] *EHRLR* 141. This article is reproduced as chapter 15 in this book.

This concerns attempts by constitutional law to regulate the powers of state bodies, including potentially even the legislature, in the field of racial discrimination. The second level is the non-constitutional level. This often concerns the relations between private individuals and entities, such as employers, landlords and companies providing goods and services to the public, such as railway companies. These situations may involve state bodies or they may involve private entities. Sometimes the law, usually in the form of legislation, rather than constitutional provisions, attempts to prohibit racial discrimination in such areas of human activity.

In the United States in the middle of the nineteenth century we see early attempts by the law to address racial discrimination both at the constitutional level and at the non-constitutional level. In the five years after the Civil War ended in 1865, as part of the process known as 'Reconstruction', by which the states which had seceded in 1861 to form the Confederacy were brought back into the Union, three important constitutional amendments were passed. In 1865 the Thirteenth Amendment abolished slavery. In 1868 the Fourteenth Amendment (among other things) guaranteed against the States the 'equal protection of the laws'. What that means is something to which I will have to return. In 1870 the Fifteenth Amendment prohibited racial discrimination in the exercise of the right to vote.

As well as those laws, which operate at the constitutional level, the US Congress enacted a number of statutes seeking to prohibit racial discrimination at the non-constitutional level. The Civil Rights Act of 1866 conferred what might be regarded as the most basic rights on newly freed slaves, for example the right to form contracts and to own property. These were 'civil' rights in the truest original sense, things that most of us hardly even think about, they seem so obviously to be an incident of what each of us is entitled to do as a person. But of course many human beings had until 1865 not been recognised in the US as persons at all: they had themselves been regarded as chattels, a piece of property to be bought and sold.

The issue of racial discrimination often arose in the context of segregation on America's early railroads. Even before the Civil War, courts had been required to consider the issue and had held that railroads were bound by the common law requirement that public carriers should accept all customers subject only to reasonable regulations imposed for public convenience. However, racial segregation in railway carriages was generally considered to be a reasonable regulation. According to Michael J Klarman, 'the prevailing view of courts was that [segregation] qualified as a reasonable policy'.[9]

In 1865 Massachusetts became the first state to forbid racial discrimination in public accommodations. In 1875 the US Congress enacted legislation (the Civil Rights Act of that year) which was generally understood to forbid segregation by common carriers but the Supreme Court invalidated it in 1883. However, segregation did not come to either the railways or to other forms of public transportation quickly or uniformly across even the Southern States. Florida enacted the first state railroad segregation law in 1887 and was followed by other states. Segregation of streetcars began in earnest in 1900 and had become well established by 1906.

---

[9] *From Jim Crow to Civil Rights: The Supreme Court and the Struggle for Racial Equality* (Oxford, OUP, 2004) 17.

As Michael Klarman observes segregation in schools and in railway travel were not necessarily the same issue.[10] Black people had been almost universally excluded from public (in other words state) schools even at the time of the Fourteenth Amendment after the Civil War. As I have mentioned the Fourteenth Amendment guarantees the 'equal protection of the laws'. Nineteenth century public education had been more segregated than railroad transportation. Even before the Civil War and even in northern states black people had either been excluded altogether from public schools or had been segregated. Massachusetts was the only state which forbade school segregation by law. Other northern states did so in the 1870s and 1880s. As has often been pointed out, even the US Congress which enacted the Fourteenth Amendment was itself segregating public schools in the District of Colombia, for which Congress is responsible, since Washington DC is not within the territory of any of the states.

Another of the important constitutional amendments passed in the aftermath of the Civil War was the Fifteenth Amendment, which provides that the right of citizens to vote 'shall not be denied or abridged by the United States or by any State on account of race, color, or previous condition of servitude'. This was not wholly without teeth. For example, in 1904, a court in Georgia invalidated a law forbidding black people from voting in municipal elections.[11] It would also be a mistake to assume that, in the years immediately after the end of the Civil War, black people (most of whom had formerly been slaves) were immediately subject to disfranchisement. In fact the process took much longer and was initially uneven. In 1880 a majority of black people were still voting in most southern states. Black people held office in the state legislatures. In some areas black voters were in fact in the majority. However, the political participation of black people in southern states declined dramatically after 1890. A number of legal measures were deployed to achieve this end. Most southern states adopted literacy tests, which had a disproportionate effect on black people even if they were applied fairly, given the higher rates of illiteracy among them. These were reinforced by 'understanding clauses', which required a person to understand a constitutional provision which was read to them. Other devices that were used included 'grandfather clauses', which exempted a person from literacy tests if they would have been eligible to vote before 1867 and sometimes required a voter to have been a former soldier or their descendant. Some states adopted a poll tax of one or two dollars.

The issue of segregation in public schools never in fact came before the US Supreme Court at the relevant time. The issue of segregation in the railways did come before the Supreme Court and in *Plessey v Ferguson*[12] the Supreme Court by a majority of 7–1 infamously upheld such segregation laws. The Supreme Court announced the notorious doctrine of 'separate but equal': in other words it held that mere segregation of accommodation on the railways did not render accommodation for black people unequal. Justice Harlan dissented. Interestingly he had himself been a slave owner.

---

[10] ibid, 19.
[11] ibid, 33.
[12] 163 US 537 (1896).

Voting restriction laws which were not on their face discriminatory were upheld by the Supreme Court, for example in *Williams v Mississippi*.[13] On this occasion even Justice Harlan joined the opinion of the Court. As a result of such measures black voting was reduced virtually to nil by around 1900. So things remained until the 1950s.

On 17 May 1954, in what is arguably the most famous decision ever handed down by the US Supreme Court, the Court held in *Brown v Board of Education of Topeka, Kansas*[14] that racial segregation in public schools is inherently unequal and so violated the Equal Protection Clause of the Fourteenth Amendment. It rejected the *Plessey* doctrine that there could be facilities which were separate but equal. The Court held, on the basis of social science data which was put before it in the form of a 'Brandeis brief' that racial segregation in schools imposed a badge of inferiority on black children. That was the reason why they were being kept segregated from white children at school. In giving the unanimous judgment of the Court, Chief Justice Warren famously pronounced that:

> We conclude that, in the field of public education, the doctrine of 'separate but equal' has no place. Separate educational facilities are inherently unequal.[15]

As I have mentioned, the District of Columbia is not a State and therefore is not bound by the Fourteenth Amendment. In fact there is no equal protection clause which on its face binds the Federal Government of the US. For that reason, in the companion case of *Bolling v Sharpe*,[16] the Supreme Court held that the Due Process clause of the Fifth Amendment impliedly imposes the duty of equal treatment on the Federal Government also. In that way the Supreme Court was able to hold that racial segregation in the public schools in Washington DC was also unconstitutional just as it was in the States.

The way in which *Brown v Board of Education* came to be decided is itself a fascinating story which I do not have time to recount this evening. Anyone interested in the subject should read the Pulitzer prizewinning account of it by Richard Kluger, *Simple Justice* (first published in 1975).[17] The decision owed much to the ingenuity, hard work and courage of the team of lawyers, led by Thurgood Marshall, of the NAACP. *Brown* represented the culmination of decades of careful strategic thinking and litigation. In due course, Thurgood Marshall was appointed by President Johnson to be the first African-American judge on the US Supreme Court.

So we see in American history that the law on racial segregation went from permitting it to take place in the middle of the nineteenth century, to requiring it to take place from about 1890, to prohibiting it in the middle of the twentieth century.

The mere fact that a court has spoken, even the highest court in the land, does not necessarily mean that its orders will be complied with on the ground. The difficulties which were encountered in the implementation of the decision in *Brown*

---

[13] 170 US 213 (1898).
[14] 347 US 483 (1954).
[15] At 495.
[16] 347 US 497 (1954).
[17] (London, Penguin Random House, 2004).

and subsequent decisions of the US Supreme Court in the 1950s and 1960s are well known. For example, at Little Rock, Arkansas in 1957 President Eisenhower had to send in the National Guard to ensure that black school children could go to school as ordered by the courts.

The constitutional case law of the US Supreme Court of that era culminated in a decision in 1967: *Loving v Virginia*.[18] With hindsight it seems almost incredible now that it was only some fifty years ago that the US Supreme Court finally struck down what were called anti-miscegenation laws, in other words laws which made it a criminal offence for persons of different racial origins to marry. The case of *Loving* has been depicted in at least two films, the most recent of which was made in 2017.

So that was what occurred at the constitutional level in the US in the post-war era. At the non-constitutional level the campaign to achieve an end to racial discrimination led to the enactment by Congress of the Civil Rights Act of 1964. At that time this was the most comprehensive legislation of its kind that I am aware of anywhere in the world. It prohibited racial discrimination in such areas as employment, housing and the provision of goods and services to the public.

In due course, in caselaw interpreting the Civil Rights Act, the US Supreme Court held that it prohibited what became known as 'indirect' discrimination as well as direct discrimination.[19] The legal concept of indirect discrimination went on to influence the law both in the United Kingdom and in the European Union. It is now a familiar concept to us. Essentially it prohibits measures which on their face are racially neutral but which have a disproportionate impact on a particular racial group unless that difference of treatment can be objectively justified.

Curiously (at least to an outsider) the concept of indirect discrimination has been held to be inapplicable in the US constitutional context. In *Washington v Davis*[20] the US Supreme Court held that the Equal Protection clause of the Fourteenth Amendment does not prohibit indirect racial discrimination, only direct.

Staying with the constitutional level for a moment, in the meantime, during the Second World War, the US Supreme Court had decided one of the most notorious cases in its history: *Korematsu v United States*.[21] This was a majority decision of 6–3 judges. In that case the Court upheld the Executive Order by which the President detained American citizens of Japanese descent in detention camps in the United States. The minority included Justice Murphy and Justice Jackson, both of whom had served as Attorney General in the administration of President Franklin D. Roosevelt, the same President whose executive order was now under challenge.

Justice Murphy said:

> I dissent ... from this legalisation of racism. Racial discrimination in any form and in any degree has no justifiable part whatever in our democratic way of life. ... It is utterly revolting among a free people who have embraced the principles set forth in the constitution of the United States.[22]

---

[18] 388 US 1 (1967).
[19] *Griggs v Duke Power* 401 US 424 (1971).
[20] 426 US 229 (1976).
[21] 323 US 214 (1944).
[22] At 242.

Korematsu continued to be a highly controversial decision right up to this year, when it was finally overruled by the unanimous decision of the US Supreme Court in *Trump v Hawaii*.[23] Although the actual decision in that case, which upheld the ban on entry into the US of people from certain countries, most of which have a majority of Muslim citizens, has itself provoked controversy, and was decided by a narrow majority of 5–4 judges, it is important to recognise that the Court unanimously held that its previous decision in *Korematsu* had been wrongly decided on the day that it was decided and ever since. The wrong that was done during the Second World War has at long last been recognised by the highest court in the US.

LEGISLATION IN THE UK

It was against that international background, in particular in the USA, that the first Race Relations Act was passed by Parliament in this country in 1965. The British statute was much more limited than the US Civil Rights Act of the previous year. It was limited in its scope; limited as to who could take action under it; and limited in respect of the remedies which could be granted by the courts.

The 1965 Act did not cover areas of social activity such as housing or employment. It applied to what it called 'places of public resort', including hotels and restaurants but it did not apply to private boarding houses. It did not apply to shops.

The grounds on which discrimination were prohibited were colour, race, and ethnic or national origins. It was subsequently held by the House of Lords in *Ealing London Borough Council v Race Relations Board*[24] that the phrase 'national origins' did not include nationality. Later, as we shall see, in 1976 Parliament amended the law to include discrimination on the ground of nationality. The phrase 'ethnic origins' was later still construed by the courts to include both Sikhs and Jewish people.[25]

Under the 1965 Act it was not possible for an individual to enforce the obligations created by it directly. Rather there was a body called the Race Relations Board which was set up to monitor the work of local conciliation committees. Where discrimination continued, the matter could be referred to the Law Officers, who could apply for an injunction from the court. The Act made clear that it did not create any criminal liability.

The Act was strengthened in 1968 but substantially widened in the Race Relations Act 1976. As I have mentioned, nationality was added as a prohibited ground of discrimination. The scope of the Act was extended to cover employment, education and the provision of goods and services. Furthermore, Parliament adopted the concept of indirect discrimination which had been developed in American caselaw. Finally, the 1976 Act conferred rights on individuals and enabled them to obtain a range of remedies from either the County Court or what was then called the Industrial Tribunal, now the Employment Tribunal. Those remedies included compensation, including compensation for injury to feelings.

---

[23] 585 US – (2018).
[24] [1972] AC 342.
[25] *Mandla v Dowell-Lee* [1983] 2 AC 548; *R (on the application of E) v Jewish Free School* [2010] 2 AC 728.

The Race Relations Act 1976, as originally enacted, did not apply to barristers. The Act was not extended to cover barristers, for example the way in which barristers' clerks distributed work to members of chambers, until 1991, with the coming into force of the Courts and Legal Services Act 1990.

As you will appreciate, what I have said so far about the legislation against racial discrimination in this country essentially covered what I have described earlier as non-constitutional issues. The legislation did not apply to actions of the state itself when exercising public functions. This was made clear in a decision of the House of Lords called *Amin*,[26] in which it was held that the provision of services to the public did not include the performance of public functions which only the state provides, for example the legislation did not apply to the exercise of immigration functions. Although that was a case under the Sex Discrimination Act 1975, the provision that fell to be construed in that case had an equivalent in the Race Relations Act.

This was all to change in 2000, when Parliament enacted the Race Relations (Amendment) Act to implement some of the key recommendations made by Sir William MacPherson after the Stephen Lawrence Public Inquiry in 1999. The amended Act prohibited racial discrimination by public authorities in the exercise of their public functions. The Act also introduced an amended version of section 71, which has become known as the 'Public Sector Equality Duty', which has now found its way into the Equality Act 2010, in section 149, and applies to a range of other protected characteristics under that Act. The Public Sector Equality Duty is a positive duty. It requires public authorities to have due regard to the need to promote equality of opportunity. It was intended to meet the problem of 'institutional racism' which had been identified in the Stephen Lawrence Inquiry Report by ensuring that the potential impact of policies and decisions on ethnic minorities was not overlooked.

The Public Sector Equality Duty was described as being an important one and 'a salutary requirement' by Lady Justice Arden in the case of *Elias* in 2006.[27] In that case I was leading counsel for Diana Elias, who was one of the most interesting clients I ever had. She was in many ways a child of the British Empire. Her family were Jewish and had gone from what was then called Mesopotamia to settle in southern India, where she was born. She could speak Hindi – much better than me. Later her family moved to Hong Kong, which is where they were when the Japanese captured it in late 1941. Some British inhabitants were able to escape to Australia but at that time Australia practised racial discrimination in who would be admitted and so people who were not classified as being of European origin were prevented from reaching Australia. Diana Elias and her family were among those civilians who were interned by the Japanese. Unspeakable things happened at the internment camp. Of course they were British subjects, which is why they were interned by the Japanese, who were at war with the British Empire.

After the War Diana Elias come to the UK and became a British citizen. She had a family here. In the early part of this century the British Government introduced an *ex gratia* compensation scheme for British subjects who had been interned by the Japanese in the Far East during the Second World War. You might have thought that

---

[26] *R v Entry Clearance Officer, Bombay, ex p. Amin* [1983] 2 AC 818.
[27] *R (Elias) v Secretary of State for Defence* [2006] 1 WLR 3213, at para 274.

Diana Elias was exactly the sort of person who would qualify for that compensation. But no. The Government's scheme provided that in order to qualify a person had to have been born in the UK or have at least one parent or grandparent who had been born in the UK. That was how the Government decided who counted as 'British' for this purpose. As Diana Elias put it in her witness statement, she was British enough to be interned but not British enough to be compensated.

Her claim for judicial review succeeded in the High Court on the ground that the Secretary of State's policy constituted indirect racial discrimination. The Secretary of State's appeal was dismissed by the Court of Appeal, Lord Justice Mummery giving the lead judgment.

Even with those legislative amendments which extended the reach of the racial discrimination legislation to the exercise of public functions, we still did not have in this country the equivalent of constitutional protection against for example discrimination in legislation itself. However, in one sense that has changed since the coming into force of the Human Rights Act 1998. As is well known, this gives effect in domestic law to the main rights to be found in the European Convention on Human Rights. Those rights include the right to equal treatment in the enjoyment of other Convention Rights, which is in Article 14. Accordingly, it has become possible for even primary legislation to be scrutinised against the standards of the Convention, albeit that the remedy which can be granted is a declaration of incompatibility rather than (as would be possible for example in the US) a power to strike down primary legislation.

An example of such a declaration of incompatibility being granted where legislation was found by the House of Lords to be incompatible with the prohibition of discrimination on grounds of nationality can be found in the so called 'Belmarsh' case *A v Secretary of State for the Home Department*.[28] In that case, which followed the enactment of emergency legislation passed after the attacks of 9/11, which conferred power on the Secretary of State to authorise the detention of suspected international terrorists but only if they were foreign nationals, the House of Lords held (by a majority of 8–1) that Part 4 of the Anti-Terrorism, Crime and Security Act 2001 was incompatible with the Convention rights. In giving the lead speech, Lord Bingham of Cornhill said that the legislation was discriminatory on grounds of nationality and that discrimination was not objectively justified.

Parliament then amended the 2001 Act to remove Part 4 and replaced it in 2005 with a system of 'control orders', a system which itself has subsequently been repealed and replaced by TPIMs under the Terrorism Prevention and Investigation Measures Act 2011.

The Race Relations Act has now been replaced by the single Equality Act 2010. There is no longer a Commission for Racial Equality, which had been created by the 1976 Act.

Instead, since 2007 there has been a single Equality and Human Rights Commission, which is now responsible for all the protected characteristics in the 2010 Act, not only race but sex, disability and so on.

---

[28] [2005] 2 AC 68.

The Race Relations Act 1976 was an important piece of legislation in this country. It conferred legal rights on individuals and provided for potentially strong remedies to be granted by courts and tribunals. That does not mean that Parliament had some kind of magic wand, which has created an equal society in our country. Nevertheless, the Act did set out what kind of society we wish to be.

When people look around them there is sometimes frustration that the equality legislation in this country has not brought about the equal society that it appeared to promise. I think the reason for this may lie in part in the difference between racial discrimination and racial equality. Making discrimination unlawful does not necessarily lead to equality. There may be many reasons for this: educational, economic and cultural. There are perhaps also limits on what the law alone can achieve.

The first reason for this is the risk of unconscious bias. It can often be difficult to prove that there has been discrimination on racial grounds. As Lord Nicholls said in *Nagarajan* few people are prepared to admit, even to themselves, that they have views which are based on racial prejudice.[29] He said:

> All human beings have preconceptions, beliefs, attitudes and prejudices on many subjects. ... We do not always recognise our own prejudices. Many people are unable, or unwilling, to admit even to themselves that actions of theirs may be racially motivated.

We have all become much more aware of the concept of unconscious bias. We all have unstated assumptions we make about the world around us and the people we come across. Judges now receive training about the risk of unconscious bias.

The second reason I would suggest is that there are limits to what discrimination law can do to achieve true equality because the causes of inequality may be much more structural ones in wider society which are beyond the control of an individual.

The model of discrimination law which is reflected in the Race Relations Act 1976 and its successor, the Equality Act 2010, is one that has the following features. It enables an individual to complain about an individual act of racial discrimination in a relevant field of human activity which is within the scope of the Act, for example employment, education or housing. It requires there to be unfavourable treatment of that individual as compared to an actual or hypothetical comparator and it requires that less favourable treatment to have been on racial grounds.

As Professor Sandra Fredman puts it in her book *Discrimination Law*:

> racism and other forms of discrimination extend far beyond individual acts of prejudice. Such prejudices are frequently embedded in the structure of society, and cannot be attributed clearly to any one person.[30]

Essentially we have a model of law which seeks to guarantee equality of opportunity, in other words legal equality. It is a very important model and its importance should not be under-estimated. One only has to recall what went before, in the 1960s, to appreciate the value of such a prohibition on discrimination. Those who have felt the humiliation of discrimination know only too well the importance of prohibiting it as a matter of law.

---

[29] *Nagarajan v London Regional Transport* [2000] 1 AC 501, at 511–12.
[30] (2nd edn, Oxford, OUP, 2011) 14.

However, equality of opportunity, important though it is, simply means that, once a person is in a race, the best person will win. What it does not address is the question: who is in the race in the first place and how do you get there?

There may be larger forces at work, which are well beyond the capacity of any individual to do anything about. They may be economic. For example, the fact that estate agents can no longer lawfully discriminate against a person on racial grounds does not mean that that person will have the money to buy a house in an expensive area.

Some statistics which have been published by the government may be of interest in this context.[31] UK households were divided into five equally sized groups or 'quintiles', based on their income. The average household income ranged from £9,100 in the lowest quintile to £45,900 in the highest quintile (after housing costs were deducted). Over half of households from the Asian, black and other minority ethnic groups fell into the two lowest income quintiles. 42 per cent of white British households fell into the two highest quintiles, this being the highest percentage of all ethnic groups. Only 20 per cent of black people fell into the two highest quintiles, this being the lowest percentage of all ethnic groups. The reasons for these differences in income are complex and well beyond my expertise and the remit of this lecture. However, such differences of income may form one of the structural features of our society which I have mentioned.

CONCLUSION

Let me conclude. The Race Relations Act and its current counterpart in the Equality Act had a purpose and effect which went beyond the mere creation of legal rights and duties, important though that was. It was a piece of social legislation which had an important symbolic effect in setting out what Parliament regards as a fundamental value in our society. Parliament sent out a very clear message that racial discrimination would not be tolerated in this country and that the principle of racial equality is fundamental to our society.

---

[31] As at 16 August 2018, available on www.gov.uk under the heading 'Ethnicity facts and figures'.

Religion and the Law

In 2008 I took part in a seminar organised by the NGO Justice on religion and the law. My brief contribution took the form of a comment responding to a longer paper which was given by the Bishop of Durham (Dr N T Wright). In this paper I mentioned the law which was enacted in France prohibiting the wearing of religious symbols in public buildings, including schools. That law was subsequently challenged – unsuccessfully – in the European Court of Human Rights in a number of cases, including J Singh v France *(App. No. 25463/08, 30 June 2009); but was the subject of a successful complaint to the UN Human Rights Committee by a Sikh child, who was not permitted to attend a state school in France if he wore a turban:* Bikramjit Singh v France *UN Doc CCPR/C/106/D/1852/2008 (Decision of 1 November 2012). Opinions of that Committee, which are issued under an optional protocol to the International Covenant on Civil and Political Rights, which France has ratified but the UK has not, are not binding and so the law in France has not been changed. At the time of this paper I was a practising barrister. It was first published in* [2008] JUSTICE *journal, issue 1, 33.*

I AM GRATEFUL for the invitation to address you this evening although I feel singularly unqualified to do so on this important topic. I do not claim any specialist knowledge about theology in general, nor even about Sikhism in particular. I have a passing acquaintance with the law, although Lord Hoffmann (having had to endure my submissions in court earlier this week) may have reason to doubt even that.

I have listened with great interest to what the Bishop of Durham has had to say this evening. I agree with much of what he has said but by no means all. In particular I agree that in this country we need to be able to have serious debate about issues such as the relationship between faith and the law in a way which is thoughtful, respectful of the views of others and not conducted in a shrill or abusive way.

I approach these issues from the perspective of a lawyer with a particular interest in human rights. Human rights thinking does not necessarily provide answers to difficult questions but what it does seek to do is set out a framework of values so that problems can be addressed in a principled way. The Universal Declaration of Human Rights (UDHR) begins, in Article 1, with the fundamental statement that: 'All human beings are born free and equal in dignity and rights'. The UDHR was adopted in 1948 but of course its roots go back much further than that, not just to the Enlightenment but I would suggest to older traditions in western thought including the Judaeo-Christian tradition. But it was intended to be and I believe is a statement of values which have universal application. The drafting committee deliberately included members from different parts of the world and not just from the west. Certainly, it would not seem at all alien in an eastern country like India, which is not only the largest democracy in the world but has a written constitution, a bill of rights and a supreme court charged with enforcing them which is held in the highest regard both within India and around the world. India is interesting because it is a religious country but a secular state, in which freedom of religion is guaranteed. There are many faiths, not only Hindus, who form a large majority of over 80 per cent but one of the largest Muslim populations in the world, and also smaller communities of Christians, Jews and Parsis as well as Sikhs. It is not always appreciated in the west that there are more Christians in India than there are Sikhs.

Returning to this country, it seems to me that one of the hallmarks of a liberal democracy is that the law must respect fundamental human rights, including both freedom of religion and the freedom not to believe. It also includes the right to freedom of expression. These rights are important for three main reasons.

First, they facilitate the development of the individual human being. A person's freedom of thought and conscience is absolute. No one can be made to think or believe something because the state or others in authority force them to do so.

Secondly, they contribute to what is conventionally called the 'marketplace of ideas', so that society itself may benefit from the various and perhaps conflicting views which are aired.

Thirdly, they help to maintain social peace, in particular in a society where there are people of many (perhaps conflicting) faiths and many who have no faith at all – and do not wish to have any faith imposed upon them.

It is important to appreciate what I am not saying. I am not saying that these rights are unlimited. Liberty is not the same thing as licence. Individuals do have the responsibility to respect the rights of others around them too. Article 29 UDHR recognises that. Although in human rights law freedom of thought is absolute, the right to express those thoughts and the right to manifest one's religion are not absolute. Like many human rights, they may be qualified so far as necessary in a democratic society. This is where the principle of proportionality comes in. The European Court of Human Rights has frequently said that there is a need to strike a fair balance between the rights of the individual and the general interest of the community. The Court has also emphasised that a democratic society which is committed to human rights is not simply one in which the will of the majority will always prevail. It is rather a society which is characterised by tolerance, pluralism and broad-mindedness.

In the particular context of religious freedom this means, in my view, that it is not necessarily open to the state to use the coercive power of the law to ban the wearing of religious symbols in public institutions. It has often been said that everyone must be treated equally before the law. Of course that is right. But equality is not the same thing as uniformity- it includes the notion of diversity. Sometimes to treat people in the same way irrespective of their differences has the effect of treating them unequally. Our law recognises that in the context of disability discrimination and sex discrimination.

It is therefore arguable that the French law on religious symbols violates the European Convention on Human Rights because it breaches the principle of proportionality and also the principle of equality. There is nothing new or surprising about the notion that the law should recognise the right of individuals to act in accordance with their own faith or conscience. For example, when abortion was legalised in 1967 Parliament saw fit to acknowledge that some hospital staff could simply not act contrary to their conscience and should not be required to do so. The law is well able to make reasonable adjustments to allow everyone to participate in society on an equal basis.

But there is another dimension to this. Just as human rights law protects religious groups from oppression by the state, so it protects individuals within religious groups too. Although a pluralistic society allows space for faith groups to organise themselves in accordance with their own beliefs there are limits to this. Religious groups have no more right to abuse the rights of women or gay people than anyone else does. Vulnerable individuals and sub-groups within religious groups are entitled to invoke the protection of the general law of the land.

How then should the law of the land respond to the diverse society we now live in? I would like to end with a quotation from a judgment in the Court of Appeal which seems to me to indicate the way. It is the judgment of Munby J in an immigration case called *Pawandeep Singh v Entry Clearance Officer*.[1] At paragraph 62 he said:

> The fact is that we live in a secular and pluralistic society. ... One of the paradoxes of our lives is that we live in a society which is at one and the same time becoming both increasingly secular but also increasingly diverse in religious affiliation.

At paragraph 64 he continued:

> We live in a society which on many social, ethical and religious topics no longer either thinks or speaks with one voice. These are topics on which men and women of different faiths or no faith at all hold starkly differing views. All of those views are entitled to the greatest respect but it is not for a judge to choose between them. The days are past when the business of the judges was the enforcement of morals or religious belief.

[1] [2005] QB 608.

Privacy and National Security

Privacy and Personal Autonomy

This paper was first given in 1999 (when I was still a barrister) at a private seminar at the US Supreme Court, organised by the American Bar Association and the Bar Council of England and Wales. It was first published in 2000 in a book under the auspices of the American Bar Association, Common Law, Common Values, Common Rights. *I gave a brief comparative analysis of the right of privacy in American and English law. In essence the right of privacy can exist at two levels. The first is the constitutional level: this is the level at which the right has gained prominence in American cases (sometimes highly controversial ones) about issues such as abortion. Such cases tend to be concerned with privacy in the sense of personal autonomy. The second level is concerned with more traditional notions of privacy, in particular the protection of seclusion and personal information. This second level also tends to be concerned with intrusion on privacy interests by the media.*

INTRODUCTION

THERE IS NO right to privacy as such in English law. There is as yet no constitutional right to privacy like the one recognised by the US Supreme Court in cases such as *Griswold v Connecticut*.[1] Nor is there a common law tort (or torts) of breach of privacy such as the ones recognised in many American states *(Restatement of Torts (2d)* (1977), Sections 652A–6521). In *Kaye v Robertson*,[2] Glidewell LJ said: 'It is well-known that in English law there is no right to privacy, and accordingly there is no right of action for breach of a person's privacy'. However, things are not always as they seem.

For one thing, privacy is a vitally important value in English culture and this has been reflected in the common law. As was said in *Semayne's Case*,[3] 'the house of everyone is to him as his castle and fortress'. Many of the nominate torts, such as trespass to land and private nuisance indirectly protect privacy interests. Bodily autonomy is protected through the torts of assault, battery, and false imprisonment. Personal information is protected to some extent by the law of defamation, injurious falsehood, passing off, and breach of copyright. Equity has not been slow to assist in this task: most notably the equitable wrong of breach of confidence will often protect personal information from unjustified disclosure and may in time develop into a fully fledged right to privacy.

[1] (1965) 381 U.S. 479.
[2] [1991] F.S.R. 62.
[3] (1604) 5 Co. Rep. 91a.

Furthermore, the legislature has from time to time acted to protect privacy in an increasingly intrusive age: for example, the Data Protection Act 1998, which implements a directive of the European Community, protects personal information held on computers and in other 'personal data filing systems'.

Finally, English law is about to undergo a transformation with the incorporation of the European Convention on Human Rights ('ECHR') into national law by the Human Rights Act 1998, which is expected to come into force in October 2000, Article 8 of the ECHR expressly guarantees privacy rights in the following terms:

1.   Everyone has the right to respect for his private and family life, his home and his correspondence.
2.   There shall be no interference by a public authority with the exercise of this right except such as is in accordance with the law and is necessary in a democratic society in the interests of national security, public safety or the economic well-being of the country, for the prevention of disorder or crime, for the protection of health or morals, or for the protection of the rights and freedoms of others.

THE COMMON LAW

The common law has protected privacy interests in two ways. First, it has relied on the general principle that a person is free to do whatever he or she wishes to unless it is proscribed by some positive rule of law. The corollary has been that if the state wishes to intrude upon a person's personal autonomy, including his or her privacy, it must be able to point to some legal authority to do so. The classic example of this was *Entick v Carrington*,[4] which was in substance an early case on search and seizure. There Lord Camden, the Chief Justice of the Common Pleas, said:

By the laws of England every invasion of land, be it ever so minute, is a trespass. No man can set his foot upon my ground without my licence.

He went on:

[I]f this point should be determined in favour of the jurisdiction, the secret cabinets and bureaus of every subject in the Kingdom will be thrown open to the search and inspection of a messenger, whenever the secretary of state shall think fit to charge, or even to suspect, a person to be the author, printer, or publisher of a seditious libel.

And of the suggestion that the doctrine of 'state necessity' would permit the secretary of state to do what was otherwise unlawful, Lord Camden was dismissive:

[T]he common law does not understand that kind of reasoning, nor do our books take notice of any such distinction.

The Court's distaste for general warrants was later reflected in the Fourth Amendment to the US Constitution.

---

[4] (1765) 19 State Trials 1029.

It is not only in historic cases that one finds the importance of privacy in English law stressed. In a resounding judgment Sir Nicolas Browne-Wilkinson V-C said in *Marcel v Commissioner of Police for the Metropolis*:[5]

> [I]f the information obtained by the police, the Inland Revenue, the social security offices, the health service and other agencies were to be gathered together in one file, the freedom of the individual would be gravely at risk. The dossier of private information is the badge of the totalitarian state.

The common law principle that a person is free to do what he or she likes unless there is some specific legal authority given to the state to interfere with liberty is still of practical importance. It is reflected in recent cases such as *Secretary of State for the Horne Department v Robb*,[6] in which it was held that an adult of sound mind has a fundamental right to self-determination in the common law, so that the prison service could not force-feed a prisoner who was on hunger strike. Thorpe J said: '[E]very person's body is inviolate and proof against any form of physical molestation'.

The second main technique used by the common law to protect privacy interests is to make certain invasions of privacy legally actionable. Thus, trespass to land clearly helps to protect a person's privacy in the home, although it is directly concerned with the protection of property. This is important because any officer of the state, including the police, must be able to justify entering upon a person's land without consent, by referring to some legal authority. If no such authority exists, they commit a trespass and will be liable in damages. Similarly, a person who divulges personal information received in confidence will commit an equitable wrong (breach of confidence). If it is not too late to prevent the disclosure, the courts will in principle grant an injunction to restrain publication, although of course they are sensitive to the importance of freedom of expression in a democratic society and will not prevent disclosure of information which is in the public interest.

But the common law approach to the protection of privacy suffers from two major defects. The first is that, where there is some rule of positive law which permits an interference with privacy interests, there is no fundamental right to privacy which can be invoked to 'trump' that rule. The second is that there is no cause of action for breach of privacy as such: if the act complained of cannot be brought within, the boundaries of a nominate tort, the law will afford no protection to privacy. A notorious example is *Malone v Commissioner of Police for the Metropolis*,[7] in which the English court held that there was nothing unlawful about police interception of telephone communications, since there is no right to property in telephone conversations and there is no general right to privacy in English law. The case went to the European Court of Human Rights, which held that there was a violation of Article 8 of the Convention for the simple, but fundamental, reason that the interference with telephone privacy was not 'in accordance with the law' (*Malone v United Kingdom*[8]). The case forced the United Kingdom Parliament to introduce a

---

[5] [1992] Ch. 225.
[6] [1995] Fam. 127.
[7] [1979] Ch. 344.
[8] (1985) 7 E.H.R.R. 14.

statutory code to regulate telephone taps with the Interception of Communications Act 1985. Another example, which has not yet been overturned by statute, is *Hunter v Canary Wharf Ltd*,[9] where the House of Lords held that the tort of private nuisance can be relied cm only by a person who has an interest in land and not by (for example) a lawful visitor to that land. If that person's privacy is invaded, the English tort of nuisance will not afford any protection.

STATUTORY PROTECTION OF PRIVACY

Parliament has from time to time sought to provide protection for certain privacy interests. This is in step with what has happened in other societies, including the United States: the complexity of modern society and the development of new technologies (including the widespread use of personal computers and of video surveillance cameras) has led to specific statutory protection in (for example) the Data Protection Act (originally enacted in 1984 and revamped in 1998).

In contrast to the United States, however, many of the controversies over privacy interests have not had to be litigated through the courts because the legislature has sought to resolve the moral and political conflicts raised by such issues as abortion and gay rights. Abortion was legalised in specified circumstances by the Abortion Act 1967. The main requirements are that two registered medical practitioners must certify that the continuation of the pregnancy poses a greater risk to the woman's physical or mental health than termination. Although abortion is not available on demand it is relatively easy to obtain in the first trimester and can be obtained up to twenty-four weeks into a woman's pregnancy (or later if there is a risk to her life). Moreover, abortion is available, as most medical treatment is, on the National Health Service (which is publicly funded).

Homosexual acts between adults over 21 were legalised by the Sexual Offences Act 1967, provided they are consensual and take place in private. In 1994 the age of consent for homosexuals was reduced to 18. This will soon be reduced to 16, in response to a case brought in the European Commission of Human Rights, which will ensure equality with heterosexuals. In recent years the most controversial issue arising from the privacy rights of gay people has been the total ban on homosexuals from the armed forces. This ban was upheld by the English courts in *R v Ministry of Defence, ex p. Smith*,[10] but has been held to violate Article 8 of the ECHR by the European Court of Human Rights in *Lustig-Prean and Others v United Kingdom* (27 September 1999). The ban on gays in the armed forces has been lifted by the British government in response to that judgment and it is intended to introduce a code governing sexual conduct in the armed forces, which will apply to both heterosexuals and homosexuals. The judgment of the European Court serves as a powerful reminder of the inadequacy of the English common law in protecting privacy rights of the most intimate character because of its doctrinal limitations. This inadequacy

---

[9] [1997] A.C. 655.
[10] [1996] Q.B. 517.

has been recognised by both the courts and now by Parliament, which has decided to 'bring rights home' by incorporating the ECHR into national law.

Another controversial area – but one in which Parliament has not yet acted – is the law on transsexuals. The European Court of Human Rights has held that a person's choice of sexual identity comes within the scope of the right to respect for private life in Article 8 of the ECHR. However, it has refrained to date from holding that the stance of English law, which regards a person's sex as being fixed by reference to biological criteria at birth *(Corbett v Corbett)*,[11] is incompatible with Article 8; eg, *Sheffield and Horsham v United Kingdom*.[12] However, the trend is clearly in that direction and it is widely predicted that, under the pressure of the Human Rights Act, English law will have to recognise a person's change of sex after gender reassignment surgery.

EUROPEAN CONVENTION ON HUMAN RIGHTS (ECHR)

In *Niemietz v Germany*,[13] the European Court of Human Rights interpreted the scope of private life in Article 8 of the ECHR as being wide when it said that it 'must also comprise to a certain degree the right to establish and develop relationships with other human beings'. Furthermore, the European Court has held that the obligations which are imposed on a state by Article 8 are not merely negative in character but may be positive as well. In *X and Y v The Netherlands*,[14] the Court said that the positive obligation will extend to requiring action to protect an individual from the acts of other private parties:

> The Court recalls that although the object of Article 8 is essentially that of protecting the individual against arbitrary interference by the public authorities, it does not merely compel the State to abstain from such interference: in addition to this primarily negative obligation, there may be positive obligations inherent in an effective respect for private or family life. These obligations may involve the adoption of measures designed to secure respect for private life even in the sphere of the relations of individuals between themselves.

In *Spencer v United Kingdom*,[15] a case about the publication of photographs taken with a telephoto lens of a famous person who was recovering at a private clinic, the European Commission of Human Rights took the view that the law of confidence has moved on sufficiently in the English case law to provide a remedy which must be exhausted before any complaint of breach of privacy can he made to the European Court of Human Rights, in Strasbourg. The Commission said that it

> would not exclude that the absence of an actionable remedy in relation to the publications of which the applicants complain could show a lack of respect for their private lives. It has regard in this respect to the duties and responsibilities that are carried with the right

---

[11] [1971] P. 83.
[12] (1999) 27 E.H.R.R. 163.
[13] (1993) 16 E.H.R.R. 97.
[14] (1986) 8 E.H.R.R. 236.
[15] (1998) 25 E.H.R.R. C.D. 105.

to freedom of expression guaranteed by Article 10 of the Convention and to Contracting States' obligation to provide a measure of protection to the right of privacy of an individual affected by others' exercise of their freedom of expression.

THE HUMAN RIGHTS ACT

The Human Rights Act will create a right to privacy against the state: this is equivalent to the constitutional right to privacy recognised in American jurisprudence. Cases such as *Malone* and *Lustig-Prean* should no longer have to go to Strasbourg before privacy interests are adequately protected by English law. But the Human Rights Act may have an even more profound effect on the English common law. It may lead to the development of a right to privacy which is equivalent to the American torts of breach of privacy: such a right would be available not just against the state but also against the privately owned media.

The Human Rights Act makes it unlawful for any 'public authority' to act in a way which is incompatible with the Convention rights, including Article 8. 'Act' includes a failure to act, giving effect in national law to the European concept of positive obligations. This could be especially important when one bears in mind that courts are included within the definition of 'public authorities'. This means that the courts must not infringe privacy rights when they make orders such as for disclosure of documents or searches. However, it probably goes further. The courts will probably be under a positive obligation to protect an individual's privacy from other individuals and from private corporations. This could be the spur to the creation of a common law right to privacy. This is likely to happen, initially at least, through the development, of existing causes of action, in particular the doctrine of breach of confidence. However, it is open to the House of Lords to recognise a general right to privacy in the English common law. This was left open by a majority of the judges in *R v Khan (Sultan)*,[16] in which Lord Nicholls of Birkenhead said:

> I prefer to leave open for another occasion the important question whether the present, piecemeal protection of privacy has now developed to the extent that a more comprehensive principle can be seen to exist.

CONCLUSION

The seminal article by Warren arid Brandeis ('The Right to Privacy'[17]) is often cited as the genesis of the torts of breach of privacy in American law. It is ironic that the article relied upon many cases in English jurisprudence, including *Prince Albert v Strange*.[18] It would be fitting if privacy were recognised as a right in English law in the new century. There is every sign that it will be.

---

[16] [1997] A.C. 558.
[17] (1890) 4 *Harv. L.R.* 193.
[18] (1849) 2 DeGex and Sm 652.

The English common law stands at the beginning of a new dawn in the year 2000. It is about to be transformed by the Human Rights Act. It is in the field of privacy that the Human Rights Act may have the greatest impact. It will make it unlawful for any public authority to breach the right to respect for private life in Article 8 of the ECHR. It may go further and have indirect effect against private individuals and corporations. It is likely to be used as the catalyst for the development of existing causes of action so as to create a general right to privacy in English law. There could be no better illustration of the interaction between the Human Rights Act and existing law or of the continuing ability of the common law to reinvent itself to meet the needs of a changing society.

Privacy and the Media After the Human Rights Act

This article was based on a paper given at the Bar conference in October 1998 (when I was still a barrister). At that time the Human Rights Act was in the process of being enacted (it received Royal Assent in November 1998 and came into full force on 2 October 2000). This article was first published in [1998] EHRLR 712. In it I explored to what extent the HRA would lead to the development of a right of privacy not only against public authorities but the private media. At that time it was received wisdom that there was no right of privacy in English law. I suggested that this would have to change as the result of a combination of two factors: first, the concept of positive obligations in the ECHR case law, so that the state sometimes has a duty to protect the right of privacy against intrusion from the media; and, secondly, the inclusion of courts in the definition of 'public authorities' in section 6 of the HRA. At the time of this article even the case law in Strasbourg was yet to state clearly that there is a positive obligation on the state to protect an individual's privacy against the media but this has since become clear: see eg Von Hannover v Germany (2005) 40 EHRR 1. In domestic law that development has also taken place, in particular in the decision of the House of Lords in Campbell v MGN Ltd [2004] UKHL 22; [2004] 2 AC 457. It has now become commonplace for courts in this country to talk of a tort of 'misuse of private information': see eg ZXC v Bloomberg LP [2020] EWCA Civ 611; [2021] QB 28. It should also be noted that a case to which I referred in this article (Peck) later went to Strasbourg, where the European Court of Human Rights held that there had been a violation of Article 8 (that was a case concerning a public authority and not the private media): Peck v United Kingdom (2003) 36 EHRR 41.

INTRODUCTION

I T IS TRITE to say that there is no right to privacy as such in English law. In *Kaye v. Robertson* Leggatt LJ said that this right 'has so long been disregarded here that it can be recognised now only by the legislature'.[1] The Government have

---

[1] [1991] F.S.R. 62 at 71. See also Glidewell L.J. at 66: 'It is well-known that in English law there is no right to privacy, and accordingly there is no right of action for breach of a person's privacy'.

confirmed that they do not intend to introduce a statutory right of privacy as such. However, the European Convention on Human Rights, which is currently being incorporated into domestic law by the Human Rights Bill,[2] contains a right to 'respect for private life'.[3] This article will consider whether, and to what extent, this will lead to a right to privacy in English law. In particular it will address the question whether incorporation of the European Convention on Human Rights will create a right to privacy as against the media.

Since *Kaye* the debate about whether there is a right to privacy in the English common law (including rules of equity for this purpose) has intensified rather than diminished. For example, in *Hellewell v Chief Constable of South Yorkshire*[4] Laws J. said that:

> If someone with a telephoto lens were to take from a distance and with no authority a picture of another engaged in some private act, his subsequent disclosure of the photograph would, in my judgment, as surely amount to a breach of confidence as if he had found or stolen a diary in which the act was recounted and proceeded to publish it. In such a case, the law would protect what might reasonably be called *a right of privacy*, although the name accorded to the cause of action would be breach of confidence.

As that passage makes clear, that case was concerned – directly at least – with the law of breach of confidence, a recognised cause of action in existing law. It illustrates the point that English law does currently afford some protection to privacy interests (other examples are provided by the law of trespass to land, private nuisance, defamation, injurious falsehood, passing off and breach of copyright) but it does not follow that there is a right to privacy as such.

The classic formulation of the tort (or more accurately torts) of breach of privacy in American law was set out by Prosser as follows: (1) intrusion on seclusion, solitude or private affairs; (2) publication of embarrassing private facts; (3) publicity which portrays a person in a false light; and (4) appropriation of a person's name or likeness.[5] While the piecemeal protection provided by English law is reasonably good at dealing with (2) and (3) and to some extent (4), it is initial intrusion on a person's seclusion or private affairs, especially by the media, ever on the look-out for an interesting or titillating photograph or 'human interest' story, that is inadequately addressed in the English common law. In particular it is doubtful that English law would currently prohibit breach of privacy in the sense of an initial act of intrusion on privacy (for example, by taking photographs of a private act or situation without more) as opposed to the subsequent disclosure of the fruits of the intrusive act (as when photographs are sold to a newspaper or published by it). On the facts of *Kaye*, for example, it was the acts of photographing and interviewing Mr Kaye while he lay in his hospital bed suffering from severe head injuries which were offensive to

---

[2] References in this article to the Human Rights Bill, which was introduced in the House of Lords, are to the Bill as amended by the House of Commons and published on 2 July 1998. At the time of writing, the Bill had completed the Committee stage in the Commons.

[3] Article 8 of the ECHR, which is reproduced in Sched. 1 to the Bill, provides: '1. Everyone has the right to respect for his private and family life, his home and his correspondence'.

[4] [1995] 1 W.L.R. 804 at 807H (emphasis added).

[5] William L Prosser, 'Privacy' (1960) 48 *Calif. L.R.* 383 at 389.

the conscience as much as (if not more than) the subsequent publication of the interview and photographs.

In *R v Khan (Sultan)*[6] the House of Lords was not directly concerned with whether there is a cause of action for breach of privacy in English law. It was concerned with whether, in the context of a criminal prosecution, evidence obtained (arguably) in breach of the right to respect for private life in Article 8 of the European Convention on Human Rights ought to have been excluded from the trial. The House of Lords held that there was no rule requiring automatic exclusion of illegally obtained evidence, thus confirming its decision in *R v Sang*.[7] The House went on to hold that the issue of privacy was relevant to the exercise of the trial judge's discretion under section 78 of the Police and Criminal Evidence Act 1984 to exclude evidence where fairness requires it. Three members of the House expressly left open the question whether there is a general right to privacy in English law. In particular, Lord Nicholls of Birkenhead said:

> I prefer to leave open for another occasion the important question whether the present, piecemeal protection of privacy has now developed to the extent that a more comprehensive principle can be seen to exist.[8]

The limits of this patchy framework of protection through established causes of action should also be noted. After *Khorasandjian v Bush*[9] the Court of Appeal was widely applauded for developing the law of private nuisance in an imaginative way so as to create in effect a tort of harassment, where a person engaged in persistent and unwanted telephone calls to the plaintiff. This was thought to provide an indirect means of protection for one of the many interests embraced within the concept of privacy. However, the House of Lords has recently overruled *Khorasandjian* in part, re-establishing the principle that generally only a person with an interest in land can sue for private nuisance.[10]

It also needs to be borne in mind that English public law may indirectly protect privacy interests as well.[11] However, the attempt to use public law in this way has recently suffered a setback in the decision of the High Court in *R v Brentwood Borough Council, ex parte Peck*.[12] Harrison J. held that, in the absence of a right to privacy in English law, the Council in that case had not acted unlawfully in disclosing video footage which it had obtained by means of a closed circuit television camera and which showed the applicant's attempt to commit suicide to a broadcasting company, which later showed the footage on television.

---

[6] [1997] A.C. 558.

[7] [1980] A.C. 402.

[8] [1997] A.C. 558 at 582H-583A.

[9] [1993] Q.B. 727.

[10] *Hunter v Canary Wharf Ltd* [1997] A.C. 655, especially at 690–94 (Lord Goff of Chieveley), 698 (Lord Lloyd of Berwick), 704–07 (Lord Hoffmann, who saw *Khorasandjian* as properly a case about intentional harassment and not about nuisance) and 725–26 (Lord Hope of Craighead). Lord Cooke of Thorndon dissented on this issue.

[11] See R Singh, *The Future of Human Rights in the United Kingdom: Essays on Law and Practice* (Oxford, Hart Publishing, 1997), ch 5.

[12] *Times Law Reports*, December 18, 1996 (Harrison J.). The Court of Appeal refused leave to appeal and the case is proceeding to Strasbourg. *Cf R v Chief Constable of the North Wales Police, ex p. AB* [1998] 3 W.L.R. 57.

EXTRA-JUDICIAL REMARKS

The judges have not been silent on the question in their extra-judicial remarks either. In particular, in an important speech delivered at the National Liberal Club on May 21, 1996, the Lord Chief Justice said:

> Should there be a law to protect rights of personal privacy? To a very large extent the law already does protect personal privacy; but to the extent that it does not, it should. The right must be narrowly drawn, to give full effect to the right of free speech and the public's right to know. It should strike only at significant infringements, such as would cause substantial distress to an ordinarily phlegmatic person. My preference would be for legislation, which would mean that the rules which the courts applied would carry the imprimatur of democratic approval. But if, for whatever reason, legislation is not forthcoming, I think it almost inevitable that cases will arise in the courts in which the need to give relief is obvious and pressing; and when such cases do arise, I do not think the courts will be found wanting.[13]

As the Lord Chancellor has remarked in Parliament, the courts are, 'regardless of incorporation [of the European Convention on Human Rights] very likely to develop a common law right of privacy themselves'.[14]

In November 1997 Dame Mary Arden added her voice to the growing body of judicial opinion in favour of a right to privacy. She said:

> There is considerable uncertainty over the future of the law of privacy. There are many new situations which the courts may have to resolve. In my view, after so many years of rhetoric on this sensitive subject, the time has come for an informed debate as to the appropriate limits to legal remedies for breach of the right to privacy if the courts find that such a breach is indeed actionable as such. As a start, I have endeavoured to raise some of the issues that I consider will have to be resolved. As I see it the problems are capable of solution. The law that is developed will have to have many qualities: it will have to be measured, reflective and flexible, and it will have to strike a proper balance between the right to privacy and freedom of expression. I think that all this can be achieved through the courts. Now that I have laid out one way in which it can be done it is for those who disagree with this point of view to participate in debate.[15]

Significantly, Dame Mary Arden was speaking after the publication of the Human Rights Bill and sought to ask some questions about what the enactment of that Bill will mean for the continuing debate about a right to privacy in English law. That is the question which is the main subject of this article. To answer that question, it is important first to see what the European Convention on Human Rights itself requires in the field of privacy. Then it is important to see how the Human Rights Bill incorporates the European Convention on Human Rights in order to see whether and, if so, how it will generate a right to privacy in domestic law.

---

[13] Lord Bingham of Cornhill, 'Should There Be a Law to Protect Rights of Personal Privacy?' [1996] *E.H.R.L.R.* 450 at 461–62.

[14] *Hansard*, H.L. Deb., November 3, 1997, col. 1230. Lord Irvine of Lairg L.C. was addressing the concerns of the press in his speech introducing the Human Rights Bill in the Second Reading debate.

[15] Dame Mary Arden, 'The Future of the Law of Privacy' (1998–99) 9 *K.C.L.J.* at 19.

WHAT THE EUROPEAN CONVENTION ON HUMAN RIGHTS REQUIRES

Article 8 of the European Convention on Human Rights guarantees the right to respect not only for a person's private life but also for their family life, correspondence and home. It is an article of wide scope. It protects many aspects of private life which are not directly the subject of this article, including sexual intimacy[16] and control over a person's identity.[17] In *Niemietz v Germany*[18] the Court of Human Rights said that the scope of private life in Article 8 was wide when it said:

> The Court does not consider it possible or necessary to attempt an exhaustive definition of the notion of 'private life'. However, it would be too restrictive to limit the notion to an 'inner circle' in which the individual may live his own personal life as he chooses and to exclude therefrom entirely the outside world not encompassed within that circle. Respect for private life must also comprise to a certain degree the right to establish and develop relationships with other human beings.

As Professor Feldman has put it:

> People disagree about the values which privacy-related rights protect. This offers opportunities for creative advocacy to bring within Article 8 a range of interests which are otherwise inadequately protected. Some see control over personal information as the core of privacy. Others give greater weight to personal autonomy, dignity, or moral integrity, which are central to liberalism. Privacy related rights have extended beyond their original concern – threats to private space, particularly the home – to encompass personal security, self-fulfilment, and identity, including the organisation of family life and relationships, sexual *mores*, and some business activities.[19]

However, this article will focus on the right to privacy in the more traditional senses of control over personal information and freedom from intrusion on seclusion. It is this kind of privacy interest which is usually affected by some of the less acceptable activities of the media. It therefore provides an insight into whether the incorporation of the European Convention on Human Rights will make much difference to what the media can do in the field of privacy.

In proceedings brought in Strasbourg it is the Contracting State alone which can be a party to a complaint brought by an individual. It must not be forgotten that the European Convention on Human Rights is an international treaty and, although it is unusual in that it permits individuals (and not only other States) to bring complaints under it, it is binding only on States Parties and not on private individuals or companies such as those which publish newspapers. In the parlance of European

---

[16] As in the cases on the rights of homosexuals to engage in consensual acts between adults in private: see *Dudgeon v United Kingdom*, Series A, No. 45 (1981) 4 E.H.R.R. 149; *Norris v Ireland*, Series A, No. 142 (1988) 13 E.H.R.R. 186; *Modinos v Cyprus*, Series A, No. 259 (1993) 16 E.H.R.R. 485.

[17] As in the cases on the rights of transsexuals to have their change of sexual identity recognised by the state: see *Rees v United Kingdom*, Series A, No. 106 (1986) 9 E.H.R.R. 56; *Cossey v United Kingdom*, Series A, No. 184 (1990) 13 E.H.R.R. 622; *B v France*, Series A, No. 232-C (1992) 16 E.H.R.R. 1; *X, Y and Z v United Kingdom*, (1997) 24 E.H.R.R. 143; *Sheffield and Horsham v United Kingdom*, (Judgment of July 30, 1998).

[18] Series A, No. 251-B, (1993) 16 E.H.R.R. 97, para 29.

[19] D Feldman, 'The Developing Scope of Article 8 of the European Convention on Human Rights' [1997] *E.H.R.L.R.* 266 at 266–67 (footnotes omitted).

Community law, it has 'vertical' but not 'horizontal' effect. As Professor Barendt has noted, Article 8(2) only requires justification for an interference with the rights in Article 8(1) by a 'public authority':

> For this reason it is doubtful whether the provision could be invoked to help someone who claimed that his privacy was violated by the media or by a private investigator.[20]

However, the position is not quite so straightforward. The Court of Human Rights has held that the obligations which are imposed on a State by the Convention are not merely negative in character but may be positive as well. This has been said to be particularly so of Article 8, which does not prohibit just 'interferences' by the State with privacy but imposes an obligation to 'respect' that right, thus importing a positive obligation to ensure its effective protection. The Court has said that the positive obligation will extend to requiring action to protect an individual from the acts of other private parties:

> The Court recalls that although the object of Article 8 is essentially that of protecting the individual against arbitrary interference by the public authorities, it does not merely compel the State to abstain from such interference: in addition to this primarily negative obligation, there may be positive obligations inherent in an effective respect for private or family life. These obligations may involve the adoption of measures designed to secure respect for private life even in the sphere of the relations of individuals between themselves.[21]

In such contexts a fair balance has to be struck between the interests of the individual and the general interest. A fair balance would include recognition of the rights of others, including the right to freedom of expression, itself guaranteed in Article 10 of the European Convention on Human Rights, and in particular freedom of the press, which has been described by the Court of Human Rights as being an essential foundation of a democratic society.[22]

Professor Feldman has suggested that the positive obligation imposed by Article 8 on states may require legal regulation of the collection and use of personal information by private agencies:

> It is possible that the Court will hold that states, which must already take proper steps in relation to files which they hold, must also ensure that private agencies do the same. Harassment by the press presents special problems, because of the uneasy relationship between privacy rights and press freedom. In view of the high value which the Court usually attaches to freedom of the press, legislation curbing the activities of journalists in order to protect Article 8 rights would be liable to violate Article 10. However, the more closely a press intrusion affects the rights of others, including the right to respect for private and family life, the more likely it is that the Court may hold that the state is permitted, if not bound, to limit the Article 10 rights of the press to protect that right, and to provide an effective remedy for arguable infringements of Article 8(1).[23]

---

[20] E Barendt, 'Privacy as a Constitutional Right and Value' in P Birks (ed), *Privacy and Loyalty* (Oxford, Clarendon, 1997) 12.

[21] *X and Y v The Netherlands*, Series A, No. 91 (1986) 8 E.H.R.R. 235, para 23. See also the cases on transsexuals (*supra* n 18).

[22] See *eg Sunday Times v United Kingdom*, Series A, No. 30 (1979–80) 2 E.H.R.R. 245.

[23] D Feldman, 'The Developing Scope of Article 8 of the European Convention on Human Rights' [1997] *E.H.R.L.R.* 266 at 272 (footnotes omitted). See also D Feldman, 'Privacy-related Rights and their Social Value' in P Birks (ed), *Privacy and Loyalty* (Oxford, Clarendon, 1997) 47.

The fact that the State may, because of the absence of legal regulation of intrusions on privacy, breach its obligations under Article 8 is illustrated by two cases about interception of telecommunications: *Malone v United Kingdom*[24] and *Halford v United Kingdom*.[25] *Halford* is of particular interest because it concerned not a public telephone system (as in *Malone*) but an internal office system which was listened to by the applicant's employers (the police) with whom she had a long-running and well-publicised dispute about sex discrimination. The Court of Human Rights held that the absence of any legal regulation in domestic law of intrusion on such internal telephone systems violated Article 8(2), which permits interference with a right under Article 8(1) only if it is in accordance with the 'law'. The Court also held that there had been a violation of the applicant's rights under Article 13 of the Convention, to have an effective remedy in national law for breach of her rights under Article 8; the absence of legal regulation meant that she had no legal remedy.[26]

It will be noted, however, that both *Malone* and *Halford* concerned interception of telephone conversations by the police, obviously a public authority. The issue which *Halford* leaves to be decided is whether it would be a breach of Article 8 to fail to protect an individual's privacy where the facts are exactly the same as in *Halford* but the employer is a private company rather than a public authority. It is submitted that it should make no difference to the result (or the reasoning in support of it) in Strasbourg. The state should still be liable for breach of its own positive obligation. However, it does not follow that an action can be brought (whether in Strasbourg or in a national court after the Human Rights Act comes into force) against the private entity itself. The cause of action in Strasbourg will still be against the State. To use an analogy from European Community law, this type of action is more akin to an action against a Member State for failing to transpose a directive properly into national law where the directive would have protected an individual against another individual or company[27] than to actions brought against private entities themselves under provisions of EC law which have horizontal direct effect.

It has to be acknowledged that until recently the case law from Strasbourg has not been encouraging to those who wished to assert that the right to privacy includes an obligation on the State to protect privacy against intrusion by private entities. In *J. S. v United Kingdom*[28] the European Commission of Human Rights rejected an application where an insurance company had engaged in covert surveillance of the complainant. However, this decision could be explained on the basis that the insurance company was justified in its actions because it was seeking to protect its position in relation to litigation. In *Bausson v France*[29] the Commission rejected a complaint where telephone conversations had been recorded by the co-accused and used in criminal proceedings against him. This case is interesting because the mere 'fact that the courts become involved at some stage does not, therefore, necessarily engage the responsibility of the State under Article 8'.[30]

---

[24] Series A, No. 82 (1985) 7 E.H.R.R. 14.
[25] (1997) 24 E.H.R.R. 523, especially para 51.
[26] ibid, para 65.
[27] Cases C-6 and 7/90 *Francovich v Italy* [1991] E.C.R. I-5357.
[28] App. No. 19173/91, decision of January 8, 1993.
[29] App. No. 21120/93, Decision of February 1, 1993.
[30] SH Naismith, 'Photographs, Privacy and Freedom of Expression' [1996] *E.H.R.L.R.* 150 at 157.

In *Winer v United Kingdom*[31] the Commission rejected a complaint about newspaper reporting on the ground that the causes of action available in national law, in particular defamation, were sufficient to protect against invasions of privacy. However, the decision is explicable by reference to its particular facts. Clearly, there will be some invasions of privacy where an action for defamation will not lie: for example, where the story is intrusive on private life without any public interest in its publication but is true. It is also interesting to note that in *Winer* the Commission took the view that the English law cause of action for breach of confidence did not provide an adequate remedy which had to be exhausted before recourse to Strasbourg, on the ground that it was (at that time) insufficiently certain.

The above case law has led one commentator to conclude that:

> Essentially, then, the Commission seems to take the view that positive obligations under Article 8 are fulfilled if remedies offering a degree of protection to the aggrieved individual are available and the national courts at least take into account the privacy aspect. As far as the United Kingdom is concerned, it is true that there are a number of specific remedies for specific wrongs ... but it is doubtful whether any of these is appropriate in respect of a true statement, let alone a photograph, and this point was not satisfactorily dealt with in the *Winer* case ... In spite of some indications that the Commission would give priority to the right of privacy over freedom of expression in appropriate circumstances, it is by no means clear that the European Convention on Human Rights supplies the protection which is lacking at the national level.[32]

However, in its recent decision in *Earl Spencer v United Kingdom*[33] the Commission has taken the view that the law of confidence has moved on sufficiently in the English case law to provide a remedy which must be exhausted before any complaint to Strasbourg. The case arose from media interest in the private affairs of Earl Spencer and his then wife, who suffered from eating disorders and was being treated at a clinic when she was photographed by the press. The Commission held that the reason why the application was inadmissible was that the applicants had failed to exhaust their domestic remedies under Article 26 of the European Convention on Human Rights. This pre-supposes that there are effective remedies under domestic law which are there to be exhausted. The Commission said that it:

> would not exclude that the absence of an actionable remedy in relation to the publications of which the applicants complain could show a lack of respect for their private lives. It has regard in this respect to the duties and responsibilities that are carried with the right to freedom of expression guaranteed by Article 10 of the Convention and to Contracting States' obligation to provide a measure of protection to the right of privacy of an individual affected by others' exercise of their freedom of expression.

On the decisive point in the case, namely that the applicants had failed to exhaust their domestic remedies, the Commission said that:

> The parties' submissions indicate that the remedy of breach of confidence (against the newspapers and their sources) was available to applicants and that the applicants have not

---

[31] (1986) 48 D.R. 154.
[32] SH Naismith, 'Photographs, Privacy and Freedom of Expression' [1996] *E.H.R.L.R.* 150 at 158.
[33] (1998) 25 E.H.R.R. CD 105.

demonstrated that it was insufficient or ineffective in the circumstances of their cases. It considers that, insofar as relevant doubts remain concerning the financial awards to be made following a finding of a breach of confidence, they are not such as to warrant a conclusion that the breach of confidence action is ineffective or insufficient but rather a conclusion that the matter should be put to the domestic courts for consideration in order to allow those courts, through the common law system in the United Kingdom, the opportunity to develop existing rights by way of interpretation.

This could be seen as a 'green light' to those judges who would like to develop the common law (in particular the law of breach of confidence) so as to recognise a right of privacy. One further piece of encouragement from Strasbourg for those who wish to see such a right enforceable even as against the private media is to be found in paragraph C7 of Resolution 428 (1970) of the Parliamentary Assembly of the Council of the Europe (the Council is the body which sponsored the European Convention on Human Rights and supervises its implementation) which provides:

> The right to privacy afforded by Article 8 of the Convention of Human Rights should not only protect an individual against interference by public authorities, but also against interference by private persons including the mass media. National legislation should comprise provisions guaranteeing this protection.[34]

Before leaving the subject of what the European Convention on Human Rights requires of Contracting States, it should be noted that many (but by no means all) of the comments about positive obligations have been influenced by the presence in the European Convention on Human Rights of two provisions: Article 1, which requires States to 'secure to everyone within their jurisdiction the rights and freedoms' in the substantive parts of the European Convention on Human Rights; and Article 13, which provides that:

> Everyone whose rights and freedoms as set forth in this Convention are violated shall have an effective remedy before a national authority notwithstanding that the violation has been committed by persons acting in an official capacity.

Neither of these two provisions is to be enacted into domestic law by the Human Rights Bill, which sets out the rights which it incorporates in Schedule 1. However, this will not necessarily mean that Strasbourg jurisprudence in which reference is made to these two provisions will be irrelevant to the courts' consideration of the issues before them under the Human Rights Bill. Domestic courts will be required to have regard to relevant case law from Strasbourg by clause 2 of the Bill. In answer to a question posed by Lord Lester of Herne Hill at the Committee stage of the Bill's progress in the House of Lords, the Lord Chancellor said that:

> The courts may have regard to Article 13. In particular they may wish to do so when considering the very ample provisions of Clause 8(1) ... Knowing the remedial amplitude

---

[34] See further A Clapham, *Human Rights in the Private Sphere* (Oxford, Clarendon, 1993) 102–03, where it is suggested that resolutions such as this one are an important guide to evolving standards of human rights in Member States of the Council of Europe. They might be called a source of 'soft law'.

of the law of the United Kingdom, I cannot see any scope for the argument that the English or Scots law is incapable within domestic adjectival law of providing effective remedies.[35]

As Lord Lester put it: 'This will be a fascinating debate for lawyers to read in *Hansard*'.[36]

THE HUMAN RIGHTS BILL

The five main features of the Bill relevant to this article can be summarised as follows.

First, clause 1 provides that the substantive Convention rights reproduced in Schedule 1 to the Bill shall have effect for the purposes of the Human Rights Act.

Secondly, clause 6(1) makes it unlawful for any public authority to do anything which is incompatible with Convention rights. Despite its simplicity, this provision will have profound effect generally and in relation to privacy in particular. It lies at the heart of the Bill. It is the principal method chosen by the Government to incorporate (ie give direct effect to) the rights in the European Convention on Human Rights. In the field of privacy, it will have the effect of reversing cases such as *Peck*.[37] It will no longer be necessary for an applicant for judicial review to argue that a public authority such as the respondent there has acted irrationally or for an impermissible purpose. It will suffice to argue that it has acted incompatibly with the right to respect for private life by disclosing information of a private character and, unless such disclosure was justified under Article 8(2), has thereby acted unlawfully.

The phrase 'public authority' clearly includes bodies which are obviously public such as central government departments and local authorities. Both the Lord Chancellor and the Home Office have made it clear, during the debates on the Bill in Parliament, that this means that *all* the activities of local authorities and central government departments will be subject to the Human Rights Act.[38] They will not be able to say (as they can under our present law of judicial review) that some of their acts are private in nature, as when they act in their capacity as employers.[39] This will be important where public authority employers seek to use their power to interfere with the privacy of their employees, for example by listening in to their telephone conversations in the office.

But clause 6 goes further. It defines public authority to include any body *certain* of whose functions are public.[40] In relation to this kind of hybrid body it will be only its

---

[35] *Hansard*, H.L. Deb., November 18, 1997, cols 476–77.

[36] *Hansard*, H.L. Deb., November 18, 1997, col 480. These statements need to be read with some caution, however, because of the exchanges between Sir Nicholas Lyell MP and the Home Secretary (Jack Straw MP) in the House of Commons when the Conservatives put down a probing amendment to include Article 13 in the Bill, which they withdrew apparently on the basis that they were reassured that *Hansard* would not be used to look at Article 13 in the way suggested by Lord Lester: *Hansard*, H.L. Deb., May 20, 1998, cols 975–87.

[37] *R v Brentwood BC, ex p.Peck*, *Times Law Reports*, December 18, 1996.

[38] *Hansard*, H.L. Deb., November 24, 1997, cols 758–59 (Lord Williams of Mostyn, the Parliamentary Under-Secretary of State, Home Office) and col. 796 (Lord Irvine of Lairg L.C.); *Hansard*, H.C. Deb., February 16, 1998, col. 775 (Jack Straw M.P., the Home Secretary).

[39] See eg *R v East Berkshire Health Authority, ex p. Walsh* [1985] Q.B. 152 CA.

[40] Clause 6(3)(b).

public functions which are subject to the Human Rights Act, not its private acts.[41] It is likely that a corporation such as the BBC will be a 'public authority' for the purposes of the Bill and it may be that Channel 4 will be.[42] As will be seen below, bodies that are created not by statute or prerogative but nevertheless exercise some public functions, such as the Press Complaints Commission, will be included in the definition of 'public authority'.

Clause 6 does not stop there. The phrase 'public authority' includes courts and tribunals.[43] This means that when the courts are deciding cases based not on a statute but on the common law, which is their own creation, they will have to do so in a way which is consistent with the European Convention on Human Rights. The Bill will make rights effective not just against the government, local authorities and other public bodies but also in some contexts against private companies and individuals. In this way the Bill will achieve what Andrew Clapham has called the 'privatisation' of human rights.[44] It also meets the traditional criticism from the 'old left' that the European Convention on Human Rights is merely a liberal charter based on the false premise that the only threat to human rights comes from the state and not from the accumulation of private wealth and power as well.

The third important feature of the Human Rights Bill is that it provides a very full clause on remedies for breaches of the European Convention on Human Rights. The court or tribunal in which a human rights argument is raised will be entitled to give whatever remedy which is within its power and which it considers just and appropriate to put right the breach in question.[45] This could include injunctive relief and an account of profits, both of which could be important remedies in the context of privacy.

The Bill goes on to provide that the remedies for breach of a Convention right may include damages to compensate for the loss suffered.[46] In assessing whether to award damages and, if so, how much, the court will have to have regard to the principles on compensation developed by the Court of Human Rights under Article 41 (formerly Article 50) of the European Convention on Human Rights, which allows it to award 'just satisfaction' to a successful applicant in Strasbourg.

The fourth main feature of the Bill is that, while national courts and tribunals will have to take the jurisprudence of the Commission of Human Rights, Court of Human Rights and the Council of Ministers into account, they will not be bound by it.[47] This leaves open the intriguing possibility that courts in the United Kingdom could develop their own bill of rights, in respect of which the case law from Strasbourg will be the starting-point but not the finishing-point by any means. In practice, they are unlikely to give any less protection to human rights than the Strasbourg case law requires, since they will know that the road to Strasbourg will still be available to a disappointed litigant. However, since the European Convention on Human Rights

---

[41] Clause 6(5).

[42] See the views of Lord Williams of Mostyn (the Parliamentary Under- Secretary of State, Home Office): *Hansard*, H.L. Deb., November 3, 1997, col. 1309, but note that he went on to say that: 'I stress that that is a matter for the courts to develop as the jurisprudence develops'.

[43] Clause 6(3)(a).

[44] A Clapham, 'The Privatisation of Human Rights' [1995] *E.H.R.L.R.* 20; see also A Clapham, *Human Rights in the Private Sphere* (Oxford, Clarendon, 1993).

[45] Clause 8(1).

[46] Clause 8(2).

[47] Clause 2.

provides a floor and not a ceiling for rights throughout the Council of Europe (there are now 40 States Parties to the European Convention on Human Rights, including some of the former Communist countries of Eastern Europe), it is perfectly possible that the courts of this country will provide greater protection for human rights under the Bill than is strictly required by the case law from Strasbourg. This might be true particularly in the field of privacy, where judges who have spoken on the subject clearly feel that they were hampered by the absence of incorporation of the European Convention on Human Rights from developing a free-standing right to privacy in English law.[48] They will be free to develop their own case law on the scope and effect of Article 8, provided that they do not go so far in protecting privacy that they take the protection given to freedom of expression below the threshold required by Strasbourg case law.

The final important feature of the Bill is that it precludes the possibility of complaint being made in a national court or tribunal that Parliament has failed to legislate or that a Minister has failed to propose legislation to Parliament.[49] It is not even possible under the Bill for the higher courts to declare that a failure to legislate is incompatible with the (positive) obligations contained in the European Convention on Human Rights. Accordingly, if the courts consider after incorporation that the absence of a right to privacy against the privately-owned media is in breach of the United Kingdom's positive obligation under Article 8, they will either have to assume responsibility themselves for fulfilling that obligation or they will have to acknowledge that there has been a failure to bring rights home fully and that they are powerless even to make a declaration of incompatibility. It is likely that they will themselves fill the gap in protection.

When the Bill was being debated in the House of Lords, the Lord Chancellor clearly envisaged that the courts would be free to, and probably would, use the European Convention on Human Rights to develop a right to privacy in the common law.[50] He said with justification that it would be better that they should do this under the incorporated European Convention on Human Rights than without it. They would then be required to balance the rights in Article 8 and Article 10. In particular they would have to take account of the importance which the Court of Human Rights has attached to freedom of the press to investigate political and other matters in the public interest. They would also have to take account of the distaste expressed in the jurisprudence of the Court of Human Rights for 'prior restraints', such as interlocutory injunctions that can be obtained in an emergency when a newspaper is about to go to print.

PROPOSED AMENDMENTS FROM LORD WAKEHAM

When the Bill was considered by the House of Lords at Committee stage, two sets of amendments were proposed by Lord Wakeham, who chairs the Press Complaints

---

[48] See eg Lord Bingham of Cornhill C.J., 'Should There Be a Law to Protect Rights of Personal Privacy?' [1996] *E.H.R.L.R.* 450.

[49] Clause 6(6).

[50] *Hansard*, H.L. Deb., November 3, 1997, cols 1229–30.

Commission (PCC), a self-regulatory body set up by the press themselves, which has a voluntary code of conduct, governing privacy as well as other aspects of media behaviour. The first set of amendments would have had the effect of excluding courts and tribunals from the definition of 'public authority' where the dispute was otherwise between two private parties. This would have meant that an individual could bring an action based on Article 8 against a public authority (such as the police) but not against a newspaper company. Its consequences would have been far-reaching. They would potentially have placed the United Kingdom in breach of its international obligations under the European Convention on Human Rights whenever it is the actions of a court (itself a part of the State for the purpose of international law) which place the United Kingdom in breach in Strasbourg. This has happened more often than it may be popular now to mention, as in the *Sunday Times* cases, the *Spycatcher* litigation and the *Goodwin* case.[51]

Lord Wakeham explained and justified his proposal in this way:

> My amendment aims to stop the development of a common law of privacy. Such a law could never be as effective as self-regulation in safeguarding the rights of individuals. And such a law would seriously erode the freedom of the press, which has been a pillar of our democracy since the first Bill of Rights in 1689.[52]

A second set of amendments proposed by Lord Wakeham would have removed the PCC from the definition of 'public authority' in the Bill. Lord Wakeham explained his proposals as follows:

> If the PCC's adjudications on matters of privacy could be subject to subsequent action by the courts, my task of seeking to resolve differences, to obtain a public apology where appropriate or, if necessary, to deliver a reprimand to an erring editor would no longer be a practical proposition because the courts would be able to intervene after our work had finished. That would ensure that from day one the newspapers' approach to a complaint of invasion of privacy would be highly cautious and legalistic. The courts may also be able to award monetary compensation. My chances of making self-regulation work for the benefit of ordinary people, and without cost to them, would be minimal.[53]

The Lord Chancellor said in response to these amendments that:

> As I have often said, the judges are pen-poised regardless of incorporation of the Convention to develop a right of privacy to be protected by the common law. This is not me saying so; they have said so. It must be emphasised that the judges are free to develop the common law in their own independent judicial sphere. What I say positively is that it will be a better law if the judges develop it after incorporation because they will have regard to Articles 8 and 10, giving Article 10 its due high value ... In my view, the courts may not act as legislators and grant new remedies for infringement of convention rights unless the common law itself enables them to develop new rights or remedies. I believe that the true view is that the courts will be able to adapt and develop the common law by relying on existing domestic

---

[51] *Sunday Times v United Kingdom* Series A, No. 30 (1979–80) 2 E.H.R.R. 245; *Sunday Times v United Kingdom (No. 2)* Series A, No. 217 (1992) 14 E.H.R.R. 229; *Observer and Guardian Newspapers v United Kingdom* Series A, No. 216 (1992) 14 E.H.R.R. 153; *Goodwin v United Kingdom*, judgment of March 27, 1996 (1996) 22 E.H.R.R. 123.

[52] *Hansard*, H.L. Deb., November 24, 1997, col. 772.

[53] *Hansard*, H.L. Deb, November 24, 1997, col. 773.

principles in the laws of trespass, nuisance, copyright, confidence and the like, to fashion a *common law right to privacy.*[54]

The Lord Chancellor's views are supported by Murray Hunt, who says:

> This inclusion of courts and tribunals in the definition of public authorities who are subject to the obligation in section 6(1) to act compatibly with the Convention is of great significance for the horizontality of Convention rights under the Human Rights Act. Kentridge A.J. in *Du Plessis* saw the absence of reference to 'the judiciary' in cl.7(1) of the interim South African Constitution to be of great significance as an indicator that court judgments were not to be equated with state action and that the doctrine of horizontal effect was therefore not to be imported into South African law. By the same token, the *inclusion* of courts in section 6(1) of the Human Rights Act must bear a converse significance … By making courts and tribunals 'public authorities' it imposes a *duty* on them to act compatibly with the Convention, including when they decide purely private disputes between private parties governed solely by the common law.[55]

As Murray Hunt says later in the same article, this will not mean that courts will be free – let alone required – to invent new causes of action. That would be to defy the will of Parliament, which will clearly have decided not to make its provisions directly binding on everyone, including private bodies.

In contrast, Professor Sir William Wade, QC appears to be of the view that the duties imposed on courts by clause 6 of the Bill will lead inescapably to horizontal effect, including the creation of a right to privacy against the private media:

> It would be a poor sort of 'incorporation' which exempted private individuals and bodies from respecting the fundamental rights of their fellow-citizens and drove them back to Strasbourg with all its cost in time and money – the very evil which 'incorporation' is supposed to remedy. It must surely be correct to read the Bill as requiring courts and tribunals to recognise and enforce the Convention rights, taking account of the ECHR materials catalogued in clause 2, and subject only to contrary primary legislation … This will be a statutory duty in all proceedings, *whether the defendant is a public authority or a private person.*[56]

It is submitted that the views of Murray Hunt are to be preferred to those of Professor Sir William Wade, QC. The courts will not be free, let alone required, to create wholly new causes of action based directly on Article 8 against the private media. However, they will be entitled, and perhaps required, to develop existing causes of action in such a way as to protect privacy against such media.

Lord Wakeham's amendments were withdrawn in the face of the Government's determination to protect the integrity of the scheme which it had chosen for the incorporation of the European Convention on Human Rights.[57] By the time the Bill

---

[54] *Hansard*, H.L. Deb.,November 24, 1997, cols 784–85.

[55] M Hunt, 'The "Horizontal Effect" of the Human Rights Act' [1998] P.L. 423 at 439–40. The reference to *Du Plessis* is to the decision of the South African Constitutional Court in *Du Plessis v De Klerk* (1996) 3 S.A. 850, which was a defamation action between private parties in which an issue was raised about the right to freedom of expression in the interim Constitution.

[56] Sir William Wade, Q.C., 'The United Kingdom's Bill of Rights' in University of Cambridge Centre of Public Law, *Constitutional Reform in the United Kingdom: Practice and Principles* (Oxford, Hart Publishing, 1998) 63 (emphasis added).

[57] The Lord Chancellor did indicate that his door was still open to the PCC for discussion and this was welcomed by Lord Wakeham: *Hansard*, H.L. Deb., November 24, 1997, cols 786–87.

went to the House of Commons, the Home Secretary (who has primary responsibility for the Bill) had reached an understanding with Lord Wakeham, which led him to announce that the Government itself would introduce amendments of a more limited character to assuage the concerns of the media. When the Bill was introduced into the House of Commons for its Second Reading, the Home Secretary said:

> The components of such an amendment would be, first, an explicit provision that no relief or remedy is to be granted regarding Article 8 on respect for private life unless the respondent is either present or represented, or the applicant has taken all practicable steps to alert the *newspaper* against whom the application is brought. That would virtually rule out pre-publication injunctions being granted *ex parte*; secondly, an explicit provision that in any case in which a person applies for relief or a remedy on article 8 grounds related to respect for private life, and the granting of a remedy would raise issues concerning an Article 10 Convention right, the court must have particular regard to freedom of expression – this would be consistent with the jurisprudence of the European Court, which already lays great emphasis on Article 10 rights, but it could also constitute a useful signal and reminder to the United Kingdom courts; thirdly, a requirement for the court – in the case of an application involving journalistic, literary or artistic material, also to take into account the extent of the public interest in the publication in question, whether the newspaper had acted fairly and reasonably, and whether it had complied with the provisions of the Press Complaints Commission's code.[58]

There is always a danger when legislating in such specific detail in what is otherwise a human rights bill of general application that the Bill will fail to 'bring rights home' fully. However, in many ways the Home Secretary's announcement did no more than to reflect the existing case law of the Court of Human Rights.

Given the long history of our courts giving insufficient weight to freedom of expression, reflected in the various findings of violations of Article 10 in Strasbourg, it is reasonable for Parliament to draw the courts' attention to the high regard in which freedom of expression is held by the Court of Human Rights.

At Committee stage in the House of Commons, the Government brought forward its own amendment to give effect to the Home Secretary's announcement by way of inserting a new clause 12 into the Bill.[59] Clause 12, which has the sidenote 'Freedom of expression', reads:

(1) This section applies if a court is considering whether to grant any relief which, if granted, might affect the exercise of the Convention right to freedom of expression.

(2) If the person against whom the application for relief is made ('the respondent') is neither present nor represented, no such relief is to be granted unless the court is satisfied –

   (a) that the applicant has taken all practicable steps to notify the respondent; or
   (b) that there are compelling reasons why the respondent should not be notified.

(3) No such relief is to be granted so as to restrain publication before trial unless the court is satisfied that the application is likely to establish that publication should not be allowed.

---

[58] *Hansard*, H.L. Deb., February 16, 1998, col. 777 (emphasis added). It is noteworthy that the Home Secretary was clearly envisaging that there could be cases brought against newspapers based on Article 8 under the Human Rights Bill.

[59] Note that when it was introduced the amendment was numbered new clause 13: *Hansard*, H.L. Deb., July 2, 1998, col. 534.

(4)   The court must have particular regard to the importance of the Convention right to freedom of expression and, where the proceedings relate to material which the respondent claims, or which appears to the court, to be journalistic, literary or artistic material (or to conduct connected with such material), to –

    (a)   the extent to which –

        (i)   the material has, or is about to, become available to the public; or

        (ii)   it is, or would be, in the public interest for the material to be published;

    (b)   any relevant privacy code.

(5)   In this section –

'court' includes a tribunal; and

'relief' includes any remedy or order (other than in criminal proceedings).

Fortunately, the amendment actually brought forward by the Government, unlike the Home Secretary's announcement, does not make reference to whether the media have acted 'fairly and reasonably'. This is to be welcomed because, in so far as claims which may be brought against the media under the Bill, the test of fairness and reasonableness is looser than the European Convention on Human Rights test of whether an interference with a fundamental right is 'necessary in a democratic society', ie whether it corresponds to a pressing social need and is proportionate to that need. While the other matters which the court would have to take into account under the Home Secretary's announcement may be thought to be directly relevant to whether that test is met, to include reference to fairness and reasonableness might have risked substituting a different test altogether. If it were held in Strasbourg that a different, and lower, test had been applied in a particular case there would be a violation of Article 8.

It is also to be welcomed that there is no express reference to compliance with the PCC's Code of Conduct as a matter to be taken into account. Clearly that Code will be one example of what the amendment calls a 'private code'. It would have been undesirable for the Bill to enter into any greater detail. After all, the PCC may change its structure or name over the years. More importantly, there may well be other privacy codes that ought to be taken into account, such as those promulgated by the Broadcasting Standards Council and perhaps the Independent Television Commission.

The amendment made by the new clause 12 enables courts to strike the right balance between the Convention right to freedom of expression, including the public interest in publication of certain material, with other interests such as the right to privacy. In particular it makes it difficult to obtain prior restraints or 'gagging orders', and makes it virtually impossible to obtain them *ex parte*. The amendment is preferable to the way in which Lord Wakeham's amendments would have sought to protect the press. Unlike those amendments, the new clause is consistent with, rather than contrary to, the scheme of the Bill, which is universal: it gives no public body a privileged position in the context of human rights.[60] It also gives no particular Convention right priority over any other.

---

[60] As the Home Secretary pointed out in introducing the amendment, the new clause applies to the exercise of freedom of expression by anyone and is not limited to cases to which a public authority is a party: *Hansard*, H.L. Deb., July 20, 1998, col. 536.

As will be apparent from the debates on the Bill in Parliament, it now appears to be accepted by the Government (rightly) that the PCC will fall within the meaning of 'public authority' in clause 6(3) of the Bill.[61] However, it is important to see what this means. It is rarely going to be the case that the PCC itself is going to be accused of violating someone's right to privacy. But if it violates anyone's rights under the European Convention on Human Rights, eg a journalist's freedom of expression, it is right that it should be answerable for that. Sometimes the PCC will have a positive obligation under Article 8 of the European Convention on Human Rights to protect people's privacy from newspapers. But this is what it is designed to do in any event. If it does its job effectively, it will have nothing to fear from the courts.

It is also important to bear in mind that, in those cases that do come before the courts, whether on judicial review from the PCC or directly, they are themselves public authorities under the Bill. They must comply with the European Convention on Human Rights – and this means all of the Convention, not just one part of it. They will have to balance the right to privacy against the right to freedom of expression in Article 10 of the Convention. They will also have to bear in mind the case law from Strasbourg. The Court of Human Rights has often stressed that freedom of the press is essential to a democratic society, in particular when the press are investigating the working of government or other matters in the public interest. The Court has also frowned upon the use of prior restraints (ie injunctions or gagging orders) which prevent news from being published, because it recognises that news is often a perishable commodity. Legitimate and fearless reporting therefore has nothing to fear from the European Convention on Human Rights. Far from it – incorporation of the European Convention on Human Rights will give to journalists and newspapers the guaranteed right to freedom of expression for the first time in our history. The British press has secured many important victories in Strasbourg – the *Thalidomide* case brought by the *Sunday Times* in the 1970s and the *Spycatcher* cases brought in the late 1980s by various newspapers including the *Observer* and the *Guardian* are among the most memorable.[62] It has helped to achieve the high level of protection afforded to freedom of expression in the Strasbourg case law. Everyone who supports freedom of the press should welcome the Bill which brings these hard-won rights home.

CONCLUSION

The enactment of the Human Rights Bill will mark 'the beginning of a new constitutional chapter' in the history of the United Kingdom.[63] In the field of privacy it will perhaps have the greatest impact. It will make it unlawful for any public authority

---

[61] *Hansard*, H.L. Deb., November 24, 1997, cols 784 and 786 (Lord Irvine of Lairg L.C.). See also *Hansard*, H.L. Deb., July 2, 1998, cols 544–45 (the exchange between Sir Norman Fowler M.P. and the Home Secretary).

[62] *Supra* n. 52.

[63] *Hansard*, H.L. Deb., November 3, 1997, col. 1256 (Lord Scarman).

(in the wide sense used in the Bill) to breach the right to respect for private life in Article 8 of the European Convention on Human Rights. It may go further and be at least indirectly applicable against private individuals and companies. It is likely, in the light of recent authority from the Commission of Human Rights and extrajudicial comments of judges in the United Kingdom, to be used as the springboard for the development of existing causes of action so as to fill the gaps in the patchy protection of privacy in English law.

Holding the Balance: National Security, Civil Liberties and the Role of the Investigatory Powers Tribunal[1]

This lecture was given in 2019 at the School of Oriental and African Studies, in memory of Kay Everett, a remarkable solicitor who had changed course from being a commercial solicitor to practising human rights law. In this lecture I took the opportunity to explain the history and work of the Investigatory Powers Tribunal, of which I was appointed President in 2018. The Tribunal was created in 2000 and is in substance a court which deals with complaints which include those made against the intelligence services. It is not to be confused with the office of the Investigatory Powers Commissioner, which was created by the Investigatory Powers Act 2016: although that office includes "judicial commissioners", they do not sit to adjudicate on disputes as the Tribunal does. Their functions include the approval of warrants of various types under the 2016 Act and the carrying out of inspections. After this lecture was given, the Supreme Court reversed the decision of the Court of Appeal in R (Privacy International) v Investigatory Powers Tribunal *and held that the Tribunal is in principle amenable to judicial review*: [2019] UKSC 22; [2020] AC 491. *Although important, particularly for decisions in the past, this will have less impact in the future than might be thought because in the meantime Parliament has created a mechanism for appeals against the decisions of the Tribunal. The first such appeal was heard by the Court of Appeal in January 2021:* Privacy International & Ors v Secretary of State for Foreign and Commonwealth Affairs & Ors [2021] EWCA Civ 330.

I T IS A genuine pleasure to give this year's Kay Everett Memorial Lecture. Kay Everett was a truly remarkable person. I doubt if there are many others who would have the courage to do what she did. Midway through her career with a 'magic circle' firm of solicitors, she decided to embark on an LLM here at SOAS on the subject of human rights law. She then devoted her life and career to helping others by making use of that knowledge and experience. Her life was sadly cut short when she was only 43 but her memory lives on and inspires others.

[1] I would like to thank Jonathan Glasson QC for his comments on an earlier draft of this lecture.

The theme of my lecture this evening will be the work of the Investigatory Powers Tribunal (or 'IPT'). I was appointed President of that Tribunal in September last year. I hope you will find it interesting to hear about the history and work of this Tribunal. It is a tribunal whose work is perhaps not as well known as it should be. It is also a relatively rare kind of tribunal in that its jurisdiction extends to all four constituent nations of the United Kingdom.

The activities over which the IPT has jurisdiction include surveillance, interception of communications and the use of covert human intelligence sources ('CHIS' as they are known in the jargon or 'informants' as they are known more colloquially). The public authorities which are within its remit include the police, local authorities and central government departments. Perhaps most significantly, its jurisdiction includes complaints made by members of the public against one of the security and intelligence agencies.

The IPT has been described by one commentator (Ian Cobain) as the 'most secretive court' in this country.[2] On the other hand, the very fact that the IPT exists, to review the legality of the actions of bodies which necessarily have to operate in secret, may itself be a tribute to the rule of law in this country.

As one academic commentator, Paul F Scott, has put it in his recent study, *The National Security Constitution*:

> Where the pursuit of national security ends reaches further into the constitutional landscape than was previously the case, that fact is often in large part the consequence of there having been formalised in law (and, by extension, in constitutional law) processes and actions which would previously not have taken place, or would have happened without legal authority. ... What is presented here as the emergence (or acceleration) of a national security constitution is in many ways the consequence of developments which are themselves, from the point of view of the rule of law – or, if that is too diffuse a value, the bare commitment to legality – unambiguously positive.[3]

The IPT was created by the Regulation of Investigatory Powers Act 2000 ('RIPA'). It succeeded several earlier bodies, including the Interception of Communications Act Tribunal, which had been created in 1985.

The IPT's first President was a Court of Appeal judge, Lord Justice Mummery, who served from its inception in 2000 until his retirement in 2013. Its second President was a High Court judge, Mr Justice (later Sir Michael) Burton, who served from 2013 until 2018. RIPA also makes provision for there to be a Vice-President of the IPT, a post which is currently vacant but which we hope will be filled in the near future. In addition, there are other members. Those other members currently include two serving High Court Judges from England and Wales; a retired High Court Judge from Northern Ireland; and senior practitioners from England and Wales and Scotland.

SOME HISTORY

The history of spying long predates modern technology such as telephones and computers. The leading historian of intelligence matters, Christopher Andrew,

---

[2] *The History Thieves* (London, Portobello Books, 2016) 287.
[3] (Oxford, Hart Publishing, 2018) 4.

suggests that the history of espionage can be traced back to Moses in the Old Testament. In his recent magisterial history of intelligence, he says that: 'The first major figure in world literature to emphasize the importance of good intelligence was God'. After Moses had led his people out of captivity in Egypt in search of the Promised Land, he was told by God to send spies to the land of Canaan, 'which I give unto the children of Israel'.[4]

In England, by Elizabethan times, if not before, we can already see the phenomena of interception of communications and code-breakers. Francis Walsingham, who was Queen Elizabeth I's principal Secretary of State between 1573 and 1590, was particularly keen to keep a careful eye on what was being said in letters written by Mary, Queen of Scots. Indeed, it was a letter which had been intercepted and which appeared to endorse a suggestion that Queen Elizabeth should be assassinated that led to Mary's death warrant. According to Professor Andrew, it was in 1592, in Shakespeare's play *Richard III*, that the first use of the word 'intelligence' is to be found in its modern sense of 'secret information'.[5]

During the brief time when England was a republic, in the Commonwealth era after the Civil War, a Deciphering Branch was created. It was to last from 1653 until Victorian times.

The General Post Office was created in 1660 after the restoration of Charles II. It seems clear that from its inception postal communications were liable to be intercepted by agents of the state. This practice was recognised for the first time in an Act of 1711 in the reign of Queen Anne.

In 1844 it was discovered, after a scandal concerning the interception of the post of the Italian exile Giuseppe Mazzini, that this practice was not uncommon. There was outrage in the House of Commons that something so un-English could have been happening in this country. This led to the abolition of the Deciphering Branch and the Secret Office of the Post Office. According to Christopher Andrew this had the consequence that, at the outbreak of the First World War, Great Britain did not have a code-breaking facility. It quickly found that it needed one.[6]

In the meantime, in 1909 there was established the Secret Service Bureau. Of course its existence was not announced or even acknowledged for many decades. At first it consisted of just two officers, one responsible for domestic matters and the other for foreign intelligence. The original officers, Sir Vernon Kell and Sir Mansfield Cumming became respectively the first heads of the Security Service (MI5) and the Secret Intelligence Service (MI6). It is in honour of Cumming that to this day the Chief of MI6 is known as C – not M, as in the James Bond stories.[7]

The third agency which now forms part of the UK intelligence community is the Government Communications Headquarters (GCHQ), whose origins lie in the Government Code and Cypher School, created after the First World War and which famously worked at Bletchley Park during the Second World War, although this was kept secret for many decades after the war.

[4] *The Secret World: A history of intelligence* (London, Allen Lane, 2018) 13.
[5] ibid, 187.
[6] ibid, 380–83. See also David Omand, *Securing the State* (London, Hurst & Co, 2010) 277.
[7] Andrew (n 4) 483.

What is important for present purposes is that the security and intelligence agencies are subject to the law of the land, including the requirements of RIPA and the Human Rights Act 1998 ('HRA'). By putting complaints under those Acts against one of the agencies into the IPT Parliament has sought to ensure both that such complaints can be made to an independent judicial body; and that the interests of national security are protected.

THE IMPACT OF THE EUROPEAN CONVENTION ON HUMAN RIGHTS ('ECHR')

In 1979, in *Malone v Metropolitan Police Commissioner*, an action concerning interception of telephone calls, pursuant to a warrant issued by the Home Secretary, failed in the High Court on the simple ground that, unlike interception of the post, there was no interference with rights of property. Sir Robert Megarry V-C held that there was no right to privacy at common law.[8] The case of *Malone v United Kingdom* went to the European Court of Human Rights, where it succeeded in 1984.[9] It was that decision which led to the first statute regulating the interception of telephone communications: the Interception of Communications Act 1985. It was the 1985 Act which established a tribunal which was one of the three predecessors of the IPT.

The law in this area was first developed by the European Court of Human Rights in the seminal case of *Klass v Germany*.[10] At paragraph 42 the Court observed that 'powers of secret surveillance of citizens, characterising as they do the police state, are tolerable under the Convention only insofar as strictly necessary for safeguarding the democratic institutions'. The Court stressed that, although states need to be able to respond to threats of terrorism, this does not mean that they 'enjoy an unlimited discretion to subject persons within their jurisdiction to secret surveillance' (paragraph 49). In the same passage the Court emphasised that surveillance poses the risk of undermining or even destroying democracy 'on the ground of defending it' and so states 'may not in the name of the struggle against espionage and terrorism, adopt whatever measures they deem appropriate'.

It is important not to lose sight of the underlying values which are protected by the right to privacy. As a recent academic article by Kirsty Hughes, 'Mass Surveillance and the European Court of Human Rights'[11] puts it, at page 598, privacy is not only an individual right. It also:

> has important societal benefits, in particular it acts as a bulwark against totalitarianism, it provides the space in which ideas (particularly controversial ideas) can be formed, developed, explored and expressed, it fosters social relations, and by protecting privacy we protect those that are typically subject to the most intrusive measures including ethnic and religious minorities, and those of low socio-economic status. Thus privacy contributes to a democratic, intellectually vibrant, harmonious and egalitarian society.

[8] [1979] Ch 344.
[9] (1985) 7 EHRR 14.
[10] (1979–80) 2 EHRR 214.
[11] [2018] *EHRLR* 589.

THE ORIGINS AND HISTORY OF THE IPT

The IPT was established under section 65(1) of RIPA. That Act came into force on 2 October 2000. It is no coincidence that that was the same date on which the Human Rights Act came into full force. This is because RIPA was intended to ensure compliance with this country's obligations under the ECHR so far as they relate to investigatory powers. That Act therefore fits into the framework of human rights law which was also created at that time.

Importantly, section 65(2) provides that the IPT is the only appropriate forum in relation to proceedings against any of the intelligence services for any acts alleged to be incompatible with the Convention rights. In the case of the intelligence services, therefore, the jurisdiction of the IPT is not confined to investigatory powers as such. It covers all conduct of the intelligence agencies which is alleged to breach section 7 of the Human Rights Act.

Under section 67(2) and (3)(c), the IPT must apply the principles applicable by a court on an application for judicial review. However, as has now become clear since 2000, the principles applicable on judicial review include an allegation that a public authority has acted unlawfully under section 6 of the Human Rights Act. Accordingly, the IPT has the same jurisdiction to consider breaches of the Convention rights as an ordinary court would do in a claim for judicial review.

However, the IPT does not have the power to make a declaration of incompatibility in respect of primary legislation. This is because it is not a 'court' within the meaning of section 4 of the Human Rights Act.

In his report of 2015, *A Question of Trust*, David (now Lord) Anderson QC did make a recommendation (at paragraph 14.106 and Recommendation 115) that consideration should be given to conferring the power to make a declaration of incompatibility on the IPT but this was not accepted when Parliament enacted the Investigatory Powers Act 2016 ('the 2016 Act'). That said, it should be noted that David Anderson felt that a possible alternative reform would be to introduce a right of appeal from the IPT, which would then render it less important that the IPT itself may not grant a declaration of incompatibility. That recommendation was accepted by Parliament, in enacting section 242 of the 2016 Act.

Under section 67(8) of RIPA it had been provided that there was to be no appeal from a decision of the IPT 'except to such extent as the Secretary of State may by order otherwise provide'. No such order was made at the time. However, an order has now been made, bringing into force the amendment made by section 242 of the 2016 Act: the new appeal route was introduced from 31 December 2018. Since the courts to which an appeal will lie, including the Court of Appeal of England and Wales, do have the power to make a declaration of incompatibility, it should not be a practical problem that the IPT does not have that power.

The question whether the jurisdiction of the IPT in relation to conduct of the security and intelligence agencies is an exclusive one came before the Supreme Court in *R (A) v Director of Establishments of the Security Service*.[12] In that case the claimant was a former senior member of the Security Service who had written

---

[12] [2009] UKSC 12; [2010] 2 AC 1.

a book about his work with the Service and wished to publish it. He was bound by strict statutory and contractual obligations as well as duties of confidentiality and he was required to obtain the consent of the Director of Establishments of the Security Service before he could publish. The Director refused to give his consent to publish parts of the book. The claimant commenced judicial review proceedings in the High Court alleging that this was contrary to his right to freedom of expression in Article 10 of the ECHR. The Supreme Court held that only the IPT had jurisdiction to hear claims under section 7(1)(a) of the Human Rights Act and section 65(3)(a) of RIPA did not limit that exclusive jurisdiction to proceedings arising out of the exercise of one of the regulated investigatory powers in that Act itself. The judgment of the Court was given by Lord Brown JSC.

At paragraph 14 of his judgment Lord Brown made the particular point that the doctrine of 'neither confirm nor deny' ('NCND') meant that it is important that cases against the security and intelligence services should be brought not in the ordinary courts but in a specialist tribunal that has the appropriate procedures to handle such cases.

Furthermore, Lord Brown responded to the criticisms which were made of the IPT's procedures, in particular the suggestion that they were 'flatly contrary to the basic principles of open justice', as follows at paragraph 26 of his judgment:

> Claims against the intelligence services inevitably raise special problems and simply cannot be dealt with in the same way as other claims. This, indeed, has long since been recognised both domestically and in Strasbourg.

In that context Lord Brown went on to quote what Lord Bingham had said in *R v Shayler*,[13] at paragraph 26:

> The need to preserve secrecy of information relating to intelligence and military operations in order to counter terrorism, criminal activity, hostile activity and subversion has been recognised by the European Commission and the Court in relation to complaints made under article 10 and other articles under the Convention ... The thrust of these decisions and judgments has not been to discount or disparage the need for strict and enforceable rules but to insist on adequate safeguards to ensure that the restriction does not exceed what is necessary to achieve the end in question. The acid test is whether, in all the circumstances, the interference with the individual's Convention right prescribed by national law is greater than is required to meet the legitimate object which the state seeks to achieve.

HEARINGS IN PRIVATE OR PUBLIC?

Until very recently the Tribunal's Procedural Rules were those set out in the rules enacted at its inception in 2000. The language of Rule 9(6) of those original rules was clear and unqualified:

> The Tribunal's proceedings, including any oral hearings, shall be conducted in private.

That language was mandatory and on its face admitted of no exceptions.

[13] [2002] UKHL11; [2003] 1 AC 247.

Nevertheless, on 23 January 2003 the Tribunal gave its judgment in the matter of applications number IPT/01/62 and IPT/01/77, which were rulings on preliminary issues of law. As the Tribunal observed at paragraph 1, this was the first occasion on which the Tribunal sat in public. As later became apparent, the case was about a Mr Kennedy.

The relevant provision in the Rules was challenged by Guardian Newspapers Limited under the Human Rights Act, relying upon the right to a fair and public hearing in Article 6, as well as Articles 8 and 10 of the ECHR.

The Tribunal comprised the then President (Mummery LJ) and Vice-President (Burton J) and they gave a joint judgment.

Rule 9(2) of the 2000 Rules provided that:

> The Tribunal shall be under no duty to hold oral hearings, but they may do so in accordance with this Rule (and not otherwise).

The Tribunal reached the conclusion that the absence from the Rules of an absolute right to either an *inter partes* oral hearing, or failing that, to a separate oral hearing in every case was within the rule-making power in section 69(1) of RIPA. It was also compatible with Articles 6, 8 and 10 of the ECHR: see paragraph 161 of its judgment.

However, when it came to the absolute requirement that hearings must be in private in Rule 9(6), the Tribunal concluded that this was *ultra vires* the enabling power in section 69 of RIPA. Accordingly, it did not bind the Tribunal: see paragraph 173 of its judgment. The Tribunal concluded that there was no conceivable ground for requiring legal arguments on pure points of procedural law to be held in private: see paragraph 171.

The Tribunal also concluded that, unless and until the Rules were amended by the Secretary of State, the Tribunal would have a discretionary power under section 68(1) to hear legal arguments in public under Rule 9(3). This was, however, subject to the important qualification that the Tribunal continued to be subject to its duties in both RIPA and Rule 6(1). Rule 6 required the Tribunal to carry out their functions in such a way as to secure that information is not disclosed to an extent, or in a manner, that is contrary to the public interest or prejudicial to national security or other interests specified in section 69(6)(b) of RIPA. There is a similar provision in the 2018 Rules: Rule 7(1).

In its judgment in that early case, the Tribunal also referred to the inherently secret nature of much of its work.

As the Tribunal observed at paragraph 52 of its judgment:

> In general, the work of the security services must be carried out in secret in order to safeguard national security as an important policy objective. National security may be compromised and harmed by the disclosure of the fact of surveillance.

It was for that reason that the Tribunal concluded that the long standing policy of successive Governments that they 'neither confirm nor deny' whether interception or surveillance has taken place was lawful and compatible with the Human Rights Act. That policy was set out, for example, in a White Paper in 1988 (Cm 408), at paragraph 43:

> As a general policy, Governments do not comment on assertions about security or intelligence: true statements will generally go unconfirmed, and false statements will normally go undenied.

This flowed from the general and fundamental considerations which were set out in paragraphs 59–60 of the Tribunal's judgment. At paragraph 59 the Tribunal said that:

> Cases potentially involving national security are at the cutting edge of Convention rights. One of the main responsibilities of a democratically elected Government and its Ministers is to safeguard national security. Intelligence gathering by the use of investigatory powers is an essential part of that function. Otherwise, it may not be possible to forecast and foil attempts to overthrow democratic institutions and laws (including Convention rights) by undemocratic means. Interception of communications and surveillance are obvious methods of gathering intelligence. Legitimate security and intelligence systems are allowed to use those methods, on the basis that they must operate within the law, in order to protect the very rights and freedoms guaranteed by the Convention.

To counter-balance those legitimate considerations, at paragraph 60 the Tribunal observed that:

> As the exercise of investigatory powers potentially conflicts with individual rights of person, property and privacy there must be a proper means of safeguarding individuals from, and providing redress for, unjustified infringements of their rights. It is the function of the Tribunal to enquire into and determine the lawfulness of any use of investigatory powers and to provide redress where appropriate. They must do so impartially, operating as an independent body discharging judicial functions within the legislative framework of RIPA and the Rules, as properly interpreted by the Tribunal in the light of the Convention requirements of fair trial and open justice.

In similar vein, in the Court of Appeal case of *R (Privacy International) v Investigatory Powers Tribunal*,[14] at paragraph 38, Sales LJ said:

> It is implicit ... that Parliament considered that the IPT can be trusted to make sensible decisions about matters of this kind and on questions of law which arise and need to be decided for the purpose of making determinations on claims or complaints made to it. There is nothing implausible about this. The quality of the membership of the IPT in terms of judicial expertise and independence is very high, as set out in Schedule 3 to RIPA ... The IPT has been recognised to be 'a judicial body of like standing and authority to that of the High Court': see *R (A) v Director of Establishments of the Security Service* [2010] 2 AC 1, para 22, per Laws LJ; and see para 57, per Dyson LJ and para 32, per Rix LJ.

Ever since its decision in *Kennedy* in 2003, the IPT has developed the practice of holding a hearing in public if that is possible and is compatible with the public interest. In particular, it will often hold a hearing in public to consider a question of law on the basis of assumed facts without (at that stage) deciding whether those facts are true or not.

IS THE TRIBUNAL PART OF THE TRIBUNAL SYSTEM?

The IPT is not part of the general tribunal system in this country which was established by the Courts, Tribunals and Enforcement Act 2007. That Act implemented the proposals which had been made in 2001 by Sir Andrew Leggatt in his

---

[14] [2017] EWCA Civ 1868; [2018] 1 WLR 2572.

review of Tribunals, '*Tribunals for Users: One System, One Service*'. Sir Andrew addressed the position of the IPT expressly at paragraph 3.11 of his report, where he said:

> This Tribunal is different from all others in that its concern is with security. For this reason it must remain separate from the rest and ought not to have any relationship with other Tribunals. It is therefore wholly unsuitable both for inclusion in the Tribunals System and for administration by the Tribunals Service. So although the Chairman is a Lord Justice of Appeal and would be the senior judge in the Tribunals System he would not be in a position to take charge of it. The Tribunal's powers are primarily investigatory, even though it does also have an adjudicative role. Parliament has provided that there should be no appeal from the Tribunal except as provided by the Secretary of State. [See section 67(8) of RIPA]. Subject to Tribunal rules made by the Secretary of State the Tribunal is entitled to determine its own procedure [section 68(1)]. We have accordingly come to the conclusion that this Tribunal should continue to stand alone; ...

THE ROLE OF COUNSEL TO THE TRIBUNAL

Over the last 12 years or so the Tribunal has developed the practice of instructing Counsel to the Tribunal, not in every case but in certain cases. It is important to note that Counsel to the Tribunal does not represent any of the parties in a case but nor is he or she a 'special advocate' of the kind that is now familiar in other contexts, for example the Special Immigration Appeals Commission. The closest analogy is probably with counsel to a public inquiry.

The original Tribunal Rules of 2000 made no mention of Counsel to the Tribunal. Nevertheless, the Tribunal has, at least since 2006, used its broad power to regulate its own procedure under section 68(1) of RIPA to instruct Counsel to the Tribunal. The first occasion on which I am aware this happened was in *C v The Police and Secretary of State for the Home Department* (IPT/03/32), in which the Tribunal had to consider whether it had jurisdiction to deal with police employment related surveillance cases.

The Attorney General was asked to appoint an advocate to the Tribunal. This followed the practice and procedure which is familiar from the Attorney General's Memorandum of 19 December 2001, 'Requests for the Appointment of an Advocate to the Court', a term which has replaced what used to be called the *amicus curiae*.

Since that time the practice has developed whereby the Tribunal simply instructs Counsel to assist it without the need for appointment by the Attorney General. In *Liberty/Privacy International v Secretary of State and others*,[15] Counsel to the Tribunal (Martin Chamberlain QC) made written submissions, which are recorded in the Tribunal's judgment, in which he set out the role of Counsel to the Tribunal and distinguished it from the role of a special advocate. He said:

> A special advocate is appointed (normally, but not necessarily, pursuant to statute) to represent the interests of a party at hearings from which that party is excluded. A special

---

[15] [2014] UK IP Trib 13 77-H; [2015] 1 Cr App R 24.

advocate is required to be partisan. He or she makes such submissions (if any) as he considers will advance the interests of the excluded party. If the special advocate reaches the view that it would not advance the interests of the excluded party to make submissions at all (as has happened in a few cases), then the proper course is to decline to make submissions at all, even though this leaves the Tribunal without assistance.

… Counsel to the Tribunal performs a different function, akin to that of *amicus curiae*. His or her function is to assist the Tribunal in whatever way the Tribunal directs. Sometimes (eg in relation to issues on which all parties are represented), the Tribunal will not specify from what perspective submissions are to be made. In these circumstances, counsel will make submissions according to his or her own analysis of the relevant legal or factual issues, seeking to give particular emphasis to points not fully developed by the parties. At other times (in particular where one or more interests are not represented), the Tribunal may invite its counsel to make submissions from a particular perspective (normally the perspective of the party or parties whose interests are not otherwise represented).

That description of the role of Counsel to the Tribunal has clearly formed the basis for the definition of such counsel which is now to be found expressly in Rule 12 of the Tribunal Procedure Rules 2018, which have recently come into force (on 31 December 2018). Rule 12(1) provides that:

The Tribunal may appoint Counsel to assist the Tribunal in their consideration of any complaint or section 7 proceedings where –

(a)   the complainant is not legally represented;
(b)   the respondent objects to the disclosure of documents or information to the complainant;
(c)   the Tribunal intends to hold a hearing (in whole or in part) in the absence of a complainant; or
(d)   in any other circumstance in which the Tribunal considers it appropriate to do so.

Rule 12(2) provides that the Tribunal may request Counsel to the Tribunal to perform various specific functions, which are listed, including cross-examination of a witness called by the respondent in the absence of the complainant; to ensure that all the relevant arguments on the facts and the law are put before the Tribunal and, generally, to perform any other function that would assist the Tribunal.

Interestingly, in the context of the new appeal procedure to which I will refer later, Counsel to the Tribunal also now has the role (made mandatory in the Rules by Rule 12(3)) to seek to identify any arguable error of law in relation to any decision or determination made by the Tribunal consequent upon a hearing held (in whole or in part) in the absence of the complainant. Rule 12(4) provides that, where Counsel to the Tribunal does identify an arguable error of law in accordance with that provision, Counsel must notify the Tribunal and, when so notified, the Tribunal must, subject to its general obligation to protect the public interest (in Rule 7 of the 2018 Rules), disclose the arguable error of law to the complainant.

In an interesting article published by Martin Chamberlain in the University of Toronto Law Journal,[16] 'Special Advocates and *Amici Curiae* in National Security Proceedings in the United Kingdom', he again emphasises, at page 505, the difference

[16] ((2018) 68 UTLJ 496).

between the special advocate, who must be partisan and is not there to assist the Court, and an *amicus*, whose function is to assist the Court or Tribunal. It is interesting to observe that, in that article, reflecting the views of some others, for example JUSTICE, he notes criticisms which have been made about the effectiveness of the special advocate system in closed material proceedings. Nevertheless, there have also been suggestions that, in the IPT, there should be the opportunity to have a special advocate whose function would be to represent the complainant, at least in addition to Counsel to the Tribunal, whose function (as I have mentioned) is primarily to assist the Tribunal and is not to represent the complainant in a partisan way.

The recent judgment of the Strasbourg Court in the *Big Brother Watch* case noted, it would appear with approval, the role of Counsel to the Tribunal and how it can help to ensure that the overall procedure is fair.

THE DECISION OF THE EUROPEAN COURT OF HUMAN RIGHTS IN
BIG BROTHER WATCH UK v UNITED KINGDOM

The European Court of Human Rights considered the role of the IPT in secret surveillance cases in *Kennedy v United Kingdom*, decided in 2010.[17] The Court held that proceedings before the IPT had been compliant with Article 6, since any procedural restrictions were proportionate to the need to keep secret sensitive and confidential information and did not impair the very essence of the applicant's right to a fair trial. However, the Court expressed some concerns about whether proceedings before the IPT should be regarded as an effective remedy so as to require the procedure to be exhausted under Article 35 of the ECHR before an application could be made to Strasbourg.

In its recent judgment in *Big Brother Watch* the Court returned to these issues.[18] It observed that the IPT's ruling in *Kennedy* had come very early in its history. In fact it was the first time that the IPT had sat in public. In the 15 years which had passed since that time, the Court considered that the experience of the IPT and the very real impact its judgments have had on domestic law in practice meant that the concerns expressed by the Court in *Kennedy* about its effectiveness as a remedy for complaints about the general compliance of a secret surveillance regime were no longer valid: see paragraph 253 of the judgment. In that context, at paragraph 255, the Court was influenced by the consideration that the IPT was the only tribunal with jurisdiction to obtain and review 'below the waterline' material. The Court said that an examination of the IPT's extensive caselaw since *Kennedy* demonstrates the important role that it can and does play in analysing and elucidating the general operation of secret surveillance regimes. It noted that in the *Liberty* proceedings the IPT played a crucial role first in identifying those aspects of a surveillance regime which could and should be further elucidated, and then recommending the disclosure of certain 'below the waterline' arrangements in order to achieve that goal.

[17] (2011) 52 EHRR 4.
[18] Applications 58170/13, 62322/14 and 24960/15, judgment of 13 September 2018.

Furthermore, at paragraph 258, the Court noted that it would appear that, where the IPT has found a surveillance regime to be incompatible with the ECHR, the British Government has ensured that any defects are rectified and dealt with.

Therefore the Court concluded, at paragraph 265, that as a general rule the IPT has shown itself to be a remedy, available in theory and practice, which is capable of offering redress to applicants complaining of both specific incidences of surveillance and the general compliance of surveillance regimes with the ECHR. As a consequence, applicants to Strasbourg will normally be expected to exhaust their domestic remedies by pursuing the opportunity to bring proceedings in the IPT first. Nevertheless, in the special circumstances of the cases before it, and given what the Court had earlier said in *Kennedy*, the Court was prepared to hold that the particular applications before it were not inadmissible under Article 35(1) of the ECHR.

The Court went on to consider whether proceedings before the IPT comply with Article 6 of the ECHR. It noted that neither the Commission nor the Court has found to date that Article 6(1) of the ECHR applies to proceedings relating to a decision to place a person under surveillance. It noted further that the IPT has itself gone further than the Court in this regard. In its joint ruling on preliminary issues of law in the British-Irish Rights Watch case the IPT accepted that Article 6 applies to a person's claims under section 65(2)(a) and to his complaints under section 65(2)(b) of RIPA since each of them involves the determination of his civil rights.

The European Court itself found it unnecessary to reach any firm conclusion on the applicability of Article 6 since it concluded that the complaint was manifestly ill-founded in any event. The complaint under Article 6 was therefore held to be inadmissible.

At para. 510 of its judgment the Court reaffirmed what it had said in *Kennedy*, namely that the procedures of the IPT are compatible with Article 6 since any restrictions on the applicant's rights are both necessary and proportionate and they do not impair the very essence of Article 6. In particular, the Court observed, the IPT had deployed its extensive powers to ensure the fairness of the proceedings. There was scrutiny of all the relevant material, open and closed. Material was only withheld from the applicants where the IPT was satisfied that there were appropriate public and national security reasons for doing so. Finally, the IPT had appointed Counsel to the Tribunal to make submissions on behalf of the applicants in the closed proceedings.

Big Brother Watch was a decision of a chamber of the European Court of Human Rights. Earlier this month, on 4 February 2019, the Court decided that the case will be referred to the Grand Chamber. We await the judgment of the Grand Chamber with interest.

THE 2018 PROCEDURE RULES

As I have mentioned, for the first time since its creation in 2000, the IPT's Procedure Rules were recently revised and are now to be found in the Investigatory Powers Tribunal Rules 2018 (SI 2018 No. 1334). The old rule which had required all hearings to be in private has been abolished. Rule 10 now provides that the Tribunal is under no duty to hold a hearing but may do so; and that it may be held wholly or partly in private. Rule 13 provides that the Tribunal may receive evidence in any form, and may receive evidence that would not be admissible in a court of law. Rule 11 provides for representation at hearings. As I have mentioned earlier, Rule 12 expressly refers for the first time in the Rules to Counsel to the Tribunal.

Rule 7(1) retains the provision that:

> The Tribunal must carry out their functions in such a way as to secure that information is not disclosed to an extent, or in a manner, that is contrary to the public interest or prejudicial to national security, the prevention or detection of serious crime, the economic well-being of the United Kingdom or the continued discharge of the functions of any of the intelligence services.

Under section 67(7) of RIPA the IPT has a broad power to grant such remedies as it thinks fit. They can include the quashing of a warrant and the award of compensation.

An important change has been made by Rule 15 of the 2018 Rules and makes detailed provision for those circumstances in which a notification of a decision by the IPT may contain reasons. This duty remains subject to the general duty in Rule 7(1). Where the IPT make a determination in favour of the complainant, they must provide the complainant and respondent with the determination including any findings of fact: see Rule 15(2). Where the Tribunal make a determination which is not a determination in favour of the complainant, the Tribunal must, if they consider it necessary in the interests of justice to do so, provide the complainant and respondent with 'a summary of the determination': see Rule 15(3).

As I have mentioned, the 2016 Act amends RIPA to create for the first time the opportunity to appeal against decisions of the IPT. The 2018 Rules give effect to this in Rules 16–18. The appropriate appellate court will be, in England and Wales, the Court of Appeal. In Scotland it will be the Inner House of the Court of Session. At present it will not be possible for there to be an appeal to the Court of Appeal of Northern Ireland but such appeals may go to another appropriate appellate court. This is because there is currently no devolved administration in Northern Ireland and its consent would be required to bring this legislation into force in respect of Northern Ireland. The grounds on which an appeal may be made (with the leave either of the IPT or the relevant appellate court) are that there is an error of law which raises an important point of principle or practice, or that there is some other compelling reason for granting leave.

The introduction of the possibility of an appeal does not have retrospective effect. It only applies to decisions taken since 31 December 2018. Accordingly, for those decisions which were made before that date, it may still be important to know whether the IPT is amenable to judicial review. That question is currently the subject of an appeal being considered by the Supreme Court, whose judgment is awaited. Both the Divisional Court and the Court of Appeal held that judicial review is not available because there is an effective ouster clause in section 67(8) of RIPA: see *R (Privacy International) v Investigatory Powers Tribunal*.[19,20]

---

[19] [2017] EWHC 114 (Admin); [2017] 3 All ER 1127; [2017] EWCA Civ 1868; [2018] 1 WLR 2572.

[20] For differing academic views on this issue see Tom Hickman, 'The Investigatory Powers Tribunal: a law unto itself?' [2018] *Public Law* 584 and Robert Craig, 'Ouster Clauses, separation of powers and the intention of Parliament: from *Anisminic* to *Privacy International*' [2018] *Public Law* 569.

Whatever the outcome of the case in the Supreme Court it is worth noting two passages in the judgment of Sales LJ in the Court of Appeal because they set out some general features of the nature of litigation before the IPT. At paragraph 7, Sales LJ said:

> The context in which the IPT functions is one in which there is particular sensitivity in relation to the evidential material in issue and the public interests which may be jeopardised if it is disclosed. The intelligence services may have valuable sources of information about terrorist organisations, organised crime and hostile activity by foreign powers which would be lost if those targets of investigation and monitoring became aware of them. Human sources, such as informers, might be killed or threatened with serious harm if their identities (or even the possibility of their existence) were revealed. Technological capacities to obtain information might be rendered useless if it were revealed they existed and new strategies to evade them or block them were developed. Opportunities for exploitation of simple lapses of care on the part of targets which allow the intelligence services to obtain valuable information about them would be lost if the targets learned about them and tightened up their procedures. The aspects of the public interest which would be jeopardised if these things occurred, as referred to in rule 6(1),[21] are of the most pressing importance.

At paragraph 10 Sales LJ said:

> The legislative regime for the IPT deliberately creates a judicial body with powers to examine in private and without disclosure any relevant confidential evidence which cannot safely be revealed to the complainant, which body is at the same time subject to an imperative overriding rule which forbids it from requiring disclosure of such material. In this way, the regime provides a guarantee that the important aspects of the public interest referred to above are safeguarded while at the same time enabling the IPT to examine the merits of claims against the intelligence services and others on the basis of the relevant evidence in a closed proceeding.

STATUTORY REGULATION OF THE INTELLIGENCE AGENCIES

As we have seen, the existence of the various intelligence agencies in this country was not publicly acknowledged until the 1980s. Times have changed greatly since then. In 1989 the Security Service Act placed MI5 on a statutory footing. Five years later, the Intelligence Services Act 1994 placed both MI6 and GCHQ on a statutory footing. The 1994 Act also established a Parliamentary Committee, the Intelligence and Security Committee, to monitor the work of all three UK intelligence and security agencies. For the first time, members of both Houses of Parliament were to be involved in the scrutiny of the expenditure, administration and policy of the secret agencies.[22] The ISC is currently chaired by the former Attorney General, Dominic Grieve QC MP.

Sir David Omand has held various offices, including Permanent Secretary at the Home Office and the Cabinet Office and also Director of GCHQ. Since retirement from public service he has been a visiting professor at King's College, London and has contributed to bringing the field of intelligence studies into the academic world, in particular through his book *Securing the State*. In that book he quotes one

---

[21] Now rule 7(1) of the 2018 Rules.
[22] Omand (n 6) 264.

British Ambassador from 1785, who wrote to the Secretary of State in London about his involvement with secret agents:

> I abhor this dirty work, but when one is employed to sweep chimneys, one must black one's fingers.[23]

Sir David Omand welcomes the fact that the intelligence agencies must operate within the law, in particular respecting human rights:

> Human rights are a public good, as is security. The balance to be struck by wise government is not between security and rights, as if to argue that by suspending human rights security could be assured. The balance has to be within the framework of rights, recognising that the fundamental right to life, with the legitimate expectation of being protected by the state from threats to oneself and one's family, is an important right that in some circumstances must be given more weight than other rights, such as the right to privacy of personal and family life. This is a choice that society is able to make when there is a serious terrorist threat ... In those circumstances, checks and balances of good government should come into play to provide confidence that the balance is a genuine one and that red lines are not being crossed. Remaining within the framework of rights is important, however, not least as a constant reminder that there are rights, such as the right not to suffer torture, which cannot be derogated.[24]

The framework of supervision also includes the office of the Investigatory Powers Commissioner, which was created by the Investigatory Powers Act 2016. The first holder of that office is Sir Adrian Fulford, a serving judge of the Court of Appeal. Sir Adrian leads a team of 15 Judicial Commissioners and a larger team of staff; and has a Technical Advisory Panel.[25] The Commissioners have various roles under the 2016 Act, including the grant of judicial warrants where the Act requires them in addition to warrants issued by the Secretary of State for various investigatory practices. The Commissioners' duties are, however, essentially administrative and their decisions are subject to review by the IPT.

It can therefore be seen that each of the three branches of the state, Parliament, the executive and the judicial branch, has a role to play in the legal regulation and supervision of the intelligence agencies.

As Sir David Omand puts it:[26]

> I have argued that intelligence gathering is now a recognised, avowed activity of Government. But there is a need to balance secret actions for the good of the city with upholding the reputation of being the city of the good. There has to be a level of public acceptance of the activity and how it is conducted – and more importantly, perhaps, public acceptance that there is regulatory mechanism that can prevent excesses and abuses, and processes for a rapid independent way of putting things right when they go wrong.

It will be a matter for others to judge but I would hope that the IPT plays its part in that process of reassuring the public and maintaining the rule of law in this country.

---

[23] ibid, 265.
[24] ibid, 267.
[25] For more detail see the first annual report by the IPC, relating to 2017 (HC 1780).
[26] Omand (n 6) 285.

Fairness and National Security[1]

This was the Miriam Rothschild and John Foster lecture of 2020, a series that was begun in 1986. John Foster was a Conservative MP with an interest in human rights and Miriam Rothschild was a trustee of the lecture series initially established in his honour. The subject of my lecture was the balance that has to be struck between fairness and national security. I traced the history of the development of the law in this area, in various contexts: criminal law, civil law, immigration law and in various kinds of tribunal proceedings. One aspect of this development which I looked at was the introduction of the special advocate system in 1997, when the Special Immigration Appeals Commission was created, and its subsequent expansion to other types of legal proceedings. After this lecture was given, the Supreme Court decided the case of R (Begum) v Special Immigration Appeals Commission [2021] UKSC 7; [2021] 2 WLR 556, in which it decided, in the context of a decision to deprive a person of citizenship on national security grounds, that the right to a fair and effective appeal is not a 'trump card'.

INTRODUCTION

THANK YOU FOR inviting me to give this year's lecture.[2] I am honoured to follow in the footsteps of some very distinguished predecessors, to many of whom I owe an intellectual debt. In looking at the list of previous speakers I noticed that some of them were not lawyers. I think this would have appealed to both John Foster and Miriam Rothschild, who would have appreciated that the subject of human rights is far too important to be left only to lawyers.

The subject of my lecture will be Fairness and National Security. By fairness lawyers usually mean what used to be called the rules of natural justice, that is the right to procedural fairness when decisions of the executive or the courts are taken which are adverse to a person's interests. It is a fundamental aspect of a just legal system that a court or tribunal must act fairly. This is so axiomatic that one hardly needs Article 6 of the European Convention on Human Rights ('ECHR') for this purpose. Indeed, in some ways the scope of Article 6 is more limited than the common law principles of natural justice or fairness. For example, much ink has been spilt in Strasbourg on the concept of what is a 'determination of civil rights': it is only when a decision constitutes a determination of civil rights, or where there is a criminal charge, that the

---

[1] Lord Justice of Appeal and President of the Investigatory Powers Tribunal.
[2] I would like to thank my former Judicial Assistant, Lucy Jones, for research for this lecture.

requirements of Article 6 apply. By way of contrast, English law principles of natural justice apply to administrative decision-making as well. It is many decades since our own administrative law was freed from the shackles of questions such as whether a decision was 'judicial' or 'quasi-judicial'. Those constraints on the scope of procedural fairness in domestic law were swept away in the early 1960s, in particular in the decision of the House of Lords in *Ridge v Baldwin* (1962).[3] Indeed, as long ago as 1911, in *Board of Education v Rice*[4] it had been said that the duty to listen fairly to both sides 'is a duty lying upon every one who decides anything'.

In this lecture, however, I will focus on fairness in courts and tribunals. What interests me – and I hope will interest you too – is how, and to what extent, the normal rules of fairness in judicial proceedings have had to be modified or adapted to accommodate the needs of national security.

THE USUAL FEATURES OF A FAIR HEARING

Before considering the ways in which the interests of national security may require modification of the usual features of a fair hearing in a court or tribunal, it is perhaps worth setting out in outline what those traditional features are:

– First, all the parties are entitled to be present at the hearing.

– Secondly, the parties are entitled, at least in those forums in which legal representation is permitted, to be represented by lawyers whom they have chosen for themselves.

– Thirdly, the parties and their lawyers are entitled to see and hear all of the evidence and arguments made by the other parties.

– Fourthly, the hearing is usually conducted in open, and may be watched by members of the public, including the media, who have an important role in reporting what happens in proceedings so as to inform the wider public. The principle of open justice is a fundamental principle of both the common law and Article 6 of the ECHR.

– Fifthly, a judgment is usually delivered in a public way. The reasons given by a judge for reaching a decision are accessible to the parties and to the public.

– Sixthly, there is usually some form of disclosure, in both civil and criminal cases. By criminal cases I mean cases in which a prosecution is brought, usually by the state, alleging that a person has committed a criminal offence, such as murder or robbery. By civil cases I mean other kinds of dispute between citizens or between the citizen and the state, as when a person seeks judicial review of the actions of government. This obligation of disclosure means that documents which are in the possession of one party, but which it does not itself wish to deploy in support of its own case, nevertheless will usually have to be disclosed to the other party

---

[3] [1964] AC 40.
[4] [1911] AC 179, at 182 (Lord Loreburn LC).

because they are relevant and may help to advance the other party's case or undermine the case against it.

As we shall see, to some extent each of these main features of a traditional judicial process has had to be modified in cases involving national security. We are now accustomed to closed hearings, at which one party will not be present and so will not see the whole of the evidence or arguments. Their interests will usually be represented by a special advocate, who is not usually permitted to communicate with them after seeing closed material. The media and the public will not be able to observe a closed hearing or report on it. At the end of the hearing there will often be a closed judgment as well as an open judgment.

I remember when I was in practice that I did a case at which my client and I were excluded from the hearing for most of the day and at the end of the day we were informed that my client's appeal had been allowed but for reasons that could not be disclosed to us, since they were set out in a closed judgment. Since becoming a judge I myself have conducted closed hearings, in the High Court, in the Special Immigration Appeals Commission ('SIAC') and now in the Investigatory Powers Tribunal ('IPT').

THE IMPORTANCE OF FAIRNESS

In *John v Rees*,[5] at page 402, Megarry J said, in a famous passage, that there are some who would decry the importance which the courts attach to the observance of the rules of natural justice. When something is obvious, they may say, why force everybody to go through the tiresome waste of time involved in framing charges against a person and giving them an opportunity to be heard? The result, they may say, is obvious from the start. Megarry J eloquently answered that question in the following way:

> As everybody who has anything to do with the law well knows, the path of the law is strewn with examples of open and shut cases which, somehow, were not; of unanswerable charges which, in the event, were completely answered; of inexplicable conduct which was fully explained; of fixed and unalterable determinations that, by discussion, suffered a change. Nor are those with any knowledge of human nature who pause to think for a moment likely to underestimate the feelings of resentment of those who find that a decision against them has been made without their being afforded any opportunity to influence the course of events.

In similar vein Bingham LJ said in *R v Chief Constable of Thames Valley Police, ex parte Cotton*,[6] at paragraph 60: 'This is a field in which appearances are generally thought to matter'. Further, 'where a decision-maker is under a duty to act fairly the subject of the decision may properly be said to have a right to be heard, and rights are not to be lightly denied'.

---

[5] [1970] Ch 345.
[6] [1990] IRLR 344.

SOME HISTORY

I would like to begin by going back in time to the law as it was at around the time when I first started in practice at the Bar in 1990. There are three topics in particular that I would like to mention at this stage.

The first is that it was very difficult, if not impossible, for a court to go behind the assertion by the executive that something was in the interests of national security. Such questions were not regarded as justiciable in the courts. This was so even where ordinarily there could have been no doubt that the rules of natural justice required a fair hearing. An example of this can be found in the decision of the Court of Appeal in *R v Secretary of State for Home Affairs, ex parte Hosenball*,[7] which concerned a decision by the Home Secretary to deport a person on grounds of national security. He was not entitled to see the national security case against him. Nor was he entitled to make representations before an independent court or tribunal. There was no such thing in those days as SIAC or special advocates. If the decision of the executive was challenged, the High Court itself did not see the closed material as we would now call it. The most that a person could expect was that there was an informal panel (known colloquially as the 'Three Wise Men'), which advised the Home Secretary.

In *R v Secretary of State for the Home Department, ex parte Cheblak*,[8] a decision at the time of the first Gulf war, the applicant brought an application for both *habeas corpus* and judicial review against the decision to deport him on the ground that this was conducive to the public good for reasons of national security. The Court of Appeal confirmed what had been said in *Hosenball*.

In giving the main judgment Lord Donaldson of Lymington MR cited the statement made by the Home Secretary in Parliament on 15 June 1971, in which he had set out the procedure in such cases, which included the panel of three advisors. Interestingly, at the time of *Cheblak* the panel included a serving judge of the Court of Appeal, Sir Anthony Lloyd, who later became a Law Lord. At the time he was also the Vice-Chairman of the Security Commission, which reported to the Prime Minister on the work of the security services. Lord Donaldson observed that the Home Secretary was fully accountable to Parliament for his decisions and, as part of that accountability, for any failure to heed the advice of the non-statutory panel. He was also subject to the jurisdiction of the High Court. Nevertheless, he said,

> the exercise of the jurisdiction of the courts in cases involving national security is necessarily restricted, not by any unwillingness to act in protection of the rights of individuals or any lack of independence of the executive, but by the nature of the subject matter. National security is the exclusive responsibility of the executive.

Lord Donaldson also cited Geoffrey Lane LJ in *Hosenball*, at page 783, where he had said:

> There are occasions, though they are rare, when what are more generally the rights of an individual must be subordinated to the protection of the realm.

---

[7] [1977] 1 WLR 766.
[8] [1991] 1 WLR 890.

Later Lord Donaldson described the approach adopted by the advisory panel as an 'independent quasi-judicial scrutiny'. He noted that all of its members had the necessary security clearance to enable them to take an active role in questioning and evaluating the weight of the evidence and information which formed the basis of the Home Secretary's decision.

It is interesting to observe, albeit with the enormous benefit of hindsight, that a generation later we have become used to members of an independent court or tribunal being able to see national security material without the need for the relative informality which was thought to be necessary at that time. By way of example, that is what I do when I sit as President of the IPT.

The approach that was taken in cases such as *Hosenball* and *Cheblak* had long been the approach of the courts. In a case arising during the course of the First World War, *The Zamora*,[9] Lord Parker of Waddington said that:

> Those who are responsible for the national security must be the sole judges of what the national security requires. It would be obviously undesirable that such matters should be made the subject of evidence in a court of law or otherwise discussed in public.

Nevertheless, in *The Zamora* itself, at 108, Lord Parker said that it was not sufficient that the Government could have acted for reasons of national security. It had to adduce evidence that it had in fact acted on those grounds.

In my experience when I was in practice in the early 1990s, and sometimes represented the Home Secretary in court, where there was such evidence on behalf of the Government, for example in the form of an affidavit from a civil servant, that was sufficient to bring the curtain down and no further investigation could or would be undertaken by the court into the underlying evidence.

The second point I want to make is that in the early 1990s it was established doctrine that, even where otherwise the rules of natural justice would apply, they might be abrogated by the demands of national security. It was not simply a question of modifying them. The best example of this is perhaps the decision of the House of Lords in *Council of Civil Service Unions v Minister for the Civil Service* (1984), often referred to as the GCHQ case.[10]

This arose from the well-known decision of the then Prime Minister (Margaret Thatcher) to ban membership of trade unions at the Government Communications Headquarters (or GCHQ). The House of Lords held that, in principle, the decision was amenable to judicial review. This itself was in its time a breakthrough in administrative law. Previously it had been thought that the exercise of a prerogative power was not amenable to judicial review, although the existence and extent of the prerogative power were. Furthermore, the decision was and remains important because it established that a legitimate expectation of procedural fairness could be created not only by an express promise of consultation but by a past practice of consultation. There had for many years been consultation of the trade unions at GCHQ before fundamental terms and conditions of service there were altered. On this occasion,

---

[9] [1916] 2 AC 77; at 107.
[10] [1985] 1 AC 374.

however, the ban had been decided upon without any consultation with the unions. In principle that would therefore have been a breach of the requirements of natural justice. The case, however, turned upon the fact that the interests of national security were invoked by the Government of the day to explain why there had not been consultation. This was raised in evidence after the High Court had decided the case against the Government. Both the Court of Appeal and the House of Lords accepted that argument.

The third topic I want to mention at this stage is the concept of public interest immunity ('PII'). The normal obligation of disclosure has for a long time been subject to questions of PII, which is a broader concept than the interests of national security. This concept was already well-established in our law by the early 1990s. It had replaced the earlier absolute concept of Crown Privilege as a result of the decision of the House of Lords in *Conway v Rimmer* (1966).[11] It had become established therefore that there is no absolute immunity from disclosure of certain documents simply because the Government says so. Although an executive certificate is required that it would not be in the public interest for a document to be disclosed in litigation, the decision is ultimately one for the court, which must balance the public interest in non-disclosure against the public interest in the fair administration of justice.

PII issues can arise not only in civil proceedings but also in criminal cases. It is not unusual, as my own experience shows when I used to sit as a criminal judge in the Crown Court, for the prosecution to make an application that material which would otherwise be disclosable to the defence ought not to be disclosed because it would be contrary to the public interest. This can happen, for example, in relation to the identity of the source of certain information. In an extreme case, that person's life may be at risk.

The significant point about PII is that, if the application by the prosecution or other party requesting non-disclosure is granted, the result is that *neither* party can make use of that material. The material which is not disclosed to the defence cannot be adduced by the prosecution and is never seen by the jury, which is the tribunal of fact in a trial in the Crown Court. The grant of PII does not have the consequence that the court can take that material into account when reaching its decision on the merits of a case.

THE DIFFERENT WAYS IN WHICH THE LAW HAS RESPONDED TO NATIONAL SECURITY ISSUES

Over the last 50 years or so the law of this country has responded to the threat posed by terrorism and other threats to national security in a variety of ways. Depending on which response is taken as a matter of substantive law, the impact on procedural fairness has also varied.

---

[11] [1968] AC 910.

The Criminal Justice System

The first type of response has been to treat people suspected of terrorism and similar offences no differently from others who are suspected of breaching the criminal law. In principle they have been put on trial and, if convicted after a fair trial, have been punished accordingly. This was essentially the response which the UK took towards the problem of terrorism in Northern Ireland. As is well known, the criminal justice system there was modified, in particular by dispensing with juries in 'Diplock courts', but the essence of the trial process was maintained.

This was subject to one major exception, which was the use of internment in Northern Ireland in the early 1970s. Time does not permit me to go into that important topic today but I will be coming back to the use of powers to detain terrorist suspects without trial later, when I consider what happened after the events of 9/11 in 2001.

Human rights issues have arisen nevertheless even in the ordinary criminal justice process. For example, in *Jasper v United Kingdom*[12] complaint was made that the defence had not been given disclosure of evidence obtained by the interception of communications. The Strasbourg Court held, by a narrow majority of nine to eight, that there had been no breach of Article 6 because the principle of 'equality of arms' had been respected. Neither the prosecution nor the defence can use intercept evidence at trial. This is because, as a matter of law, no evidence can be adduced which discloses the contents of a communication which has been obtained following the issue of an interception warrant: see section 56 of the Investigatory Powers Act 2016 ('IPA') and its predecessors in the Interception of Communications Act 1985 and the Regulation of Investigatory Powers Act 2000. (There are exceptions to this general rule, which are set out in Schedule 3 to the IPA). This is one consequence of the long-standing policy in this country that the fact that interception of communications has taken place in any particular case should remain secret and not be disclosed to the subject of that interception. This is because of the need to protect the continuing value of interception as a means of gathering intelligence.

An example of where the criminal justice process had to be adapted to take account of the interests of national security is to be found in *Re Guardian News and Media Ltd and Others*,[13] in which the Court of Appeal (Criminal Division) had to consider a very unusual trial which was about to take place at the Central Criminal Court. The trial judge had ordered that the entirety of the trial should be held *in camera* and that the defendants should remain anonymous. The Court of Appeal modified that procedure in part by permitting the identity of the defendants to be published and also by enabling a number of accredited journalists to attend the trial *in camera* in order to be able to report the proceedings later.

In giving the judgment of the Court, at paragraph 10, Gross LJ said that one aspect of the rule of law is open justice. Open justice, he said, is both a fundamental principle of the common law and a means of ensuring public confidence in our legal

---

[12] (2000) 30 EHRR 441.
[13] [2014] EWCA Crim 1861; [2015] 1 Crim App R 4.

system; exceptions are rare and must be justified. Any such exceptions must be neces-sary and proportionate. He also drew a distinction between open justice and natural justice. At paragraph 12, he said that concerns as to natural justice may arise under closed material procedures, where a party is excluded from the proceedings, but such concerns do not arise when the hearing is *in camera*.

He also observed that national security is itself an interest of the first importance. It is in the interests of justice, he said, that the Crown should not be deterred from prosecuting cases of suspected terrorism by the risk of material, which is properly secret, becoming public through the trial process. Considerations of national security will not by themselves justify departure from the principle of open justice. However, open justice must give way to the more fundamental principle of the paramount object of a court, which is to do justice. Accordingly, where there is a serious possibil-ity that the administration of justice would be frustrated, for example by deterring the Crown from prosecuting the case, a departure from open justice may be justified: see paragraph 17 of his judgment.

Deportation

The second approach which has been taken by the state, in the case of foreign nation-als, is to consider deporting them on grounds of national security. We have already come across this in the cases of *Hosenball* and *Cheblak*. This was considered by the European Court of Human Rights in *Chahal v United Kingdom* (1996).[14] In that case the system which had developed in this country and was endorsed in cases such as *Cheblak* was held to be in breach of Article 6. That decision led to the establishment in 1997 of SIAC, to afford the person affected a fair procedure before an independent court, albeit not the ordinary courts but a specialist tribunal created for this purpose, which is chaired by a High Court judge.

Special Advocates

The adoption of special advocates in the United Kingdom was another response to the judgment of the European Court of Human Rights in *Chahal*.

The Strasbourg Court stated as follows:

> The Court recognises that the use of confidential material may be unavoidable where national security is at stake. This does not mean, however, that the national authorities can be free from effective control by the domestic courts whenever they choose to assert that national security and terrorism are involved ... [T]here are techniques which can be employed which both accommodate legitimate security concerns about the nature and sources of intelligence and yet accord the individual a substantial measure of procedural justice. (paragraphs 130–31)

The Strasbourg Court was influenced in that case by its understanding of a procedure used in certain closed material proceedings in Canada, which involved the use of a

---

[14] (1997) 23 EHRR 413.

security-cleared counsel appointed by the court, who cross-examined the witnesses and generally assisted the court to test the strength of the state's case. It appears that the Court's reference to Canadian practice mistakenly suggested that these special counsel appeared before Canadian federal courts in immigration cases. The Court probably had in mind the use of special security-cleared counsel before the Security Intelligence Review Committee.[15]

In the definition used by the House of Commons Constitutional Affairs Committee in 2005, a special advocate is a specially appointed lawyer (typically, a barrister) who is instructed to represent a person's interests in relation to material that is kept secret from that person (and their ordinary lawyers) but analysed by a court or equivalent body at an adversarial hearing held in private.[16]

The special advocate has the advantage that he or she can see closed material and attend a closed hearing. They will represent the interests of the excluded person in the absence of the open representatives. But in general they cannot communicate with that person once they have seen the closed material. This means that the special advocate cannot know what answers that person may have to the matters raised in the closed material.

Since 1997, the variety of schemes in which special advocates may be used has been expanded by Parliament. Some examples include:

– The Proscribed Organisations Appeals Commission, which was created by section 4 of the Terrorism Act 2000. I think I may be one of the few people who ever appeared before that body when I was in practice.

– The Pathogens Access Appeals Commission: the Attorney General may appoint 'a person to represent the interests of any person who will be prevented from hearing or inspecting any evidence' on grounds of national security (Pathogens Access Appeals Commission (Procedure) Rules 2002, SI 2002/1845, rule 8).

– Local planning inquiries: if the Secretary of State decides that a local planning authority is to be held in secret on national security grounds, the Attorney General may appoint a special advocate to represent the interests of any person prevented from being there (Planning and Compulsory Purchase Act 2004, section 80).

– Employment Tribunals: a minister may, 'if he considers it expedient in the interests of national security', direct an Employment Tribunal to hold a secret hearing (Employment Tribunals (Constitution and Rules of Procedure) Regulations 2004 (SI 2004/1861) Schedule 1, paragraph 54; see now Employment Tribunals (Constitution and Rule of Procedure) Regulations 2013 (2013/1237) Schedule 1, paragraph 94).

The Canadian system which influenced the decision of the Strasbourg Court in *Chahal* may in fact have been similar not so much to the special advocate model but to the model which we have adopted in the IPT, of having Counsel to the Tribunal ('CTT'), who is appointed by the Tribunal and not by the Law Officers. Moreover, the CTT is permitted to carry on communicating with both parties throughout the

[15] J Ip, 'The Rise and Spread of the Special Advocate' [2008] *PL* 717, 719.
[16] House of Commons Constitutional Affairs Committee, *The operation of the Special Immigration Appeals Commission (SIAC) and the use of Special Advocates.* HC Paper No. 323-I (Session 2004/05), para 44.

proceedings, even after seeing closed material, without the need for communications with the claimant to be agreed by the respondent or, in default of agreement, sanctioned by the Tribunal. The role of CTT is now expressly recognised in rule 12 of the IPT Rules 2018 (SI 2018/1334).

As we shall see later, the Supreme Court has held that it is not for the courts to extend the special advocate system beyond the boundaries which Parliament has chosen to draw for its use thus far; therefore the procedure can only be introduced by legislation.[17] However, the procedure need not be expressly authorised by statute; necessary implication of the power will suffice.[18] In 2005 the House of Lords held that the Parole Board was impliedly authorised to adopt the special advocate procedure in deciding whether to release a mandatory life prisoner on licence.[19]

Furthermore, the Supreme Court has held that its own statutory powers under the Constitutional Reform Act 2005, in section 40(2) and (5) to decide an appeal 'from any order or judgment of the Court of Appeal' and to determine 'any questions necessary ... for the purposes of doing justice in an appeal' were sufficient to confer the required power for it to hold a closed hearing.[20]

As we have seen, SIAC and the concept of special advocates were first introduced to deal with the problem revealed by the decision in *Chahal* so that there would be a fair procedure to challenge a decision to deport a person, for example on grounds of national security.

But even where there is such a fair procedure, if in fact that person cannot be deported, the state has had to find other ways of dealing with that person while they remain in the UK. The difficulty has arisen in those cases where deportation is not practicable because there is a real risk of torture or other treatment contrary to Articles 2 or 3 of the ECHR if that person is deported. This was in fact another aspect of the decision in *Chahal* itself. The state has tried to address this difficulty in a variety of ways.

Detention Without Trial

The first approach which was taken, after the events of 9/11 in 2001, was to permit the Home Secretary to certify that a suspected international terrorist should be detained without charge in circumstances where that person could not be deported. This led to the well-known decision of the House of Lords in *A v Secretary of State for the Home Department* (2004),[21] often known as the 'Belmarsh case', because the applicants in that case were detained at Belmarsh prison. In that case a declaration

---

[17] *Al Rawi and ors. v Security Service and ors* [2011] UKSC 34; [2012] 1 AC 531, para 47 (Lord Dyson JSC).

[18] HWR Wade and CF Forsyth, *Administrative Law* (11th edn, Oxford, Oxford University Press, 2014) 434.

[19] *R (Roberts) v Parole Board* [2005] UKHL 45; [2005] 2 AC 738, the special advocate procedure was impliedly authorised by the Criminal Justice Act 1991, Schedule 5, para 1(2)(b), granting power to the Parole Board to 'do such things ... as are incidental to or conducive to the discharge' of its functions.

[20] *Bank Mellat v HM Treasury (No. 2)* [2013] UKSC 38; [2014] AC 700, at 729–62 (jurisdiction judgments).

[21] [2004] UKHL 56; [2005] 2 AC 68.

of incompatibility was made under section 4 of the Human Rights Act 1998 by the House of Lords in respect of Part 4 of the Anti-Terrorism, Crime and Security Act 2001 ('the 2001 Act'), principally on the ground that the legislation applied only to foreign nationals and was therefore discriminatory.

In the light of that decision Parliament decided to repeal Part 4 of the 2001 Act and replaced it with a system of 'control orders'.

Control Orders and TPIMs

The control orders regime was established by the Prevention of Terrorism Act 2005 ('the 2005 Act'). The 2005 Act empowered the Home Secretary to make a 'control order' against any individual. A control order specified and imposed a range of obligations upon the controlled person. These could be of various kinds but generally specified the individual's residence, imposed a curfew requirement and restricted their communications with others. It was a criminal offence to contravene any obligation (section 9(1) of the 2005 Act).

Control orders proved controversial and they have now been replaced by TPIMs. These changes were effected by the Terrorism Prevention and Investigation Measures Act 2011 ('the 2011 Act'). A TPIM may be imposed by the Home Secretary when she 'reasonably believes that the individual is, or has been, involved in terrorism-related activity' and she 'reasonably considers that it is necessary, for purposes connected with protecting members of the public from a risk of terrorism, for terrorism prevention and investigation measures to be imposed on the individual' (section 3(1), (3) of the 2011 Act).

A TPIM may only be imposed with the permission of the court unless the Home Secretary considers that the matter is urgent (section 3(5)); the court then determines whether the TPIM is 'obviously flawed' (section 6(3)(a)). Provision has been made for special advocates and closed hearings to deal with intelligence material. If the court grants permission for a TPIM, it must set a date for a 'review hearing', the open part of which the individual who is the subject of the TPIM is allowed to attend (section 8). At this hearing the court will apply the 'ordinary principles of judicial review' (section 9(2)). A TPIM may remain in force for up to two years (section 5).

The powers of the Secretary of State are somewhat weaker under the TPIM regime than they were under the control order regime. In particular there is no longer the power to 'relocate' the subject, curfews have been renamed 'overnight residence measures' and the subject is now entitled to access to a fixed-line telephone and the internet in their home (Schedule 1 to the 2011 Act).[22]

TPIMs, like control orders before them, are considered by the High Court and not by a tribunal. The challenge to a control order or, since 2011, to a TPIM, is therefore made in the ordinary courts. However, there are procedural rules which have modified the way in which the court must conduct its hearing which are similar to the rules

---

[22] For further see, C Walker and A Horne, 'The Terrorism Prevention and Investigations Measures Act 2011: one thing but not much the other?' [2012] *Crim LR* 421.

which govern procedures in tribunals such as SIAC and the IPT. In particular, there is a rule which is common to each of those jurisdictions that the court or tribunal must ensure that information is not disclosed contrary to the public interest. This would be so, for example, if it is made contrary to the interests of national security.

The requirements of fairness in the context of control orders made under the 2005 Act were considered in two important cases. The first was the decision of the Grand Chamber of the European Court of Human Rights in *A v United Kingdom*.[23] The second was the decision of the House of Lords in *Secretary of State for the Home Department v AF (No. 3)*.[24]

In *AF* the House of Lords considered that the approach taken by the Court of Human Rights in the case of *A* had to be applied in the context of control orders.

The position of people subject to control orders such as *AF* had previously been considered by the House of Lords in *Secretary of State for the Home Department v MB*.[25] However, the position had to be revisited in the light of the judgment of the Court of Human Rights in the case of *A*.

The case of *A* itself concerned those who had been detained without charge under the 2001 Act after 9/11. The Court of Human Rights considered that in that context Article 5(4) of the ECHR imports substantially the same fairness guarantees as Article 6(1) does in criminal cases: see paragraph 217 of its judgment. Against that background, the Court said that it was essential that as much information about the allegations and evidence against each applicant should be disclosed as was possible without compromising national security or the safety of others. Where full disclosure was not possible, Article 5(4) required that the difficulties this caused should be counter-balanced in such a way that each applicant still had 'the possibility effectively to challenge the allegations against him'.

Further, the Court considered that, while a special advocate can perform an important role in this regard, he or she could not perform this function in any useful way unless the detainee was provided with sufficient information about the allegations made against him to enable him to give effective instructions to the special advocate.

In summarising the effect of the Strasbourg decision on control order proceedings, Lord Phillips of Worth Matravers concluded in this way, at paragraph 65 of *AF*:

> The Grand Chamber has now made clear that non-disclosure cannot go so far as to deny a party knowledge of the essence of the case against him, at least where he is at risk of consequences as severe as those normally imposed under a control order.

Lord Brown of Eaton-under-Heywood summarised the position pithily, at paragraph 116:

> In short, Strasbourg has decided that the suspect must *always* be told sufficient of the case against him to enable him to give 'effective instructions' to the special advocate, notwithstanding that sometimes this will be impossible and national security will thereby be put at risk. (Emphasis in original)

---

[23] (2009) 49 EHRR 625.
[24] [2009] UKHL 28; [2010] 2 AC 269.
[25] [2007] UKHL 46; [2008] AC 440.

He continued, at paragraph 120:

> Plainly A does not require the disclosure of the witness's identity or even their evidence, whatever difficulties that may pose for the suspect. What is required is rather the substance of the essential allegation founding the Secretary of State's reasonable suspicion.

Deprivation of Citizenship

Another approach which is sometimes available to the state is to exclude a person who is considered to be a threat to national security from coming into the UK in the first place. This may even be done in the case of a person who has held British nationality. This has led to some cases in which the Home Secretary has deprived a person of their British citizenship on the ground that this is conducive to the public good.[26] This can be done in a case where that person will not be rendered stateless,[27] for example where they have dual nationality or are entitled to the nationality of another state by descent through their parents or grandparents.

The decision to deprive a person of British citizenship can itself be challenged in SIAC. Although there is no right to a fair hearing in advance of the deprivation, and bringing a challenge does not act as a suspension of the decision to deprive a person of their citizenship, it has been held that the opportunity to have recourse to an independent tribunal affords a fair procedure in this context.[28]

CLOSED MATERIAL PROCEDURES AND CIVIL LITIGATION

As I mentioned earlier, the Supreme Court has stated that the use of special advocates may only be used where authorised by statute. In *Al Rawi v Security Service*,[29] it was established that a court has no power to approve a closed hearing in an action for damages, holding that the common law does not allow such a procedure, and that only Parliament could authorise it.[30] That case arose out of the detention of the claimants at various foreign locations, including Guantanamo Bay. They alleged that the UK's Security Service had been complicit in their ill-treatment there. Lord Dyson JSC, who gave the main judgment for the majority in that case, noted that closed material procedures and the use of special advocates continued to be controversial precisely because they involve 'an invasion of ... fundamental common law principles'.

That decision led, in 2013, to the enactment of the Justice and Security Act, which extended the possibility of using 'closed material procedures' to all civil proceedings in the High Court and above. The central provision in the legislation is section 6, which sets out the conditions in which the court may make a declaration that the

---

[26] Section 40(2) of the British Nationality Act 1981, as amended by the Immigration, Asylum and Nationality Act 2006.

[27] Section 40(4) of the British Nationality Act 1981.

[28] *Al-Jedda v Secretary of State for the Home Department* [2014] SC/66/2008, at paras 158–59 (Flaux J).

[29] [2011] UKSC 34; [2012] 1 AC 452.

[30] [2012] 1 AC 531, para 47 (Lord Dyson JSC).

proceedings are proceedings in which a closed material application may be made to the court.[31] In broad terms, the conditions are that, first, a party to the proceedings would be required to disclose sensitive material to another person (whether or not a party to the proceedings); and, secondly, that it is in the interests of the fair and effective administration of justice in the proceedings to make a declaration.

More recently, *Al Rawi* was distinguished by the Supreme Court in *R (Haralambous) v Crown Court at St Albans*,[32] at paragraphs 53–59, where Lord Mance DPSC observed that a closed material procedure must be available in judicial review cases arising from a lower court or tribunal in which Parliament has authorised such a procedure. He considered that the proper analogy was not with ordinary civil proceedings, as in *Al Rawi*, but with appeals, as in *Bank Mellat*. As I mentioned earlier, in that case the Supreme Court held that it could itself hold a closed hearing in order to hear an appeal from a lower court in which there had been a closed judgment.

CONCLUSION

By way of conclusion, I would suggest that our legal system has come a long way in less than 30 years, since the time when I was in the early years of my practice at the Bar. At that time, it was very difficult for the courts to go behind the invocation of national security; and the normal requirements of procedural fairness were overridden by the interests of national security.

Today, there is a more nuanced approach, so that the normal features of a fair hearing may have to be modified to accommodate the interests of national security but there is a core irreducible minimum of fairness that cannot be extinguished. I am well aware that there continue to be concerns, expressed in academia, in Parliament and elsewhere, for example about the limitations of the special advocate system.

If one compares what happens in closed proceedings, whether in the ordinary courts or in specialist tribunals like SIAC or the IPT, to what we would expect in normal cases, clearly there are many features which would be unacceptable were it not for the important public interests on the other side of the balance, including the interests of national security. But if one compares what happens now to what went before, in particular before the decision of the Strasbourg Court in *Chahal* in 1996, it might be said that the glass is half full rather than half empty.

---

[31] For application of the legislation, see *CF v Security Service* and *Mohamed v Foreign and Commonwealth Office* [2013] EWHC 3402 (QB); [2014] 1 WLR 1699 and *R (Sarkandi) v Secretary of State for Foreign and Commonwealth Affairs* [2014] EWHC 2359; [2016] 3 All ER 837; see also *De Smith's Judicial Review* (8th edn, London, Sweet and Maxwell, 2018) chapter 8.

[32] [2018] UKSC 1; [2018] AC 236.

International Law

The Use of International Law in the Domestic Courts of the United Kingdom*

This was the 2005 MacDermott lecture, given at Queen's University, Belfast at a time when I was still a barrister. Lord MacDermott was a distinguished lawyer and judge, who had been both a Lord of Appeal in Ordinary ('Law Lord') and Lord Chief Justice of Northern Ireland. It was first published in (2005) 56 NILQ 119. I chose as my topic issues of international law in domestic courts, something which formed a large part of my practice as a barrister at that time, particularly issues arising from the Iraq war of 2003. After this lecture had been given, several of the cases mentioned in it proceeded to higher courts. R v Jones (Margaret) [2006] UKHL 16; [2007] 1 AC 136 was decided by the House of Lords in 2007: the defendants in those criminal cases failed in their argument that they had a potential defence in that they were acting reasonably to prevent a crime under international law (the crime of aggression). R (Al-Skeini & Ors) v Secretary of State for Defence was decided by the House of Lords in 2007 [2007] UKHL 26; [2008] AC 153: the applicants succeeded in part and this led to the Baha Mousa Public Inquiry, conducted by Sir William Gage, who published his report in 2011. The applicants eventually succeeded in full in the European Court of Human Rights in 2011: Al-Skeini v United Kingdom (2011) 53 EHRR 18, which decided that events in that part of Iraq which was occupied by the UK could in principle fall within its 'jurisdiction' for the purposes of Article 1 of the ECHR.

INTRODUCTION

WHILE INTERNATIONAL LAW might traditionally have been confined to regulating relations between States, its scope today is ever expanding. One example of that expansion is the extent to which – more and more – international law is being invoked before domestic courts by individuals, corporations

* Given at Queen's University Belfast on 20 April 2005. I would like to thank Max du Plessis, a member of the Matrix research panel, for assistance in preparing this lecture.

and non-governmental organisations. Certainly international law remains by and large about the affairs of States, but it is also, and increasingly, aimed at non- State entities and individuals – whether because of international human rights treaties, environmental regulation, or international criminal law rules, to name but three developments since World War II.

In recent years the United Kingdom's courts have seen a number of high profile domestic cases involving international law arguments. We shall see that the courts' receptiveness to international law arguments has been mixed, and that the mixed reaction has revolved around the courts' concerns about two principal issues. The first is the question of international law's proper place in domestic law: that is, the extent to which it is correct to invoke international law in the first place. And to the extent that international law was correctly invoked in the case at hand, the second issue becomes relevant, namely, whether other considerations preclude the court from ruling on the questions that the international law arguments raise. The second issue might be described as being one of justiciability, and has tended to lead to the exercise of judicial restraint.

THE PROPER PLACE OF INTERNATIONAL LAW IN UK DOMESTIC LAW

Beginning with the first issue – the place which international law properly occupies within the domestic legal system – we must appreciate that international law, as a law made principally by and between States, does not provide norms that can be automatically pleaded before domestic courts. There are two main sources of international law: treaty law and customary international law. Parties in national courts have first to negotiate their way around various principles before they can safely call international treaties or customary international law into service in their domestic cases. The principles are varied and complex, but certain recent cases provide useful illustrations of the most important principles and help to explain the interaction of international law and domestic law.

If we start with the classic source of international law – treaties – we see that treaties which the Executive enters into at the international level do not without more become part of our domestic law, and cannot be relied upon directly as sources of legal rights. This 'dualist' position – as it is sometimes called – means that any rule or principle of international law can only have effect within the domestic legal system if it is expressly and specifically 'transformed' into municipal law by the use of an appropriate constitutional machinery, such as an Act of Parliament.[1]

The prerogative power of the Crown, which in the United Kingdom possesses the constitutional authority to enter into treaties, cannot be impugned by the courts.[2]

---

[1] See generally Malcolm Shaw, *International Law* (5th edn, Cambridge, Cambridge University Press, 2003) 129. Terminology may lead to confusion in this context: it has become commonplace for English lawyers to refer to the need for a treaty to be 'incorporated' but international lawyers use the term 'transformation' to contrast it with the doctrine of 'incorporation', which makes rules of customary international law automatically part of the common law and does *not* require enactment by Parliament: see further *Trendtex Trading v Bank of Nigeria* [1977] 1 QB 529, 554 (Lord Denning MR).

[2] See *Council of Civil Service Unions v Minister for the Civil Service* [1985] AC 374, 418. The exercise of the prerogative power to enter into a treaty is considered beyond judicial review, so that the desirability

The position is as Lord Oliver of Aylmerton described it in *J H Rayner v Department of Trade and Industry*:

> [A]s a matter of the constitutional law of the United Kingdom, the royal prerogative, whilst it embraces the making of treaties, does not extend to altering the law or conferring rights on individuals or depriving individuals of rights which they enjoy in domestic law without the intervention of Parliament. Treaties, as it is sometimes expressed, are not self-executing. Quite simply, a treaty is not part of English law unless and until it has been incorporated into the law by legislation.[3]

A knock-on effect of what Lord Oliver has described is that while the treaty or its relevant provisions might be directly transformed by a specific statute – think for instance of how the rights in the European Convention on Human Rights have been 'brought home' by the Human Rights Act 1998[4] – it is the specific statute to which courts will thereafter give effect.[5]

The implications are important. Lord Hoffmann has said the following in *R v Lyons and Others*:[6]

> International law does not normally take account of the internal distribution of powers within a State. It is the duty of the State to comply with international law, whatever may be the organs which have the power to do so. ... In domestic law, however, the position is different. The domestic constitution is based upon the separation of powers. In domestic law the courts are obliged to give effect to the law as enacted by Parliament. This obligation is entirely unaffected by international law.[7]

The facts in *Lyons* concerned the convictions in the Guinness trial, convictions which had depended, to a large degree, on answers that the accused had given to DTI inspectors armed with statutory powers to compel answers. In two separate judgments the European Court of Human Rights held that their right against self-incrimination under Article 6 of the Convention had been violated; their trials were thereby rendered unfair. However, those judgments did not result in the quashing of the convictions. That is a matter for national law. The applicants, understandably, sought the quashing of their convictions, arguing that the English courts were organs of the state and therefore obliged to give effect to the state's international obligations, in particular the obligation to give effect to a judgment of the European Court of Human Rights.

---

of entering into a treaty cannot be challenged in the courts (see *R v Secretary of State for Foreign Affairs ex p Rees-Mogg* [1994] QB 552).

[3] [1990] AC 418, 550. See too *Halsbury's Laws of England*, 'War and Armed Conflict', Vol 49(1), 4th Edition, para 517.

[4] The text of the Convention rights are set out in Schedule 1 of the Human Rights Act 1998 and given effect largely by sections 3 and 6.

[5] See also the statement of Lord Hoffmann in *R v Lyons and Others* [2003] 1 AC 976, para 47, discussed immediately below: '[I]t is firmly established that international treaties do not form part of English law and the English courts have no jurisdiction to interpret or apply them ... Parliament may pass a law which mirrors the terms of the treaty and in this sense incorporates the treaty into English law. But even then, the metaphor of incorporation may be misleading. It is not the treaty but the statute which forms part of English law' (para 27). See also, in the context of an appeal from the Court of Appeal of Northern Ireland, *In re McKerr* [2004] 1 WLR 807, para 25 (Lord Nicholls of Birkenhead); para 48 (Lord Steyn); para 63 (Lord Hoffmann); para 74 (Lord Rodger of Earlsferry); and para 90 (Lord Brown of Eaton-under-Heywood). Cf. *R (S) v Secretary of State for the Home Department* [2004] 1 WLR 219, para 66 (Lord Rodger of Earlsferry).

[6] [2003] 1 AC 976, para 47.

[7] Para 40.

The House of Lords disagreed. It held that the admissibility of the evidence which had been lawfully introduced against the defendants according to the domestic law at the time of their trial could not be impugned under the European Convention on Human Rights. Lord Hoffmann, while expressing admiration at the resourcefulness of counsel's argument, held that its 'foundations rest upon sand'. The statutory language governing the admission of the evidence was clear: it permitted no room for the application of international law standards.

The effect of this traditional dualist position regarding treaties is that there is very little room for the legal practitioner to draw upon the treaty in a municipal case.[8] Very little room, however, does not mean no room at all. So long as a statute does not clearly trump the application of international law, there are certain situations where an unincorporated treaty may still find its use in an advocate's legal arsenal, by and large through its 'indirect' effect in domestic law. For a start, the presumption of compatibility in UK law secures a place for unincorporated treaties in the sphere of domestic law. There is a presumption that where there is an ambiguity, domestic law will be interpreted in a way which does not place the United Kingdom at odds with its international obligations. As Lord Bridge of Harwich explained in *Brind*:[9]

> [I]t is already well settled that, in construing any provision in domestic legislation which is ambiguous in the sense that it is capable of a meaning which either conforms to or conflicts with the Convention, the courts will presume that Parliament intended to legislate in conformity with the Convention, not in conflict with it.

Subsequent developments suggested that ambiguity is in fact not needed but rather that there is a presumption that Parliament does not intend by general words to infringe human rights, in the absence of express language or necessary implication to the contrary. This is sometimes called the 'principle of legality': see *R v Secretary of State for the Home Department, ex p. Simms*.[10] Even now that the Human Rights Act is in force in the UK, this doctrine has a continuing role to play in relation to the numerous international human rights treaties which have been ratified but not incorporated by statute into domestic law, eg the 1989 UN Convention on the Rights of the Child. In the recent case of *A v Secretary of State for the Home Department*, in which the House of Lords held that the UK's derogation from Article 5 of the ECHR was unlawful, Lord Bingham of Cornhill referred at length to international materials which he accepted were 'not legally binding on the United Kingdom'[11] and yet which he found to be illuminating in answering the questions before the House. Such materials are sometimes called 'soft law' and I predict that our higher courts will become increasingly receptive to their use in the future.

The presumption of compatibility may operate in various ways before the UK courts, whether to assist in clarifying the common law,[12] or in the interpretation of

---

[8] Note, however, that it has recently been suggested that the dualist approach may require 'critical re-examination' in the context of human rights treaties: *In re McKerr* [2004] 1 WLR 807, para 50 (Lord Steyn).

[9] *R v Secretary of State for the Home Department ex p. Brind* [1991] AC 696 at 747.

[10] [2000] 2 AC 115, 131 (Lord Hoffmann).

[11] [2005] 2 WLR 87, para 63.

[12] See *R v Mid Glamorgan Family Health Service ex p. Martin* [1995] 1 WLR 110, 118 H, per Evans LJ.

legislation,[13] or in determining the lawful remit of executive discretion.[14] And, in appropriate cases, the presumption allows for an unincorporated treaty to be used as a guide to UK judges of the correct path their decisions ought to take; that is, as an influence upon judicial discretion and in shaping the common law concept of 'public policy'.

Kuwait Airways Corporation[15] may now be regarded as the leading authority on this subject. After its invasion of Kuwait on 2 August 1990, the Iraqi regime passed resolutions proclaiming Iraqi sovereignty over Kuwait. Upon seizing Kuwait Airport, Iraqi forces removed ten commercial aircraft belonging to Kuwait Airways Corporation and flew them to Iraq. Thereafter Iraq passed resolution 369 which purported to transfer ownership of the commercial aircraft to Iraqi Airways Company. Kuwait Airways Corporation brought proceedings in England for return of the aircraft or payment of damages, and the matter came before the House of Lords. One of the defences raised by Iraqi Airways Company was that resolution 369 was to be recognised as a foreign 'act of state' – a governmental act affecting property which was recognised under Iraqi law – and which was to be respected. The manner in which Kuwait Airways Corporation responded to this defence was to rely on the UK's obligations, pursuant to an unincorporated treaty, the UN Charter and its prohibition on the use of force, and the resolutions of the Security Council condemning the invasion of Kuwait as a breach of international peace and security. Lord Steyn's description of the counter-argument by Iraqi Airways that no reliance could be placed on unincorporated treaties, was terse:

> Marching logic to its ultimate unreality, counsel for IAC submitted that the UN Charter and Security Council Resolutions are not incorporated into our law and must be disregarded.[16]

Coming to the opposite conclusion, Lord Steyn held that it would be 'contrary to the international obligations of the United Kingdom were its courts to adopt an approach contrary to its obligations under the United Nations Charter and under the relevant Security Council Resolutions' and that it thus followed that 'it would be contrary to domestic public policy to give effect to Resolution 369 in any way'.[17] In similar vein Lord Nicholls of Birkenhead said:

> The leading example cited in this country ... is the 1941 decree of the National Socialist Government of Germany depriving Jewish émigrés of their German nationality and, consequentially, leading to the confiscation of their property. Surely Lord Cross of Chelsea was indubitably right when he said that a racially discriminatory and confiscatory law of this sort was so grave an infringement of human rights that the courts of this country ought to refuse to recognise it as a law at all: *Oppenheimer v Cattermole* [1976] AC 249, 277–278. When deciding an issue by reference to foreign law, the courts of this country must have a residual power, to be exercised exceptionally and with the greatest of circumspection, to

---

[13] See *R v Secretary of State for the Home Department ex p. Venables* [1998] AC 407 at 499, *per* Lord Browne-Wilkinson.
[14] See *R v Secretary of State for the Home Department ex p. Norney* [1995] Admin LR 861 at 871, *per* Dyson J.
[15] [2002] 2 AC 883.
[16] Para 114.
[17] ibid.

disregard a provision in the foreign law, when to do otherwise would affront basic principles of justice and fairness ... Gross infringements of human rights are one instance ... But the principle cannot be confined to one particular category of unacceptable laws.[18]

The decision of the House of Lords on the 'extraordinary facts'[19] in *Kuwait Airways* suggests that in certain cases litigants may indeed rely upon an unincorporated treaty as a source of international law before a domestic UK court, and that such a source acts as a guide to the development of judicial policy. Of equal importance is the Court's stance on the question of justiciability, a vitally important topic to which I will return.

Having touched on the direct and indirect effect of treaty law in the domestic sphere, we now need to ask ourselves about that second source of international rules – customary international law. Customary international law consists of rules which are not to be found in treaties but arise from a combination of state practice and what is called *opinio juris* (a sense of obligation that the practice is required rather than just voluntary).[20] What is the status of customary international law before domestic courts? English courts have since the eighteenth century stated that customary international law is part of the common law.[21] This doctrine proceeds from the idea that international law is part of the municipal law automatically without the need for the interposition of a constitutional ratification procedure: therefore no Act of Parliament is required to transform it into domestic law. The most famous exposition of this stance is that of Blackstone, who declared in his Commentaries that:

> [T]he law of nations, wherever any question arises which is properly the object of its jurisdiction, is here adopted in its full extent by the common law, and it is held to be a part of the law of the land.[22]

Strictly speaking, this statement is too wide because, as we have seen, it is not true of treaties. But as far as customary international law is concerned, the doctrine has been applied in numerous cases in England.[23] As such, the general rule[24] is that customary

---

[18] At 1078–79.

[19] See the description by Janeen Carruthers and Elizabeth Crawford, '*Kuwait Airways Corporation v Iraqi Airways Company*' (2003) 52 ICLQ 760 at 760.

[20] See generally *R (European Roma Rights Centre) v Immigration Officer at Prague Airport* [2005] 2 WLR 1, para 23 (Lord Bingham of Cornhill).

[21] *Triquet v Bath* (1764) 3 Burr 1478.

[22] 'Commentaries', IV, Chapter 5, cited in Shaw (n 1) 129.

[23] See Peter Malanczuk, *Akehurst's Modern Introduction to International Law* (7th revised edn, New York, Routledge, 1997) 69. However, it is worth noting that since English courts look largely to English judgments as the main evidence of international customary law, in practice there is somewhat of a blurring between the incorporation and transformation doctrines.

[24] There are a number of situations, however, which constitute exceptions to the general rule, and in which English courts cannot apply customary international law. For example, if there is a conflict between customary international law and an Act of Parliament or judicial decision, the English Act of Parliament or judicial decision prevails. However, where possible, English courts will interpret Acts of Parliament so that they do not conflict with customary international law (Malanczuk (n 23) 69). It is also accepted that English courts are probably free to depart from earlier judicial precedents laying down a rule of international law if international law has changed (see *Trendtex Trading Corporation v Central Bank of Nigeria*, [1977] QB 529).

international law is part of the common law, and this then 'provides lawyers a hook on which to hang their public international arguments'.[25]

It goes without saying, however, that any alleged rule of customary law must be proved to be a valid rule of international law and not merely an unsupported assertion. As Lord Macmillan put it in *The Christina*,[26] for the courts to apply a rule of customary international law, it must have 'attained the position of general acceptance by civilised nations as a rule of international conduct, evidenced by international treaties and conventions, authoritative textbooks, practice and judicial decision'.[27] So, in *Pinochet*, the House of Lords – while denying immunity to Senator Pinochet as a *former* head of state – nonetheless discerned sufficient evidence of state practice and *opinio juris* to conclude that under customary international law a state is entitled to expect that its *serving* head of state will enjoy a measure of immunity from the jurisdiction of the courts of other states.[28]

Of course, the evolving nature of customary international law and associated difficulties of proof provide at one and the same time an opening and a risk. Lawyers are provided with an opening to be creative in making arguments involving customary international law. But in the background is the attendant risk that such creativity will not be matched by the court's conclusion on the status of the rule that has been called into service, or by the court's willingness to go where no other court might have gone before. An example of this difficulty is provided by the *Abbasi* case – another decision which we shall return to in our discussion of justiciability. Mr Abbasi, a British national who was captured by US forces in Afghanistan, was until this year detained at Guantanamo Bay in Cuba. He and other detainees had found it impossible to obtain any relief before the US courts to establish definitively their status and to challenge continued detention. The applicants sought by judicial review in England to compel the Foreign and Commonwealth Office to exercise its international law power of diplomatic protection and to make representations on Mr Abbasi's behalf to the US Government.

In respect of the diplomatic protection point, the applicants, while conceding that customary international law at the time of the hearing did not provide Mr Abbasi with a definitive right to diplomatic protection, argued that there was nothing preventing the Court from developing such a right within domestic law. Citing a range of sources which suggested that international law is moving towards the recognition of such a right, the applicants submitted, boldly, that 'our municipal law should lead so that international law may follow.' The Court of Appeal, however, balked at this task, and

---

[25] See Sam Wordsworth, 'Public International Law in the English Courts', p 1, available at <www.oxford-lawsoc.com/files/verdict/MT03/Sam%20Wordsworth%20Art.doc>.

[26] [1938] AC 485.

[27] At 497.

[28] *R v Bow Street Metropolitan Stipendiary Magistrate, ex p. Pinochet Ugarte (No. 3)* [2000] 1 AC 147. That finding has been affirmed by the recent decision of the International Court of Justice in its *Arrest Warrant* decision (*Democratic Republic of Congo v Belgium* [2002] ICJ Rep 8. See especially para 58 where the ICJ found that it was unable to deduce under customary international law 'any form of exception to the rule according immunity from criminal jurisdiction and inviolability to incumbent [senior Government officials like Ministers of Foreign Affairs and Heads of State], where they are suspected of having committed war crimes or crimes against humanity'.

declared that '[i]t is clear that international law has not yet recognised that a State is under a duty to intervene by diplomatic or other means to protect a citizen who is suffering or threatened with injury in a foreign State'. As such, said Lord Phillips MR, 'it does not seem to us that [the applicant] can derive any assistance from established principles of international law'.[29]

JUSTICIABILITY

Discussion of *Abbasi* brings me to the second issue confronting a lawyer in the UK when attempting to advance international law arguments before a domestic court. As I said earlier, even if international law is correctly invoked in the case at hand, other considerations may preclude the court from ruling on questions of international law. Two recent decisions – one of which is *Abbasi*, the other the *CND* case – paint the picture vividly. They reveal that the sensitive nature of foreign relations and national security weigh heavily with domestic courts when confronted with international law arguments.

In *Abbasi* we have seen that the applicants sought an order for diplomatic protection from the UK Government. In pressing this claim, the applicants put arguments before the Court of Appeal to show that the United States was in the process of violating their human rights and that, in the circumstances, the Foreign Secretary was under a duty under domestic public law to take positive steps to redress the position, or at least give a reasoned response to the request for assistance. One of the arguments raised by the Government was that the Court was being improperly asked to make a ruling on the legality of US conduct at Guantanamo Bay – in effect, a ruling which would find the United States to be acting in violation of international law. According to the argument for the Foreign Secretary[30] this would run contrary to the classic statement of judicial restraint made by Lord Wilberforce in *Buttes Gas & Oil v Hammer*.[31] Lord Wilberforce there stated that there is 'a general principle that the courts will not adjudicate upon the transactions of foreign sovereign states', and deemed it 'desirable to consider this principle … [as] one of judicial restraint or abstention'.[32]

The Court of Appeal in *Abbasi*, in a progressive jurisprudential move, rejected the Government's broad contention. It did so by relying first on the House of Lords' judgment in the *Kuwait Airways* case,[33] which we have already encountered, and which updates the law on judicial restraint. A passage in the judgment of Lord Nicholls in *Kuwait Airways* identified the modern limits to the principle of judicial restraint.

---

[29] *R (Abbasi) v Secretary of State for Foreign and Commonwealth Affairs* [2003] UKHRR 76, para 69. See also, in the context of action which was said to be taken to prevent a crime against peace (namely the invasion of Iraq in March 2003), *R v Jones (Margaret)* [2005] QB 259, where the English Court of Appeal (Criminal Division) held that there was no sufficiently settled definition of a crime of aggression under international law so as to be a 'crime' in domestic law within the meaning of section 3 of the Criminal Law Act 1967. The case is due to be heard by the House of Lords in February 2006.

[30] See para 32 of the judgment.

[31] [1982] AC 888.

[32] ibid, at 931.

[33] *(nos. 4 and 5)* [2002] 2 AC 883, para 26.

One of those limits, said Lord Nicholls in reference to the Iraqi invasion, is that the judiciary need not 'shut their eyes to a breach of an established principle of international law committed by one state against another when the breach is plain'.[34]

The Court in *Abbasi* went further by drawing on immigration law. In asylum cases, where the issue is often whether the applicant for asylum has a well-founded fear of persecution if removed to a third country, the Court pointed out that 'consideration of the claim for asylum frequently involves ruling on allegations that a foreign state is acting in breach of international law or human rights'.[35]

The Court of Appeal was openly concerned about 'Mr Abbasi's predicament' – in particular, the undisputed fact that Mr Abbasi was (at that time)[36] being denied access to court to challenge the legality of his detention. And it allowed itself an opening to review steps taken by the UK Government to relieve this predicament on the basis that '[i]n apparent contravention of fundamental principles recognised by both [the US and the UK] and by international law, Mr Abbasi is at present arbitrarily detained in a "legal black hole"'.[37]

Abbasi thus provides a foothold for a lawyer in the UK facing the mountain of judicial restraint. One senses the height of this mountain, however, from the eventual decision given. The Court of Appeal was sufficiently concerned about 'Mr Abbasi's predicament' to find that he had a legitimate expectation that the Government would consider making representations to the United States. But beyond this, it would not go. On the facts it found that Mr Abbasi's case had indeed been considered by the Foreign and Commonwealth Office, and, finding refuge on the top of the mountain, concluded as follows:

> On no view would it be appropriate to order the Secretary of State to make any specific representations to the United States, even in the face of what appears to be a clear breach of a fundamental human right, as it is obvious that this would have an impact on the conduct of foreign policy, and an impact on such policy at a particularly delicate time.[38]

If there were any doubts about the continuing potency of the doctrine of judicial restraint, then the *CND* case[39] ought to lay them to rest. The decision, given in December 2002, relates to the controversial invasion of Iraq by US-led forces in March 2003, which was already widely anticipated; and involved an investigation by the courts of the legality of the proposed use of force by the Crown. The Campaign for Nuclear Disarmament brought an application against the Prime Minister and others, seeking a declaration on whether UN Security Council Resolution 1441 authorised states to take military action in Iraq. In the words of Simon Brown LJ:

> In short, the court is being invited to declare that the UK Government would be acting in breach of international law were it to take military action against Iraq without a further Resolution. It is, to say the least, a novel and ambitious claim.[40]

---

[34] Para 26, *Kuwait Airways*.

[35] At para 53.

[36] Now *cf. Rasul v Bush* 542 US – (2004).

[37] Para 64.

[38] Para 107(ii).

[39] *R (Campaign for Nuclear Disarmament) v The Prime Minister of the United Kingdom and Others* [2002] EWHC 2777 (Admin) (17 December 2002).

[40] Para 2.

The international law that the applicant invoked before the Court was limited to customary international law, more specifically, the breach of the *ius cogens* norm outlawing the use of force in international relations. The term *ius cogens* refers to peremptory norms of international law which are so fundamental that they permit of no derogation by any state. Following from our earlier discussion about the proper place of international law within UK domestic law, this is significant. CND, anticipating that the Government would maintain that any use of force was authorised on the Government's understanding of existing unincorporated Security Council resolutions, placed its reliance on customary international law. In this way CND was able to argue that its claim was based on a breach of law over which the Court had jurisdiction, since, as we have seen, customary international law is part of domestic law.

The Divisional Court rejected the application, and did so on two principal bases which appear to be interrelated. The first problem, said the Court, is that the applicants' reliance on customary international law did not avoid the real problem at hand, namely, the proper interpretation of Resolution 1441 – an unincorporated international instrument. The Court concluded that the applicants sought 'a ruling on the interpretation of an [unincorporated] international instrument, no more and no less', and could not therefore 'escape the rule which *Lyons* exemplifies by seeking to invoke the principle of customary international law'.[41]

The second problem, in the Court's eyes, was that the issues raised in the case were not justiciable. With the question: '[h]ow could our assumption of jurisdiction here [to interpret unincorporated Resolution 1441] be regarded around the world as anything other than an exorbitant arrogation of adjudicative power?'[42] Simon Brown LJ disclosed what the Court saw as the real obstacle confronting the applicants. That obstacle was the 'general rule' that, 'in the interests of comity, domestic courts do not rule on questions of international law which affect foreign states'.[43] The rule of non-interpretation of unincorporated international legal standards appears to look like more than a principle of judicial restraint and to be a rule of jurisdiction – at least in the sense that the court regards itself as having none.[44] And certainly this appears to be the case in the *CND* decision. The Court found itself declining to embark upon the determination of the issue because to do so 'would be damaging to the public interest in the field of international relations, national security or defence'.[45]

The applicants had submitted that 'the only proper course for government to take is to conduct its international relations openly in accordance with whatever advice it has received', a view that Simon Brown LJ took to 'represent a singularly utopian view of international affairs'.[46] Perhaps, as the world order is in danger of rupture following the deeply controversial Iraqi conflict, one of the goals will be to ensure that international relations are conducted more openly, and the pressure on governments, including our own, is mounting. Sir Franklin Berman, a former chief legal adviser to

---

[41] Para 37.
[42] Para 37.
[43] Para 38.
[44] Colin Warbrick, 'International Law in English Courts – Recent Cases' (2003) 52 *ICLQ* 815, 823.
[45] Para 47(ii).
[46] Para 45, *CND case*.

the FCO, is reported to have said the following in the context of the government's refusal to disclose its full reasons for going to war:

> For a decision to go to war, especially when the government claims to be acting on behalf of the international community, they ought to explain in the necessary detail the basis on which they were acting.[47]

As is well-known, the debate about disclosure of the advice given by the Attorney General as to the legality of the attack on Iraq in 2003 continues unabated. Professor Philippe Sands has recently published a book, *Lawless World*, in which he discusses the question at length and concludes that: 'I suspect that the cloud will continue to hang over those most closely associated with the advice until it is published in full'.[48]

The decisions in *Abbasi* and *CND* reveal that, where there is evident tension between reliance on international law and the policy considerations relied upon by the Executive, domestic courts will not allow the international law arguments to resonate too loudly.

What are we to make of this self-imposed judicial caution? If one thinks back to our discussion of *Kuwait Airways*, and Lord Steyn's willingness to have recourse to the unincorporated UN Charter's prohibition on the use of force and the relevant Security Council resolutions in that case, it might be questioned why, for example, the Court in *CND* was so reluctant to do the same. Certainly the UN Charter's prohibition on the use of force relied on by Lord Steyn reflects the same principle of customary international law that the court was asked to have regard to in the *CND* case.

One difference, it would seem, is that the House of Lords had not been asked to interpret the real meaning of the unincorporated instruments, while the judges in *CND* felt that that is precisely what was required of them in relation to Resolution 1441. What appears to have been crucial is the fact that in *CND* the application of international law prohibiting the use of force did not dovetail with the Executive's policy considerations. In this light the House of Lords' judgment in *Kuwait Airways* can also be more readily understood. The House of Lords knew that its decision would accord with the policy considerations of the Executive. One of those considerations, as expressed by Sir Franklin Berman (then FCO Legal Adviser) in a letter before the Court, was that the UK considered itself bound by the Security Council resolutions which condemned the invasion of Kuwait as a breach of international peace and security[49] – the Executive's policy considerations were a mirror of the international law arguments pleaded before the House.

What is not clear then is whether lawyers in cases to come will achieve success with facts any less 'extraordinary' than those in *Kuwait Airways* and involving international law arguments which chime any less with the Executive's policy

---

[47] The Guardian, 'War QC sticks to his guns', Monday, March 1, 2004, available at <www.guardian.co.uk/guardianpolitics/story/0,3605,1159222,00.html>.

[48] Philippe Sands, *Lawless World: America and the Making and Breaking of Global Rules* (London, Penguin, 2005) 201. After this lecture was delivered, the text of the Attorney General's advice of 7 March 2003 was released by the Government after extracts from it had been leaked and were published in the media.

[49] See para 114, *Kuwait Airways*.

considerations. The best that might be hoped for is an ability to scale the mountain of judicial restraint in the appropriate circumstances. *Abbasi* as we have seen provides something of a foothold. A domestic court is free to express a view in relation to what it conceives to be a clear breach of international law, particularly in the context of human rights.[50] But even in *Abbasi* the lawyers failed to scale the mountain face in respect of their request. More disconcertingly, the *CND* decision suggests that climbing might not even be worth the effort.

In the national context, courts readily accept that they are the guardians of the domestic law and the constraints it places on government action, even in the face of national security considerations the Executive might advance. As Colin Warbrick has recently pointed out: 'however difficult an adverse judgment might be for the execution of the government's chosen policy, the court will not decline to give its judgment and will expect it to be followed'. Lord Steyn has had recent occasion to highlight this role for the courts in the context of the detention of prisoners at Guantanamo Bay.[51] Speaking extra-judicially about the terrible injustices in modern times that national governments have 'perpetrated in the name of security on thousands who had no effective recourse to law',[52] Lord Steyn stressed that 'instinctive trust in public servants, executive or judicial, has been replaced by a culture requiring in principle openness and accountability from all entrusted with public power'.[53]

But in the realm of international law and foreign policy, things appear so far to be different. And where international law and government's foreign policy do not openly mirror each other, the mountain of judicial restraint takes shape. The effect of this edifice, it appears to me, is that the constraints of international law stand the risk of being sacrificed on the altar of government's chosen policy, no matter how bad, ill-conceived, or partisan that policy might be. In Professor Warbrick's words:

> [I]t appears that the judges in *CND* took the position that international law is a part of the process of international relations, not a fetter upon it. While the judgment does not go quite so far as to say that the government needs the freedom to act contrary to international law, it does take a robust view of how international law works in the service of policy.[54]

Professor Warbrick's words allow me an opening to express some of my own opinions surrounding this question. I believe that we should be wary of allowing international law to be subservient to the demands of national security or the conduct of foreign affairs. The demands of international law should ordinarily come before the demands of comity, which may otherwise be a cloak for *realpolitik*; and international law should provide the framework of rules within which international relations are conducted. While other countries might allow or believe otherwise, international law ought to be a fetter on the way the UK conducts its foreign affairs. To believe otherwise is to place the type of 'instinctive trust' in public servants, executive or judicial, that Lord Steyn was talking about in the context of domestic policy. I think the time

---

[50] Para 57, *Abbasi*.
[51] See Johan Steyn, 'Guantanamo Bay: The Legal Black Hole' (2004) 53 *ICLQ* 1.
[52] At p 2.
[53] At p 5.
[54] Colin Warbrick, 'International Law in English Courts – Recent Cases' (2003) 52 *ICLQ* 815, 824.

may have arrived for us to strive also for a culture of openness and accountability in the international context, and to use the courts to interrogate whatever instinctive trust may remain in those entrusted with public power in the field of foreign policy and international relations.

THE FUTURE

Let me look towards the future. The Iraq war and the subsequent occupation of Iraq remain the most high profile sources of litigation that domestic courts have to confront. Two examples may suffice.

The first relates to the very issue that was at the core of the *CND* decision – the legality of the war. In cases involving protestors in Southampton Magistrates' Court and Bristol Crown Court rulings have been made applying the *CND* decision even to criminal charges brought against individuals who wished to argue that they acted as they did to prevent an illegal war. In the judgment of Grigson J, given at Bristol Crown Court in the case of *R v Pritchard and others* (12 May 2004), it was held that the principle of non-justiciability in *CND* applies even where a domestic court has to decide whether or not a defendant has a defence available to a criminal charge. The Court of Appeal (Criminal Division) dismissed an appeal in July 2004.[55] However, it did say:

> There is, it seems to us, considerable force in the argument that the *CND* case does not, in itself, provide the answer to justiciability in the present case.[56]

The second type of case to come before the courts has been brought by the families of Iraqi civilians killed by British soldiers.[57] The Divisional Court heard six test cases last year in which three preliminary issues arose: (1) whether the ECHR applied to British forces in Iraq in the circumstances of those cases; (2), whether the HRA applied; and (3) if so, whether the procedural obligation under Articles 2 and 3 of the ECHR to conduct an investigation into deaths and alleged torture which may have been caused by state agents was breached in those cases. Judgment was given on 14 December 2004.[58]

The Divisional Court held, first, that only one of the cases before it fell within the jurisdiction of the UK, the case of Mr Mousa, on the ground that he was detained by British forces in a prison and so there was sufficient control over him to bring him within their jurisdiction. The Court held, secondly, that Mr Mousa's case also fell within the scope of the Human Rights Act, which to that extent does have some extra-territorial effect. Thirdly, the Court held that there had been a breach of the

---

[55] *R v Jones (Margaret)* [2005] QB 259. The case is due to be heard by the House of Lords in February 2006.

[56] Para 14 (Latham LJ, giving the judgment of the Court). Another case, decided by the Divisional Court after this lecture was delivered, also considered similar legal issues: *Ayliffe v DPP* [2005] EWHC 684 (Admin) (21 April 2005).

[57] See The Independent, 'Britain on trial for Iraqis killed by its troops', 1 March 2004, available at <http://news.independent.co.uk/low_res/story.jsp?story=496536&host=3&dir=60>.

[58] *R (Al Skeini) v Secretary of State for Defence* [2005] HRLR 3.

procedural obligation in Articles 2 and 3 in that there had not been an adequate and timely investigation of his alleged torture and killing by British soldiers. I hope I summarise the decision fairly if briefly but I will not comment on it in detail because the case is going to the Court of Appeal. For present purposes, what is of interest is that the Court was inevitably required to adjudicate on intricate questions of international law relating to the concept of a state's 'jurisdiction' because that is the concept used in Article 1 of the ECHR.[59]

These examples illustrate the contemporary relevance of international law issues in UK courts. They also illustrate, as do the other cases I have spoken about, the importance of the issues at stake. Democracies face threats to national security, and controversial decisions about foreign policy are taken all the time. In the climate of our extraordinary times, however, it is not only our security and questions of foreign policy that are at issue. At issue also is the very nature of our democracy and its response to acts of war and international terrorism. Speaking of the outrage against international and human rights law that Guantanamo Bay represents, Lord Steyn asked whether our government ought to make plain publicly and unambiguously the utter lawlessness at Guantanamo Bay. To Lord Steyn the answer might be found in John Donne's famous vision of no man being an island unto itself – where 'any man's death diminishes me, because I am involved in Mankind'.[60]

Certainly, for effect to be given to this vision then comity and the precarious nature of international relations must in principle remain subservient to the demands of justice and the standards set by the world's law. And while Lord Steyn's challenge is limited to the UK government and its politicians, the difficulty remains for lawyers, once they have correctly invoked applicable international law in UK courts, to convince judges that the challenge is one that applies also to the judiciary.

Lord Hoffmann said in *Rehman*, 'it is important neither to blur nor to exaggerate the area of responsibility of the executive' and the courts may have to decide 'issues which at no point lie within the exclusive province of the executive'.[61] I would suggest that questions of pure law, as opposed to the merits of a policy, are for the courts and certainly not within the exclusive province of the executive.

WHY DOES INTERNATIONAL LAW MATTER IN THE PRESENT CONTEXT?

I would like to try to answer the question as follows:

(a) It matters to governments, which say that they wish to comply with international law and that they are doing so – that has certainly been the position of the British Government in relation to the Iraq war of 2003. In a democracy they should be accountable for that view.

(b) It matters to our armed forces – who are well-disciplined and trained to comply with the law, including international law. It has emerged that in the week

[59] Note that, although Article 1 itself is not included in Sch 1 to the Human Rights Act 1998, the Divisional Court considered that it was relevant to the scope of the Act.
[60] Johan Steyn, 'Guantanamo Bay: The Legal Black Hole' (2004) 53 *ICLQ* 1, 15.
[61] *Secretary of State for the Home Department v Rehman* [2003] 1 AC 153, para 54.

leading up to the invasion of Iraq in March 2003 Lord Boyce (then Chief of the Defence Staff) required firm reassurance from the Attorney General that the invasion would be lawful. As Professor Sands puts it in his recent book, Lord Boyce 'wanted to be sure that military chiefs and their soldiers would not be "put through the mill" at the International Criminal Court'.[62]

(c)   It matters to the public – for example, opinion polls suggested that many people wished to see a UN resolution clearly authorising the use of force on Iraq (the so-called 'second resolution') before the UK took part in any invasion. That may not be enough for some people, who would still have doubted the morality or political wisdom of attacking Iraq, but at least it would have been a good start.

(d)   It matters because we should live up to our own standards. If we do not, we simply give sustenance to those who believe that the rule of law is a sham which is used by Western powers to cloak the naked use of power. Defiance of the law encourages others around the world to use violence too. This is dangerous in an increasingly dangerous world.

I can do no better than to end with a quotation from an American judge, Justice Brennan, who was a judge for many years on the US Supreme Court and said:

> Mutuality … serves to inculcate the values of law and order. By respecting the rights of foreign nationals, we encourage other nations to respect the rights of our citizens. Moreover, as our Nation becomes increasingly concerned about the domestic effects of international crime, we cannot forget that the behavior of our law enforcement agents abroad sends a powerful message about the rule of law to individuals everywhere. As Justice Brandeis warned in *Olmstead v United States* 277 US 438 (1928):
>
> 'If the Government becomes a lawbreaker, it breeds contempt for law; it invites every man to become a law unto himself; it invites anarchy. …' Id., at 485 (dissenting opinion)
>
> … If we seek respect for law and order, we must observe these principles ourselves. Lawlessness breeds lawlessness.[63]

---

[62] Sands (n 48) 197.
[63] *Verdugo-Urquidez* 494 US 259 (1990) at 285.

'We Have it in Our Power to Begin the World Over Again': The Contribution of Lauterpacht and Jackson to the Post-War Legal Order

This lecture was given to the University of Bristol law club in March 2021. It gave me the opportunity to bring together the stories of two men who have long inspired me: Sir Hersch Lauterpacht and Justice Robert Jackson. They met several times during and in the aftermath of the Second World War. Although they were from very different backgrounds their lives in many ways represent the history of the world in the first half of the twentieth century, with its convulsions and upheavals. Despite everything they were hopeful people and helped to create the post-war legal order, which included the creation of the United Nations, the prohibition of war as an instrument of international relations and the establishment of individual human rights at the heart of international law.

INTRODUCTION

THANK YOU FOR inviting me to be your Patron for this year and to give this lecture at the University of Bristol.[1] I am sorry that we cannot be together in the great city of Bristol. For now we have to meet virtually but, as you will know, I have fond memories of the University, as I used to walk past it every day when I was going to school next door.

I have taken my title from the pamphlet 'Common Sense' by Thomas Paine, which he published soon after his arrival in America in 1776 and which is regarded by many as providing one of the inspirations for the War of Independence. What, however, I want to talk about today is a different era, during and after the Second World War, when the world turned its face against the horrors of the holocaust and a war of aggression and chose to create a new world order, based on peace and fundamental human rights. I want to look, in particular, at the lives of two men who had very different backgrounds but who came to meet during the Second World War and made

---

[1] I would like to thank Professor Philippe Sands QC for his comments on a draft of this lecture.

a vital contribution to the creation of the new order after that war. Those two men were Sir Hersch Lauterpacht and Justice Robert Jackson. The lives of these two men in a sense reflect the history of the first half of the twentieth century, with its upheavals and convulsions; they saw wars, revolutions, and the collapse of old empires. They were both born in the late nineteenth century and died at relatively young ages in the middle of the twentieth.[2]

Sir Hersch Lauterpacht was born in 1897 in what was then the Austro-Hungarian Empire. He came to this country in 1923, arriving at Grimsby, with a not very good command of the English language (at least not the spoken language), and became an academic, initially at the LSE. In just 14 years, by 1937 he was the Whewell Professor of International Law at the University of Cambridge and the editor of the leading work on international law by Oppenheim. In 1954 he was appointed as a Judge of the International Court of Justice, and knighted in 1955. He died in 1960.

Robert Jackson was born in 1882 in rural Pennsylvania. He was not able to obtain a law degree (or indeed any kind of degree) but was able to become a lawyer, in effect by doing an apprenticeship. He served as Attorney General in the administration of President Franklin D. Roosevelt. The President then nominated him to become an Associate Justice of the Supreme Court of the United States in 1941. In 1945 he was asked by President Truman to be the Chief Prosecutor at the war crimes trial of the Nazi high command at Nuremberg. He died in 1954, shortly after the US Supreme Court had given its unanimous judgment in *Brown v Board of Education of Topeka, Kansas*,[3] of which he would have been justly proud, as it declared racial segregation in schools to be unconstitutional in breach of the Equal Protection clause of the Fourteenth Amendment. As we shall see, Justice Jackson's commitment to racial equality in American law was arguably ahead of its time. He was also a great believer in the dignity of the human individual even if that person is unpopular with the majority in society.

THE EARLY LIFE OF LAUTERPACHT

Lauterpacht was born on 16 August 1897 in Zólkiew, which was at that time in the Austro-Hungarian Empire. His father was a timber merchant. In 1911 his family moved to nearby Lemberg. In 1914 the Russian army occupied the city but were expelled in 1915 by the Austro-Hungarian army. After the end of the First World War the city became part of Poland and was renamed Lwów. It is now Lviv in Ukraine.

---

[2] I have relied in preparation for this lecture on some books which I hope you will find of interest: *East West Street* by Philippe Sands (London, Weidenfeld & Nicolson, 2016); *The Internationalists and their plan to outlaw war* by Oona Hathaway and Scott Shapiro (London, Allen Lane, 2017); the biography of Sir Hersch Lauterpacht by his son, Sir Elihu Lauterpacht (Cambridge, Cambridge University Press, 2010); *Jurists Uprooted* (edited by Jack Beatson and Reinhard Zimmerman) (Oxford, Oxford University Press, 2004); and the biography of Robert H Jackson by Gail Jarrow (Honesdale, Calkins Creek, 2008).
[3] 347 US 483 (1954).

At the age of 18 Lauterpacht started the study of law at the university in Lemberg but, partly as a result of anti-Semitism, he moved in 1919 to Vienna, where he studied with Hans Kelsen, who was working with the Austrian government on the drafting of a constitution for the new Republic of Austria.

Lauterpacht last visited Lwów in 1928. Much of his family continued to live there until the Second World War. Most of his family were killed during the war although he did not know what had happened to them until the end of the war.

THE EARLY LIFE OF ROBERT H JACKSON

In dedicating her biography of Robert Jackson to the memory of her grandparents Gail Jarrow says:

> Along with Robert H Jackson, they were part of a remarkable generation that lived through two World Wars and several smaller ones, the Great Depression and unprecedented changes in society and technology. Through it all, they never gave up trying to make the world a better place for their children and grandchildren.

Robert Houghwout Jackson was born on 13 February, 1892, in Spring Creek, Pennsylvania. Although his family was not poor, it was not wealthy or privileged either.

When he was five years old, the Jackson family moved to Frewsburg, New York. That is where Robert Jackson had most of his schooling. He graduated from Frewsburg High School in 1909. He wanted to have more education and went to spend an extra year at the High School in Jamestown, which is in the western part of New York State and where he then practised law. Today there is a centre dedicated to the memory of Justice Jackson in Jamestown. It has a website with useful archive material and other resources about his life and legacy to the world.

Robert Jackson never obtained a law degree; indeed he obtained no degree at all. However, he did study law for two years in Albany, the state capital of New York, and he learnt how to be a lawyer by doing an apprenticeship in Jamestown. The mother of his girlfriend and future wife Irene told her that:

> He is too skinny and he's never going to amount to anything!

How wrong a person can be.

After Franklin D Roosevelt was elected President during the Great Depression in 1933, Jackson accepted an invitation to work for the administration in Washington DC. In due course he was appointed Solicitor General and then Attorney General. As we shall see later, it was while he was Attorney General that he first met Professor Lauterpacht.

After his term as Attorney General, in 1941 Jackson was appointed by President Roosevelt to be an Associate Justice of the US Supreme Court. It was predicted by many that he was destined to become Chief Justice but this was not to be. He served on the Court until his untimely death in 1954.

While he was a serving Justice, in 1945 he was asked by President Harry S Truman to become the Chief Prosecutor at the Nuremberg War Crimes Trial, which began on 20 November 1945. On that day the charges were read out against the defendants, who included Goering. The following day, Jackson gave his opening speech. He said:

> These prisoners represent sinister influences that will lurk in the world long after their bodies have returned to dust. We will show them to be living symbols of racial hatred, of terrorism and violence, and of the arrogance and cruelty of power.

As we shall see, Jackson's speech at Nuremberg chimed with his long-standing commitment to racial equality and the control of the abuse of power by the state. But his experience at Nuremberg also taught him of the dangers of totalitarianism and the risk to democratic societies posed by it.

SOME OF JUSTICE JACKSON'S FAMOUS JUDGMENTS

West Virginia State Board of Education v Barnette[4] concerned a rule, which was very common in American society at one time, which required schoolchildren to salute the flag of the United States and offer their pledge of allegiance to the Republic at the start of each school day. Failure to comply was deemed by law to be an act of insubordination, which required expulsion from school. The child was then regarded as being a 'delinquent' because she was unlawfully absent from school and her parents could be prosecuted and punished by a fine or a term of imprisonment of up to 30 days.

The plaintiffs in that case were two girls who were Jehovah's Witnesses. Their families did not feel that they could salute the flag because of their religious beliefs. In a case just three years earlier, in 1940, the US Supreme Court had decided that the US Constitution did not forbid such a rule: *Minersville School District v Gobitis*.[5] The issue came before the Court again in 1943, by which time of course the US had entered the Second World War. In the meantime, there had been some changes in the composition of the Court and one of the new members of the Court was Justice Jackson. This time the Court held, by a majority of six to three, that the rule requiring schoolchildren to salute the flag did violate the Constitution. Justice Jackson gave the judgment of the Court.

At paragraph 26 he said:

> The very purpose of a Bill of Rights was to withdraw certain subjects from the vicissitudes of political controversy, to place them beyond the reach of majorities and officials and to establish them as legal principles to be applied by the courts. One's right to life, liberty, and property, to free speech, a free press, freedom of worship and assembly, and other fundamental rights may not be submitted to vote; they depend on the outcome of no elections.

In a chilling passage at the end of paragraph 31, in which Justice Jackson had in mind the totalitarian regimes of Europe at that time, he said:

> Those who begin coercive elimination of dissent soon find themselves exterminating dissenters. Compulsory unification of opinion achieves only the unanimity of the graveyard.

---

[4] 319 US 624 (1943).
[5] 310 US 586 (1940).

At paragraph 32 he said:

> We set up government by consent of the governed, and the Bill of Rights denies those in power any legal opportunity to coerce that consent. Authority here is to be controlled by public opinion, not public opinion by authority.

Finally, at paragraph 34, he said:

> If there is any fixed star in our constitutional constellation, it is that no official, high or petty, can prescribe what shall be orthodox in politics, nationalism, religion, or other matters of opinion or force citizens to confess by word or act their faith therein.

We cited this passage in our decision in the Divisional Court in *R (BBC) v Secretary of State for Justice*,[6] paragraph 40: that was a case about the right to freedom of expression in Article 10 ECHR.

The next case to which I will refer is *Korematsu v United States*.[7] This case arose out of the decision taken by the US military in the Second World War to detain American citizens of Japanese ancestry without charge. The detention was for an indefinite period in centres that were described as concentration camps far from a person's home. That decision was taken pursuant to an Executive Order by the President, who was of course Franklin D Roosevelt, who had appointed Robert Jackson to the Supreme Court. By a majority of six to three this was upheld by the US Supreme Court. There were powerful dissents from three judges, including Justice Jackson. Many decades later, in 2018, the decision of the majority was unanimously held by the Supreme Court to have been 'gravely wrong' (Roberts CJ), not only now but on the day that it was decided: *Trump v Hawaii*.[8]

In *Korematsu* the majority held that the decision was a lawful military one in time of war, to which great deference had to be paid, and was not vitiated by racial discrimination. The minority view was that it was unconstitutional.

At 242–43 Justice Jackson said:

> Korematsu was born on our soil, of parents born in Japan. The Constitution makes him a citizen of the United States by nativity, and a citizen of California by residence. No claim is made that he is not loyal to this country. There is no suggestion that, apart from the matter involved here, he is not law-abiding and well disposed. Korematsu, however, has been convicted of an act not commonly a crime. It consists merely of being present in the state whereof he is a citizen, near the place where he was born, and where all his life he has lived.

He went on to explain that:

> A citizen's presence in the locality, however, was made a crime only if his parents were of Japanese birth. Had Korematsu been one of four – the others being, say, a German alien enemy, an Italian alien enemy, and a citizen of American-born ancestors, convicted of treason but out on parole – only Korematsu's presence would have violated the order. The difference between their innocence and his crime would result, not from anything he did, said, or thought, different than they, but only in that he was born of different racial stock.

---

[6] [2012] EWHC 13 (Admin); [2013] 1 WLR 964.
[7] 323 US 214 (1944).
[8] 138 S Ct 2392 (2018), at 2423.

The third case I want to mention, *Railway Express Agency v New York*,[9] is important but not so much for the actual decision on its facts, which were unremarkable: they concerned a state regulation of advertising on vehicles. One of the arguments made was that the regulation discriminated as between the owner of a vehicle, who could advertise its own business, as compared with the owner of a business which wanted to advertise someone else's business. The Supreme Court dismissed the challenge. What is of longer term interest is the concurring judgment of Justice Jackson about the Equal Protection clause of the Fourteenth Amendment, not least because it has been cited with approval by the House of Lords in this country.

At pages 112–13 he said:

> Invocation of the equal protection clause, on the other hand, does not disable any governmental body from dealing with the subject at hand. It merely means that the prohibition or regulation must have a broader impact. I regard it as a salutary doctrine that cities, states and the Federal Government must exercise their powers so as not to discriminate between their inhabitants except upon some reasonable differentiation fairly related to the object of regulation. This equality is not merely abstract justice. The framers of the Constitution knew, and we should not forget today, that there is no more effective practical guaranty against arbitrary and unreasonable government than to require that the principles of law which officials would impose upon a minority must be imposed generally. Conversely, nothing opens the door to arbitrary action so effectively as to allow those officials to pick and choose only a few to whom they will apply legislation and thus to escape the political retribution that might be visited upon them if larger numbers were affected. Courts can take no better measure to assure that laws will be just than to require that laws be equal in operation.

That passage was cited with approval and applied by the House of Lords in the 'Belmarsh' case: *A v Secretary of State for the Home Department*,[10] at paragraph 46 (Lord Bingham of Cornhill).

The last case I want to mention, *Terminiello v Chicago*,[11] was a case concerning freedom of speech and freedom of assembly. The case was of the kind that the police and courts have had to deal with in this country too, where a public meeting is the subject of a counter-demonstration; feelings run high on both sides and there may be public disorder. In that case the speaker was convicted under an ordinance of the City of Chicago about breaches of the peace. According to the majority judgment given by Justice Douglas, the speaker 'vigorously, if not viciously, criticised various political and racial groups he denounced as inimical to the nation's welfare': paragraph 2. He contended that his conviction was in breach of his right to freedom of speech in the First Amendment. This argument was accepted by the majority of the US Supreme Court but not by Justice Jackson, who was one of the dissenters in a court that was narrowly divided five to four.

In his dissenting judgment, Justice Jackson drew on his experience of appearing as prosecuting counsel at the Nuremberg trials. He recited the facts of the case at length, observing that the police had had to deal with what was in effect a riot,

---

[9] 336 US 106 (1949).
[10] [2004] UKHL 56; [2005] 2 AC 68.
[11] 337 US 1 (1949).

with a speech that provoked a hostile mob and incited a friendly one, and threatened violence between the two (paragraph 32). At paragraph 70, Justice Jackson set out what some members of the crowd had shouted at the meeting in response to what the speaker had said, for example: 'Kill the Jews'. The speaker denied that he was a fascist but Justice Jackson considered that his speech followed with fidelity that was 'more than coincidental' the pattern of European fascist leaders (paragraph 71).

At paragraph 74 he recalled what had been said by Hitler in *Mein Kampf* about winning power by first winning the battle for the streets:

> First laughed at as an extravagant figure of speech, the battle for the streets became a tragic reality when an organized *Sturmabteilung* [storm troopers] began to give practical effect to its slogan that 'possession of the streets is the key to power in the state'.

He ended his judgment, at paragraph 107, with these stirring words:

> The choice is not between order and liberty. It is between liberty with order and anarchy without either. There is danger that, if the Court does not temper its doctrinaire logic with a little practical wisdom, it will convert the constitutional Bill of Rights into a suicide pact.

THE FIRST MEETING BETWEEN LAUTERPACHT AND JACKSON

The first meeting between Lauterpacht and Jackson took place while Jackson was still Attorney General, in December 1940. Lauterpacht was on a long and gruelling lecture tour of the United States at the invitation of the Carnegie Institute for Peace. Although he lectured on international law at 15 law schools, one of the purposes of his tour was to encourage American support for the war effort. At that stage the US had not entered the war and a large part of American public opinion, including among international lawyers, was in favour of a strictly neutral stance as between the belligerent parties. The administration of President Roosevelt was not of that view and wished to do everything it could properly do to assist Great Britain and its allies while complying with the obligations of a neutral state. This was what led in 1941 to the Lend-Lease scheme, by which the US lent equipment to Britain in exchange for the use of British facilities around the world.

Jackson, who was Attorney General at the time, was keen to hear from Lauterpacht what were the limits of what the US, as a neutral state, could lawfully do in order to assist the Allies short of war. To this end, Lauterpacht prepared a memorandum for him, which Jackson used more or less verbatim as the basis for a lecture he gave to the Inter-American Bar Association in Havana on 27 March 1941. Jackson's lecture was described at the time by the *New York Times* as 'extraordinarily significant'.

The view which Lauterpacht expressed, and with which Jackson agreed, was that the strict requirement of impartiality which the old law of neutrality may have imposed on a non-belligerent, no longer applied. This was because of the fundamental change which had been made to the international legal order by the Paris Peace Pact of 1928, sometimes referred to as the Kellog-Briand Pact, after the names of the US Secretary of State and the French Foreign Minister of the time. Most states of the world had become parties to the Pact, including Germany and Italy.

The Peace Pact is the subject of a fascinating study by Hathaway and Shapiro called *The Internationalists and their plan to outlaw war*, which traces the history of international law governing the use of force between states from the time of Grotius. For the first time in history, the Pact prohibited war as an instrument of policy in international relations. Before 1928 the waging of war was not only permitted by international law, it was regarded as a substitute for judicial enforcement of rights and obligations precisely because there was no enforcement mechanism of the traditional kind available to states.

The general prohibition on the use of force in international relations is now contained in Article 2(4) of the Charter of the United Nations, which was created at the end of the Second World War. It is also a norm of customary international law and indeed is part of the *ius cogens*, in other words a peremptory norm of law which permits of no derogation. It is subject to two well-known exceptions: the right of self-defence and where the use of force is authorised by a relevant resolution of the UN Security Council. There is continuing debate about whether there is a third exception: where the use of force is necessary for humanitarian reasons.

As we shall see, after the US entered the Second World War in response to the Japanese attack on Pearl Harbor on 7 December 1941, both Lauterpacht and Jackson (who was by now a judge) continued to reflect on the legal order which should follow that war. In particular, they both considered whether it would be possible to put individuals on trial for the atrocities which had been committed during the war. These became known as war crimes and crimes against humanity. They also turned their minds to a new concept: crimes against peace. They reached the conclusion that there was such a concept. Not only that. It was not an example of retrospective law-making, since the Peace Pact of 1928 had already prohibited war as an instrument of international policy well before the German invasion of Poland in 1939. Furthermore, they came to the conclusion that there could be individual criminal responsibility in international law for the planning and waging of a war of aggression, that is a war which was unlawful.

FURTHER MEETINGS BETWEEN LAUTERPACHT AND JACKSON

Lauterpacht and Jackson met again during the War, in Washington DC in early 1942. As early as 1942 discussions had started about the possibility of putting Nazis on trial for crimes under international law. In late January 1942 Jackson, who was by now a judge but who still had the ear of the administration of FDR, gave a speech at the Waldorf Hotel in Washington on 'International Lawlessness'. Lauterpacht had helped him write it and attended the lecture as a guest.

In June 1942 a Committee on War Crimes was established, chaired by the well known international lawyer, Arnold McNair, who had been Lauterpacht's mentor at the LSE in the 1920s and who now invited Lauterpacht to become a member. There was also a United Nations War Crimes Commission, established by the Allies.

After the surrender of Germany in May 1945, the Allies stepped up preparations for a trial of Nazi war criminals. With that in mind, Jackson and Lauterpacht met again, this time in Britain. President Harry S Truman, who had succeeded FDR just before the end of the War, appointed Jackson to be the chief prosecutor for the US at the trial. In July Jackson and Lauterpacht met in London at Jackson's hotel; and then in Cambridge, where Lauterpacht lived and worked. In August 1945 the Allies agreed the terms of the Charter of the International Military Tribunal. Article 6 was particularly important, as it set out the jurisdiction of the tribunal. Although the wording was the subject of intense debate between the Soviets, French, British and Americans, Lauterpacht's idea of adopting three titles to describe the different kinds of crime alleged, which was championed by Jackson, was accepted. In particular, the term 'crimes against humanity' entered the lexicon for the first time, a formulation that was proposed by Lauterpacht and which reflected his commitment to the idea that all human beings, at all times and places, are, as individuals, entitled to the protection of minimum rights under the law.

For Jackson the most important part of the indictment for the forthcoming trial related to the crime of aggression, that is the planning and waging of an unlawful war. To his mind the atrocities which the Nazis had committed flowed from that underlying crime. But it was far from clear that there was such a crime in international law at that time. The French delegation at the meeting of the Allies in London in the summer of 1945 was highly sceptical of the idea. When one French professor of international law, Jules Basdevant, had suggested in San Francisco earlier that summer that the proposed crime of aggression was *très fragile*, Jackson noted in his diary: 'God save us from professors!' But, as Hathaway and Shapiro observe, in the end it was professors who saved Jackson – in particular Lauterpacht, who came up with the concept and title of crimes against peace, which came to form the first part of the indictment at Nuremberg.

It was another professor, and former judge of the Austrian Supreme Court, Hans Kelsen, who had taught Lauterpacht many years earlier at Vienna and who was by now an exile in the US before becoming a distinguished professor at Berkeley, who also saved Jackson. On Kelsen's advice, Jackson insisted that Article 6 of the Charter of the IMT had to include express reference to the individual criminal responsibility of the defendants. Without that, important as the Peace Pact was, all that it would have helped to establish was that the state was no longer entitled to wage war as an instrument of international policy. That was not enough for the purposes of the forthcoming trial. It was not the state of Germany which would be in the dock at the Palace of Justice in Nuremberg; it was to be individuals. The original draft indictment named as the first defendants: Hitler, Mussolini, Himmler and Goebbels. They had all either been killed or committed suicide before they could be tried. The fifth defendant, Goering, survived long enough to be put on trial at Nuremberg although he later committed suicide. There were other defendants who did face trial.

Lauterpacht and Jackson were both present at Nuremberg for the trials. Lauterpacht was there to assist the British prosecution team, led by the Attorney General in the new Labour government, Sir Hartley Shawcross, and his predecessor, the Conservative Sir David Maxwell-Fyfe, who later became Home Secretary in the 1950s and, as Viscount Kilmuir, was Lord Chancellor. As I have mentioned, Jackson was the chief prosecutor for the US.

HUMAN RIGHTS

During the war, in July of 1942 Lauterpacht was invited by the American Jewish Committee to write a book on the international law of human rights, a topic which he was to make very much his own. The traditional view of international law was that it governed relations between states only and had nothing to say about the rights of the individual. It was also thought that what a state did to its own nationals was a matter which fell within its own sovereignty and not the concern of other states. The book which Lauterpacht eventually published in 1945 was called *The International Bill of the Rights of Man*.[12] It was to become a classic.

It was republished in 2013 with an introduction by Professor Philippe Sands. Although there had been attempts made previously to draft such declarations, this was the first systematic attempt to draft an international declaration on human rights which was intended to be legally binding on states. The text of the draft which Lauterpacht produced is closer to the International Covenant on Civil and Political Rights, which was adopted by the UN in 1966 and is an international treaty, than it is to the 1948 Universal Declaration of Human Rights, which was a resolution of the UN General Assembly and does not, strictly speaking, have legal force.

Lauterpacht was, more than any other lawyer of his time, responsible for suggesting that the focus of international law had to change from the protection of states to the recognition that the individual human being is 'the ultimate unit of all law'.

Lauterpacht's preface to the 1945 edition of his book began by noting that Churchill had said that one of the purposes of the war was 'the enthronement of the rights of man'. Lauterpacht said:

> The great contest, in which the spiritual heritage of civilisation found itself in mortal danger, was imposed upon the world by a power whose very essence lay in the denial of the rights of man as against the omnipotence of the state.

Lauterpacht was well aware of the nature of totalitarian regimes, whose ideology regarded the individual human being as being completely subsumed within the state. For stirring images which reflect such ideologies, one only has to see the propaganda film, *Triumph of the Will*, made for the Nazis by Lefi Riefenstahl. It was no accident that, after the war, the Allies chose to hold the trial of the Nazi war criminals in Nuremberg, which had been the stage of so many of their rallies in the 1930s.

In his book Lauterpacht explicitly drew on the idea of natural rights in western thought going back to Ancient Greece and Rome, through the writings of Thomas Aquinas and in particular to Locke in the seventeenth century.

The intellectual heritage to which Lauterpacht was heir is reflected throughout his book, for example in the following passage at page 16:

> The state ... has no justification and no valid right to exact obedience except as an instrument for securing the welfare of the individual human being.

---

[12] Republished edition (Oxford, Oxford University Press, 2013).

At page 17 he said that the power of the state and of its rulers is derived ultimately from the assent of those who compose the political community, and that there are limits to the power of the state to interfere with the individual's right to do what he conceives to be his duty.

At page 193 of the book Lauterpacht even considered how such an international bill of rights could be enforced within the constitutional traditions of a country such as the UK, which appeared to recognise no limits on the power of Parliament. He said that in such circumstances the courts would not have the power to declare invalid any legislation which was inconsistent with the Bill of Rights but would be able to make a formal pronouncement declaring it to be inconsistent. Some people have argued that that was the intellectual origin of the concept of a declaration of incompatibility, which is now to be found in section 4 of the Human Rights Act.

Finally, I should mention what Lauterpacht said about equality. At page 115, he said that the claim to equality before the law is 'in a substantial sense the most fundamental of the rights of man'. This passage was quoted by Lord Bingham in the Belmarsh case in 2004, at paragraph 46. It is perhaps fitting that both Lauterpacht and Jackson were quoted in that case by Lord Bingham on the importance of the principle of human equality.

CONCLUSION

The legacy of Lauterpacht and Jackson, although not theirs alone, includes the following:

- The prohibition of war as an instrument of policy in the conduct of international relations.
- The crime of aggression.
- Individual criminal responsibility for war crimes, crimes against humanity and other similar crimes.
- The international law of human rights.
- The fundamental nature of the principle of equality.

Perhaps most important of all – they were creative lawyers, who devoted their legal knowledge and skills to the service of humanity, at the most challenging of times. They were never deterred by the criticism that something had never been done before. They asked the questions 'why not?' and 'how can we do it?'

Epilogue: The Nature of the Judicial Process 100 Years on

BENJAMIN CARDOZO WAS born in 1870 and died in 1938. For the last six years of his life he was a Justice of the US Supreme Court but he is best known for the period he spent as a member of the Court of Appeals for the State of New York from 1917, in the last five years as Chief Judge. In 1921 he published the Stores Lectures which he had delivered at Yale University as a book: *The Nature of the Judicial Process*.[1]

I thought that a century later it would be worth considering this classic work by one of the great judges of the Anglo-American world. Inevitably some of the language in the book now sounds dated but I think it continues to have relevance to the way in which we do our work as judges.

The book is divided into four lectures. Lecture 1 consists of an introduction and a discussion of what Cardozo called 'the method of philosophy'. I think he meant by that logical reasoning. Lecture 2 concerns what he called 'the methods of history, tradition and sociology'. In Lecture 3 he returned to the method of sociology and also talked about 'the Judge as a legislator'. Finally, Lecture 4 concerned adherence to precedent and 'the subconscious element in the judicial process' as well as a conclusion.

Clearly the book is not about everything that judges do. It is not intended to be a manual for judges. Indeed it would be uninteresting if it were. In particular, Cardozo does not talk about one important aspect of what judges do, namely the finding of facts, particularly in civil cases. That is generally an under-explored aspect of the judicial process. The best essay of which I am aware on that subject was published by Lord Bingham in his book *The Business of Judging*: 'The Judge as Juror: The Judicial Determination of Factual Issues'.[2] What Cardozo's book is primarily about is the way in which judges decide issues of law. In other words it is a book about judicial reasoning on questions of law and not a general encyclopaedia about the judicial process. It is also primarily about appellate courts rather than courts of first instance because it is usually appellate courts (and in particular final courts of appeal) which have responsibility for the development of the law. At page 163, Cardozo himself recognised that 'the bulk of the business of the courts' does not raise a new question of law but consists of the application of established rules of law to the facts of a particular case.

[1] Yale University Press, 1921.
[2] Oxford University Press, 2000, Ch.1.

At page 112 Cardozo said:

> My analysis of the judicial process comes then to this, and little more: logic, and history, and custom, and utility, and the accepted standards of right conduct, are the forces which singly or in combination shape the progress of the law. Which of these forces shall dominate in any case must depend largely upon the comparative importance or value of the social interests that will be thereby promoted or impaired. One of the most fundamental social interests is that law shall be uniform and impartial. There must be nothing in its action that savours of prejudice or favour or even arbitrary whim or fitfulness. Therefore in the main there shall be adherence to precedent.

But, Cardozo continued, symmetrical development of the law may come at too high a price:

> Uniformity ceases to be a good when it becomes uniformity of oppression. The social interests served by symmetry or certainty must then be balanced against the social interests served by equity and fairness or other elements of social welfare.

As these passages indicate, much of the book is about the development of the common law, in particular private law. Cardozo recognised that judges do sometimes act as legislators. They make the law. But he was adamant that the judge

> legislates only between gaps. He fills the open spaces in the law. ... Nonetheless, within the confines of these open spaces and those of precedent and tradition, choice moves with a freedom which stamps its action as creative. The law which is the resulting product is not found, but made. The process, being legislative, demands the legislator's wisdom. (pages 113–15).

Cardozo was also adamant that:

> The judge, even when he is free, is still not wholly free. He is not to innovate at pleasure. He is not a knight-errant roaming at will in pursuit of his own ideal of beauty or of goodness. He is to draw his inspiration from consecrated principles. (page 141)

Apart from the common law, Cardozo was also interested in the interpretation of legislation. In this regard, his views would probably today be more in keeping with modern practice in European legal systems, rather than the American one, where the 'original intent' theory has become more prevalent again. At pages 84–85 Cardozo quoted Kohler:

> The interpretation of a statute must by no means of necessity remain the same forever.

Cardozo was also interested in the difference between statutory interpretation and the interpretation of a constitution. This was of course of particular relevance in the American context. At page 83 he said:

> Statutes are designed to meet the fugitive exigencies of the hour. ... A *constitution* states or ought to state not rules for the passing hour, but principles for an expanding future. (Emphasis in original)

That is also a good example of one of the reasons why I still think this book continues to deserve reading today. It is quite simply because of the beauty of Cardozo's prose.

One of the most interesting features of the book is the numerous references by Cardozo to foreign jurists, in particular French and German writers, often in the original language. I wonder how many judges in this country today would be as familiar as he was with academic writings not only in the English speaking world but elsewhere?

The final point I want to make is that Cardozo was well aware that judges, like other human beings, act not only on the basis of conscious reasoning but also 'subconscious forces'. At page 12 he said that:

> Every one of us has in truth an underlying philosophy of life, even those of us to whom the names and the notions of philosophy are unknown or anathema. There is in each of us a stream of tendency, whether you choose to call it philosophy or not, which gives coherence and direction to thought and action. Judges cannot escape that current any more than other mortals. All their lives, forces which they do not recognise and cannot name, have been tugging at them – inherited instincts, traditional beliefs, acquired convictions; and the resultant is an outlook on life, a conception of social needs, a sense ... of 'the total push and pressure of the cosmos,' which, when reasons are nicely balanced, must determine where choice shall fall. ... We may try to see things as objectively as we please. Nonetheless, we can never see them with any eyes except our own.

Towards the end of the book, Cardozo returned to this topic of subconscious forces. At pages 174–75 he said:

> The spirit of the age, as it is revealed to each of us, is too often only the spirit of the group in which the accidents of birth or education or occupation or fellowship have given us a place. No effort or revolution of the mind will overthrow utterly and at all times the empire of these subconscious loyalties.

I think that insight continues to have relevance today, as debates continue about the importance of diversity in judicial decision-making, not only diversity in the obvious sense (for example race or gender) but cognitive diversity and diversity of experience.

But to Cardozo this did not mean that law descends into mere subjectivity or the preferences of individual judges. Particularly because he had in mind the work of appellate courts, which fashion the law from time to time, Cardozo took hope in the collective nature of the enterprise:

> The eccentricities of judges balance one another. One judge looks at problems from the point of view of history, another from that of philosophy, another from that of social utility, one is a formalist, another a latitudinarian, one is timorous of change, another dissatisfied with the present; out of the attrition of diverse minds there is beaten something which has a constancy and uniformity and average value greater than its component elements. (page 177)

I have found that to be true of my own role as a judge in the Court of Appeal. I have often thought that the end product of our discussions after a hearing is more valuable precisely because different judges, with different legal and other backgrounds, have contributed to the decision. In my view, the whole is greater than the sum of its parts.

Index